PARTISANSHIP, GLOBALIZATION, AND CANADIAN
LABOUR MARKET POLICY

Studies in Comparative Political Economy and Public Policy

Editors: MICHAEL HOWLETT, DAVID LAYCOCK, STEPHEN MCBRIDE, Simon Fraser University

Studies in Comparative Political Economy and Public Policy is designed to showcase innovative approaches to political economy and public policy from a comparative perspective. While originating in Canada, the series will provide attractive offerings to a wide international audience, featuring studies with local, sub-national, cross-national, and international empirical bases and theoretical frameworks.

Editorial Advisory Board

For a list of books published in the series, see page 391.

RODNEY HADDOW AND THOMAS KLASSEN

Partisanship, Globalization, and Canadian Labour Market Policy

Four Provinces in Comparative Perspective

UNIVERSITY OF TORONTO PRESS
Toronto Buffalo London

© University of Toronto Press Incorporated 2006
Toronto Buffalo London
Printed in Canada

ISBN 13: 978-0-8020-9090-4
ISBN 10: 0-8020-9090-7

Printed on acid-free paper

Library and Archives Canada Cataloguing in Publication

Haddow, Rodney
  Partisanship, globalization and Canadian labour market policy : four
  provinces in comparative perspective / Rodney Haddow and Thomas
  Klassen.

  (Studies in comparative political economy and public policy)
  Includes bibliographical references and index.
  ISBN-13: 978-0-8020-9090-4
  ISBN-10: 0-8020-9090-7

  1. Labor market – Canada – Provinces.   2. Labor market – Canada –
  Provinces – Case studies.   3. Globalization – Economic aspects –
  Canada.   I. Klassen, Thomas R. (Thomas Richard), 1957–   II. Title.
  III. Series.

  HD5728.H33 2006   331.12'0971   C2005-907524-4

This book has been published with the help of a grant from the Canadian
Federation for the Humanities and Social Sciences, through the Aid to
Scholarly Publications Programme, using funds provided by the Social
Sciences and Humanities Research Council of Canada.

University of Toronto Press acknowledges the financial assistance to
its publishing program of the Canadian Council for the Arts and the
Ontario Arts Council.

University of Toronto Press acknowledges the financial support for
its publishing activities of the Government of Canada through the
Book Publishing Industry Development Program (BPIDP).

We dedicate this book to the memory of our fathers, Vernon Haddow (1922–2003) and Gerhard Klassen (1915–1967)

Contents

Acknowledgments

Research for this manuscript was funded by a Standard Research Grant from the Social Sciences and Humanities Research Council of Canada (grant no. 410–2001–1777; Rodney Haddow, principal investigator; Thomas Klassen, co-investigator; Steffen Schneider, collaborator). Many people helped us with this book. Most important were the more than 100 individuals who were interviewed in Toronto, Edmonton, Vancouver, Victoria, Montreal, and Quebec City, as well as in several German cities. These interviews were an essential complement to printed sources in preparing the case studies. At least 20 separate interviews were conducted in each of the four Canadian provinces, including at least 3 each with representatives of organized business and labour in the province; at least 3 interviews were also conducted with provincial ministerial officials in each province who possessed an intimate knowledge of each of the six policy fields examined here. All of these people receive our anonymous and heartfelt thanks. Stephen McBride at Simon Fraser University has been consistently supportive of this research project. Veronique Roy contributed excellent research assistance for the Quebec and BC chapters, by thoroughly researching available media sources and public documents, and compiling excellent summaries of her data. Ursule Critoph, Jeff Taylor, and Donna Wood provided valuable background information for the Alberta chapter. Anja Kirsch and Christine Seeliger, also research assistants, played an important role at different phases of the preparation of the manuscript. Dan Buchanan helped prepare some of the quantitative data utilized in the book, as well as material for the discussion of social assistance in Ontario. Jan Kainer, at York University, gave advice regarding pay equity. As always, of course, any errors or shortcomings in the analysis offered herein are the fault of the authors. We especially appreciate the valuable contribution of the chapter on Germany by Steffen Schneider. Some material in chapter 4 appeared in a different format in our article, 'Partisanship, Institutions and Public Policy: The Case of Labour Market Policy in Ontario, 1990–2000,' published in the *Canadian Journal of Political Science*, vol. 37 (2004), pp. 137–160. Finally, we thank the staff at the University of Toronto Press for their work in bringing the manuscript to press.

PART ONE

Context

1 Partisanship, Globalization, and Political-Economic Institutions in Labour Market Policy-Making

Globalization is now widely believed to have reduced the 'degrees of freedom' available to policy-makers in developed capitalist nations. The present study contributes to the debate about this contention. It examines the limits of the possible in one such nation – Canada – in a policy field that represents a crucial test of globalization's putative effect. This book compares the impact of partisan differences among governing parties on labour market policy-making from 1990 to 2003 in four Canadian provinces: Ontario, Quebec, British Columbia, and Alberta. Measuring partisanship's impact on policy-making allows us to assess the room to manoeuvre now available to governments in liberal democracies: Can electorates make different choices, reflecting their distinctive preferences, in areas of public policy that are important for their families and communities? Two specific queries are posed. First: *To what extent does the complexion of governing parties in these jurisdictions (centre-left or centre-right) affect labour market policy outcomes?* Second: *Has globalization brought about radical retrenchment in this field?*

Before addressing these questions, this chapter examines how institutions shape political life. Two aspects of institutions are of concern, corresponding to our two questions. First, the comparative political economy literature discussed below suggests that the impact of partisanship on policy-making is different in institutionally distinct settings, and that these different sites 'select for' – work in favour of the potential success of – correspondingly distinct policy choices. Moreover, in relation to the first of our questions, this literature contends that *partisanship's impact on policy-making will be stronger in some settings than in others.* By defining this setting for the jurisdictions studied here, we will be able to venture hypotheses about variations among them concerning how partisanship affects policy outcomes. Three dimensions of the institutional context of political economies – welfare states, production regimes, and party systems – are the focus of our attention. The importance of each is explained in the main body of this chapter. An analysis of the institutional setting for the four provinces along these three dimensions is provided in chapter 2, where hypotheses about the likely relation of partisanship to policy-making in each of them are also developed. Second, in recent years comparative political economy scholarship has faced new challenges to its central contention that institutions differ and that these differences matter. It is now often argued that globalization has reduced or eliminated differences among states, as they converge on market-oriented policy choices. Disputing this view, many comparative political economists argue that institutional differences remain important and that globalization will have quite different implications for policy outcomes in distinct milieus. This chapter therefore also examines this debate in the current political economy literature and indicates how *globalization might be expected to affect policy-making differently in different settings* depending on their pre-existing welfare states, production regimes, and party systems. In light of this, chapter 2 also develops hypotheses regarding the impact of globalization on policy-making for each case. By focusing on the years since 1990, we assess globalization's impact during the time it is usually argued to have had its greatest impact in reducing government discretion.

The hypotheses developed in chapter 2 on the two questions defined above are then tested for each province in the case studies that form the core of the book (chapters 4 through 8). These are preceded, in chapter 3, by a description of the federal government's evolving role in labour market policy in Canada, and of the main areas of provincial policy-making. An appreciation of these themes will help the reader understand the policy developments that are addressed more analytically in subsequent chapters. Chapters 4 through 7 respectively address most labour market fields examined here for Ontario, Quebec, British Columbia, and Alberta. For reasons explained below, chapter 8 concentrates on one field – social assistance for employable persons – for all four provinces. These jurisdictions differ institutionally in important ways that will shed important light on how institutions mediate the impact of partisanship and globalization on policy-making. But they also have much in common. Consequently, features of these two relationships – conditioned by institutions that are similar among the cases – will not be fully elucidated by comparisons among them. Chapter 9, contributed by Steffen Schneider, in contrast examines simultaneous developments in Germany and in three of its *Länder* (states); the relevant institutions in Germany historically have diverged fundamentally from those in Canada. This case will help us understand our Canadian cases better by illustrating how differently the nexus of institutions, partisanship, and globalization has played out in an institutionally very different nation. Finally, chapter 10 will assesses all of this study's findings, returning to the theoretical concerns set forth in this chapter.

Framework of the Study

The main conceptual themes addressed in this study are summarized in this section, and provisionally located in relation to relevant theoretical literatures and debates. The rest of the chapter elaborates upon these topics.

Freedom, Equality, and the Welfare State

A familiar imagery identifies equality and freedom as the foremost alternatives that divide voters in Western nations. The former choice connotes that government must intervene in market relations to reduce the inequalities and hazards that they give rise to; the latter implies a preference for permitting agents to benefit, or suffer, more fully from the market-based distribution of rewards.[1] These nations frequently are referred to as capitalist democracies, a term that captures the fundamental tension that gives rise to this choice.[2] They grant formal political equality to all citizens, creating pressures to equalize the distribution of social and economic advantages as well. On the other hand, markets play a crucial role in establishing the primary allocation of material rewards in these settings, a practice that appears almost inexorably to increase inequality in the distribution of rewards. Prior to universal male suffrage, there was much speculation about whether political equality could be reconciled with economic inequality. In the event, they were harmonized, and the welfare state was the tool used to accomplish this feat.[3] Defined broadly to include all government interventions that modify the distribution of income and advantages in capitalist economies from what it would be in a notional free market, uninfluenced by government, welfare states establish the terms of this accommodation of equality and freedom. They encompass the tax structure, allowances and services for mothers and children, social assistance, housing policies, disability measures, public health insurance and pensions, and public regulation of occupational benefits.

In the 1960s and 1970s, many accounts of welfare state development adopted a functionalist viewpoint, arguing that social programs in different nations represented broadly similar responses to the imperatives of industrialism or capitalism.[4] But subsequent scholarship, now associated most prominently with the work of Gøsta Esping-Andersen, supports the view that the accommodation of democracy and markets varied markedly among capitalist democracies.[5] Partisan influences explained much of this variability. This literature attributes great importance to the ability of distinctive political coalitions to build alternative welfare state designs in response to divergent conceptions of the proper balance of equality and freedom. The significance of the recent literature on globalization, in this light, is to suggest that this plurality of choices may no longer be viable, in the face of an emerging imperative to follow a common path towards reducing barriers to free markets.

Labour market policies are a particularly important test of globalization's impact. Such policies include 'those actions that affect the supply and demand for labour as well as the labour process itself.'[6] They encompass industrial relations, employment standards, workers' compensation, and occupational health and safety, as well as active measures and passive assistance for employable persons. These can alter the distribution of market income and benefits. For instance, active labour market policies (ALMP) – designed to 'improve access to the labour market and jobs, develop job-related skills, and to promote more efficient labour markets,'[7] – can enhance the employability of low-skill unemployed workers, making it easier for them to find employment and increasing their potential earnings. Labour market initiatives are therefore widely understood to be part of the welfare state. Yet, to a greater extent than for most of the social measures listed above, these initiatives often are seen as directly serving efficiency objectives alongside, or even instead of, equity ones. It is often argued that ALMP should primarily address skill shortages, rather than assisting marginal workers. Labour market policy thus occupies an ambiguous position between 'social policy' (with its focus on equity) and 'economic policy' (which concentrates on efficiency and growth). One might therefore expect it to be contested in the partisan arena even more fundamentally than other welfare state measures. The traditional partisan confrontation between advocates of more security and champions of greater freedom is likely to be reinforced by an additional contention regarding the very purpose of labour market measures: should they primarily enhance equity or foster market efficiency? The latter option will become increasingly prominent if, as globalization theorists suggest, policy-makers are driven by international economic pressures to favour efficiency over equity.

Methodology

The term *historical institutionalism* describes approaches to the study of politics that frequently employ qualitative methods to examine political phenomena over time, and that seek to understand the nexus between agency and constraining institutions in politics.[8] Much comparative research on capitalist democracies has adopted this methodology, including Esping-Andersen's. Historical institutionalists now frequently complement their qualitative research with quantitative methodologies.[9] Quantitative studies alone can encompass a large number of cases. But the more cursory understanding of each case that they permit means that purely quantitative studies are less able to provide a rich account of the distinctive role of institutions in shaping developments in different polities. Because qualitative scholarship, by contrast, usually starts with detailed descriptive accounts, it requires the selection of a limited number of cases.[10] These are subject to a 'controlled comparison' where selected cases differ in relation to a few institutional parameters; the objective is to ascertain the relationship between these variations and policy outcomes.[11] The present study is inspired by historical institutionalism and uses a primarily qualitative and historical-narrative methodology of this type.

Case Selection

The Canadian provinces represent a very promising subject for a comparative study of labour market policy. These jurisdictions are responsible for most aspects of labour market policy for most workers in Canada. That the provinces share identical constitutional responsibilities, a common political history within the Canadian state, and similar welfare states facilitates a controlled comparison. In comparing developments between the selected cases, and within each over the time-period studied, it is easier to isolate the effect of partisanship and globalization on policy-making than would be possible if the cases were entirely institutionally distinct. On the other hand, there are also important institutional differences among the cases (see chapter 2), the consequences of which are the primary focus of our study. Quebec's production regime departs from the liberal model that prevails in the three English-speaking provinces in important respects; there are also significant variations among the latter. Differences among the party systems of the four provinces, the third institutional order examined here, are more profound and interpenetrate with variations among provincial production regimes. The German developments discussed in chapter 9 transpired in a setting that is consistently very distinct institutionally from Canada; they further indicate how institutional differences condition the role of partisanship and globalization in policy-making.

The four provinces selected for study are the most populous in Canada and are capable of exercising their authority in the labour market field. This is less true, for instance, of Canada's four Atlantic provinces, long more dependent on Ottawa for leadership in active and passive labour market policy. The partisan divide in the four provinces examined is also relatively easy to characterize in traditional left-right ideological terms, again in comparison with the Atlantic jurisdictions, and, to a degree, with federal politics in Canada. Since 1990, moreover, these four provinces have had distinctive political histories. Ontario experienced a political transition from a government of the centre-left (New Democratic) to one of the centre-right (Progressive Conservative) in the middle of the 1990s; shortly beforehand, Quebec went in the opposite direction, replacing a centre-right (Liberal) government with one of the centre-left (Parti Québécois). Alberta was governed by a party of the centre-right throughout the period of study (Progressive Conservative); British Columbia was ruled by the centre-left New Democrats for most of the period, but these were replaced by their Liberal, centre-right, rivals in 2001. The cases provide a broad mix of ideologically distinct parties in power throughout the period of our study. The selected German Länder also reflect a range of partisan scenarios: centre-right hegemony (Bavaria), centre-left predominance (North Rhine-Westphalia), and a mixture (Saxony-Anhalt).

We have sought comprehensiveness in identifying specific sub-fields for study within the ambit of labour market policy because provincial governments have wide-ranging responsibilities in this field. Developments are examined regarding all six of the main components of this domain: industrial relations, employment standards (defined broadly to include pay and employment equity), workers compensation, occupational health and safety, active labour market policy, and passive labour market policy for employable persons. Our focus has been narrowed in one important respect, however. We address only measures that affect the private sector labour market. Policies that pertain to both private and public sector workers therefore are considered. But we do not examine public sector industrial relations, a contested domain in all jurisdictions, or features of other sub-fields of labour market policy (such as ALMP) where these exclusively address public sector employees. There are several reasons for this exclusion. Provincial public sector industrial relations has been much studied in Canada in recent years;[12] it seems to have received more attention than any other aspect of provincial labour market policy. Moreover, policy regarding the private sector appears to us to be more important as a test of the question that preoccupies this study: To what extent do centre-left and centre-right parties offer distinctive approaches to the relationship between equality-enhancing intervention and the unhindered marketplace in a context where globalization is thought to have privileged the latter over the former? Aspects of public sector labour relations and human resource management touch upon these matters. Downsizing government is justified by a putative need to lighten the fiscal burden represented by the state. Contracting out and privatization allegedly do the same, and import efficiency-enhancing market principles into public sector management. But our main concern is with the impact of government policy on labour market equity and efficiency at the macro level, in relation to the political economy as a whole. And, again, efforts to remodel the public sector itself to be more efficient and market-friendly are already the focus of a significant body of research.[13] Because the labour market responsibilities of German Länder are largely confined to ALMP, and because there is only space in the one chapter devoted to that nation to address part of the changes occurring there – albeit, the most important part, we would argue – discussion of the German case concentrates on ALMP.

We now elaborate upon the implications of existing historical institutionalist research for our study. The next three sections of this chapter treat the welfare state literature that emerged around Esping-Andersen's work, and the complementary institutionalist literatures on production regimes and party systems. These, respectively, define the social policy, and the economic and partisan institutional settings that condition labour market policy. The fourth and fifth sections then address the import of globalization for policy-making, and return to, and highlight, the main theoretical concerns of our study.

Partisan Origins and Institutional Consequences of Welfare State Diversity

Welfare states were ubiquitous in the capitalist democracies by the 1960s. This gave credence to the view that social security systems emerged in response to a functional imperative for these societies – a response to the 'logic of industrialism' (according to structural-functionalist thinking) or to the ideological and reproductive requirements of capitalism (according to many Marxists).[14] However, it was clear on closer examination that welfare states were highly disparate, and that these dissimilarities could not be explained by variables, such as the level of economic development, that were easily reconciled with a functionalist logic. Political variables quickly suggested themselves as an alternative. But here too the evidence was less than conclusive. When welfare states were treated simply as a matter of 'more' or 'less,' with the difference between the two being measured largely in terms of levels of social expenditure, the partisan stripe of governing parties could only explain a part, some argued a very small part, of welfare state variety.[15] Petry et al. concluded that the ideological stripe of the governing party in the Canadian provinces explained some of the observed variations among them in public expenditures, but that this pattern was inconsistent and by no means robust.[16]

Yet raising public expenditures is not itself usually an objective for the political left any more than for the right. Historical institutionalist research on the welfare state sought clues about the impact of politics on social security precisely in these concrete motivations, and in the variable circumstances that allowed one or another set of objectives to be inscribed in social security arrangements. This required detailed historical and qualitative comparisons of a limited number of cases. For Esping-Andersen, the post-war capitalist welfare states broadly corresponded to three distinct types, each tracing its origins to a distinctive political setting.[17] While the precise number and composition of welfare state regimes has subsequently been disputed, in broad terms his approach is now widely adopted by historical institutionalist welfare state research.[18] *Social democratic* welfare states (typical of Scandinavia) emerged where centre-left parties aligned with the labour movement

were hegemonic; these parties engineered political coalitions with crucial middle class groups – initially farmers, later white-collar employees. The welfare state's coverage was extensive and had a strongly
universalist hue. Most social measures were available to all. Supplementary public insurance schemes for more affluent citizens did emerge,
but these developed on top of basic public provision and were intended
to complement the latter, rather than provide private sector alternatives. This design was consistent with the core objective of working
class politics in capitalist democracies for most of the twentieth century,
which was to foster social equality and solidarity. *Conservative* regimes
(common to most of Continental Europe, including Germany) developed where non-bourgeois conservative political interests controlled
the state at the welfare state's origins. These offered highly variable
publicly funded and contribution-based benefits to an array of social
categories, in order to foster loyalty among them to the existing order.
But they also reinforced group-specific identities within these categories that fragmented citizens' sense of belonging, rather than encouraging the solidarity sought by social democrats. The middle classes were
again crucial: granted particularly generous arrangements, these strata
developed a particular loyalty to them, and a strong sense of distinction
from blue-collar workers. *Liberal* welfare states (in the Anglo-Saxon
world, including Canada), finally, differ considerably from both of the
above, each of which is centred on non-market priorities, albeit distinctive ones. These emerged under the political influence of business-
dominated parties, which wished to maximize citizens' reliance upon,
and loyalty to, the free market. Here, public provision was comparatively underdeveloped and tended to be used as a last line of defence
for those unable to provide for themselves. Selective and poverty-
oriented measures are most common in the liberal order. The vital
middle class cohort, benefiting from the relatively ample private measures that emerge in the absence of public alternatives, seeks to protect
these against government encroachment, and to defend itself against
the higher taxes needed to improve public provision for others.

A pervasive criticism of Esping-Andersen's initial characterization of
regimes was that his definition of the welfare state was too narrow,
focusing excessively on income security measures and neglecting each
regimes' implications for families and labour markets. Conceding this
point,[19] Esping-Andersen subsequently extended his typology to address these phenomena; the implications of his elaborated model for
labour markets, our core preoccupation, are addressed here.[20] *Social*

democracy sustains its commitment to equality and expensive universal measures only because its labour market measures maximize employment, and provide unemployed and less skilled individuals with the training needed to find work at adequate wages. In terms of the policy fields addressed in this study, this implies a strong reliance on active labour market measures. There is less need for passive measures, which, in any case, focus on facilitating labour market re-entry. An industrial relations system that features strong and centralized unions fosters nationwide and equality-enhancing wage and benefit bargaining. Combined, these measures should encourage high levels of labour market participation and wage equality, and substantial labour market participation among women. With these parameters in place, employment standards legislation plays a more modest role in protecting the currently employed. *Conservative* welfare states also are reluctant to embrace the free market; but the alternative values that they embody are quite different. Considerably influenced by Catholic social teachings, conservatism stresses the importance of the family, and the pivotal role of the male breadwinner. Consequently, active measures are modest, or are focused largely on vocational training for male workers; labour market participation rates are low, above all because female employment is not encouraged. Passive measures play a crucial role in sustaining family viability in times of need. Conservative regimes differ among themselves in their level of unionization and protection of union rights, but they generally lie between their social democratic and liberal alternatives in this respect; industrial bargaining is also moderately centralized. Consistent with the male breadwinner model, employment standards are used energetically to protect existing (predominantly male) workers against redundancy. In its wariness to embrace non-market principles, *liberalism* again differs sharply from its rivals. Active measures are limited, as markets are relied upon to create an efficient distribution of workers and skills. Passive measures, while more needed because of the paucity of alternative social security, tend to provide niggardly benefits and are designed to encourage, or coerce, a return to employment at whatever wage may be available. Unions are relatively weak, and industrial relations legislation more restrictive, in these settings. Employment standards are again very modest, and frowned upon as representing imprudent interference with labour market efficiency, the ultimate guarantor of high employment and economic growth. Like social democracy, though in a radically different way, liberal welfare states far exceed the conservative ones in their levels of labour market participation, among women as well as men. There is, on the other hand, generally much more inequality and poverty. The two remaining features of labour market policy covered by this book – workers' compensation and occupational health and safety – are closer in design and purpose to the core income maintenance and social security measures addressed by Esping-Andersen in his earlier work. One would therefore expect them to be broad and generous in coverage under social democracy; ample, but only for workers in core economic sectors, in conservative settings; and least well developed where liberal principles prevail.

The comparative welfare state literature is less informative regarding the style of state-societal relationship in public policy-making that characterizes each welfare state type, a theme addressed more by the scholarship on production regimes treated below. Philip Manow nevertheless argues that the occupational focus of social measures in conservative settings makes it much more likely than in liberal ones that the labour market partners – above all, business and labour – will play an important role in designing, administering, and reforming these measures. In liberal welfare states, by contrast, social security measures are less likely to be tied to occupational status; here, social policy debates are more likely to happen in the arena of partisan politics.[21] These two policy-making styles, respectively, characterize nations with corporatist and pluralist systems of interest intermediation;[22] the latter distinction therefore applies to welfare state policy-making as it does to aspects of production regimes.

Distinct political coalitions underlie different welfare state regimes. But once a welfare state design has emerged, the political loyalties that it embodies and reinforces become a force in their own right, a constraint on subsequent change. 'The welfare state is not just a mechanism that intervenes in, and possibly corrects, the structure of inequality; it is, in its own right, a system of stratification. It is an active force in the ordering of social relations.'[23] Welfare states tend to perpetuate themselves. Social democracy's universalism, and its high taxes, not only reduce inequalities much more than other regime types, but also foster cross-class cohesion, a strong political bulwark against a reversal of this change. The liberal model reduces inequality the least, and requires the lowest taxes; by targeting public measures disproportionately at a socially marginal underclass, it also ensures that these programs will remain modest and their clients suspect. Pierson's research on the politics of retrenchment in the British and American welfare states nevertheless found that, where these liberal regimes had extended significant benefits to middle class voters before 1980, these measures proved highly resilient to erosion by hostile neo-liberal politicians.[24] During the 1960s and 1970s social democratic politicians in West Germany and Austria attempted to adjust in a more egalitarian direction the diverse and uneven entitlements that characterized these mature conservative welfare states. Here, too, the pre-existing order, and the political loyalties that it embodied, proved more potent than the agency of incumbent politicians.[25]

Such research findings suggest that, once institutionalized, welfare states are immutable. Referring to welfare state changes until the late 1990s, Esping-Andersen concluded that 'political alternation may very well have caused roll-backs in a program here or some policy redesign there, but there is almost no case of sharp welfare regime transformation.'[26] Whether mature welfare state regimes have indeed proven unalterable recently is a main focus of Huber and Stephens's recent comparative study. Drawing on both qualitative-historical and quantitative data, their book concludes that during the 1980s and 1990s 'cutbacks were widespread [in industrial welfare states] but in large part modest, or at least not system transforming, except in the United Kingdom ... and New Zealand ... Labour market deregulation and welfare state retrenchment in these countries did substantially increase poverty and inequality.'[27] None of the social democratic and conservative welfare states which did most to challenge market principles experienced sufficient retrenchment to move into the liberal category. Huber and Stephens insist that their theoretical position is midway between one that treats mature welfare states as institutionally inviolate, and an opposing view that they are as open to partisan adjustment as they were at their point of origin.[28] But, in the event, they explain their two exceptional examples of regime transformation as reflecting exceptional features of the British and New Zealand cases: control of highly centralized government systems by ideologically determined parties in a context of severe economic distress. Broadly speaking, Huber and Stephens's findings support the argument that the variety built into welfare states at their origins has persisted in the face of the homogenizing and marketizing pressures of globalization.[29]

While in principle understanding welfare state development as reflecting an interplay of agency and structure and of partisanship and institutions, much of the comparative welfare state research, like historical institutionalist scholarship more generally, arguably privileges the latter over the former in institutionally mature settings. Colin Hay and Daniel Wincott argued some years ago that in practice historical institutionalist scholarship stresses institutions over agency, though in principle it need not do so.[30] Kathleen Thelen recently took up this theme systematically, arguing that this scholarship often treats institutional change as an 'all or nothing' affair, failing to detect 'institutional changes that fall short of breakdown.'[31] She proposes that processes of 'layering' and 'conversion' entail that institutions that emerged with one set of purposes in a particular historical setting, shaped by then-dominant political interests and ideas, might later acquire entirely new goals without being fundamentally altered, goals that make them consistent with 'currently prevailing power relations and cultural norms.'[32] Much existing institutionalist research, she suggests, is insufficiently sensitive to this ongoing role of agency in institutionally developed contexts. In view of these considerations, it is essential that we remain attentive to the possibility that institutional change in the cases examined here is greater than the historical institutional models discussed in this chapter would anticipate. We return to this question in chapter 10, when we reflect upon the implications of our findings for further research.

Comparing Production Regimes: The Varieties of Capitalism

Labour market policy is in an integral part of the welfare state, and divergent welfare state designs have distinctive implications for labour market structure and institutions. But labour market policy has an 'in-between' status, between social policy and economy; it is used to foster growth and efficiency, as well as redistribution and equity. The origins and variety of labour market institutions therefore are also addressed by scholarship on production regimes, which examine the institutionally distinctive foundations of economic life in capitalist democracies, or, to use a now-common idiom, 'the varieties of capitalism.' This literature is distinct from, and much less settled on a common approach than, the comparative welfare state research discussed above. Certain aspects of labour market institutions, such as the relevance of corporatist and pluralist systems of intermediation and the kinds of skills formation typical of particular political economies, nevertheless are treated in much greater detail by production regime research. An account of the institutional backdrop to labour market policy-making therefore must include a discussion of this scholarship. Moreover, there are important parallels between regime typologies proffered by production regime and welfare state scholarship. This section reviews recent developments in the former tradition, links them to the welfare state literature, and identifies a composite model of the institutional background to the policy developments examined in this study. Here again, we attend to the implications of theoretical models for the interface between partisanship and its constraining context.

Among the available typologies of capitalism, the two-regime model advanced by David Soskice is the most influential. Soskice divides the capitalist democracies into uncoordinated or liberal market economies (LMEs) and business-coordinated market economies (CMEs).[33] The distinction is determined by the extent to which the business community is capable of collaborating within itself, and with other economic actors. Where this potential is limited (mostly in the Anglo-Saxon world), LMEs emerge; where it is substantial (most of Continental and Northern Europe, and East Asia), CMEs are typical. In CMEs, interaction among economic actors is structured by trust-based relationships that endure over time and that are relatively immune to disruption by short-term price signals. In LMEs, market signals motivate most transactions; they are fluid and changeable.

The distinction has implications for four specific aspects of capitalist economies, two of which pertain directly to the labour market: industrial relations, education and training systems, company finance, and the rules governing inter-company relationships. In CMEs, labour-management negotiations are handled at the level of industry sectors; vocational skill formation is well developed and actively managed by business and labour; firms typically belong to networks of enterprises that share a bank, or banks, and a stable shareholder base; and firms participate in long-term relationships with suppliers, customers, and research institutions, and work with other firms in the same industry to sustain international competitiveness. In LMEs, industrial relations are usually conducted at the enterprise level and are fractious, and union power is generally weaker; advanced education emphasizes general skills rather than vocational ones, and the latter are not financed or overseen as actively by the labour market partners; firms are more likely to obtain financing from fluid capital markets and short-term loans; and firms are highly protective of their autonomy in making strategic decisions.[34] Soskice's characterization of differences between CMEs and LMEs in active and passive labour market policy is supported by other research. Estevez-Abe et al. uncovered a persistent preference for greater technical skills training and generous unemployment insurance benefits in CMEs; LMEs privilege general education and training, and offer modest passive benefits.[35] Ashton and Green discerned a clear difference between mostly Anglo-Saxon nations that have settled on a 'low skills' equilibrium, supplemented by extensive general post-secondary education; and a 'high skills' alternative, where advanced technical skills are stressed, which persists in Germany and Japan.[36] For Soskice and his collaborators, neither production regime is intrinsically superior to the other. Because of their reliance on enduring relationships, CMEs are likely to have a comparative advantage in 'incremental innovation,' especially characteristic of capital and durable consumer goods manufacturing. LMEs, comparatively unburdened by long-term commitments, will more likely succeed in 'radical innovation,' which typifies many high technology service and manufacturing industries.[37]

Soskice acknowledges significant variation among nations that belong to each of these broad categories, especially among the CMEs.[38] Until the 1980s, the Scandinavian nations practised industrial relations coordination at the national level, rather than the sectoral one. Changes in that decade, induced by business pressure, devolved collaboration to the sectoral level, eliminating this distinction.[39] But there remain important differences between Scandinavian and other Continental European political economies.[40] More fundamental distinctions are observed between Continental European CMEs, where inter-firm coordination occurs at the industry level, and the CMEs of East Asia, where it transpires at the level of often supra-sectoral families of firms (such as the Japanese *keiretsu* and South Korean *chaebol*), and where 'the state play[s] a framework-setting role.'[41] The state is also attributed a more significant role in most of the CMEs of southern Europe, and of France. Soskice expresses particular ambivalence about the latter nation, terming it 'a "state-business-elite coordinated-market economy"' in which '[c]ompanies can coordinate their activities ... but not independently of the state.'[42] It is in relation to this group of nations, where the state plays a particularly significant economic role, that many comparative political economists depart from Soskice, preferring a three-model typology. In addition to liberal and coordinated models, Vivien Schmidt identifies 'state-enhanced capitalism'; David Coates refers to 'state-led capitalism.' This category includes Soskice's 'group-coordinated' East Asian nations, and, for Schmidt at least, France and Italy.[43] While coordination is more extensive in these state-enhanced production regimes than in

LMEs, the state plays an important role in fostering collaborative activity in the four areas identified by Soskice. In France, for instance, Schmidt distinguishes an ongoing, though weakened, role for the state in industrial planning, stimulating inter-firm collaboration, and fostering education and training, though it has largely abandoned its erstwhile functions in industrial relations.[44] We do not propose to arbitrate between these contending two- and three-model typologies here; nevertheless, in chapter two we employ a distinction among three tendencies in capitalist economies: market-oriented, coordinative, and state-enhanced. This is certainly supported by the scholarship discussed in this paragraph, and, as we have seen, is not inconsistent with a more elaborated version of Soskice's model.

In distinguishing regime types, production regime research emphasizes different features of social and economic organization than does the welfare state scholarship discussed earlier. For the latter, the determinants of welfare state type are broad and enduring political coalitions. Such coalitions are related to the size and strength of, and the historical relationship among, the major social classes. In its earliest incarnations, welfare state scholarship laid particular emphasis on the size of the working class and the strength of the labour union movement and of social democratic political parties.[45] Soskice explicitly rejects these variables as determinants of production regimes, focusing instead on 'the role that firms and employer organizations play in the coordination of the economy'; business is endowed with this organizational capacity in CMEs, and largely lacks it in LMEs.[46] Yet these two typologies address different components of the same social order. If each is plausible, presumably there should be a defensible way of reconciling them, by subsuming one under the other or by means of a meta-theory able to account for the regularities uncovered by each in terms of a yet-deeper generative principle. To the best of our knowledge, no such rapprochement exists. Nevertheless, it would be particularly valuable in relation to production regime scholarship. Referring to much of this scholarship, and Soskice's in particular, Schmidt expresses a 'significant critique of the firm-centred approach ... It runs the risk of presenting reality as static, with the two variants of capitalism as systems maintaining a kind of homeostatic equilibrium.' Soskice presents the distinction between organized and unorganized business communities as a fait accompli, and does not account for its historical origins or identify the potential basis of its future development. It does not account for the 'dynamics of change in economic practices,' and for how these 'have affected the structures of business, government and labour relations.'[47] Consequently, the production regime literature is even more vulnerable than is comparative welfare state research to the above-noted objection of being insufficiently attentive to agency's role in shaping institutional design and change. Soskice provides no historical account of how distinctive regimes reflect different patterns of power resource mobilization over time in various countries. If, as Anthony Giddens argues, accounting for agency is essential for dynamic social models,[48] then connecting the production regime literature to welfare state scholarship's potentially greater (though still arguably deficient) attention to generative processes could foster an increased emphasis on these 'dynamics of change' in the former.

It is beyond the scope of this study to attempt this feat here. Charles Maier's classic account of the 'preconditions of corporatism' nevertheless suggests how it might be done. While Soskice disputes that CMEs share a background in corporatism and the strong labour movements and left parties associated with it, Maier provides a complex historical account of the origins of corporatism and of its ability to generate cooperative industrial relations. The latter is a key feature of CMEs, at least of the industry-coordinated northern European ones that conform to this type most comfortably. In Maier's account, it is a combination of labour and left party strength *and* of national 'vulnerability,' a result of war and economic openness, which fostered corporatism in these post-war European nations.[49] A broader account of the underpinnings of LMEs and of the other variants of CMEs might, similarly, identify how social and political balances of forces at specific historical conjunctures shaped the institutional order; and it might also be more sensitive to how these originating power-political dynamics might themselves subsequently change, laying the seeds for subsequent institutional evolution.

While no rapprochement theory now exists, what has been attempted, more modestly, is a *synthesis* of the production regime and welfare state literatures. First ventured by Kitschelt et al., this approach does not reconcile their generative principles, but simply observes complementarities between institutions identified by each.[50] Each typology relies on a distinction between a relatively liberal and market-oriented institutional order and another (or others) that embodies different principles. Anglo-Saxon nations predominated in the liberal variants in each case. Liberal welfare states, then, are clearly associated with LMEs. The Scandinavian social democratic welfare states emerged

Table 1.1: Comparing Political Economies[51]

Production Regime	Welfare State	Party System	Membership
Liberal market economy	Liberal	2-party; polarized	Anglo-Saxon nations
Erstwhile nationally coordinated CME	Social democratic	1-party dominant; left party	Scandinavia
Industry-coordinated CME	Conservative	3-party; Catholic, social dem., liberal	Northern Europe
State-enhanced	Conservative[52]	As above or clientistic[53]	Southern Europe, France, East Asia

where nationally coordinated CMEs existed, particularly suited to generating the egalitarian and universalist outcomes prized by social democrats. While coordination in these nations was decentralized to the sectoral level in the 1980s, they continue to represent another model. The 'core' sector-coordinated CMEs of northern Europe are all also endowed with conservative welfare states, not surprisingly, in view of Manow's observation of the role of social partnerships in administering these social policy regimes. If, following Schmidt and Coates, one identifies a third, 'state-enhanced' regime that includes some East Asian and Mediterranean nations, and France, this represents a fourth cluster of nations. Most of its members can be said to have conservative welfare states, though they vary considerably in design. This synthetic model is summarized in table 1.1

Located at the confluence of social and economic policy, labour market policy-making is shaped by institutions relevant to each. The synthetic model adopted here allows us to examine the impact of these different institutional settings in an integrated manner. They define the parameters – reflected in pre-existing social policy arrangements and the political loyalties that they embody, and in patterns of cooperative or competitive and market-based relations among economic actors – that partisan actors confront when pursuing preferred labour market policies.

Party Systems and the Configuration of Partisan Preference

For historical institutionalists, institutions not only define the limits of the possible for agents; they mould agency itself. 'Not only the *strategies* but also the *goals* actors pursue are shaped by the institutional context.'[54] For Hall and Taylor, 'institutions provide strategically-useful information, [but] also affect the very identities, self-images and preferences of the actors.'[55] We have already witnessed this. Welfare states shape voter preferences – building solidarity around the egalitarian benefits of social democratic welfare states and the status-segregated ones of conservative regimes, and granting little political appeal to the marginal provisions that typify liberalism. Politicians must consider these parameters, strategically, in defining their electoral platforms. More fundamentally, institutions indelibly affect these politicians' own aspirations; left-of-centre politicians in social democratic milieus will be more attracted to initiatives designed to attract women into the core workforce than will their counterparts in patriarchal conservative welfare states.

Herbert Kitschelt developed this dimension of institutionalism a step further. Distinctive patterns of party system formation, he argues, are associated with each type of production regime and welfare state. (A focus on this nexus between party systems and other features of national or provincial political economies is absent from recent Canadian scholarship on party systems; in this study, we therefore use Kitschelt's comparative framework in modelling our examination of the mediating impact of partisanship on labour market policy-making.)[56] By configuring the terms of political debate, party systems shape the strategies and the ultimate ends pursued by parties. Social democratic and liberal welfare states, while on opposite ends of most measures of welfare state development, each have partisan debates that are dominated by economic and distributive issues (the size and redistributive capacity of the welfare state). In social democratic polities, the party system typically includes a robust equality-favouring party of the centre-left, which faces one or more weaker and fragmented centre-right liberal parties. Liberal party systems feature a strong liberal party confronting a social democratic alternative. Divided in this way between left and right, party politics in liberal settings generally is more polarized regarding the merits of increasing or curtailing welfare state benefits than is the case elsewhere. Moreover, in the current era of globalization, these party systems are more likely to give rise to pressures for radical neo-liberal retrenchment. 'Without strong liberal parties in Western democracies that place the issue on the agenda and compel their competitors to take a position, decisive [neo-liberal] reform programmes have rarely gotten off the ground.'[57] By contrast, in conservative welfare states, which typically emerge in nations where religious or regional divisions traditionally were strong, partisan debate centres mostly on socio-cultural issues, such as 'religion, environmental quality of life, multiculturalism, or moral conduct.'[58] Three broad political formations typically exist: along with the liberal and social democratic ones present elsewhere, there exists an often hegemonic Christian Democratic party. Economic and distributive issues are of secondary importance here, and – in a context where cooperation among government, business, and labour is frequently an important feature of welfare state policy-making and administration – there is often a broad consensus among the main parties on economic issues. In a fourth, 'clientistic' setting, in contrast to the first three, parties do not primarily divide in programmatic terms; instead, 'parties engage in a direct exchange with citizens where those who provide votes and financial resources to the party receive tangible, selective benefits in return.'[59] This pattern exists in Japan and in most other developed East Asian welfare states.[60] In these cases, ample welfare states are unlikely to have arisen; whatever measures do exist, however, are unlikely to be the focus of sharp partisan disagreement. Kitschelt's theory of party systems can be synthesised with the models discussed in the previous sections (see table 1.1). Each of the first three political economy types is associated with one of the three programmatic party system models. The state-enhanced category includes some nations (France and southern Europe) with three–party systems broadly of the type that exist in sectoral CMEs; politics in this category's East Asian exemplars is more clientistic.

The party system that typifies liberal welfare states is of particular importance for this study; it differs from alternative party systems in ways that are crucial for the two research questions defined at the beginning of this chapter, which we address in this study. First, in relation to the first question, it is in liberal settings that partisanship is likely to have the strongest ongoing effect on policy-making in mature welfare states. Lacking effective corporatist arrangements to displace problem-solving from the legislative setting (as in sectoral CMEs), a pervasive societal commitment to social security (national CMEs), or clientistic practices that blunt programmatic partisan rivalries (some state-enhanced political economies), liberal milieus are especially susceptible to partisan polarization around economic and distributive issues. In a liberal context, 'where support for social provision is relatively thin and the electoral arena plays a dominant role, partisan control of

Table 1.2. Party Systems, Predicted Policy 'Swings,' and Retrenchment Potential

Party System	Predicted short-term policy 'swings'	Potential for globalization-induced retrenchment
Liberal: 2-party; high economic polarization	High	High
Social democratic: 1-party dom.; high polarization	Low	Low
Conservative: multi-party; low economic polarization	Low	Low
Clientistic: 1-party dom.; low polarization	Low	Low

government and the degree to which institutions concentrate political authority become critical factors.'[61] *We should therefore expect partisanship – expressed in divergent party programs and in policy alterations after a change in government – to be more prominent the more liberal is the political-economic setting.* Consequently, what will be termed here the *short-term partisan 'swings,'* which occur after changes in government, are likely to be substantial. Due to the weakness of the welfare state's opponents (in social democratic settings), the consensus that prevails around the welfare state (conservative welfare states), or the lack of programmatic politics (clientism), this is much less true elsewhere. With reference to the second question, this partisan arrangement offers advantages to market-oriented liberals in an era when retrenchment is an option, reinforcing the advantage that accrues to them by virtue of the fact that existing social security arrangements embody only a moderate degree of solidarity. In each case, identified above, where Huber and Stephens detected radical retrenchment during the 1980s and 90s (the United Kingdom and New Zealand), such a strong liberal party was present in an economically polarized party system. *The party systems of liberal settings therefore grant a particular privilege to market-oriented options in an era when globalization has created the potential for severe welfare state cuts;* as an environment, it has considerable potential to foster *long-term policy retrenchment.* Lacking the combination of an economically polarized party system and a powerful market-oriented liberal party, other party systems are less likely to experience radical retrenchment. The distinctive implications for four different party systems for each of these two dimensions of partisanship's impact on policy-making are summarized in table 1.2.

Because liberal settings privilege business interests in informal, pluralist systems of interest intermediation, it should come as no surprise that case studies of liberal welfare state development frequently note that social democratic parties, when in power, sometimes attempt to construct corporatist decision-making arrangements. This was true, for example, in the United Kingdom in the 1970s and in Australia during the 1980s. Given their inconsistency with pre-existing institutions, it is also not surprising that such efforts rarely are successful for long.[62] They nevertheless conform to a certain logic. Confronting an institutional setting that chronically disadvantages their pro-welfare agenda, social democratic governments might reasonably be expected to attempt to adopt foreign systems of interest intermediation that characterize political economies where this agenda has developed further and is under much less threat. It would be reasonable to look for this pattern, as well, in the cases examined here.

Globalization, Partisanship, and Institutional Variety

There is now a voluminous literature on globalization, a phenomenon first identified by scholars in its specifically contemporary form in the late 1980s. While often considered to encompass cultural, military, and political aspects, as well as economic ones,[63] it is the latter that are the object of greatest attention. 'Economic globalization,' for Robert Gilpin, involved 'a few key developments in trade, finance and foreign direct investment by multinational corporations.'[64] Rapid expansion of these was facilitated by technological (cheaper and faster transportation links and telecommunications) and political developments (the willingness of leading states in the global economy to pursue free trade and deregulation). For many observers these trends have emasculated the nation state. 'In a highly integrated global economy, the nation-state, according to this interpretation, has become an anachronism and is in retreat.'[65] Kenichi Ohmae argues that globalization 'has swallowed most consumers and corporations, made traditional national borders disappear, and pushed bureaucrats, politicians, and the military towards the status of declining industries.'[66] This view is contested. Robert Boyer and J. Rogers Hollingsworth state, flatly, that 'the conventional wisdom about the convergence of all societies belonging to the same borderless world is erroneous.'[67] Paul Hirst and Grahame Thompson affirm, similarly, that 'government policies to sustain national economic performance retain much of their relevance' and that 'national governments can still *compensate* for the effects of internationalization and for the continued volatility of the financial markets.'[68]

This debate has complex implications for the role of institutions in mediating the impact of partisanship and globalization on public policy-making, our central concern. Sensitive to the variety of capitalist democracies, scholars associated with the literatures discussed in this chapter generally reject the view that globalization is eliminating this multiplicity. But there are two distinct questions at issue. As we have seen, these literatures argue that capitalist democracies possess different institutional arrangements with respect to their welfare states and production regimes. Most authors also emphasize the role that partisanship and its social foundations played in constructing and sustaining institutional plurality.[69] Historical institutionalists might therefore dispute the globalization argument on two different fronts. They might contend that (a) *pace* Ohmae's characterization of politicians as a 'declining industry,' partisanship remains important in policy-making; and (b) that globalization is not eliminating institutional variety. Each argument has, in fact, been made, though they sometimes may have been conflated. The first two subsections below respectively provide separate accounts of the debate about the ongoing role of partisanship and about continued institutional distinctiveness. The latter also reviews evidence of possible further divergence or *polarization* between regime types. A third subsection addresses comparative regime economic *performance* in the wake of globalization.

Whither Social Democracy?

If globalization has curtailed the potential for partisanship to affect policy outcomes, this should be reflected particularly clearly in the fate of social democratic parties. It is these, more committed than other mainstream formations to collectivist and egalitarian objectives, whose agenda is most threatened by globalization's putatively market-oriented and liberalizing thrust. Indeed, it is now widely argued that social democracy largely has lost its ability to pursue its traditional objectives. Summarizing most contributions to a recent volume devoted to this question, Andrew Glyn foresees 'governments of the Left succumbing to remorseless pressure, both ideological and from the economic constraints faced, to accept orthodox policies – priority to inflation control, limitation of overall tax burdens, labour-market de-regulation.'[70] Gerassimos Moschonas's extensive study of post-war so-cial democracy is equally pessimistic. While European social democratic parties experienced electoral success during the 1990s, Moschonas con-tends that they have increasingly adopted market-oriented goals. 'Mod-erately neo-liberal economic policies; a certain working-class electoral defection; the loosening of the link with the unions; the middle-class entry into the organisation; class images diluted in favour of catch-all strategies ... The new social-democratic construct – marked by the strong presence of the neo-liberal component on the ideological and programmatic level, and by the middle classes on the organisational level – is buckling under its own weight.'[71] Other observers paint an equally bleak portrait.[72]

Many are more optimistic about social democracy's room for ma-noeuvre, but are uncertain about where that room can be found, or describe it in terms that suggest it requires accommodating much of the agenda of social democracy's liberal opponents. For Adam Przeworski, 'the constraints that paralyse social democrats are not as tight as they tend to believe.' Yet he admits to not knowing what alternative now exists to market-oriented policies, venturing only that social democratic success 'requires innovative ideas, the courage of conviction, and luck.'[73] For Fritz Scharpf, since Keynesian macro-economic policies are no longer viable in view of the 'large cycles of international capital markets,' social democrats must resign themselves to encouraging an ample re-turn to capital, and to not seeking to reduce this return to the advantage of labour. Social democrats must pursue 'socialism in one class.'[74] To confront high unemployment, he recommends more job creation or the reduction of working hours. Social democracy must abandon its 'focus on the distribution of unclaimed gains from capitalist growth' and 'explicitly [accept] the full harshness of worldwide economic condi-tions.'[75] Ton Notermans argues, conversely, that it is precisely through macro-economic policy, above all an expansive monetary stance, that social democrats can reduce unemployment. However, he also suggests that globalization has rendered ineffective the mechanisms that previ-ously prevented low unemployment from causing high inflation. Macro-economic stimulus must therefore be combined with 'micro-economic liberalism;' in the context of global markets, the latter would ensure wage discipline.[76] Such recent European developments as the 'aban-donment of interventionist supply-side policies in favour of deregula-tion and privatization, and in particular the ongoing process of market liberalisation' appear to be examples of this stance.[77] Again proposing a directly contradictory macro-economic policy, one based on Scandinavian developments, Torben Iversen contends that 'decentralisation and monetarist macroeconomic policies in the future must be part of the institutional foundations for social democracy, *despite* their antithetical relationship to traditional socialist ideals.' Moreover, 'the failure of [the social democratic model of the past] resulted from a perpetuation of egalitarian ideals that went beyond what was compatible with sustained international competitiveness.'[78] In view of proposals of this type, antithetical and seeming to reduce significantly the distance between social democracy and neo-liberalism, many might ask, with Perry Anderson, 'What kind of movement will it change into?' as it accommodates globalization.[79]

Some comparative political economy scholars, by contrast, contend that partisanship remains important. Carles Boix's research, which concentrates on economic policy (including labour market measures) is particularly ambitious. Boix concedes that contemporary macro-economic policy variations can be explained by 'different domestic institutional arrangements,' rather than by 'political coalitions, or partisan strategies for that matter.'[80] But with respect to micro-economic interventions, including spending on education, vocational training, and public investment, the story is quite different. Indeed, regarding these 'supply-side' policies, partisanship has come to play an even greater role since the 1970s. 'Left-wing governments have responded [to the collapse of demand-management techniques] by calling for more public investment and larger education and vocational-training programs and by defending, in some cases, the strategic role of public firms in an increasingly competitive world economy.' The right, by contrast, developed an ever-deeper attachment to market solutions.[81] Geoffrey Garrett's research is intended to support a similar conclusion. 'Globalization,' he asserts, 'increased the political incentives for left-wing parties to pursue economic policies that redistribute wealth and risk in favour of those adversely affected ... by market dislocations. ... The historical relationship between left-labour power and big government has not weakened with market integration.'[82] Garrett correlates spending levels in a variety of policy fields with a measure of 'left-labour power,' which combines scores for left-party control of executive and legislative seats and 'for labour market institutions (which aggregates standardized scores for union density, the number of unions in the largest labour confederation [etc.]).'[83] He observes that 'the greater the combined power of the left and organised labour, the higher public expenditures were. ... [and] the partisan distinctiveness of government spending increased with the greater integration of national economies into global markets.'[84]

Institutional Resilience ... or Polarization?

Colin Hay contends that Garrett confuses two arguments: on the one hand, the claim that partisanship still matters; and, on the other, the quite distinctive contention that the institutional variety that typified capitalism before globalization's emergence has persisted since. Garrett's research, he claims, supports the latter view, while being presented as a defence of the former. It really suggests, for Hay, that 'social democratic outcomes are dependent on social democratic institutions (in particular, encompassing labour market movements) which cannot be acquired overnight.'[85] While 'social democratic corporatism is 'selected for' in nations characterized by social democratic corporatist institutions and traditions,' neo-liberal policies are 'selected for' elsewhere.[86] Is Hay's argument justified? Garrett's measure of 'left-labour power' does, to repeat, combine measures of left power with indices of union strength and centralization; the latter characteristically are much higher in CMEs and social democratic welfare states than in liberal milieus. At the very least, then, Garrett's data do not indicate partisanship's impact on policy-making independently of institutional factors, as Boix's attempt to. They reflect the combined effect of short-term partisan and long-term institutional influences, and, to this extent, provide at least as much evidence of the resilience of institutional diversity as they do of partisanship's continuing potential.

That distinctive regimes have persevered in the face of globalization is widely argued by comparative welfare state and production regime scholars. Huber and Stephens, we have observed, concluded that only in two cases have recent changes altered the broad design of a nation's welfare state, and these were Anglo-Saxon polities. This suggests a further possibility, also now commonly advanced by scholars in these traditions: Not only are regime types not converging in response to globalization, they are moving further apart. Many recent contributions support this 'polarization' thesis. 'Instead of the monolithic movement toward deregulation that many expect from globalization,' Hall and Soskice assert, 'our analysis predicts a bifurcated response marked by widespread deregulation in liberal market economies and limited movement in coordinated market economies.'[87] CMEs and LMEs will move further apart. Kathleen Thelen reached analogous conclusions in her review of recent industrial relations policy. She discovered 'sources of resiliency in labour institutions in the CMEs as well as ... fragility [in] traditional institutions in the LMEs. Despite important changes in some CMEs ... wage-bargaining has re-equilibrated at a rather centralised level ... While significant, these changes do not amount to wholesale deregulation, or ... the return to widespread employer unilateralism, as in the LMEs.'[88] Stewart Wood observes, in comparing recent labour market policy in Germany and the United Kingdom, that 'in an LME, where relations between firms are mediated by markets, the state will be more effective if it restores and 'sharpens' market mechanisms. In a CME, effective policy consists in supporting the institutions and networks of coordination that connect companies.'[89] In relation to various components of the welfare state, finally, Duane Swank finds that formal political institutions (executive centralisation and federalism), combined with the coordinative or pluralist institutional legacies highlighted by comparative political economy research, explain divergent responses to globalization across capitalist democracies. Globalization will put effective downward pressure on entitlements 'where welfare states are structured according to liberal programmatic principles.' Where universal or social insurance measures are well developed, however, 'and in political institutional contexts of moderate-to-strong corporatism, inclusive electoral institutions, and centralised policy-making authority, the conventionally hypothesised globalization dynamics are absent.' Here, globalization has no downward effect, 'or it is related to small positive increments in social protection.'[90]

This polarization thesis is particularly relevant for research in LMEs. If, to borrow Hay's terminology, LME's 'select for' centre-right and market-oriented policies, and CMEs 'select for' centre-left and egalitarian alternatives, the institutional bias of the former would be enhanced by globalization; that of the latter would be largely unaffected. Liberal institutions will, in effect, be 'in movement,' not only privileging centre-right options, but doing so more fully over time.

Institutional Performance

If institutions are not converging, one might nevertheless anticipate *future* convergence if one regime becomes associated with superior results, especially regarding economic growth and employment. Nations with 'inferior' institutions would have an incentive to abandon them in favour of better-performing ones.[91] If globalization is creating a systematic advantage for market-oriented arrangements, liberal institutions would presumably be favoured by such a comparison. Yet, comparative welfare state and production regime scholarship suggests that liberal capitalism has not recently performed better (or worse) then coordinative regimes. The evidence is mixed, and sometimes contradictory. Garrett finds 'no reason why social democratic corporatism should not be presented as a viable alternative to the neo-classical perspective for developing and prospering in the era of global markets.'[92] Garrett's variable of 'left-labour power' correlates with lower unemployment and higher growth than elsewhere, especially 'under conditions of high capital mobility.' Liberal settings achieved better results regarding inflation.[93]

Fritz Scharpf concludes that high overall tax levels have no negative effect on overall employment levels. But high payroll taxes do correlate negatively with low-wage private service sector employment.[94] Each welfare state model, moreover, faces specific challenges. These are no greater for social democratic settings than liberal ones. The former must fund their ample measures without discouraging lower-paying service jobs that are needed to prevent unemployment; the latter face intractably high levels of inequality and poverty. Conservative regimes confront greater problems because their tax systems favour employment-destroying payroll deductions, and because their high levels of labour market regulation also correlate negatively with job growth.[95] If social security is financed with the right taxes (on personal income, not on capital, wages, or consumption), and if labour market regulation is relaxed, Scharpf and Schmidt conclude, 'the overall size of the welfare state and the extent of redistribution remain a matter of political choice.'[96] Esping-Andersen's findings diverge from Scharpf's on one critical detail: Higher levels of labour market regulation do not, he argues, discernibly hurt the *stock* of employment available. They do reduce *flows*, however, in effect granting additional employment security to the already employed at the expense of youth, women, and those with low skills.[97] Since wholesale labour market deregulation could cause significant social harm, Esping-Andersen and Marino Regini recommend that it be avoided, in favour of 'partial deregulation, typically targeted at the 'outsiders' while leaving many prerogatives of the core workforce more or less intact.'[98] Garrett and Christopher Way acknowledge that the correlation between corporatism and superior macro-economic performance 'broke down' in the 1980s, but contend that this only occurred in nations whose labour movements are dominated by public sector unions. If the latter are not 'too strong,' 'corporatist institutions continue to promote both price stability and low rates of unemployment.'[99] Lane Kenworthy concludes that nations with relatively 'co-operative' economic institutions generally perform better economically than those that rely 'predominantly on atomistic, individualistic competition.'[100]

Comparative political economy scholarship has not refuted the claim that globalization is reducing substantially partisanship's impact on public policy, and precipitated convergence towards market-oriented institutions. But it calls both propositions into question. Globalization has not clearly eliminated the impact of partisanship; liberal and non-liberal regimes appear to have remained quite distinct in recent years, and may even have diverged further; and evidence regarding the economic 'performance' of each institutional setting gives us little reason to expect this to change soon.

Taking Stock

This is a study of the impact of partisanship and globalization on labour market policy. Consistent with the historical institutionalist approach adopted here, our first task has been to identify the institutional settings that condition how each of these affects policy. We have identified three institutional typologies as relevant for this task. Labour market policy overlaps with both social policy and the economy. Consequently, two typologies have been provided by the scholarship on comparative welfare states and production regimes. These can be synthesized in a manner that facilitates our enquiry. The third typology has addressed the party systems generally associated with these institutions. The synthesis elaborated in table 1.1 identified four regime types. For our purposes the most important distinction will be between the liberal welfare state/LME model and its more coordinative alternatives. As we will see, liberal features predominate in the welfare states and production regimes of the four Canadian provinces examined here; however, there is a partial exception in the case of Quebec, and important variations exist among the other provinces. Inter-provincial differences regarding party systems are considerable.

The welfare state and production regime literatures depict the differences that can be anticipated between liberal and non-liberal settings in the labour market field. Policy-making is likely to involve concertation among the labour market partners and government in coordinative polities; in liberal milieus, corporatist tools should be poorly developed, and the prevailing pluralist system of interest intermediation will likely favour business. Policy content should also diverge. Coordinative environments tolerate greater labour market regulation, in the context of strong labour unions and an accommodative culture, than will liberal ones. Educational systems will be geared to providing the technical vocational skills most prized in these economies; liberal regimes instead rely on markets to provide most skills, and concentrate on general education. Liberal regimes generally will also expend less on labour market measures, and, lacking comprehensive social security measures, will rely more on social assistance-type programs to provide for the neediest; there will be an incentive for these to be market-oriented and punitive. These institutional differences have implications for the six policy fields examined in this study: liberal settings will spend less on active and passive labour market policies; the former will be relatively under-emphasized compared to general education, and the latter will have market-oriented work requirements. In each of our other four domains – industrial relations, employment standards, workers' compensation, and occupational health and safety – liberal settings should favour less regulation and more modest benefits than would any other. Once mature, these institutions 'select for' one set of partisan options over others. In a liberal context, parties of the centre-right should have greater success than their centre-left rivals (typically, in a two-party landscape where economic issues predominate and partisan polarization is substantial) in effectively legislating and implementing their preferred options. Moreover, the impact of partisanship on labour market policy-making is likely to differ between liberal and non-liberal settings in ways that bear directly on the two questions with which we began this chapter. *First, short-term policy 'swings,' which result from a change in government, are likely to be considerable in liberal settings, and smaller elsewhere. Second, the labour market policy framework's relative vulnerability in liberal contexts exposes it to long-term policy retrenchment there to a greater extent than elsewhere.* Retrenchment will effectively favour centre-right agendas in ways that transcend short-term partisan 'swings,' becoming part of the long-term institutional order of liberal milieus.

The next chapter applies the framework developed here to the four jurisdictions that are the focus of our Canadian case studies. It generates specific hypotheses for each of them regarding the likely impact of partisanship on labour market policy in the short-term, and on the potential for long-term retrenchment. After the detailed description of the main components of Canadian labour market policy in chapter 3, these hypotheses are tested separately for each province for most fields in the case studies reported in chapters 4 to 7. Social assistance for employable persons is discussed separately in chapter 8 for all four provinces. As we explain at greater length at the beginning of that chapter, we began our research with the surmise that the specific context of policy-making in that sector – the leading social and political actors, and the sector's distinctive ideological, fiscal, and political features – diverged significantly from those that characterized the other five. For the same reason, we anticipated that the institutional setting for labour market policy-making in each province as it is characterized in chapter 2 may not be appropriate for understanding social assistance policy. As noted above, in chapter 9 the theoretical framework presented here is applied to Germany, and hypotheses are developed and tested regarding our two questions in relation to that case. Chapter 10 summarizes our findings and assesses their implications for further research and reflection. It also returns to the concern raised by some observers that historical institutionalism typically downplays the importance of agency in relation to structure, underestimating the extent of institutional change.

2 Welfare State, Production Regime, and Party System in Four Canadian Provinces

The institutional typologies developed in chapter 1 will now be applied to the four Canadian jurisdictions – Ontario, Quebec, British Columbia, and Alberta – addressed in this study. This is not a straightforward task, for three reasons. One of these is generic to the application of typologies to individual cases: the latter only ever 'fit' the former approximately. The other two reflect specific features of the cases examined here. First, it has proven particularly difficult to apply categories developed by the comparative welfare state and production regime literatures to Canada, and most studies have not done so in great detail. Second, by focusing on provinces, we are applying institutional categories to sub-national jurisdictions, while the studies reviewed in the previous chapter concentrated on national ones. This chapter briefly addresses each of these problems as a prelude to locating the provinces in relation to the welfare state, production regime, and party system typologies identified previously. In light of this, the last section generates hypotheses about how these provincial institutional settings can be expected to condition the impact of partisanship and globalization on labour market policy there.

We have argued that labour market programs can be viewed both as components of the welfare state and as features of the production regime. Canadian programs will be discussed briefly in the welfare state subsection below; a more extensive treatment is provided in chapter 3. Esping-Andersen notes that welfare state 'typologies are problematic because parsimony is bought at the expense of nuance.'[1] Swank warns, similarly, that 'individual welfare states depart notably from the prototype of the welfare state regime to which they are commonly assigned,' and that enquiries must 'acknowledge nuances of individual

Table 2.1. Attention to the Canadian Case in Recent Comparative Welfare State and Political Economy Studies[4]

Study	Number of cases	Canada examined?	Number of pages
Esping-Andersen & Regini (2000)	8	No	
Goodin et al. (1999)	3	No	
Hall & Soskice, pt. 2 (2001)	3	No	
Huber & Stephens (2001)	13	No	
Iversen et al. (2000)	5	No	
Kitschelt et al., pt. 3 (1999)	8	No	
Pierson et al., chaps. 9–12 (2001)	6	No	
Scharpf & Schmidt, vol. 2 (2000)	12	No	
Schmidt (2002)	3	No	
Swank (2002)	15	Yes	1 of 96

cases.'[2] Hall and Soskice observe, in relation to LMEs and CMEs, that these 'constitute ideal types at the poles of a spectrum along which nations can be arrayed.'[3] Such variations may be of secondary importance for statistical studies that examine many cases, but they require more attention in detailed qualitative discussions. In fact, the welfare states, production regimes, and party systems of the four provinces examined here, while sharing a broadly liberal design, possess important features that distinguish them from the liberal ideal type and (regarding production regimes and party systems) from each other.

The second complication in applying institutional typologies is occasioned by the Canadian setting, especially its production regimes and party systems. Canada is little attended to in most comparative studies discussed in chapter 1. It is usually included in statistical comparisons, but when these studies turn to more detailed qualitative examinations, it is rarely among those discussed. Only one study discussed in chapter 1 that relied at least in part on a case study methodology, and applied it to at least three nations from, at minimum, two different regime types, included more than a very brief (less than a page) discussion of Canada (see table 2.1).[5] Moreover, when Canadian scholars address these typologies, they express reservations about their creators' tendency to designate Canada as a liberal setting. And Kitschelt's hypothesis that liberal settings will give rise to two-party systems that polarize along economic lines does not apply to the Canadian party system. Paul Pierson recently declared, flatly, that 'we lack a convincing and detailed account of political dynamics in Canada.' He added that 'part of the explanation [of the relative modesty of recent welfare state cuts there] must be the manner in which a decentralized federal structure encouraged negotiation on the contours of adjustment between a series of national governments and powerful (and politically diverse) provincial premiers.'[6]

Canada evidently presents particular classificatory problems to students of comparative social and economic institutions. As Pierson implies, moreover, these difficulties are particularly acute in relation to the nation's politics, and they are partly attributable to the importance of inter-regional tensions in Canadian public life. In this chapter we do not propose a complete model of Canada's institutional architecture, in relation to the three dimensions reviewed in chapter 1. A rudimentary design for such a model nevertheless is required before we can develop hypotheses about the role of partisanship and globalization in shaping labour market policy in our four provinces. Its three main elements, elaborated in the first part of the three main subsections of this chapter, can be summarized briefly. First, it is in relation to its *party system* that the impact of region is greatest nationally, and where wide differences exist among the provinces.[7] Canadian politics has long been dominated by business-aligned brokerage parties. Partisan debate has focused on social (language, religion, and region), not economic (class) concerns. Where brokerage failed, influential regional third parties emerged that brought both economic and social issues to the national agenda. The prominence of language and region in national politics, along with economic grievances and the political-economic differences discussed below, resulted in distinctive party systems in the provinces. The Canadian *production regime*, secondly, has been shaped by competing centrifugal and centripetal forces. The pattern of east-west economic development fostered by the 1870s' National Policy, and the simple consequences of geography and demography in a large and sparsely populated country, resulted in asymmetrical patterns of income, industrial sector specialization and social class formation, among the provinces. In Quebec, these differences have been magnified by the province's unique political history. While a liberal pattern predominates, there are important interprovincial variations. Finally, Canada's *welfare state* diverges somewhat from the liberal model that is attributed to it. Regional variations are less significant here. One can speak of a 'Canadian' welfare state, albeit with important interprovincial variations. The broadly social democratic departures from liberalism that it embodies emerged during the welfare state's post-war construction. They reflect the influence of working class pressures, but also of regionalism, on national politics.

Regionalism's prominence in Canada's political and economic life provides us with a key for resolving our third dilemma, that we are applying the comparative institutionalist scholarship to provinces, not nations. There are, of course, significant commonalities among the Canadian provinces. These reduce the range of institutional variables that can be associated with differences identified in our case studies. Interprovincial differences nevertheless are sufficient, especially regarding production regimes and party systems, to have important implications for our research. These are addressed in the second parts of the three subsections that follow. These subsections, respectively, elaborate upon the outline of the welfare state, production regime, and partisan institutions in Canada presented above; the conclusion addresses its implications for the case studies provided in chapters 4 through 7.

Canada's 'Impure' Liberal Welfare State

Scholars agree that Canada most closely resembles Esping-Andersen's liberal regime type, but most express reservations. For Maureen Baker, while Canada and other liberal cases are similarly 'ungenerous, targeted at the poor, and funded through general taxation,' there are 'substantial variations that distinguish' them.[8] Though broadly liberal, Sylvia Bashevkin adds, 'Canada had a somewhat more robust welfare state than ... the United States.'[9] Rodney Haddow referred to Canada as 'impure-liberal' due to the presence of universal elements in its social security system.[10] John Myles and Paul Pierson, after noting that 'the United States and Canada [are] leading exemplars' of the liberal model,[11] describe quite different recent changes within each. Keith Banting contends that however similar they are from a European perspective, 'especially for the poor and for marginal social groups, the differences between Canadian and American social programmes are important.'[12]

The broadest elements in Canada's welfare state emerged after the Second World War. Previously, Dennis Guest observes, Canadian social security was 'residual,' consisting mostly of social assistance-type measures.[13] Significant departures from pure liberalism began during the 1940s, stimulated by a significant shift to the political left – reflected in growing support for the social democratic Co-operative Commonwealth Federation (CCF), predecessor to the NDP, and rising union membership – during the war. But, Jane Jenson has argued, the pervasive role of regional sensitivities, which accentuated during the post-war years, and of the brokerage style of partisanship used to address these concerns in Canada, also fostered a more than minimal welfare state.[14] The federal government, hegemonic in its relations with the provinces during the war, encouraged this expansion. Its influence diminished significantly after 1960, but its earlier predominance had a lasting effect: despite having constitutional jurisdiction in most areas, the provinces continue to have broadly similar welfare states.

The National Pattern for Social Policy

Ottawa was able to implement several elements of the post-war welfare state directly, either because the provinces granted it the necessary constitutional authority, or because it used its 'spending power' to dispense funds directly to individuals.[15] A universal family allowance was created in 1944, and, after atrophying in the face of inflation, was restored to its original value during the 1970s. A universal Old Age Security (OAS) pension was created in 1951; a contributory Canada Pension Plan (CPP), matched with a parallel program in Quebec, was launched in 1965. In other areas, Ottawa induced the provinces to establish programs that conformed to federal norms by agreeing in exchange to share program costs. This led to a nationwide 'single payer' form of public health insurance in each province. Federal cost-sharing for universities was made available with fewer conditions than in the health field; but even here, important interprovincial similarities resulted. Universities across the country became largely publicly funded, with student fees covering only a small part of costs.

    The 1980s and 1990s witnessed a retreat; the Canadian welfare state continues to be impurely liberal, but is closer to that ideal type today than it was in the 1970s. Chronically burdened by deficits after 1973, and challenged by increasingly aggressive provinces, Ottawa reduced its spending and its role in standards setting. The family allowance was eliminated; Ottawa's main child benefit now is an income-tested (selective) Child Tax Benefit (CTB). The OAS was made partly selective; the selective Guaranteed Income Supplement (GIS) is now more important for low-income pensioners. Even by its own (disputed) calculations, Ottawa now covers only about 30 per cent of the cost of the universal health care system (down from 50 per cent in the early 1970s); all provincial health schemes face severe cost and demographic pressures. In real dollars, per student university funding has fallen considerably since the 1970s, and student fees have risen substantially as a share of university costs.

The general trajectory of Canada's social policies in the post-war years can be compared to Britain's: Influenced by the 'Beveridge' model of universal provision, it moved a significant degree away from liberalism in the direction of social democracy.[16] The 1980s and 1990s then witnessed a retreat to a liberalism that is more consistent with an underlying institutional order dominated by business-oriented parties in a context of modest working class mobilization. Compared with Britain, however, neither the move away from unalloyed liberalism, nor the subsequent retreat, has been as dramatic.[17] To the extent that the Canadian welfare state has become more selective, moreover, it has not witnessed the rise of income polarization observable in other liberal countries. As Myles and Pierson observed, writing in 1997, the relative generosity of such selective measures as the CTB meant that 'the Canadian system of social transfers has been successful in stabilising the final distribution of family incomes and containing child poverty.'[18] Canada probably can still be classified as a liberal welfare state with significant social democratic features. Certainly, Esping-Andersen's own summary data on welfare state 'clusters' supported this view for 1980. While Canada shared with the United States the highest possible score of 12 for 'degree of liberalism,' based on this composite measure, it also rated a 4 (considered 'medium') for 'degree of socialism,' while the United States received a 0.[19]

The National Pattern for Labour Market Policy

The same impure-liberal pattern prevails regarding labour market policy. Estevez-Abe et al. rank Canada 13th of 18 OECD (Organization for Economic Cooperation and Development) nations in the generosity of its main passive labour market program for employable persons, and 14th of 18 in the protection provided by its employment standards; the United States is 18th in each case. Canada ranked ahead of all other Anglo-Saxon nations, except Ireland, and behind all non-Anglo-Saxon nations, with the exception of Italy regarding the former measure. Canada also has a skills profile (limited vocational training and job tenure, substantial general education) that typifies a liberal regime.[20]

Ottawa administered directly a contributory unemployment insurance (UI) scheme that it created in 1940; it was gradually expanded on several occasions thereafter, until 1971.[21] In two areas of labour market policy – passive measures for employable persons who were ineligible for UI, and active measures – post-war federal cost-sharing fostered broadly comparable policies, as it did in the health and university sectors. Beginning in the 1950s, federally cost-shared social assistance programs restricted 'workfare' in the provinces (the granting of assistance in exchange for work). Ottawa's training programs promoted a pattern favouring school-based institutional over on-the-job industrial training (the liberal norm) in the provinces, by directing federal funds to instruction provided in provincial (technical) community colleges. The post-1970s pattern of cuts was again comparable to that observed for social programs. UI benefits were reduced on numerous occasions after the mid-1970s, culminating in their replacement by the more restrictive Employment Insurance program in 1995. Ottawa terminated cost-sharing for social assistance in 1995, making it easier for provinces to implement workfare. In 1996, the federal government offered to transfer the administration of, and significant authority over, its training spending to the provinces. Overall federal spending in this area declined during the 1990s.[22]

Elsewhere in the labour market domain neither direct administration nor cost-sharing were available to Ottawa during peacetime. For most employees, industrial relations, workers' compensation, occupational health and safety, and employment standards are under provincial jurisdiction. Significant interprovincial similarities exist nonetheless. For Carolyn Tuohy, Canada shares with other liberal regimes an 'adversarial' style of industrial relations, with no significant record of success for European-style corporatism.[23] During the Second World War Ottawa was able to control the field temporarily. It 'transplanted the United States legislative framework of labour relations and collective bargaining ... until the end of the war.' Even today, according to Gene Swimmer, 'the core of all provinces' [industrial relations] legislation is extremely similar' as a result.[24] Ottawa never played a leading role in workers' compensation, but here too there is a broadly similar history. Most provinces developed their first compensation legislation during or after the First World War, again following American examples. They still share many features: administration by an independent board; employer funding of benefits in exchange for exemption from most civil liability; appeal procedures; permanent disability and survivors' benefits; and similar 'benefit formulas.'[25] An early 1990s study conducted by Labour Canada also identified several features of employment standards and occupational health and safety law that were similar among the Canadian provinces, but often absent in the United States.[26] The extent of retrenchment in these fields is examined for the four provinces studied here in chapters 4 to 7.

Provincial Variations

There is no systematic research, that we are aware of, comparing Canadian provinces across the entire range of welfare state measures. But there is evidence of notable differences in particular fields. Tuohy identified variations in relation to health insurance. All provinces can be distinguished from the United States and Britain by virtue of the 'single-payer' logic established by federal legislation. But the provincial-level accommodation between government and the medical profession required to make this logic work was accomplished differently. 'In Quebec,' the accommodation 'accorded a greater assertion of the role of the state than in any other province.' In British Columbia, 'a more polarised partisan environment, and a system of industrial relations with a highly adversarial and conflictual history all combined to create a template of adversarialism.'[27] Ontario and Alberta followed the 'adversarial' model. 'Over time, however, these ... categories began to show a degree of convergence.'[28] The mix of spending across different aspects of the health system has converged less consistently, however.

Gerard Boychuk's comparison of provincial social assistance uncovered significant differences. In 1990, BC's system conformed to a 'market performance' model, designed to 'encourage labour market participation.' Alberta's 'market/family enforcement' program 'reinforce[d] the market and family through sanctions against all state dependents.' The former generally provided higher benefits and was less stigmatizing, especially for those participating in employment preparation. Quebec's system reflected a mixture of these two sets of principles. Ontario's 'conservative' system, like the others, encouraged employment for many recipients, but granted 'differentially generous' benefits, effectively an exemption from the marketplace, to those deemed worthy.[29] Yet it is important not to exaggerate this variety. Boychuk's comparison of social assistance between Canadian provinces and American states uncovered significant divergence between American and Canadian patterns. In many respects they 'stand in stark relief' when compared.[30] As the comparative welfare state literature stresses, moreover, all social assistance schemes are, intrinsically, characteristic of market-oriented liberal welfare states.[31]

Labour market policies, we have argued, reflect both welfare state and production regime institutions. The latter vary more than the former in Canada; interprovincial variations consequently are greater regarding labour market policy than social policy. Jon Pierce's comparison of provincial industrial relations law in relation to 10 criteria determined that BC and Quebec had relatively 'liberal' (favourable to unionized workers) legislation in 1997; respectively, they possessed 7 and 5 'liberal' features in their law, as opposed to 2 and 1 'restrictive' (pro-business) ones. By contrast, Alberta's law included no 'liberal' features and 6 'restrictive' ones. Ontario had 3 'liberal' and 4 'restrictive' features. For Pierce, partisan factors largely explained the variations. 'All the [four] liberal [provinces] ... have had an NDP or PQ government for at least two full terms,' unlike all of the other six.[32] Richard Block and Karen Roberts compared 63 Canadian and American jurisdictions across a range of labour market policies, including industrial relations, workers' compensation, occupational health, and employment standards. Canadian jurisdictions generally provided greater protection, with 8 ranking among the top 14 of 63 jurisdictions examined; this upper group included British Columbia, Ontario, and Quebec, in descending order. However, Alberta was by far the lowest of the Canadian jurisdictions, ranking 51st.[33] (It should be noted, however, that all jurisdictions studied here were fundamentally liberal). Richard Chaykowski and Terry Thomason identified usually modest variations among Canadian workers' compensation programs with respect to minimum and maximum benefits and maximum earnings covered.[34]

There are differences among provincial welfare states. However, there is little reason to doubt that these represent variations on broadly liberal themes, and that, for the most part, Canada's more 'impure' form of liberalism has meant that differences *among* Canadian jurisdictions have been smaller than those *between* Canadian and American ones. To understand more fully the sources of the interprovincial differences outlined above, and to detect other – generally more profound – distinctions, we now turn to a discussion of the production regimes and party systems of our four provinces and of their national setting.

Provincial Production Regimes: Liberalism's Variable Morphology

Canada's economy, like its welfare state, is predominantly liberal, approximating Soskice's Liberal Market Economy (LME) ideal type. Michael Atkinson and William Coleman attributed to Canada 'a firm-centred industry culture [which] emphasises the self-sufficiency of the firm, the independence of management in making decisions on investment and workplace organisation, and the reliance, wherever possible, on markets for the allocation of capital and labour.'[35] This is inconsistent with a directive role for the state in economic life, and with the dense web of inter-firm relations that typifies Coordinated Market Economies (CMEs). Canadian business is weakly organized at the national or sector level, and has a limited capacity, and willingness, to collaborate with the state, labour, or other interests. Business is not incapable of having its views heard; on the contrary, its interests predominate in government decision-making. But this influence is exercised through the business-linked brokerage parties that have dominated party politics, and along the informal channels afforded by Canada's pluralist system of interest intermediation.[36]

This liberalism is reflected in the four dimensions that, for Soskice, distinguish LMEs from CMEs. 'The financial system that emerged in Canada places financial institutions, industrial corporations, and governments in distinctive spheres.'[37] In conjunction with a 'business-centred' culture, (i) this precluded the dense web of inter-firm relations, and (ii) the proximity to long-term financial capital, which typify CMEs. We have seen that Canada broadly reflects the other two features of an LME: (iii) industrial relations are decentralized and adversarial, and organized labour relatively weak; and (iv) the education and training system is dominated by institutional, not industrial, skills formation. There is little business-labour cooperation in overseeing training. Canada's federal state sometimes played a more important role in fostering national economic growth than was the case in most LMEs. But it did not adopt the strategic and directive stance that characterizes state-enhanced capitalism. Canada lacked the 'state tradition' to permit this. An entrenched tendency among state actors to defer to civil society, combined with the fragmenting qualities of federalism and of the internal organization of the federal government, 'foster[ed] a weak state tradition and discouraged anticipatory policy-making.'[38]

Yet Canada's production regime is not monolithic. The founders of Canadian political economy scholarship demonstrated that from its historical origins it embodied regional asymmetries in wealth and industrial structure.[39] The post-1870s National Policy stimulated a manufacturing economy centred in southern Ontario, and encouraged agriculture, later supplemented by resource extraction, in the western provinces. Economic variety entailed distinctive social relations in the provinces; the business community is configured differently, and organized labour possesses varying levels of strength. And because the federal government played a role – more as business' handmaiden than as strategic leader – in creating this economic geography, these regional asymmetries also profoundly affected national political life and fomented very different party systems in the provinces.

An additional factor played a crucial role in shaping Quebec's contemporary economy, making this jurisdiction distinctive. Consistent with the terms of an informal 'historical compromise' in post-Conquest Quebec between the English business community and the leading institutions for the French-speaking community, the province's private sector was long dominated by the former.[40] During the Quiet Revolution of the 1960s, this arrangement became unacceptable to the French-speaking community. The Quebec state embarked on an economic development strategy to nurture a French-speaking business class in the province. Quebec's production regime acquired statist and coordinative features that cause it to depart somewhat from the LME model in the direction of the CME and state-enhanced alternatives discussed in chapter 1.

Production regime asymmetries also entailed variations in the LMEs of the three English-speaking provinces discussed here. Ontario, the most populous and economically variegated, fits the liberal norm. Its internal diversity nevertheless encouraged 'informal bargaining' with other social interests, including organized labour. British Columbia's resource economy fostered an affluent and market-oriented business community and middle class, alongside relatively strong labour unions. Its political economy has been compared to that of an Australian state.[41] Alberta is home to a large and affluent middle class and a relatively marginal labour movement. The state has nevertheless worked closely with indigenous business to diversify the economy. This section now elaborates on these patterns, outlined in table 2.2.

Ontario

Ontario's business community is highly fragmented, in part because business organizations in the province overlap with national structures. There is no single encompassing business association. The Ontario section of the Canadian Association of Manufacturers and Exporters, the Ontario Chamber of Commerce (closely aligned with the Canadian Chamber of Commerce), and the Ontario section of the Canadian Federation of Independent Business (CFIB, for small business) are the main

Table 2.2. Institutional Setting of Policy-Making in Four Canadian Provinces

Province	Welfare state	Modified by	Production regime	Modified by	Party system	Modified by
Ontario	Liberal	Social democracy	LME	Informal bargaining (depleted?)	3-party / unstable	From 1-party prevalence to high polar.
Quebec	Liberal	Social democracy	Ambivalent/ LME	Industry CME/ statism	2-party	Low polarization
British Columbia	Liberal	Social democracy	LME	Strong labour	2-party	High polarization
Alberta	Liberal	Social democracy	LME	Industrial promotion	1-party dominant	Right hegemony
Interprov. variation	Low		Moderate		High	

supra-sectoral federations. Sector-level associations often play a more important role for their members than do broader structures. As we will see in chapter 4, when Ontario business has felt a need to speak with one voice it has had to form ad hoc umbrella organizations for this purpose. Although the labour movement possesses an encompassing federation, the Ontario Federation of Labour (OFL), it cannot coordinate the industrial relations activities of its affiliates because contract bargaining in Ontario, as elsewhere in Canada, mostly transpires at the firm level between individual companies and affiliate unions. Several important Ontario unions do not belong to the OFL, undermining the latter's credibility in such fields as construction. Moreover, as table 2.3 indicates, unionization levels are quite modest in Ontario. At 27.9 per cent, the overall level of unionization ranked ninth among the Canadian provinces in 2002, and has declined significantly since 1991.

Since the early twentieth century, the provincial state has played a modest role in economic development. The standard economic history of the province until 1939 is entitled *Progress Without Planning*;[42] its sequel, which traces developments until the mid-1980s, refers to the province's industrial strategy in the 1970s as 'empty declarations of good intentions,' and argues that 'despite repeated use of the word 'planning' ... the activities involved appear to have been little more than the co-ordination of various promotional programmes.'[43] Thomas Courchene and Colin Telmer argue that this passivity reflected the fact

Table 2.3. Union Membership by Province, 1991 and 2002

	1991		2002	
Province	%	Rank	%	Rank
Quebec	40.6	2	36.6	2
BC	38.7	3	33.1	5
Ontario	31.9	8	27.9	9
Alberta	26.4	10	22.5	10

Sources: Jon Pierce, *Canadian Industrial Relations* (Toronto: Prentice Hall Canada, 2000), p. 152; Ernest Akyeampong, *Perspectives on Labour and Income* (Ottawa: Statistics Canada), cat. no. 75-001-XPE, vol. 14, no. 3 (2002), p. 75.

that Ontario administrations long could expect the federal government to pursue macro-economic and trade policies that met the province's needs. While they believe that this has changed over the past decade, they do not envisage the province undertaking an active industrial policy.[44]

Neil Bradford points out, moreover, that the broader economic culture of Ontario is market-oriented and industrial relations are decentralized and competitive.[45] Firms are reluctant to cooperate with rivals, and generally do not belong to European-style enterprise networks or have intimate links with a bank. Before the late 1980s, the province had little experience with formal coordinate decision-making among business, labour, and the state, although these interests shared (often acrimoniously) administrative responsibilities on the labour relations' and workers' compensation boards. David Wolfe observes that significant governmental efforts to foster sector-level cooperation among Ontario firms to stimulate innovation, starting in 1985, ran against the grain of the prevailing business culture, and were largely abandoned by the Conservative government that came to power in 1995.[46] Wolfe and Meric Gertler note that Ontario's government now invests heavily in educational institutions to improve the province's human capital.[47] But, reflecting the LME pattern, on-the-job skills formation remains very modest.[48]

This liberal tableau must nevertheless be qualified. Post-war governments were much closer to the business community than to unions. But they often bargained informally with labour leaders about labour legislation. Union leaders usually had some confidence that their views would be considered. While the institutional prerequisites of formal coordinative decision-making were absent, informal bargaining softened the competitiveness and adversarialism of Ontario's LME.[49] It is hard to identify features of Ontario's political economy that accounted for informal bargaining. Sid Noel argues that Ontarians entertain a number of 'operative norms' which they expect their governments to adhere to. Among these are 'the imperative pursuit of economic success,' 'an expectation of reciprocity in political relationships,' and 'the balancing of interests.'[50] The latter 'requires that governments at least make a serious attempt to consult and accommodate divergent interests.'[51] Rand Dyck adds that 'Ontario is extremely diverse in social composition,' with a variegated economy, class structure, and distinctive patterns of intra-provincial wealth.[52] These insights suggest that informal bargaining in Ontario reflected the same factors as brokerage politics did nationally: it was the most effective way to pursue growth in a diverse polity where reconciliation was more likely than confrontation to lead to stable government. This accommodative style was also supported by Ontario's brokerage party system during the post-war years (see below).

During the period investigated in this volume, however, informal bargaining became much less evident. By the 1990s, the party system was more polarized than it had been. Informal bargaining was largely displaced, first by efforts to foster formal coordinate decision-making; then, under the post-1995 Conservative administration, by a tendency to not consult outside of the governing party's own constituencies.[53] It is too early to tell whether this change represents a permanent departure from the pre-existing institutional order, or a temporary aberration.

Quebec

Diverging from the LME ideal type much more than other Canadian provinces, Quebec's political economy nevertheless approximates the liberal model more than either its state-enhanced or coordinative alternatives. Most private financing is raised through retained earnings, capital markets, or arm's-length bank loans. Quebec firms prize their autonomy, and do not belong to formal industry groups. Entrepreneurs generally have the same firm-centred and market-oriented views as their Anglo-Saxon counterparts.[54] The province's industrial relations culture is now less confrontational than during the 1970s, but contract negotiations generally proceed at the firm level in an adversarial framework. The main exception to firm-level bargaining in the private sector is afforded by the province's decree system (see chapter 5), but these sector-level arrangements now apply to less than 5 per cent of the province's workforce.[55] Quebec's training and education system may be even more institutionally focused, and less successful at on-the-job vocational training, than its English Canadian equivalents.[56]

That Quebec's production regime is, however, 'institutionally ambivalent'[57] – statist and coordinative features subsist alongside predominant liberal ones – is reflected in the business and labour communities. Better organized than in most liberal milieus, each is also more fragmented than in northern European CMEs. The Conseil du patronat is a business association of a type that has no equivalent elsewhere in Canada; it is indisputably the leading organizational voice of business in Quebec.[58] Yet it has rivals. The Manufacturiers et exportateurs du Québec, the Quebec Chamber of Commerce, and the Quebec wing of the CFIB, as well as sectoral associations, all compete, to a degree, with the Conseil du patronat. As in other provinces, the business community often cannot fill seats on deliberative bodies, and has trouble speaking with one voice.[59] The labour movement also reveals a contradictory pattern: more workers in Quebec are unionized than in the other provinces studied here (see table 2.3); although unionization rates are higher in Newfoundland, Quebec's labour movement probably is the most influential politically in Canada. But labour is highly fragmented; it mirrors the pattern in France more than that of most CMEs. The FTQ (Fédération des travailleurs et travailleuses du Québec) is the largest union central; almost 60 per cent of private sector union members are affiliated with it, but its overall percentage of the unionized workforce barely exceeded 37 per cent in 1997. The CSN (Confédération des syndicats nationaux) then accounted for 24 per cent of unionized workers. Two other federations, the CSQ and the CSD, represented 10 per cent and 4 per cent respectively. Finally, 24 per cent belonged to unaffiliated unions.[60] Possessing different political perspectives (the FTQ is closer to the Parti Québécois and more willing to accommodate business than is the CSN), unions also often have trouble developing the shared positions generally sought after in collaborative venues.

Quebec's statism crystallized during the Quiet Revolution of the 1960s. While coordinative features had some pre-1960 antecedents,[61] in their contemporary form they developed more recently and gradually. For Gilles Bourque, these distinct trajectories correspond to separate phases of Quebec's economic development since 1960. 'For two decades, [the] first form of the "*modèle québécois*" was characterized by a hierarchical approach and [only] secondarily by partnerships.' In this context, 'state actors played a predominant role.'[62] The second phase reflects 'partnerships, in the sense of being based on new sites for coordinated action, that include the principal collective actors (state actors, unions and intermediary groups), and calls for a new social contract.'[63]

Tools were developed to foster modern, French-owned businesses during the first phase. The hydroelectric grid was nationalized in 1962; Hydro-Quebec, the provincial utility, subsequently acted aggressively to exploit the energy-generating potential of the province's north. The Société générale de financement (SGF), also created in 1962, gives financial assistance to firms. The Caisse de dépôt et de placement du Québec, created in 1965 to manage the Quebec Pension Plan's funds, became a powerful institutional investor. Other bodies, later merged to form the Société de développement industriel (SDI), also provided development assistance until being folded into Investissement-Québec in 1998.[64] While not always successful in fostering highly productive firms, these institutions did nurture a substantial increase in the share of Quebec businesses controlled by French speakers.[65] The Quebec industry ministry administers its own development programs, and attempts to provide strategic leadership.

The second phase has not displaced these entities,[66] but shifted the emphasis away from government leadership towards collaboration with the private sector. Anticipated by consensus-building exercises starting in the late 1970s, it emerged fully with the Liberal government's re-election in 1989.[67] In 1992, the province committed itself to a collaborative industrial policy inspired by Michael Porter's concept of industrial 'clusters' (*grappes industrielles*). After extensive private sector consultations, the province identified 14 clusters as priorities for its support, where it sought to foster collaboration among firms and other key actors. Instead of state leadership, the focus was now on 'improving competitiveness by forging technological alliances intended to develop and exploit generic technologies.'[68] Alongside these industrial policy developments, Quebec also, at this time, began to develop collaborative structures in the labour market field (see chapter 5).

Quebec's 'institutional ambivalence' results from the comingling of these features. On a quotidian basis, much economic activity proceeds as it would elsewhere in Canada. Firms may seek financing in the same places and on the same terms; they may have similarly arm's-length relations with competitors, suppliers, and clients; where unionized, they may engage in often acrimonious contract negotiations at the firm level; and they may seek skilled workers from public institutions. In such a 'firm-centred' setting, Quebec firms not surprisingly often express resentment of the statist and collaborative instruments constructed by Quebec governments in recent decades – and of the high taxes needed to finance them. Yet these instruments now allow public institutions to intervene directly in the investment process selectively, and to entice related firms to enter into more complex and longer-term relationships with each other and with their workers than they otherwise would. Where these actors consider such engagements successful, their subsequent behaviour and expectations likely are altered.

British Columbia

BC's economy initially depended on resource extraction, transportation, and, to a lesser extent, agriculture and fishing. The largest part of the workforce is now in the service sector, but BC's economic institutions still partly reflect this starting point. At first, the primary sectors relied heavily on small business and gave rise to a sizeable indigenous middle class. Large, often foreign-owned, resource firms have also been present since the early twentieth century. According to Keith Brownsey and Michael Howlett, the latter supplanted the former as the major influence on provincial public policy during the post-war years.[69]

Capital formation in this setting was market-oriented, based on arm's-length relations, and reliance on (often foreign) capital markets, limited state involvement in private investment, firm-level labour relations, and institution-dominated education and training.[70] Until the 1930s, the province played 'a restricted role in the provincial political economy.'[71] It then became more active, but avoided the strategic leadership role adopted in Quebec. Pursuing 'the politics of exploitation,' it provided the transportation and hydroelectric infrastructure needed to encourage private investment.[72] Centre-right governments from the 1950s to the 1970s 'control[ed] a head-strong labour movement, [kept] the tax incidence 'reasonable,' expand[ed] the economic infrastructure and fram[ed] a regulatory structure consistent with the aims of big business.'[73] Public enterprise was 'much more of a means than an end. Government [was] in business simply to stimulate private enterprise ... and to ensure an equal chance to all ... to make a profit through individual initiative.'[74] If the state was more active than in Ontario, this was because BC governments were less confident than Ontario's that Ottawa could assure an adequate setting for private sector-led growth.[75]

The 'head-strong labour movement' alluded to above is the most distinctive feature of BC's LME. The prominence of resource extraction and large transportation nurtured a strong and radical labour movement, whose strongest bastion later migrated to the public sector. As table 2.3 indicates, union membership remains above the national average, but has fallen faster than elsewhere during the past decade as resource-sector employment declined. Yet labour has had only a modest impact on BC's political-economic institutions. Centre-right parties usually win elections; the labour-aligned NDP has held power only twice: 1972 to 1975, and 1991 to 2001. It was during these periods that BC governments attempted different growth strategies. The 1970s administration – against successful business opposition – pursued elements of statism, seeking 'to control profits and capture economic rents through the creation of government monopolies over the marketing of natural gas and oil ... the provincialization of automobile insurance ... and the implementation of an accelerated mineral royalty tax.'[76] Although not as systematic as the coordinative experiments in early 1990s Ontario, the post-1991 NDP encouraged collaboration among business, labour, and other interests in a traditionally confrontational province. This was particularly true in the resource industries, especially forestry.[77] The NDP also nurtured coordination in labour market policy (see chapter 6).

Faced, historically, with militant unions, large business in BC has a more encompassing association – the Business Council of British Columbia (BCBC) – than exists in other English Canadian provinces. But it lack's the Conseil du patronat's status in Quebec as an 'association of associations.' It speaks for large corporations, and must share the spotlight with the British Columbia Chamber of Commerce, the BC wings of the CFIB and of the Canadian Association of Manufacturers and Exporters, and the British Columbia Construction Association. As in Ontario, business has sometimes had to create ad hoc umbrella bodies to lobby (NDP) governments. The British Columbia Federation of Labour (BCFL) has a higher profile than most of its counterparts in other provinces, but in an industrial relations culture dominated by firm-level bargaining, it has little power over its major affiliates, such as the woodworkers' and public sector unions.

Alberta

Alberta's production regime more closely approximates the liberal ideal type than any other in Canada. Business is not highly organized. Its main organizations include the Alberta Chambers of Commerce and the Alberta sections of the Canadian Association of Manufacturers and Exporters, and of the CFIB. Sectoral associations – especially in the energy and forestry industries – are often more visible in public affairs. Limited associational cohesion, even by liberal standards, probably owes much to the particularly business-friendly atmosphere in Alberta. In a province long governed by centre-right parties (see below), business usually gets a friendly hearing from government. The situation is quite different for labour. The level of unionization in Alberta is the lowest among the Canadian provinces (table 2.3), in spite of the province's chronically low unemployment rate. As was noted above, comparative research suggests that Alberta labour law is more business-friendly than that of any other province. According to Jeff Taylor, the post-war pattern of provincial labour law, which followed and largely reflected the federal wartime model, was only partly transplanted to Alberta. The Alberta Federation of Labour is relatively weak and isolated.[78] It is stymied by the overall weakness of labour in Alberta, and by the ability of ever-present, centre-right governments to characterize unions as a malevolent 'special interest.'[79]

Alberta is also characterized by the firm autonomy, reliance on external capital markets, and institutional education and training that typify LMEs. In one respect, however, the provincial state is quite active. Alberta's economy still largely relies on its oil and gas industry; when world markets for these collapse, the province experiences recessions. If markets are strong, enormous revenues flow into the provincial treasury. Since the 1970s, a significant part of these funds has been used to subsidize economic development, in an effort to diversify Alberta's industrial base. According to Kevin Taft, industrial subsidies first exceeded twice the per capita average for all other provinces in 1975, and surpassed 800 per cent of that average in 1983. The province was then in a deep recession and the treasury was running large deficits; but industrial spending remained more than five times higher than in the other provinces until 1988.[80] Since the late 1980s, funds have been expended more frugally; but as table 2.4 indicates, development spending remains well above the national average, and, after a period of restraint in the 1990s, has risen again recently. Réjean Landry and Chantal Blouin rank Alberta as second only to Quebec in the number of industrial assistance measures that it offered during the early 1990s; assistance was more likely than in most provinces to encourage inter-firm alliances and to concentrate on specific sectors.[81]

Table 2.4. Alberta Per Capita Industrial Development Spending with Interprovincial and National Comparisons

Province	1990	1996	2002
Alberta	$677.49	$398.83	$554.34
Quebec	260.55	300.49	401.46
British Columbia	283.16	334.36	371.62
Ontario	152.72	141.34	135.40
Canada	325.66	266.45	318.30
Alberta as % of Cdn.	208%	150%	174%

Source: CANSIM II Series data; table 3850001 (provincial and local government spending on resource conservation and industrial development); table 510001 (provincial and national populations, both sexes, all ages).

At its inception, according to John Richards and Larry Pratt, this assistance reflected a strategic vision.[82] But 'by the early 1990s,' Allan Tupper et al. contend, 'the pattern of government involvement looked more reactive and makeshift than in the 1970s; it became ... ad hoc rather than planned ... driven more by external circumstances than by design.'[83] Even in the earlier era the policy embodied a strong preference for private sector-led growth. It went well beyond the infrastructure provision typical of governments in BC and (less aggressively) in Ontario, but did not involve the use of state authority to transform the economy on behalf of a putatively broader societal interest, as in post-1960 Quebec. There has been no effort to use statist or coordinative instruments to include labour and other non-business interests in economic governance. Trevor Harrison instead uses the term *corporatism* to describe an intimate, if informal, relationship that exists among 'Alberta's business and financial elites and, to an extent, government technocrats.'[84]

Production regimes are predominantly liberal in all four of these jurisdictions, but there are important variations. In the next section we argue that variations among the party systems of Ontario, Quebec, BC, and Alberta are even larger. These often depart from the pattern that would be expected in liberal milieus, according to Kitschelt's typology. This variety does not obviate the fact that the institutions examined in the first two sections of this chapter define a fundamentally liberal setting in each province, though this is true in a more qualified sense for Quebec. Party systems nevertheless have an important effect: they colour in distinctive ways how liberalism shapes labour market policy-making.

Provincial Party Systems: The Specificity of the Political

Canada's party system has long presented anomalies to students of comparative electoral and party politics. Robert Alford's pioneering study of electoral behaviour in four Anglo-Saxon countries found that class voting in Canada was weaker than in the other nations studied. 'Class voting is low in Canada because the political parties are identified as representatives of regional, religious, and ethnic groupings, rather than as representatives of national class interests, and this, in turn, is due to a relative lack of national integration.'[85] Social concerns, in Kitschelt's terms, are therefore the main determinants of electoral preference. And they have dominated partisan debate since Confederation.[86] Not surprisingly, Canada diverges from Kitschelt's prediction that liberal political economies will posess two-party systems that are highly polarized along economic (class-related) lines. Frank Underhill hypothesized that this socially fragmented landscape gave rise to a highly clientistic, or brokerage, style of politics in Canada, where success depended on a party's ability to aggregate support from a wide range of disparate interests. The main parties nevertheless also maintain close ties to business, according to Underhill. This, in turn, has meant that social strata whose manifest interests were inconsistent with the preferences of business – especially farmers and industrial workers – have often been alienated from the brokerage parties, and supported regional and ideological 'third' parties.[87] Since the collapse of the national Progressive Conservative Party in the 1993 federal election, Canadian politics may have become unhitched from this brokerage mooring, but recent Canadian scholarship on the national party system stresses that it retains a strongly regionalist and brokerage flavour. The emergence of a more economically polarized and ideological system is now a possibility, but not yet a realized one.[88] As William Cross points out, the lack of policy and ideological focus among the main national parties in Canada is linked to their limited internal democratic accountability, electoral orientation, and modest extra-parliamentary organizations,[89] features that are difficult to change. It was in a context shaped by strong attachments to sectional interests, and of national brokerage politics only inconsistently able to reconcile them, that the provinces developed distinctive party systems. Canadian scholarship has devoted limited attention to comparing provincial party systems;[90] it has not, moreover, linked provincial partisan alignments to the other institutional settings addressed by the comparative political economy literature examined here. Below, we therefore develop our own models for the party systems of the four provinces examined in this study, incorporating insights from available research on each province's party politics.

Ontario

In a province with the least sense of 'regional identity' and of historic grievance against Ottawa, Ontario's party system has reflected the national brokerage pattern more than it has been shaped by disaffection towards it.[91] With respect to the Ontario economy, we have already seen that the resulting moderation fostered informal bargaining between government and diverse societal interests. Again resembling the post-war federal pattern, Ontario's party system included three viable political parties, with one predominating over the others. The Progressive Conservatives, who mastered the imagery, if not always the reality, of broad-based compromise, governed for 42 years between 1943 and 1985.[92] They exceeded the federal Liberals' record of success in prevailing over their brokerage rival (the Liberals in Ontario, the Conservatives federally), and over the centre-left third party (NDP in both jurisdictions). As Gad Horowitz argued in relation to the federal stage, the logic of a three-party system itself encouraged the avoidance of ideological purity and polarization. The Ontario Conservatives occupied the broad centre, marginalizing the NDP on their left, and (often) the Liberals on their right. By contrast, the two-party system in the United States, according to Horowitz, encouraged more ideological polarization between Republicans and Democrats.[93] Kitschelt, we have seen, also associates two-party systems with polarization, at least where economic issues predominate in political debate.

Just as the federal party system entered a period of uncertainty in 1993, however, there recently has also been considerable turbulence in Ontario politics. Paralleling changes in Ontario's production regime discussed above, there is now evidence of greater polarization in party politics, focused on economic issues.[94] In 1985, a minority Liberal administration displaced the Conservative dynasty, and governed with the support of the NDP. Of necessity, the Liberals moved significantly to the left during the government's two-year term; when the NDP formed the official opposition after the 1987 election, the Liberals had every incentive to continue this trajectory.[95] The Liberal administration was itself thrown out of office in 1990, and replaced by a majority NDP administration. In 'Red Tory' Ontario,[96] this would once have been considered unthinkable. The NDP pursued centre-left policies regarding labour market policy (see chapter 4). The opposition Conservatives developed a firmly market-oriented policy agenda that contrasted sharply with the NDP's. Elected in 1995, the Tories proceeded to implement this methodically, and in the face of sustained opposition from organized labour. While not yet fully reflecting Kitschelt's expectation for an LME of a two-party, economically polarized system (for the moment, three parties remain competitive), Ontario is now closer to this pattern than ever before. Yet the Conservatives' selection of an apparently more moderate leader and premier in 2002, and their replacement by a more centrist Liberal administration in 2003, may presage a return to Ontario's pre-1985 brokerage mould.

Quebec

Until 1960, Quebec's politics was bifurcated between *rouges* (Liberal) and *bleus* (initially Conservative, later Union Nationale) parties. They diverged more in terms of social (regional, religious, and ethnic) than economic (class) issues. The Liberals evolved from champions of provincial autonomy (until the 1930s) to federalism's defenders. Thereafter, party alignments also remained stable along other axes. The Liberals were more secular, modernizing and urban, and had the support of the province's English minority. The Union Nationale, which dominated politics from 1936 to 1960, was close to the Catholic Church, broadly supported the post-Conquest compromise between external business interests and the Church, and relied on rural support.[97] Thus Quebec's two-party system was not strongly polarized along left-right economic lines as Kitschelt's model anticipates for LMEs.

During the Quiet Revolution, the party system entered a transitional multi-party phase. By 1981, however, two parties again dominated, with the Liberals now confronting the pro-independence Parti Québécois (PQ). No other party has since won more than four seats in a general election.[98] A fundamentally social concern, the question of Quebec's place in the federation, is the main point of contention between the main parties. The Liberals continue to have a firm electoral base in the English-speaking and immigrant communities, the PQ in some of the same overwhelmingly French-speaking regions that supported the Union Nationale in earlier decades.

Economic issues do divide Quebec's parties more than in the past: the Liberals are identified with a centre-right, pro-market perspective, and the PQ with a centre-left, social democratic one. But this left-right divide is not as wide as in most two-party economically focused LMEs. Because the 'national question' predominates in political debate, each party attracts members and voters who, based on economic concerns alone, would support the other party. François Pétry's recent comparison of the Liberal and PQ party platforms suggests that they are quite distinctive, though the parties have probably converged considerably in ideological terms since the 1970s. He nevertheless found less compelling evidence of divergence when he examined the implementation of election and party platforms by the PQ once in power.[99] Moreover, Pétry and his colleagues elsewhere identified Quebec as one of four Canadian provinces in which there was no 'clear statistical evidence' that either electoral cycles (related to election timing) or partisan cycles (related to who is in power) affected government spending between 1974 and 1995.[100] Neil Nevitte and Roger Gibbins's study of student attitudes in several Anglo-Saxon democracies found that Canadian respondents stood out because of the French Canadian part of their sample. 'It is clear,' they found, 'that the left-right scale, as a vehicle for ideological organisation, has much less relevance for francophones than it has for anglophones.'[101] For Nelson Wiseman, 'ideological movements have been relatively fluid and unstable' in Quebec, compared to English Canada, because 'they have been overshadowed, mediated, and shaped by a relatively coherent economic nationalism.'[102] Thus, while Quebec's two-party system is not highly polarized along economic lines, as Kitschelt would predict, its exceptionalism supports his more general rule: where social issues outweigh economic ones in dividing the vote, traditional left-right polarization is moderated. The presence of significant coordinative behaviour in the Quebec production regime also attenuates tension between business and labour, the natural 'homes' of right and left agendas. And, since coordinative institutions circumscribe the unfettered working of the marketplace, and grant labour a greater role, right political options are 'selected for' less prominently in Quebec than elsewhere in Canada. As the 'left' political option, the PQ has governed far more between 1976 and 2003 (18 years out of 27) than the NDP has in the other provinces studied here.

British Columbia

BC's party system more closely approximates the economically polarized, two-party model that Kitschelt anticipates for LMEs than any other examined here. The current party system emerged in the early 1950s. The CCF was then growing in popularity, relying on the support of the robust union movement. Centre-right opposition to the CCF was divided between the Liberals and Conservatives. A complex sequence of events that was designed to avoid splitting this centre-right vote led to the emergence of W.A.C. Bennett's Social Credit Party as the alternative to the CCF.[103] Relying on the support of big business, small entrepreneurs and middle class professionals, and on its soon-established reputation for presiding over healthy economic growth, Social Credit subsequently dominated BC politics. Bennett served as premier between 1952 and 1972; Social Credit returned to power in 1975, where it remained until its annihilation in the 1991 election, which brought the NDP to power.[104] Social Credit was thereafter replaced by the BC Liberal Party as the centre-right alternative to the NDP, and came to power in 2001. In the election of that year, the NDP returned only two members to the provincial legislature; the party was restored to major party status, with 33 seats, in the 2005 election.

A strong strain of populism in Social Credit's electoral appeal restrained its market-oriented predilections. Under Bennett the party developed the range of welfare state measures that emerged elsewhere during the post-war years.[105] Left-right polarization nevertheless had clear consequences for policy-making. When the NDP briefly governed between 1972 and 1975, it launched many legislative initiatives. During the mid-1980s, Social Credit substantially curtailed public spending, arguably the first example of 'Thatcherite' restraint in any Canadian province.[106] Despite attempting to project a more 'moderate' image, the 1990s NDP government could not mollify vociferous business opposition, and the Liberals' 2001 election victory led to another round of severe budget cuts. Although the social bases of the left and right political blocs have changed substantially since the 1950s, they remain quite distinctive. Brownsey and Howlett note that service sector-based public sector unions and voters have largely supplanted blue-collar unions as the foundation of NDP support, and that the political right must now seek voters in the tertiary sector.[107] But union membership and income levels – classical correlates of left-right division in economically polarized polities – remain strong predictors of voting intentions.[108]

Alberta

Politics in Alberta long has been characterized by one-party dominance. Social Credit governed uninterrupted between 1935 and 1971, and the Progressive Conservatives have done the same since 1971. In six of the nine successive elections won by each of these dynasties, the winning party garnered more than 50 per cent of the vote. Since opposition to the dominant party is usually fragmented, the resulting legislative majorities have been overwhelming. In only two of nine elections won by each of these parties did they fail to win at least two-thirds of the seats in a general election; in most cases, opposition parties elected few legislators.[109] Since at least the 1940s, governments have been clearly centre-right and market-oriented, with close links to local and international business.[110] C.B. MacPherson's hypothesis that centre-right, one-party dominance reflected a homogeneous small business political economy, linked to an acute perception of external threat, now has few adherents.[111] A persistent sense of regional grievance, combined with the lack of a strong labour movement to challenge local business interests, nevertheless has strengthened the political right. Other contributing factors include the large proportion of immigrants from the American Midwest among the province's early settlers; and the province's post-1947 oil wealth, which permitted incumbent parties to provide very adequate welfare state benefits, by Canadian standards, while maintaining exceptionally low taxation rates and generous support for business.[112]

One-party dominance has not precluded occasional significant and rapid policy changes in Alberta. A foremost example is the substantial cuts in social spending undertaken by Conservative Premier Ralph Klein after his 1993 election victory.[113] This was preceded by a period of stagnation in the energy industry. When energy revenues declined as a result, provincial spending was not reduced fast enough to prevent significant budgetary deficits. Klein chose to eliminate the deficits and then pay down the province's accumulated debt, through substantial social program cuts, rather than by combining more modest cuts with tax increases. The opposition parties, above all the NDP, promoted the latter.[114] While the Conservatives' political hegemony appeared to be eroding during the deficit years, it was re-established in the 1997 and 2001 elections in the wake of the cuts and the return of high energy prices. Klein apparently tapped a strongly market-oriented current in the Alberta electorate, which countenances ample welfare state provision, but only in a context of strong private sector-led economic growth, balanced budgets, and very low tax rates.

Partisanship and Globalization in Provincial Labour Market Policy-Making

The institutions of each province examined in this volume are predominantly liberal. Yet this liberalism is qualified and subject to important variations. Interprovincial variations are modest regarding welfare states, which are broadly liberal – with important social democratic adulterations – across Canada. Institutional differences among the provinces studied here therefore largely result from variations in production regimes and party systems. Having reviewed these two sets of variations, above, it is now clear that they are interconnected. We will not try to *explain* why this is the case here; that is, whether provincial party systems are a 'superstructure' reflecting the provincial economic 'base,' or whether (most probably) interprovincial differences reflect a complex, historically evolving interaction between production regimes and party systems. We will, more modestly, *describe* these parallels, and anticipate their differential implications for an examination of the impact of partisanship on labour market policy-making. Specifically, we hypothesize that these implications are different in relation to the two questions, set forth in chapter 1, that are the focus of our attention in this study: first, *the degree to which these settings foster significant short-term partisan swings when a new party comes to power*; and, second, *their susceptibility to long-term, neo-liberal policy retrenchment during the current era of globalization.* Our hypotheses for each jurisdiction are summarized in table 2.5.

While *Quebec's* production regime is mainly liberal, the post-Quiet Revolution construction of statist and coordinative institutions nevertheless introduced a degree of cooperation between the social partners and the state that has no Canadian parallel. The province's party system is divided between left and right. But, consistent with the pattern in a partisan setting where a social preoccupation takes precedence over economic ones, the economic agendas of the main parties do not diverge radically. Each has fostered consensus-building relationships with and within the private sector. In this setting, *one would expect partisan swings that follow a change of government to be relatively modest*; and, in view of the 'Quebec model's' ideological hold, *the prospects for neo-liberal retrenchment, motivated by globalization pressures, real or imagined, should be low.*

In *British Columbia*, an LME that is contested by a historically strong and militant labour movement subsists in the same soil as an economically polarized party system. BC's fundamentally liberal production regime favours centre-right political solutions. And it creates a climate in which centre-right parties win most elections. Their centre-left rivals have sought to modify the prevailing institutional model when in power, as Britain's Labour Party did during the post-war years, but with equal lack of success. The distance between the economic agendas of the two main parties suggests that, first, *significant policy swings are likely following a change in government.* Second, *retrenchment politics, guided by an ideologically committed market-oriented liberal party, would seem to be a real possibility.*

Alberta departs from a 'pure' variant of liberal institutions more because of *how* business interests are privileged, and because of the extent of the left's weakness, than because these liberal features are significantly contested. In the 1970s, Alberta became preoccupied with diversifying its economy. In other respects, it is endowed with many typically liberal features: weak business organization, low taxes, and a pervasive preference for market solutions. In a partisan setting long shaped by regional resentment, and a powerful cultural preference for consensus in the face of external threats, the centre-right is politically hegemonic; for over half a century no centre-left party has contested seriously for power. Under these circumstances, we cannot test for the potential impact of short-term partisan swings; but with politics dominated by a centre-right, market-oriented political party, *the prospects for radical retrenchment are high.*

Characterizing *Ontario's* current party system is problematical, and this ambiguity has implications for secondary features of the production regime as well. Observers of Ontario politics have long characterized its political culture as 'centrist,' 'moderate,' and 'red Tory.' As we have seen, some commentators have identified a feature of its production regime as resulting from this political conjuncture. Governments in Ontario have found informal ways of addressing interests, including organized labour and other broadly oppositional ones, in policy-making. We termed this 'informal concertation,' in table 2.5. But this party system was very much shaken by the 1985 and 1990 elections. Ontario was subsequently governed by the left-leaning NDP and a rejuvenated PC party which, in a newly polarized climate, reconfigured itself as a party of the right of centre.

This institutional indeterminacy makes it harder to generate predictions along the two axes that concern us here. Institutional instability yields predictive uncertainty. Before 1985, one would have anticipated little in the way of policy 'swings' in Ontario, if only because the government never changed; and informal concertation and an inclusive political culture would have made radical retrenchment unlikely. In the new era, it is less clear. A somewhat ad hoc approach is required to address this problem, since our theoretical models provide us with no

Table 2.5: Provincial Institutions and Hypotheses Regarding Partisanship, Institutions, and Globalization

Province	Welfare state	Production regime	Party system	Predicted short-term policy 'swing'	Potential for globalization-induced retrenchment
Quebec	Liberal, SD-tinged	Ambivalent / LME ←→	2-party; low economic polarization	Low	Low
British Columbia	Liberal, SD-tinged	LME; strong labour ←→	2-party; high economic polarization	High	High
Alberta	Liberal, SD-tinged	LME; industrial promotion ←→	1-party dom.; right hegemony	N.A.	High
Ontario (pre-1985)	Liberal, SD-tinged	LME; informal concertation ←→	1-party dom; low economic polarization	[low]	[low] ↓
Ontario (post-1990)	Liberal, SD-tinged	LME; ←→ contested concertation	Fluid multi-party; high economic polarization	High	⟶ Indeterminate
Inter-provincial variation	Low	Moderate	High	–	–

consistent guidance on how to address institutionally unstable settings, but our solution nevertheless can be consistent with the logic of the models. Regarding policy 'swings,' near-term considerations – the divergence between programmatic positions of different governing parties – suggest themselves as the most likely determinant of outcomes. Because an apparently unelectable centre-left NDP came to power in 1990, followed by an equally evidently 'unOntarian' party of the right in 1995, *we anticipate large short-term policy swings after a change in government*. Regarding the prospects for retrenchment, one cannot be as certain. On the one hand, that same centre-right Conservative party would presumably be tempted to break with post-war orthodoxies and strike out in a neo-liberal direction. On the other hand, in Ontario, unlike BC, the post-war era gave rise to policy equilibriums in many areas of labour market policy, and there was no experience of a radical government of the right before 1985. These equilibriums likely moulded the expectations and behaviour of Ontario's labour market actors – in the business and labour movement, and within the state – and are reflected in the cultural patterns detected by Noel. If norms are more enduring than party systems, they would make radical retrenchment in Ontario unlikely. In view of these contradictory inferences from the theory, *we make no prediction regarding the prospects for neo-liberal retrenchment in Ontario labour market policy* after 1995.

Chapters 4 to 8 test these hypotheses against our research findings. As was noted in chapter 1, most of our data is qualitative, reflecting the qualitative nature of the institutional and policy design differences that are highlighted by comparative political economy research. This presents a particular methodological challenge for our research because testing our hypotheses requires us not only to determine *whether* policy has changed in the manner anticipated, but also to measure the *degree* of such change. Our methodology for addressing this problem is elaborated in the appendix. We begin with Peter Hall's well-known distinction among three 'orders' of policy change – those which pertain to the *'overall goals'* of policy, the *'techniques and instruments'* for realizing these, and 'the *precise settings'* of these instruments.[115] This categorization is refined by separating instances in which change of each type served to *displace* pre-existing policies from those where the new arrangements *contested* these older ones without displacing them. Where new policy features emerged but remained subordinate to older ones, such changes were termed *adjustments*. With this framework, one can distinguish three degrees of short-term partisan swing after a change in power (low, medium, and high), and five degrees of long-term retrenchment (low, low-to-medium, medium, medium-high, and high). Because short-term partisan changes usually take place within pre-existing institutional settings, while retrenchment more frequently alters these, the criteria for measuring moderate or high levels of the former are set lower than for the latter. The criteria for determining each level of change for both partisanship and globalization are summarized in table 11.1. To apply these categories to policy change in each of the policy sub-fields treated in this study, we developed an operational definition of each of Hall's 'orders' of policy change for each sub-field. Based on our understanding of the overall goals and main techniques and instruments associated with each sub-field during the pre-1990 era (discussed in chapter 3), these definitions are also explained in the appendix, followed by a summary of our case study findings in relation to each sub-field in each province. Social assistance policy change is more amenable than the others fields studied here to quantitative measurement. Consequently, data on the evolution of benefits and caseloads for employable assistance recipients is examined in chapter 8; in addition, a quantitative formula for measuring policy change in this sub-field is used in the appendix alongside a qualitative one. Chapters 4 through 8 include summary tables for the degree of policy change observed therein. But to facilitate a smoother narrative, little reference is made in these chapters to the appendix methodology. In the conclusion, where we summarize our results, this methodology is addressed explicitly.

The next chapter examines the provinces' responsibilities in the labour market field, and the historical evolution of these, including the relationship with the federal level of government. It explains the labour market policy concerns that form the 'raw material' for the case studies presented in the subsequent five chapters. These chapters use the conceptual framework developed in chapter 1, and applied to our four Canadian jurisdictions in this chapter, to examine this raw material. They assess the extent to which the institutions outlined here have 'selected for' policy options that are consistent with the prevailing institutional setting, and for parties that favour these options. And they test whether partisanship and globalization have shaped labour market policies along the provincially distinctive trajectories outlined in table 2.5.

3 Historical and Federal Context of Provincial Labour Market Policy in Canada

Labour market policy in Canada consists of a complex set of arrangements, in terms of constitutional jurisdiction, historical developments, and institutional structures. Of particular importance is the prominent role of provinces in most aspects of labour market policy, an atypical arrangement when compared to most other nations, and the reason why this book focuses on sub-national jurisdictions. The objective of this chapter is to outline the major characteristics of this field, including key historical milestones, focusing on the specific aspects of labour market policy under study in this book. It will review the nature of labour market policy in Canada, with attention to the manner in which federal-provincial arrangements have constrained and shaped policy-making. Although the chapter focuses on the six policy fields which we study in detail in this book, it also touches briefly on those labour market policy domains excluded from further analysis.

The involvement of the state in labour market policy stems, in the final analysis, from the inability of the market for labour to operate efficiently and effectively. Generally, policy seeks to increase efficiency and/or increase equity in the labour market.[1] In this book we restrict our analysis of labour market policy to those areas that affect the private sector, and to provincial jurisdiction. The following domains encompass the main areas of provincial activity:

1. Workers' compensation
2. Occupational health and safety
3. Employment standards, including pay and employment equity
4. Industrial relations
5. Active measures (such as training and skills development)
6. Social assistance for employable persons

This chapter will also briefly review passive measures (specifically employment insurance), a policy domain that is, for reasons explained later, excluded from analysis in later chapters. Finally, in order to ensure a comprehensive overview of active labour market policy, it also touches, in the last pages, on human rights and immigration.

These six domains can be grouped into three logical categories. The first three domains (workers' compensation, occupational health and safety, and employment standards) comprise the minimum obligations imposed by the state on the worker-employer relationship. They set the minimum conditions that must be met by all (or nearly all) employers and workers. There are, of course, many employment relationships that exceed these conditions in some regard, especially if workers are unionized. Labour relations policy is a distinct policy domain in that the relationship being governed by policy is between a group of workers (a union) and a specific employer. The state is setting the framework for particular processes to occur, rather than – as is the case in minimum standards – determining the outcome. The last two domains under detailed study – active measures by the provinces and social assistance for employables – have both equity and efficiency goals. In terms of equity, both are concerned with increasing the labour force success of some groups of workers, often those in receipt of income support from the state in the form of employment insurance payments and social assistance income support payments. With regard to efficiency, the emphasis is primarily on avoiding or minimizing labour supply shortages. There are other ways of grouping labour market policies for analysis. A common one is to distinguish policies that require employers and/or workers to make payments to a government agency or to workers, from those that place constraints on the actions of employers and workers. While useful for many comparative analyses, this fails to adequately incorporate active labour market policies or social assistance policies for employables.[2]

Federalism

Although Canada's constitution does not mention workplace-related matters specifically, the courts have placed that subject under provincial jurisdiction, except for those industrial sectors that are under federal jurisdiction.[3] This is because judicial decisions since Confederation have interpreted 'property and civil rights,' a provincial power, as covering a very wide field, including employment-related relationships. Thus, unlike most nations, even federations like Germany, considerable responsibility for labour markets in Canada rests with subnational jurisdictions.[4] Approximately 90 per cent of workplaces and workers in Canada are primarily covered by provincial labour market policies and legislation.

There are four types of constitutional arrangements evident in labour market policy in Canada. First, and most common, is parallel legislation, with a federal statute covering federally regulated enterprises, and a separate provincial statute covering provincially regulated workplaces. This results in a relatively airtight division of federal and provincial jurisdiction. This type of arrangement is found with regard to employment standards, occupational health and safety, labour relations, pay and employment equity, and human rights. It is not uncommon in Canada to find workplaces located side by side, and conducting similar work, that are covered by distinct legislation and policies in these domains. The second arrangement in the labour market policy field is for the federal government to have a limited or minimal policy role. This is the case with regard to workers' compensation, where the federal level has no compensation or insurance scheme for workers injured in federally regulated workplaces. Rather, federally regulated industries typically participate in the provincial workers' compensation schemes. Social assistance policy also falls into this category as the federal government has had only a small policy role, although it does provide some funding to provinces. The third arrangement is for federal and provincial policies that cover the same or overlapping client groups, as is the case in some aspects of active labour market policy. Thus, both the federal and provincial governments have, or can have, policies for youth, older workers, the disabled, and others. In most cases, program duplication is avoided and a degree of coordination of measures achieved, sometimes negotiated by local service delivery agencies. Not surprisingly, as discussed later in this chapter, there has been considerable effort in the past decade to arrive at a more clearly defined set of responsibilities in this area. Logically, the last set of arrangements is for the provinces to have a subservient or minimal role, leaving the policy domain primarily to the federal government. Employment insurance, the most important passive labour market program in Canada, belongs to this category, as it is administered solely by Ottawa. With respect to immigration, the two levels of governments share jurisdiction, but the federal government is paramount in the event of a conflict. As such, the federal government consults with provinces when setting

Table 3.1. Federalism and Labour Market Policy

Type of arrangement	Labour market policy field
Federal role only, or paramount role	Employment insurance, immigration
Provincial role only, or paramount role	Workers' compensation, social assistance for 'employables'
Federal-provincial overlap	Active labour market measures
Federal-provincial parallelism	Employment standards, occupational health and safety, labour relations, pay equity, employment equity, human rights

immigration levels and related matters. The province of Quebec has entered into a comprehensive agreement that grants it some responsibility to select immigrants and provide settlement services, but the federal government retains responsibility for defining immigrant categories, setting levels, and enforcement. In light of our focus on provincial government policy-making we do not study unemployment insurance or immigration policy in this volume. These four types of federalism arrangements are summarized in table 3.1.

The federal-provincial relationships are complex, and thus the above categorization does not capture completely the dynamics and relationships that have developed.[5] Furthermore, the relationships are constantly shifting, such that, for example, in immigration policy the provinces have gained in the past several years some increased influence over policy.

In the sections that follow, each of the six policy fields addressed in this study is reviewed. Each review begins with a brief description of the policy domain, and then moves to examine its historical development, the nature of federalism in that field, and the major issues in it. Each section concludes with a short discussion of the types of policies that left and right parties would be expected to pursue in the field.

Workers' Compensation

Workers' compensation is often described as the 'historic compromise' between labour and capital in the development of North American industrial society.[6] When introduced in the United States and Canada in the second decade of the twentieth century, workers' compensation 'set precedents for government requirements of employment-based social insurance that led to the implementation of unemployment insurance ... and eventually the entire network of modern social welfare programs.'[7] William Meredith, the judge who headed the Ontario royal commission (1910–13) that determined the nature of workers' compensation in Canada, summarized the compromise as one in which employers, employees, and the state benefit from eliminating the litigation associated with workplace injuries. In particular, the benefit to the state was to be 'the blessing of industrial peace and freedom from social unrest.'[8]

Workers' compensation in Canada is essentially an insurance scheme, operated by a public agency and funded solely by employers. The majority of workers, including part-time, seasonal, and domestic ones, are covered in most jurisdictions, although some are excluded, such as the self-employed or those deemed to be independent contractors, while the scope of injuries and diseases covered also varies from province to province.[9] The 'compromise' inherent in the scheme is that employers must contribute premiums through a payroll tax, while workers injured in the workplace are prohibited from using the legal system to seek redress, but must accept the compensation paid by the insurance scheme.

Although the federal government has the constitutional authority to operate a workers' compensation scheme for its employees and for employers under federal jurisdiction, it has decided not to do so. A federal scheme would cover relatively few workers and remove workplaces from the provincial systems, creating inefficiencies.[10] Instead, federal employees are covered by the Government Employees Compensation Act, which each province administers on behalf of the federal government. In some provinces, a few large corporations (such as banks and financial institutions) have the authority to run their own compensation schemes, but in other provinces, such as Quebec, corporations must join the provincial program. Employers operating in more than one province, such as trucking, join one provincial workers' compensation scheme, which has interprovincial agreements to cover employers operating in more than one jurisdiction.

The origin of workers' compensation in modern industrial societies lies in reforms undertaken by German Chancellor Otto von Bismarck in the 1880s. During this decade, a compulsory state-run compensation scheme was introduced, financed by both employers and workers. Beginning in 1910, state governments in the United States began to enact workers' compensation legislation, while Ontario followed in 1915 with the remainder of the provinces and territories subsequently establishing their own insurance systems.[11] Prior to workers' compen-

Table 3.2. Coverage of Provincial Workers' Compensation Schemes, 2002

Jurisdiction	Percentage of workforce covered
Quebec	93.7
Ontario	67.2
Alberta	82
British Columbia	93.5
National (weighed) average	79.7

Source: Association of Workers' Compensation Boards of Canada, Key Statistical Measures (December 2003). http://www.awcbc.org/english/board_data-key.asp.

sation legislation, workers injured in the workplace had to rely on the courts, and faced the burden of proof in showing that the employer was responsible for the injury, in seeking compensation from employers. On the other hand, employers faced the possibility of large settlements that could bankrupt an enterprise.[12] Although initially covering only the most hazardous industries, and excluding retail and office workplaces, today 80 per cent of the national workforce is covered, but such coverage varies considerably from province to province, as shown in Table 3.2.

The vast majority of nations with workers' compensation policies include such coverage with the broader social security system, making little distinction between work and non-work-related injuries and illnesses. This model, found in most European countries, ensures that all employees are covered. Relatively few countries – including Canada, the United States, Australia, and Germany – require employers to purchase separate workers' compensation insurance from either a public or private fund. Canada is one of only three countries, along with the United States and Australia, to have developed a decentralized administrative structure in which sub-national jurisdictions solely administer workers' compensation insurance.[13]

In Canada, the insurance scheme is now operated by provincial agencies at arm's-length from government and headed by tripartite (business, labour, and government) boards of directors. These agencies determine eligibility, premium and benefit policies, as well as overseeing internal appeals. Most provinces also have a separate external appeals tribunal to make final rulings on appeals. Premiums average about 3 per cent of payroll, but vary considerably from industry to industry, and sometimes from firm to firm, reflecting the past claims of the industry and of individual firms. Three types of benefits are provided by the insurance system: temporary, permanent, and fatality. The manner in which these benefits are calculated and paid has varied over time and from province to province.[14] Associated with workers' compensation is the medical rehabilitation of injured workers, as well as labour market re-entry measures for injured workers who are unable to return to their regular jobs.

As with any insurance program, key areas of policy attention and controversy are (1) the level of premiums paid by employers (2) the level and duration of payments to workers who have been injured or killed, and (3) the range of injuries and diseases that are covered. Left parties will typically support increases in premiums to ensure that payments to injured workers are higher, while seeking to expand the range of injuries covered, such as chronic stress and repetitive strain injuries, and to increase the number of workers covered. In contrast, right parties generally will seek to reduce premiums, while limiting both the benefits paid and the coverage (in terms of injuries and diseases), in keeping with the preferences of employers. As well, these parties will emphasize a swift return to the workplace for injured workers. Both left and right parties would be expected to underscore the prevention of injuries.

Occupational Health and Safety

The establishment of workers' compensation early in the twentieth century recognized 'that the market, and its parallel in the legal system – the system of tort law – is inadequate in many ways where occupational health and safety problems are involved.'[15] However, workers' compensation dealt only with injuries that had already occurred, and initially only for workers in a few industries. Industrial capitalism in central Canada continued to take its toll on the health and safety of workers, especially with the increasing use of mechanized machinery and new substances, an escalating scale of production, and the rise of factory work in the late nineteenth and early twentieth centuries.[16]

During the 1880s there were initiatives, both federally and in rapidly industrializing Ontario, supported by labour groups and reformers, to introduce legislation to regulate aspects of the newly emerging factories. The factory legislation passed in 1884 by the Ontario legislature provoked a constitutional dispute with the federal government over which level of government had constitutional responsibility for occupational health and safety, a dispute won by the province. The legislation

itself, strongly supported by unions and labour groups, was very narrow in scope but set key precedents in prohibiting the employment of
boys under 14 years of age and girls under 12. The legislation created a
number of minimum conditions with regard to ventilation, fire safety,
and safety features for machinery, as well as a rudimentary inspection
and enforcement function.[17]

In the past century, health and safety legislation has frequently been
amended, usually in response to efforts by workers; a notable workplace disaster or catastrophe that publicized unsafe workplace conditions has often acted as a catalyst. Separate legislation for different
industries (such as mining, railways, and so forth) was introduced as
industrialization proceeded, and workers and their supporters were
able to muster political support for the extension of minimal health and
safety requirements. During the 1970s and 1980s, considerable occupational health and workplace legislation was passed and policies were
developed to address new substances and compounds (such as radioac-
tive materials and asbestos), as well as new injuries and previously
non-identified illnesses such as silicosis.

This occurred not only in Ontario, but also in other provinces and at
the federal level, although there were differences based on the industrial base and other characteristics of each province. The nature of
federalism has meant that the same battles for safer workplaces have
had to be fought in each provincial jurisdiction, as well as for federally
regulated industries. The result is an uneven patchwork of policies in
Canada, one of the few nations (along with Australia) in which there are
no national standards in this domain.[18] Unlike workers' compensation,
which is a defined policy domain with a single piece of legislation,
occupational health and safety is a diluted and fragmented one. There
are several hundred federal and provincial acts that govern this field, as
well as several dozen agencies that set some aspect of policy. There are
discreet types of legislation, including hazard-specific acts such as those
dealing with different types of radiation, and industry-specific acts
such as those restricted to the mining and construction sectors.[19]

In the past several decades all jurisdictions enacted some type of
broad employment-oriented legislation that consolidated safety, prevention, and work-related injuries and illnesses policies. Such legislation (usually titled 'occupational health and safety') and associated
regulations and guidelines are typically administered by the relevant
department of labour or by the workers' compensation agency. Notwithstanding this centralization trend, some industries, such as mining,

continue to be treated separately.[20] At the federal level, occupational health and safety policy is primarily found in the Canada Labour Code (Part II), although, as in the case of provinces, some aspects remain the responsibility of departments charged with regulating specific industrial sectors, such as shipping and nuclear energy.

In all jurisdictions, government officials have the right to enter any workplace to conduct inspections as well as to issue orders to rectify dangerous conditions. However, in practice, the state's enforcement capacity is limited, in terms of staff resources and willingness to use fines and pursue prosecutions. Typically, only the most flagrant safety violations by employers, such as those that result in the death of workers, result in sanctions that have a measurable impact on the workplace or on a firm's profitability.

In addition to the centralization trend, a second tendency in the past decades has been the greater reliance on self-regulation via workplace health and safety committees in medium and large companies.[21] These committees of workers and managers are mandated by legislation or policy in nearly all jurisdictions, or required by collective agreements. There is considerable variation from province to province as to the 'the authority conferred on joint committees, and on the extent to which committees are mandatory.'[22]

Occupational health and safety policy-making involves considerable input from, and interaction with, the medical and scientific research communities. As such, this field has a large number of institutional actors: a multitude of state departments and agencies, including in some cases municipal governments fulfilling an inspection function; non-government organizations dealing with medicine and research; and business and labour (whose specific concerns and interests may be quite diverse vis-à-vis particular health and safety standards). Like workers' compensation policy, there is no national policy-making for health and safety. A degree of coordination is sometimes brought about by the efforts of labour groups, employer associations, and the medical and research community, which pressure jurisdictions to have comparable standards. It should also be noted that workplaces which are unionized often have enshrined in the collective agreement higher safety and related standards than those found in legislation.

In this book we focus primarily on the central occupational health and safety policies that apply to most workplaces, and less on the more specialized policies that relate to only one type of workplace or sector. Generally, left parties support policies that grant joint health and safety committees more, rather than less, power and scope. Such parties will also tend to increase the ability of workers to impede the production process for safety-related reasons, while mandating a relatively broad range of health and safety training for all workers. Right parties, on the other hand, can be expected to constrain the prevalence and clout of the joint health and safety committees, and limit the ability of workers to interfere with the production process. More generally, such parties will seek to lower or at least not increase occupational health and safety standards. They would seek to constrain the degree of enforcement of the applicable regulations.

Employment Standards (and Pay and Employment Equity)

Employment standards regulations cover a range of other workplace matters, excluding health and safety, of which arguably the most important are setting the minimum wage, overtime pay, the maximum hours of work (per day and per week), and minimum paid vacations. Also determined by this legislation are public holidays, unpaid meal breaks, pregnancy and parental leave, termination procedures, and pay and other related matters.

Minimum employment laws arose originally in the mining industries in England in the first half of the nineteenth century. The origin of minimum employment standards in Canada dates to the Ontario Factory Act of 1884, discussed previously, and also partially to the Mining Act passed by Nova Scotia in 1858. The motivation behind these and similar acts – such as the 1888 Ontario Shops Regulation Act – was often to place limits on the employment of children and women.[23] In 1920, Ontario passed a Minimum Wage Act, allowing the government to fix the minimum wage, and (after 1922) the maximum number of hours of work applicable to women and girls.[24] Similar legislation was enacted in the other provinces.

Nevertheless, even after the first decades of the twentieth century, most Canadian workers had few guaranteed minimum employment rights. Of greatest concern to workers in improving working conditions was reducing work time, which averaged 64 hours per week in 1870 and 60 hours in 1890, and increasing minimum wages.[25] Workers' movements tied, in part, the drive for shorter working hours to health and safety concerns by arguing that such hours would promote safer workplaces and the health of workers.[26] The Great Depression, when desperate men were willing to work for wages lower than the minimum level set by legislation for women, resulted in the application to men of some minimum wages in most provinces. As well, during the 1930s, many provinces mandated an 8-hour day and a 48-hour week as the maximum for both sexes.

During the 1940s, minimum annual vacations with pay were legislated in most jurisdictions, while by the late 1950s minimum wage regulations had come to apply to more and more workers; statutory holidays with pay were adopted in the 1960s. The 1970s witnessed the consolidation in many provinces of various laws related to minimum employment standards. The adoption in 1982 of the Canadian Charter of Rights and Freedoms caused many jurisdictions to eliminate the minimum wage rate differential between adult and young workers. The 1990s and the early years of the twenty-first century saw two types of developments: (1) amendments to legislation to provide increased flexibility in the application of minimum standards for both employers and workers, and (2) various leave provisions (following amendments to federal unemployment insurance benefits in 1990 and 2002), and other initiatives that provided increased maternity, parental, and sickness leave.[27]

As with health and safety policies, there has been a trend towards one single piece of legislation that covers the workforce, rather than the variety of statutes previously in place. However, there remain some types of workers who are excluded, in whole or in part, from the general employment standards legislation. In Ontario, some aspects of the Employment Standards Act do not apply to teachers, many professionals, provincial government employees, agricultural workers, salespersons who receive a commission, and many others, while police officers are excluded altogether. Similar exceptions are found in the other jurisdictions.

As with health and safety, there is no standardization across the provinces with respect to provisions or workers covered.[28] Indeed, of the three policy domains reviewed so far, minimum employment regulations exhibit the greatest variation from province to province, especially with regard to hours of work and overtime pay.[29] Minimum wage levels, a key component of employment standards, vary considerably from province to province, as is shown in figure 3.1. The federal government has its own minimum regulations, under the Canada Labour Code, but, in the case of the minimum wage, adopts the provincial wage in effect in the jurisdiction of employment.

Figure 3.1. Minimum Wage as a Ratio of the Average Labour Wage 1991–2003

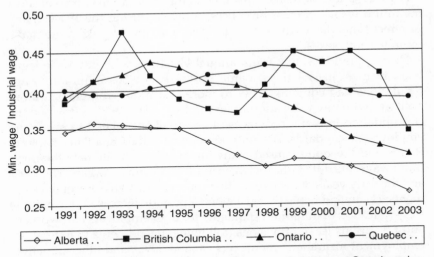

Sources: Compiled by the authors from Human Resources Development Canada and Statistics Canada data.[30]

Pay Equity

Pay equity seeks to adjust the wages of female workers, in traditionally female occupations, who have been underpaid in comparison with male workers in jobs requiring similar levels of skill. The 1970 federal Royal Commission on the Status of Women, and women's groups, provided the needed pressure for governments to address this issue, first for their own employees. Despite the dramatic increase in labour force participation among women beginning in the 1960s, women 'tended to remain segregated in traditional female-oriented occupations and there persist[ed] a significant earnings gap in general, but more specifically, also between female-dominated and male-dominated occupations.'[31] Under human rights legislation (discussed below), workers in the private sector can file complaints about pay equity.[32] In some provinces, pay equity is explicitly included in the human rights laws, while in others it operates, albeit less well, under the general anti-discrimination provisions. Yet, as we discuss later in this chapter, the complaint-based human rights legislation is not an effective tool to shape labour market policy.

In 1988, Ontario passed the first pay equity legislation in Canada that applies to the private sector.[33] These laws differed from the complaint-based model inherent in human rights legislation and policies. This legislation requires affected employers to group their workforce into classes (positions similar in term of qualifications, duties, responsibilities, and pay). If a particular class is primarily (60 per cent or 70 per cent) composed of women it is deemed a 'female job class,' potentially entitled to a wage adjustment after comparison to a job class composed primarily of men. The adjustment is based on the skill, effort, responsibilities, and working conditions of each job class. The process of determining the job classes, devising the comparisons, and adjusting pay scales is complex and often fraught with controversy, and resisted by employers.[34] Even in unionized workplaces, pay equity has had only very limited results in improving the employment incomes of women.[35]

Employment Equity

Employment equity policies seek to ameliorate the labour market chances of groups that have historically been disadvantaged. As with pay equity, individual private sector workers can file human rights complaints with the relevant human rights commission if they believe they have been discriminated against in hiring, promotion, or any other aspect of the workplace relationship, based on gender, race, disability, or other enumerated grounds. The catalyst for the first 'proactive' and not complaint-based affirmative action legislation in Canada was the report of the 1984 federal Royal Commission on Equality in Employment. The legislation that followed the commission's report was modest in scope and applied only to federal crown corporations, federally regulated firms (banks, airlines, broadcasters, railroads, and the like), and companies with federal contracts that had more than 100 employees. The only requirement of these employers is to file annually a report to the (already existing) Canadian Human Rights Commission on the composition of their workforces, with regard to the 'designated' groups – Aboriginal people, persons with disabilities, members of a visible minority, and women – and any affirmative action programs that they may have. The legislation was amended slightly in 1995 to apply also to the federal civil service. Its impact on labour market policy is nominal in that there are no targets or mechanisms for employers to alter hiring and promotion patterns, and few employers fall under its remit. Ontario became the only other Canadian jurisdiction to enact employment equity in 1993; however, the legislation was repealed in 1995 before most of its provisions were to take effect.

With regard to party preferences, left parties would be expected to increase the minimum standards in keeping with the preferences of workers and unions. These parties would also tend to support pay and employment equity legislation as a means to alleviate labour market inequities. On the other hand, right parties would take the position of most employers, who view increases in standards as directly increasing production costs and eroding competitiveness, as well as decreasing the flexibility of employers to schedule work. These parties would favour policies that lower standards and grant some ability to employers and workers in a particular workplace to negotiate specific standards themselves. They would oppose pay and affirmative action laws as unnecessary intrusions in the operation of the labour market and the employer-worker relationship.

Industrial Relations

Labour or industrial relations is a quite distinct policy domain from those reviewed above, having arisen from somewhat different dynamics and pressures. Labour relations policies are those rules and requirements imposed by the state on labour unions and employers, and particularly on the interaction of these two groups. Unlike the policy fields reviewed above, historical developments in labour relations were initially more the initiative of the federal government than the provinces, albeit significantly influenced by provincial concerns. Although the 1872 federal Trade Unions Act removed the threat of unions being prosecuted for criminal conspiracy, and subsequent legislation in 1875–76 legalized peaceful picketing, this legislation 'did nothing to compel recognition of unions by employers and left such questions to be determined by the rather asymmetrical power relation of the market.'[36]

From the first decade of the twentieth century until after the Second World War, the nation's labour relations regime was largely shaped by federal legislation, especially the Industrial Disputes Investigation Act of 1907. The main element of this legislation prohibited strikes until mandatory, but not binding, conciliation by a tripartite board was undertaken. Although this largely voluntarist framework proved of utility to already constituted unions (mostly craft), it failed to assist most industrial unions whose ability to represent workers was hindered by this largely laissez-faire legislation.[37] In the 1920s, after a constitutional ruling that labour relations was primarily a provincial matter, a hodge-podge of provincial legislation and policies was implemented that nevertheless essentially mirrored the federal regime. The constitutional decision 'promoted more fragmentation within the labour movement, because the multiplicity of legal regimes to which unions were subjected enhanced the difficulty of undertaking coordinated action.'[38]

The 1940s saw the shaping of the 'postwar compromise' legal and policy framework that has held until the present. The restructuring of the labour relations regime during this decade was fueled by a number of forces, including the experience of the Depression, the ability of labour during the Second World War to exercise greater clout, and the emergence of other components of the welfare state.[39] In 1944, under the auspices of the War Measures Act, bowing to pressure from illegal strikes in the larger provinces and with the rising political fortunes of the Co-operative Commonwealth Federation, the federal government approved Privy Council Order 1003, which institutionalized key collective bargaining rights for unions. The new federal regime was later enshrined in the federal Industrial Relations and Disputes Investigation Act of 1948. The provinces in the 1950s adopted and copied it for their own jurisdictions, although with variations from province to province.

An important component of the post-war settlement, although separate from the federal legislation, was the 'Rand formula,' which requires all members of a bargaining unit to pay union dues. This formula was the result of a ruling by Justice Ivan Rand following a long and bitter strike in Windsor, Ontario, in 1945. As a result, all collective agreements now include a clause requiring employers to deduct union dues from all members of the bargaining unit, whether or not they are members of the union. The compulsory check-off of union dues provided unions with a measure of financial stability they did not previously enjoy. This formula, when combined with the decision of the federal government to codify PCO 1003 into the Industrial Relations and Disputes Act, created the policy framework for labour relations, which has lasted relatively unaltered up to the present time.

The compromise element of the post-war settlement was a set of rules and procedures administered by the state in the form of permanent labour relations boards that governed and reviewed actions by unions and employers, such as certifying unions as bargaining agents, ensuring that workers were free to peacefully organize into a trade union, and that employers bargained in good faith. Of central consequence was the entrenchment of union certification procedures 'introduced in the postwar labour legislation in Canada to minimize disputes over union recognition and to stabilize representation rights during the initial period of a union's existence as bargaining agent. The legislation links to the bargaining rights and obligations that flow from certification the binding effect of collective agreements to which certified unions are parties.'[40] However, the regime also constrained union activities, for example, in that strikes are never legal during the term of a collective agreement, and indeed are not legal until the various provisions of the relevant labour relations legislation have been activated.

The post-war compromise allowed unionism to expand significantly in Canada. Until 1940, union membership as a percentage of the civilian labour force did not exceed 10 per cent, but beginning in 1941 membership increased steadily, to 25 per cent by the mid-1950s.[41] During the 1990s, union membership as a percentage of the civilian labour force declined gradually, from 28.7 per cent in 1990 to 25.7 per cent in 2002.[42] Union density varies considerably across Canada, as shown in table 2.3, with Alberta historically having the lowest union density, Quebec and British Columbia having higher than average density, and Ontario near the national average.

The implementation and enforcement of labour relations policy is usually left to labour relations boards – independent, quasi-judicial, administrative tribunals – created by the provinces and the federal government. Each province now has such a board, along with the federal government, whose Canada Industrial Relations Board has jurisdiction over 700,000 employees under federal jurisdiction, as well as private sector employees in Nunavut, Yukon, and the Northwest Territories. The federal and provincial boards are responsible for decisions on the certification of trade unions, illegal strikes, and lock-outs, mediating and arbitrating disputes as well as a host of related matters. A major function of these boards has been, and remains, certifying trade unions as bargaining agents.

Despite the post-war compromise, labour relations continues to be a valence issue on which left and right parties adopt quite distinct, if not opposing, positions. Right parties tend to support restrictive certification procedures that require unions to achieve a high threshold of support before and during the certification procedure, while granting employers more latitude to counter the certification efforts of the union. Also, such parties allow for employers to use replacement workers in the case of a strike. Finally, right parties are likely to impose additional steps, such as compulsory votes by union members, before a strike can commence, or to require votes by unions on collective agreement offers by management. Parties farther to the right would also be expected to question the validity of the Rand formula. Left parties, on the other hand, back less stringent certification measures that make it easier for new bargaining agents to be established, and prevent employers from using replacement workers during the duration of a strike. Such parties are also more likely to allow unions to operate with fewer impediments.

Active Measures

Active labour market policies are those designed to increase the employment opportunities for individuals, and, more generally, to match demand and supply for labour. They are considered 'active' in contrast to 'passive' measures, such as unemployment insurance or social assistance, which are financial transfers designed to mitigate the hardships of the unemployed. Active measures include three types of initiatives to stimulate employment: (1) increasing the quality of labour supply, such as through vocational (re)training; (2) increasing the demand for labour, such as through public works projects or wage subsidies to employers; and (3) improving the matching of workers to jobs, such as through counselling and job search assistance.

Unlike the four domains reviewed so far, there has been considerable federal-provincial activity in this area during the 1990s. This is a result of a long legacy of the involvement of both the federal and provincial governments in active measures, and increasing dissatisfaction (especially on the part of some provinces) with the arrangements that had arisen during the twentieth century. As discussed at the beginning of this chapter, this policy domain has the most overlap between the federal and provincial jurisdictions. In the larger provinces, active labour market policy has historically involved both the federal and provincial governments; the latter have constitutional responsibility for social and education policies, as well as for public training institutions such as technical and vocational colleges.[43] Ottawa's involvement, on the other hand, has been justified by its broader responsibility for macro-economic policies and its constitutional jurisdiction over the unemployment insurance program.

Active measures began in the late 1910s when a network of primarily provincial employment offices, partially funded by the federal government, was established that extended across most of the nation.[44] The role of these offices was mainly that of a labour exchange: finding workers for jobs, and jobs for workers. Particularly during the Depression of the 1930s, the federal government also subsidized the provision of vocational and technical education by the provinces, as well as other training initiatives. Finally, the federal government undertook large-scale employment creation schemes via public works projects, sometimes in concert with municipalities and provinces.[45]

After the launch of the unemployment insurance program in 1940, the federal government created a system of federal offices providing not only income support to the unemployed, but also labour market services.[46] These offices provided, or funded the provision through third parties, of active measures. The categories of clients served by the national employment offices were expanded substantially beginning in the 1950s to include not only those eligible for employment insurance but also groups facing particular labour market barriers: recent immigrants, people of Aboriginal descent, visible minorities, people with disabilities, women, older workers, and youth. The services provided for these clients were funded solely from general tax revenues, but delivered by the same field offices that also served those eligible for employment insurance benefits. By the mid 1980s, the federal government, through its human resources development department, had a network of 500 field offices across the nation providing employment related services.

Despite the federal measures, the larger and more affluent provinces developed their own active measures for client groups and industrial sectors that were excluded from, or inadequately served by, federal programs or that were viewed as strategic. In particular, they implemented apprenticeship and related programs, as well as services for youth, older workers, and other groups that are not eligible for unemployment insurance benefits. By the mid 1980s, provinces began to enhance the active measures offered to individuals in receipt of longer-term income support to aid them (re)enter the labour force. During the early 1990s, the provinces expanded active measures for social assistance recipients in an effort to more effectively (re)attach them to the labour market. This policy direction was largely the result of significant increases in caseloads and decreases in provincial expenditures on income security.[47] Some provinces created networks of provincial employment offices, while others enhanced the employment services offered through existing income support offices. Provinces also began to establish more programs to serve groups disadvantaged in the labour market, including youth, the disabled, Aboriginals, and others. Thus, by the mid-1990s, several provinces had established their own extensive and sophisticated local delivery networks that operated, to some extent, in parallel with the federal system.

Not surprisingly, some provinces began to argue aggressively that active labour market policy could be made more efficient and effective, and duplication eliminated, if decision-making was located closer to the local level.[48] In particular, the province of Quebec contended since the 1960s that its social and economic developments were closely linked, and that adequate integration and coordination was impossible if the federal government controlled labour market policy. Although constitutional solutions to the demand by provinces for a greater role in active labour market activities were sought during the 1980s and early 1990s, there was no resolution. Nevertheless, the federal government also began to increase the role of the private sector – business and labour – in labour market adjustment policies at the end of the 1980s by fashioning a new labour market institution.[49] The Canadian Labour Force Development Board, formally created in 1990, was a national business and labour advisory board on training issues modelled after similar arrangements in some European countries.[50] Moreover, the federal government encouraged many provinces to establish similar boards to complement the national body.[51] The boards represented a degree of decentralization in that they sought to transfer some responsibility for active labour market policy from governments to business, labour, and other groups. These corporatist boards were designed to permit the labour market partners to develop active labour market policy jointly; in Ontario and Quebec, they could even direct the delivery of provincial programs.[52] As the 1990s progressed it became apparent that most boards were proving to be unsuccessful, and indeed all but one of the boards was terminated.[53] The Quebec board has been the most successful, in part because of unique social and historical conditions in the province that foster corporatism.[54]

In late 1995, in part as a response to a referendum on sovereignty-association held by the Quebec provincial government, the prime minister committed the federal government to withdraw from labour market training. The core of the federal proposal in mid 1996 to transfer responsibilities to the provinces was twofold. First, interested provinces could deliver active measures for employment insurance clients, including employment benefits such as wage subsidies to employers, income supplements, support for self-employment, partnerships for job creation, and support for individuals to obtain training. In total, approximately $1.5 billion was available to be transferred to provinces for these measures in 1996.[55] Second, provinces could also acquire federal staff and resources in order to screen and provide employment counselling and placement to individual clients. Although the labour market development agreements signed with nearly all provinces over the next several years were administrative in nature, rather than constitutional, they represent a fundamental reordering of federal-provincial responsibilities in this policy domain. Notwithstanding the agreements, the federal government reserved several key policy levers for itself, especially decisions about funding levels and client eligibility.[56] With respect to the latter, the existing network of local federal offices continues to determine eligibility for employment insurance assistance. Only eligible clients can then receive active measures from provincial programs.

Not all provinces were interested in assuming responsibility for designing and delivering active employment measures and obtaining federal staff. Consequently, two quite distinct types of agreements have emerged: co-management and full-transfer, along with a degree of asymmetrical federalism.[57] Under the co-management model, there is no transfer of resources (either funds or staff) to the provinces; instead, a process of joint management and implementation is established. Under this model the provinces play a significant role in planning and policy development, but responsibility for actual delivery of programs is left to the existing federal officials and the local organizations with whom they sign contracts. Generally the provinces that have chosen the co-management model are the smaller ones that have historically been the net beneficiaries of federalism and have had a tradition of working closely with the federal government. The full transfer model, on the other hand, involves provinces assuming responsibility for employment benefits and support measures within the federal funding and client eligibility constraints. Typically, but not exclusively, this type of agreement has been reached with the larger provinces or those that have had more experience in designing and managing active measures.[58]

With regard to active labour market policy, parties on the left will emphasize equity concerns by focusing training and skills development initiatives and expenditures on individuals with marginal labour market attachment. Such parties may also tend to stress corporatism in an effort to involve the labour market partners in setting policy. On the other hand, right parties will tend to focus on programs and expenditures that stress efficiency. These parties may not support corporatist designs, leaving coordination to the market.

Social Assistance for Employable Persons

Social assistance policy in Canada grew out of a need to deal with levels of poverty that were overwhelming civil society. Until early in the twentieth century, the care of persons in such conditions was primarily the responsibility of churches (especially in Quebec) or other community voluntary agencies. When the state did become involved it was the municipal governments that provided minimal short-term support to the destitute. Only towards the end of the First World War did the provinces, via programs for women and children, design policies to assist the 'deserving poor.' For example, in 1920, the Ontario legislature passed the Mother's Allowance Act, which provided for a monthly payment towards the support of dependent children whose father had died or deserted them.[59] Ottawa did not become involved until 1927 when the Old Age Pension Act was passed, providing for a 50 per cent federal contribution to provincial plans offering pensions to residents over 70 years of age, and with limited means. This set the pattern for later shared-cost programs with the federal government attempting to attain national objectives in some provincial policy domains. Federal contributions to municipal and provincial programs became particularly important during the Great Depression when the lower levels of government were unable to cope with the cost of relief programs. Over the years, social assistance, initially a program of last resort for whose without any financial resources, was expanded to include the disabled, two-parent families with children, single individuals, and others. After the Second World War the provinces continued to administer most of these programs, albeit with federal funding.[60]

The creation of the Canada Assistance Plan (CAP) in 1966 institutionalized the federal government's contribution (on a fifty-fifty basis) towards the provincial welfare programs. Provinces had to abide by several federal conditions in order to receive the matched funding, including that no provincial residency requirement could be imposed; and that eligibility for assistance had to be based solely on financial need. But provinces were allowed to impose, and did to varying extents, criteria on 'employable' recipients of social assistance, such that they accept any reasonable offer of work, training, or academic upgrading offered by the government authority, or to be actively looking for work. Failure to act in such a manner could, and did, result in the suspension, cancellation, reduction, or refusal of benefits. However, it became a 'general expectation,' at least on the part of the federal government, that a work requirement would not be imposed on those in receipt of assistance.[61]

Notwithstanding the standards set under the Canada Assistance Plan, considerable variation developed between provinces concerning the adequacy of benefits and related supports. For example, even in 1990, Ontario had a conservative and patriarchal regime that reinforced the distinction between deserving social assistance recipients entitled to a pension due to disability or the presence of young children, and the less deserving entitled to lower benefits and expected to soon exit the program. Ontario was also unique in that municipal governments were required to contribute to, and deliver, social assistance to some clients.[62]

In 1990, the federal government in its efforts to reduce its deficits placed a cap on the Canada Assistance Plan that limited the growth of its contribution to provincial social assistance in Ontario, Alberta, and British Columbia (the so-called 'have' provinces) to 5 per cent per year. As a result, the provinces were paying more of the social assistance benefits from their own funds than ever before, while Ottawa contributed proportionately less. In 1996, the Canada Assistance Plan was replaced altogether with a block transfer program for health, post-secondary education, social assistance, and social services – the Canada Health and Safety Transfer. Not only was the cost-matching feature eliminated, the value of the transfer was also lower than in the Canada Assistance Plan era and the eligibility standards, other than the residency requirement, were eliminated. Each province now had a block of funding that it could allocate as it wished among its health, post-secondary education, and social assistance programs, while facing fewer constraints about how to design assistance programs.[63] Moreover, the reform of (un)employment insurance in 1996 (discussed below) further limited eligibility for unemployment benefits, a consequence of which was likely an increase in demand for provincial social assistance.[64]

Policies were implemented to increase the pressure on the 'employables' to exit the social assistance program. This was done partially by altering the definition of who was employable, so that single parents with children, for whom social assistance was originally established to prevent them from entering the labour force, were increasingly defined as employable.[65] More generally, eligibility was tightened both for groups previously eligible for the longer-term pension and for those receiving shorter-term assistance. Second, some provinces introduced more active measures and made participation in them mandatory for some employable recipients – a practice widely termed *workfare*.[66] The rationale for this was to encourage, or coerce, welfare recipients to more quickly join the labour market.

In this book, we are interested only in policies related to the employable assistance recipients, as these alone can be said to form part of the labour force. This group has received considerable political attention during the 1990s, with quite distinct partisan political agendas in most provinces.[67] With respect to the level of benefits, left-wing parties generally argue that assistance benefits should provide an income above the poverty line. On the other hand, the right holds that benefits should be set at a low level, to ensure that recipients seek employment or other means to become self-reliant. The left typically wishes to use eligibility rules to incorporate a wide variety of groups, including, perhaps, the working poor, teenagers, refugees, and post-secondary students. In contrast, the right sees social assistance as a program of last resort with limited eligibility. Left parties often contend that welfare recipients need not be coerced to exit the program, but that appropriate supports should be provided to allow them to obtain independence. By contrast, conservatives generally believe that many welfare recipients will remain on assistance unless forced, to some degree, to enter the labour market.

Other Labour Market Policy Domains

Three areas not covered above fill out the universe of Canadian labour market policy: employment insurance (passive labour market policy), human rights, and immigration. These are briefly reviewed below, to show how they interact with the six provincial labour market policy domains that are addressed in this book.

Employment Insurance, Human Rights, and Immigration

Employment Insurance is the federally run insurance scheme for employed Canadians with eligibility and benefits determined by previous employment income, amount of contributions made to the scheme, and the local unemployment rate. It is a national program begun in 1941 after a constitutional amendment allowed the federal government to operate it.[68] The insurance program increased its coverage and benefits paid until the early 1970s, with a gradual but steady erosion of benefits and eligibility since (with the notable exception of parental benefits).[69] For the past decade the scheme has been solely financed by worker and employer contributions, although in previous decades some federal general tax revenues supplemented these contributions.

In the first half of the 1990s, the program was incrementally altered to counter concerns that it was undermining work incentives by being too generous and too passive in helping the unemployed find new jobs, and, more importantly, to reduce costs. Eligibility requirements were tightened, the duration of payments was reduced, and benefits were lowered. For instance, in 1993 and 1994, the benefit rate was lowered from 60 per cent to 57 per cent and then to 55 per cent of previous employment earnings, and the average entitlement period was shortened. After 1993, the new Liberal government's social security review sought to reduce the reliance of workers on unemployment insurance, thereby achieving significant savings. Particularly severe adjustments were made to eligibility criteria affecting frequent users of unemployment insurance (now renamed Employment Insurance), who tended to be concentrated in seasonal occupations such as fishing in the Atlantic region.[70]

The provision of employment insurance is entirely a federal responsibility, and hence does not fit with our objective of analysing the role of partisanship and globalization in the provinces. But there are interactions between employment insurance and employment standards, active measures and social assistance for employables. As already noted, changes in employment insurance provisions affect provincial policies. In particular, as employment insurance eligibility has been constrained, increasing numbers of unemployed Canadians turn to social assistance, or find that they are ineligible for either program.[71]

Issues in the employer-worker relationship related to discrimination and harassment, and *human rights* generally, are subject to the Canadian Charter of Rights and Freedoms. Provincially regulated private sector employers are subject to provincial human rights legislation. Comprehensive human rights legislation was initially instituted in the 1960s (for example, the Canadian Bill of Rights passed in 1960 and the Ontario Human Rights Code in 1961), largely in response to the minorities civil rights movement that challenged the stigmatizing effects in the workplace of race, ethnicity, sexual orientation, and other putatively objective conditions, and the limitations on opportunities and freedoms associated with minority status. Until the 1980s, there was considerable variation among provinces in the extent of human rights protection.

Enactment of the Canadian Charter of Rights and Freedoms in 1982 caused the various provincial human rights acts to converge somewhat to meet the criteria established in the charter.[72] The individual complaint-based, and quasi-judicial, nature of human rights issues means that they do not have a short- or medium-term impact on the labour market. Arm's-length human rights commissions, both at the federal and provincial levels, are responsible for administering the legislation, but have no policy-making capacity, while a separate quasi-judicial tribunal rules on cases that are not resolved through mediation.[73] Although the majority of complaints are resolved without formal hearings, a very small number of cases do reach the Supreme Court of Canada and result in policy or legislative change. Human rights legislation and its enforcement remains a means for individuals to seek redress for workplace discrimination and harassment, rather than a labour market policy instrument. As such, we have excluded this policy domain from our analysis, while recognizing that human rights legislation and judicial decisions have sometimes played a role in enhancing the labour market opportunities of groups such as women, racial minorities, and others.

There is a longstanding tradition in Canada of using *immigration* policy as a thinly veiled labour market policy, such that immigration has been a staple of Canadian labour market policy for more than a century. Historically, Canadian immigration policy has been utilized to address skills shortages and inadequacies in the labour force.[74] Until the past decade the level of immigration has typically been adjusted so as to increase during times of low unemployment and decrease when unemployment was high.[75] The 'right' type of immigrant from the perspective of the labour market has always been given preference, whether to farm the Prairies, or build railroads, or, at present, for domestic work.[76] The introduction of a non-racist immigration policy during the 1960s, and the changing preferences of the final destination of highly trained immigrants, has meant that immigration became a somewhat less important tool in labour market policy. Nevertheless, the points system, which immigration applicants who are not in the family reunification or refugee categories must meet, seeks to match the human capital of immigrants with labour market conditions.

Conclusion

During the twentieth century, the provinces acquired enormous power to set policy in most areas of labour market policy. It is only with respect to one major passive measure, employment insurance, that the provinces have no role. In the six domains we have selected for analysis – workers' compensation, occupational health and safety, employment standards including pay and employment equity, labour relations, active measures, and social assistance for employables – provinces have essentially unfettered ability to make policy. In 1995, the provinces gained even further latitude to make policy with respect to social assistance recipients, with the demise of the Canada Assistance Plan, and, in active measures, with the signing of the labour market development agreements. Only regarding active measures are the provinces constrained to a degree by federal policy, and only with respect to employment insurance clients. These six domains encompass a combination of different policy tools, from solely regulatory, as in employment standards and occupational health and safety, to the brokerage role inherent in industrial relations, to a primarily income maintenance function in social assistance. Variations exist between provinces in these domains, and shifts in labour market policy have occurred in each province during the past several decades.

Given the considerable room that provinces have to manoeuvre, ideological differences among governing parties have considerable potential to shape labour market policy. The next four chapters assess empirically the extent to which partisanship and globalization, mediated by institutions, affected provincial policy-making between 1990 and 2003 in the first five main areas of provincial responsibility identified above. Chapter 8 extends the analysis to social assistance for employables in the four provinces.

PART TWO

Case Studies

PART TWO

Case Studies

4 Ontario: Policy Continuity amid Institutional Uncertainty

Ontario's post-1990 labour market policy setting is less easily character-ized in institutional terms than is the case for the other provinces examined in this study. Its political-economic institutions overlap with national ones more than is the case elsewhere: business organizations are only partly distinguishable from their national counterparts, and use organizational outlets that are often poorly differentiated from Canadian ones; and the economic role of the Ontario state has often been closely coordinated with Ottawa's. It is nevertheless clear that, as in other English-speaking provinces, Ontario's social democratic-tinged liberal welfare state is complemented by a broadly liberal market economy (LME) production regime. A more important cause of institu-tional uncertainty, for our purposes, has been Ontario's tumultuous party system. Once a bastion of political stability, apparent centre-right moderation, and one-party dominance under the Progressive Conser-vative Party, Ontario experienced dramatic political change after 1985, highlighted by the election of a centre-left NDP government in 1990, succeeded by a distinctly right-of-centre PC administration in 1995. The pre-1985 pattern was widely thought to have softened somewhat the competitive edges of Ontario's business- and market-oriented produc-tion regime, permitting what we earlier termed *informal concertation* among government, business, and labour; in the newly polarized ambi-ance of the 1990s, this feature became much less evident. With the 2002 departure from office of Mike Harris, the Tories' first post-1995 leader, followed by a Liberal victory in the 2003 provincial election, the erst-while pattern of political moderation may, perhaps, have been restored. During the period under study, however, Ontario's partisan landscape was highly and uncharacteristically polarized.

This institutional uncertainty made it problematical, in chapter two, to anticipate the likely impact of partisanship on labour market policy in Ontario after 1990; but this problem is greater regarding the long-term potential for neo-liberal retrenchment than for post-election, short-term policy swings. In a polarized partisan setting, short-term swings should be considerable, regardless of the party system's longer-term history. But whether the Conservatives' accession to power in 1995 would result in a fundamental, market-oriented departure from the post-war norm in Ontario would depend on whether this near-term partisan polarization was strong enough to overpower the post-war policy equilibrium that emerged from the earlier, and much lengthier, era of policy moderation and relative stasis. This chapter contends that it was not. A sharp shift to the political left after 1990 was followed by an equally robust countermovement after 1995; but in the labour market policy domains examined here, this return swing largely restored the pre-1985 status quo ante, rather than signifying a neo-liberal turn unprecedented in the province's post-war history.

Ontario Politics since 1990

Throughout most of the years since the Second World War, Ontario has had a three-party system. Evoking Gad Horowitz's characterization of Canada's federal party system as dominated by a centrist and broker-age-oriented Liberal Party, Nelson Wiseman attributed a similar pattern to Ontario, with the Conservative 'big blue machine' playing the role of centrist broker there.[1] As we noted in chapter 2, scholarly observers generally characterized Ontario's political culture as 'moderate,' and as requiring 'informal concentration' among diverse interests.[2] These norms fit comfortably with the dominance of the province's politics for forty-two years (1943 to 1985) by an apparently centrist party, whose success was predicated on practicing at the provincial level the kind of integrative brokerage politics that we associate with federal politics in Canada. Even before the Tories lost office in 1985, however, there were signs that this image was becoming anachronistic, as their margin of victory in elections was often narrow after the early 1970s. Ontario's expenditures across a broad range of policy fields rose very slowly after 1980, falling well below per capita averages for the Canadian provinces.[3] Finally, the Tories selected Frank Miller, a representative of the party's rural and small-town right wing, as their new leader shortly before the 1985 election.

The Peterson Liberal administrations of the late 1980s moved the province significantly to the left (see chapter 2). Spending and taxation levels grew dramatically between 1985 and 1990.[4] In the labour market policy field, the Liberals expanded spending on training and launched reforms of occupational health and safety and workers' compensation, which were precursors to later NDP measures. In a fundamental departure from Ontario practice, the Liberals created a Premier's Council, designed to enlist the province's business and labour leaders in semi-formal consultations about Ontario's economic future. The recession of the early 1980s had been the worst experienced by the province since the Great Depression, and the threat of globalization and free trade motivated the administration to seek long-term solutions to protect the province's economy. The Premier's Council's two reports, endorsed by its business and labour representatives, proposed significant changes in industrial and labour market policy. The latter, released on the eve of the 1990 election, also recommended the creation of a board to institutionalize business-labour collaboration.[5] Without significantly altering Ontario's LME institutions, these forums were explicitly designed to create policy-making tools that approximated those of Europe's CMEs.

Meanwhile, according to some observers, the Liberals allowed to atrophy the informal mechanisms for consultation that the previous Tory administration had husbanded. The Liberals' defeat in 1990 coincided with the beginning of another deep recession as Ontario's manufacturing economy experienced a fundamental structural adjustment. It was clear that the province would quickly incur a substantial budgetary deficit.[6] In this climate, a pattern of polarized partisan politics emerged in the early 1990s that diverged radically from the earlier centrist pattern. The clearest options in this polarized milieu were represented by the NDP and by a revitalized Conservative party. The general parameters of these agendas are outlined here, while their specific implications for labour market policy are addressed in subsequent sections.

The NDP's agenda envisaged continuing the policy trajectory commenced in 1985, by extending spending on education, child care, social assistance, and the non-profit sector, and implementing employment equity legislation. This was only partly reflected in *An Agenda for People*, its hastily prepared document for the 1990 election;[7] it was also revealed in positions the party had supported in opposition and announced after coming to power. While *An Agenda for People* said little about the economy, after its election victory the NDP quickly articulated an economic agenda that focused on the potential for government to help the private sector face globalization. The NDP's first post-election budget, in 1991, adopted an explicitly Keynesian perspective, promising to fight the deepening recession by increasing spending, even at the expense of expanding the province's already-exploding deficit. By 1993, however, with the province's economy only very slowly emerging from recession, the government felt compelled to reverse its fiscal course. It imposed a 'Social Contract' on the public sector, curtailing public spending by, among other things, legislating rollbacks in contracts negotiated earlier with public sector unions. With large components of its core electorate now alienated from the party, and, in the face of persistent hostility from the business community, the NDP's defeat in the 1995 election was a foregone conclusion long before the vote. Its policies regarding industrial and labour market policy followed a somewhat different trajectory. Here, it sought to work associatively with business and to induce collaborative behaviour among firms and their workers.[8] This attempt to foster more coordinative behaviour remained a hallmark of the administration until its 1995 defeat, but, in the highly polarized climate that pervaded Ontario during the 1990s, it bore little fruit.

By contrast, the Conservatives continued to move away from their erstwhile centrist stance. In 1990, they selected Mike Harris, another representative of the party's right wing, as their leader, and adopted a distinctively neo-liberal policy agenda. This culminated with the Common Sense Revolution (commonly known as the CSR), the party's program finalized in 1994 for the 1995 election campaign. The CSR was worked out in close consultation with prominent party sympathizers, especially in the business community. It proposed to reverse the political and fiscal trends of the past decade by lowering personal income taxes and balancing the budget, combined with substantial spending reductions and a smaller government; a 20 per cent reduction in social assistance benefits for employable recipients and the implementation of a form of workfare were key promises.[9] The Conservatives also championed a more market-oriented approach to the economy. They would abolish the main coordinative decision-making forums that the NDP had created, reduce business taxes, and restore prosperity by enhancing, rather than adulterating, the liberal and competitive tenor of Ontario's business culture. Buoyed by robust economic growth during the late 1990s, along with firm business support, the Conservatives maintained support among middle class and rural voters, and were re-elected in 1999. *Blueprint*, the party's official document for that campaign, promised more tax cuts and further market-oriented reform.[10] The Tories' move to the right therefore was much more successful politically, and more sustainable as policy, than the NDP's centre-left agenda had ever been.

Yet this success was not unlimited or indefinite. Conservative support fell after the 1999 election; Harris abandoned the party leadership in 2002, and was replaced by Ernie Eves, who gave some indication of wanting to pursue a course more consistent with the PC's pre-1985 image of moderation. That Ontario politics might, in fact, return to a more centrist style was made even more possible by the victory of Dalton McGuinty's Liberals in the 2003 election. As we will see below, this led to a few, mostly modest, retreats from Conservative policy. Nevertheless, to an entirely unprecedented degree, partisan conflict in Ontario during the 1990s and early 2000s, the period of focus in this study, was substantial, and permits a clear differentiation between the labour market policy agendas of left- and right-wing parties in power. The consequences of this broad political context are now discussed in detail for each of the five policy fields treated in this chapter. Developments that pertain exclusively to the public sector are not discussed. In its final section, the chapter returns to the hypotheses summarized above, and assesses the degree to which the evidence presented here is consistent with them.

Industrial Relations

An Agenda for People said nothing about labour relations; however, in opposition, the NDP supported greater protection for workers. The province's labour movement expected the new government to implement major changes in Ontario's Labour Relations Act. It had good reason to expect sympathy: one-third of the NDP caucus members had been union officials before the election.[11]

The new government's November 1990 throne speech asserted that it "will ensure that workers can freely express their right to organize."[12] The NDP's approach to this policy field crystallized the following March. Its two broad and potentially contradictory objectives would also be reflected in other areas of labour market policy. The first was to create a more 'balanced' relationship between employers and workers; since the NDP saw the current balance as favouring business, this would entail increasing union rights. Second, the NDP hoped to foster a more cooperative climate in labour relations; the labour market 'partners' would acquire a greater role in developing and implementing policy. This agenda manifested a desire to foster the kind of dialogic relations that characterize CMEs. Needless to say, the first objective could represent a major obstacle to attaining the second – relatively favoured by existing labour relations law (in a manner typical of LMEs), business would likely resist changes that favoured labour, making the pursuit of cooperation particularly difficult. Moreover, the fundamental labour market institutions in Ontario continued to be those typical of an LME after the NDP came to power – competitive relations among firms and between them and their employees, and fragmented business and labour organizations, which had little experience of cooperation.

The NDP's desire for a more collaborative labour relations culture was reflected in its March 1991 creation of a Labour Relations Act Reform Committee to revise the act substantially. The committee included three representatives each from business and organized labour, and a neutral chair. Rather than being dictated by government, the new legislation would reflect a consensus between the private sector actors. The latent tension between the NDP's two strategic goals became manifest when the labour and business participants on the committee could not agree, and submitted separate reports. Labour recommended wide-ranging changes to the act to favour unions; business endorsed the status quo, arguing that anything more than marginal changes would increase costs unacceptably.[13] The recession, already deep by 1991, enhanced the credibility of the latter argument with business's constituency and with the Ontario public.

Lacking a business-labour consensus, the government began preparing its own discussion paper on reform, a draft of which was leaked to the press in September 1991.[14] It appeared to favour labour's position by supporting the elimination of an employer's right to hire replacement workers during a strike (an 'anti-scab' law). While such a measure had long been in place in Quebec, this provision quickly became a lightning rod for business resistance to the reforms. The document also indicated support for changes that would prevent managers from performing strikers' responsibilities during a strike, permit unions to enter an employer's premises to organize, make certification possible without a certification vote if a union obtained the signatures of 50 per cent of a bargaining unit's members, and expedite the unionization of agricultural workers, security guards, and other groups. To compensate for their organizational fragmentation, the leading business federations and many firms formed an All Business Coalition, with the specific purpose of resisting these changes. When the NDP finally released its discussion paper in November, it retreated from some ideas contained in the September draft. In particular, the 'anti-scab' proposal was weakened, as firms would be allowed to move production from a striking plant to another facility. The government announced that another round of negotiations would be undertaken in 1992 to seek a business-labour consensus.[15]

Bill 40, the labour relations reform legislation, was tabled in the legislature in June 1992; it included further concessions to business. The proportion of workers needed for automatic union certification was increased to 55 per cent; the ban on replacement workers would only apply if a union received a strike mandate from 60 per cent of voting members; and certain essential services would be exempted from the ban. Yet these concessions, and the summer legislative hearings, did not soften business opposition.[16] The NDP again modified the anti-scab provision in the final legislation, passed in November 1992. The opposition Liberal Party voted against the legislation; the Conservatives promised to repeal it entirely if elected.[17] The business community argued that even in its final form Bill 40 shifted the balance of power in labour relations substantially in the direction of unions. Organized labour was equally intransigent; each step that the NDP took to soften the legislation was attacked by the Ontario Federation of Labour (OFL) as a betrayal of labour and workers. The reforms also never appear to have been fully accepted by the Ontario public.[18]

When the Conservatives won the June 1995 provincial election, they moved quickly and against no effective resistance to pass Bill 7, which reversed the changes made by Bill 40. The promise to revoke Bill 40 had been prominent in the Common Sense Revolution (CSR), and the legislation was the first by the new government to receive royal assent, in November 1995. Bill 7 eliminated the ban on replacement workers, restored the requirement that membership votes be held before a union could be certified, mandated that such a vote be held within five days of a union's application for certification, made decertification easier, reduced substantially the wage protection (earlier enhanced by the NDP) available to employees in bankrupt firms, and excluded groups of workers, such as those in agriculture and domestic work, and some professionals, to whom coverage had been extended by Bill 40.[19] In these respects, Bill 7 largely reinstated the labour relations provisions that existed in Ontario before Bill 40. In only one important area did it go further: the bill eliminated successor rights for civil servants whose jobs were transferred to the private sector, making it easier for the government to privatize services. In sharp contrast with the NDP's desire to create a more 'equitable' balance between two equally legitimate 'stakeholders' in labour relations, the Conservative legislation stressed the efficiency merits of a more market-oriented regime. The Conservative agenda for labour relations differed radically from the NDP's in form as well as in content. The CSR gave the Tories a much more detailed action plan for government than *An Agenda for People* had for the NDP. It was the product of extensive consultations before the 1995 election, but very much within the Conservatives' chosen constituency, above all the business community. The Harris government entirely abandoned the NDP's principled commitment to cooperation and bipartisanship in developing policy. The relevant consultation, the new government was fond of saying, had occurred on election day.

A similar pattern characterized subsequent legislation passed during the rest of the Conservatives' first term in office, and during its second. The Harris government backed away from a 1997 proposal to create a commission to decide which unions could bargain with the new employer when public sector jobs were privatized or transferred to the municipal or voluntary sector. This retreat was intended to reduce the prospect of a strike among some public sector unions, and softened significantly the successor rights provision of Bill 7.[20] Legislation passed in 1998 eliminated a recently acquired power for the Ontario Labour Relations Board to certify a union, where the board perceived that the employer had engaged in unfair tactics to dissuade workers from joining a union;[21] the bill also weakened construction unions by, for instance, allowing some employers to opt out of province-wide union contracts. Bill 69, tabled in April 2000, further restricted construction union powers by requiring binding arbitration for Toronto residential construction workers if a strike in that sector exceeded 46 days, and permitting more work-site flexibility for industrial construction contractors (regional groups of contractors would be permitted to negotiate with their workers variances from the existing terms of province-wide contracts); there was more consultation with affected interests in this case, during which unions persuaded the government to abandon its most radical proposal – to permit unionized construction firms to set up parallel non-union companies. But the government had already identified the legislation's main goals at the outset.[22] The binding arbitration feature of Bill 69 was renewed in September 2002.[23] Yet another bill, introduced in November 2001, required that information on how to decertify a union be posted publicly at unionized work sites, required 'cooling off' periods during union drives, and stipulated that all union officials' salaries be publicized if they exceeded $100,000 per year.[24]

Even in light of these changes, however, the Tory labour relations reforms did not represent a radical departure from arrangements that existed prior to the NDP's accession to power, though more radical reforms were proposed. For instance, the Conservatives were lobbied by some business interests and financial press commentators to abandon the Rand formula (which assures that those who choose not to join a union will nevertheless pay union dues), and to move more radically against construction unions by allowing contractors to establish non-union subsidiaries alongside their existing unionized ones. The Conservative labour minister deliberated publicly about restricting construction unions further, but did not do this. When a confidential document that appeared to imply support for abolishing the Rand formula became public in July 2000, the minister stated that he did not plan to implement it.[25] The Tories' final industrial relations bill also was intended to restore, rather than fundamentally alter, an earlier pro-business balance of power. In December 2001, the Supreme Court of Canada decided that Bill 7's exclusion of agricultural workers from industrial relations law violated the Charter of Rights and Freedoms; with the support of the Liberal Party, the Conservatives restored the exclusion with legislation that was passed the following November.[26] By the time of the October 2003 election, the pre-1990 equilibrium in the labour relations field was broadly restored. The Ontario Liberals, victorious in that campaign, had made no significant commitments to alter industrial relations law if elected.

Active Labour Market Policy

As in other Canadian provinces, occupational training in Ontario reflected the LME pattern, outlined in chapter 1, when the NDP came to power. Institutional instruction predominated over on-the-job or industrial training;[27] the education and training system as a whole was much better at providing predominantly middle class youth with a liberal, service-oriented education in universities and colleges than at offering technically and industrially oriented vocational training; the latter is especially likely to be taken up by less advantaged young people. This deficiency persisted, moreover, despite the fact that the Peterson Liberals oversaw the creation of a Ministry of Skills Development in 1985 to concentrate on industrial training. The new ministry was beset by problems from the outset; its financial resources could not rival those of the institutionally focused Ministry of Colleges and Universities, and it did not work effectively with other ministries. It lost many program responsibilities in 1989, before finally being closed in 1993.[28] NDP policy consequently would represent a second attempt to make the province's active measures more relevant for the private sector and for less advantaged Ontarians.

Yet *An Agenda for People* again gave little preliminary indication of what the NDP would do in power in this area. Shortly, however, the two elements of the CME-tinted labour market agenda defined above were extended to training: (i) training measures should be improved, with particular attention to the needs of vulnerable workers (a greater focus on equity goals); and (ii) there should be more collaborative decision making among the labour market partners. The first goal was alluded to in *An Agenda for People*, which stressed the skills needs of "workers affected by layoffs or a plant shutdown" and of "[u]nemployed workers."[29] The second commitment emerged when the NDP quickly endorsed the July 1990 proposal in *People and Skills in the New Economy*, the Premier's Council's second report (requested by the preceding Liberal administration in 1988), to create a collaborative private sector-led labour market board. In 1991, the government released its blueprint for setting up a business- and labour-dominated board to oversee many active labour market policies. Lengthy discussions were nevertheless necessary with the affected interests before legislation to launch the Ontario Training and Adjustment Board (OTAB) could be passed by the legislature in 1993. The agency that was finally brought into existence differed in important respects from the Premier's Council proposals and from preliminary thinking within the government.[30] First, the government chose to include representatives of 'equity' groups on the OTAB board, as well as business and labour; along with eight representatives from each of the latter, OTAB included spokespersons for women, visible minorities, the disabled, and francophone Ontarians; education and training institutions were also assigned two members. This was similar to the composition of the Canadian Labour Force Development Board (CLFDB), which Ottawa had created in 1991 with the intention of bring collaborative decision making to federal labour market policy. Unlike the CLFDB, however, OTAB acquired decision-making powers and a budget of $450 million. It also had a broader remit than had been anticipated originally, acquiring responsibility for training for marginalized groups, as well as for the more 'mainstream' unemployed.

By any account, OTAB was a failure.[31] There was considerable friction among the interests represented on the OTAB board from the outset; this was aggravated by the presence of equity representatives. But business and labour had enough grounds for disagreement. The NDP's industrial relations reform discussed above (Bill 40) soured relations between them. Business and labour also disagreed about a range of issues related to active measures, with labour stressing the equity objectives emphasized by the NDP. Business members preferred an efficiency focus, wishing to concentrate on filling skills shortages in key economic sectors, rather than on the needs of the disadvantaged. In policy terms, OTAB accomplished remarkably little. Working jointly with the federal government, it did launch a network of 25 local boards around Ontario; these were designed to replicate the OTAB representative model and to permit nongovernmental actors to guide the delivery of provincial and federal active measures at that level. The boards survived the NDP's departure from power in 1995; however, an external evaluation of them in 2000 concluded that they were "not progressing as anticipated," and appeared to have "embarked on a downward spiral."[32]

Stymied in its attempt to build collaborative policy-making, the NDP was forced to pursue its equity-focused training objectives well away from OTAB, using the traditional ministerial bureaucracy. Here, the NDP's ambitions were curtailed by the massive budgetary deficit that the government began to experience, which left it with little money for expensive new programs. Its biggest initiative along these lines was jobsOntario Training. Launched in 1992, it offered up to $10,000 to private sector employers for training a worker who was hired from the welfare rolls, or who had exhausted unemployment insurance eligibility. With the welfare and unemployment rolls skyrocketing in the early 1990s, jobsOntario Training quickly became a large program – expending almost $240 million in 1994 alone – and represented the government's most significant response to the plight of those left out of work by the recession.[33]

The Common Sense Revolution was categorical regarding jobsOntario Training: the Conservatives planned to eliminate it.[34] This promise was quickly implemented after the election. The CSR said nothing about OTAB, but the board's purpose of fostering coordinated decision making, rather than a reliance on market signals, ran counter to the new government's philosophy. Combined with the fact that the OTAB board's business members were already in open revolt against its other constituencies in 1995, this did not bode well for its future. OTAB was terminated in 1996.[35] The new government did not abolish the network of local boards, as these were seen as an important tool available to the province in its struggle to wrest control of federal training monies from Ottawa (see below). The CSR's prominent commitment to "cut business subsidies and reduce government grants"[36] also had implications for training. Many existing active labour market measures, including jobsOntario Training, consisted, in whole or in part, of subsidies to firms. In 1996, several programs were cancelled, including one that assisted firms in labour force planning, as well as a small labour adjustment measure for older workers, and a subsidized placement program for social assistance recipients. These cuts in the training field were significant, though they contributed only marginally to the government's expenditure-reduction agenda. The government's training budget was cut by $77 million, or 17 per cent, in 1996–97.[37]

There was little in the way of reform of training programs (as opposed to cuts) under the Conservatives; the one exception, apprenticeship, is discussed below. The financial stringency that the Tories imposed on the province was certainly one reason for this. Another factor, however, was a protracted conflict with the federal government regarding the administration of Ottawa's employment insurance-funded training expenditures in the province. Ontario was the only province at the time of writing that had not signed a Labour Market Development Agreement (LMDA) since 1997.[38] These agreements have, at the option of the province, allowed the latter to take over administration of these funds, within broad federal guidelines. In Ontario, the transfer was impeded by friction between the Harris administration and its federal counterpart. The broad lines of the Conservatives' preferred approach to training nevertheless were clear. It mirrored that of their Liberal and NDP predecessors in seeking a less institutional, more flexible training system, but it did so on quite different terms: they saw training more as a tool to meet market needs experienced by employers (an efficiency objective), than as a way of pursuing equity. As one interviewed provincial official expressed it, since the Tories came to power "employers have been brought into the equation ... The workplace determines who is ready for employment ... Government's role is to get [clients] out there ... [and give them] a hand up, rather than a hand out." This philosophy was reflected in the deliberations of the Ontario Jobs and Investment Board (OJIB), created in 1997 to provide the government with private sector advice on the economy. Though a consultative body, the OJIB was a far cry from the coordinative mechanisms preferred by the NDP. Its membership was overwhelmingly business-dominated and was determined by the government.[39] As a deliberative forum it was relatively informal, and sought to systematize, to a degree, the kind of constituency-specific consultation that the Conservatives undertook regarding the CSR document before 1995. The OJIB launched three research panels, one of which pertained to active labour market policy.[40] In its March 1999 report, the panel recommended more attention to job-relevant skills, and focused almost entirely on the efficiency-oriented goal of addressing labour market shortages.[41] The OJIB was subsequently dissolved.

The one concrete example of the Conservatives' market-oriented agenda in practice has been its apprenticeship reform. It is widely believed that skills requiring an apprenticeship will soon be in short supply across Canada.[42] The new government therefore launched a reform in 1996 designed to make the system more flexible and accessible. Components of different apprenticeships would be 'modularized' to permit multi-skilling; training periods would be shorter and provide trainees with more specific, job-relevant (and narrower) skills. Apprentices would be expected to cover more of the costs of their own training, and rules regarding the ratio of journeypersons to apprentices were curtailed.[43] Traditionally, such changes have been resisted by labour unions, which see them as tantamount to 'de-skilling'; that is, attempting to undermine the economic security of broadly trained tradesmen who complete existing apprenticeships. In the construction sector, where apprenticeship is most extensive, this resistance was fierce.[44] The Apprenticeship and Certification Act was proclaimed in 2000, but the construction trades – never on as hostile terms with the Conservatives as other unions – were exempted, and remained covered by the pre-existing legislation.[45] Here again, the effect of Conservative policy was to largely leave untouched the status quo in the province's labour market policy regime. If apprenticeship is undertaken in a more 'flexible' and 'market-friendly' manner in the future, this will only be true in economic sectors where it was not well developed previously. During the remaining years of their second term in office, the Conservatives made only minor adjustments to active measures – modestly increasing spending on apprenticeship and on assisting labour market adjustment for immigrants, and launching a web site to disseminate information about apprenticeships.[46]

In the training field, the policy framework established by the Conservatives by 2003 again resembled that which existed before 1990. And, despite the disquiet that the changes caused within the province's labour movement, Conservative policy established a broad political and policy equilibrium, not threatened by significant societal or political opposition. The Liberals' election program in 2003, outlined in the document *Plan for Change*, did promise some change; its most specific commitments were to enhance re-employment and apprenticeship programs and to create an employee training credit.[47] Even if fulfilled, these initiatives would leave unaffected the Conservatives' goals of largely abandoning labour market concertation and of making active measures more market-oriented. During the first six months after the 2003 election, and constrained by their budgetary situation, the Liberals in any case took only one modest initiative: an $18 million increase in apprenticeship financing,[48] which continued a gradual increase in spending started by the Tories.

Occupational Health and Safety

Ensuring a 'fairer' (i.e., somewhat more favourable) treatment of labour's agenda, and enhancing collaborative decision making were again the two main objectives of the NDP's approach to occupational health and safety (OHS). Here, the tension between these goals became especially evident. *An Agenda for People* was silent regarding OHS, but the NDP had long championed safer workplaces. During the 1980s, it had supported the union contention that OHS in Ontario provided inadequate protection for workers' safety and insufficient oversight of employers.[49] As in the training field, the groundwork for collaborative decision making in OHS was laid by the Liberal administration of the late 1980s. As the 1990 election approached, the Liberals were finalizing a plan to remove OHS concerns from the province's Workers' Compensation Board (WCB) and to have them addressed in a separate Workplace Health and Safety Agency (WHSA). The agency eventually acquired a bipartite structure; under a government-appointed executive chair, two co-chairs, one each from the business and labour communities, would oversee the WHSA; and its board of directors would consist of equal numbers of business and labour representatives.[50]

After the election, however, the WHSA's business representatives quickly became disenchanted and the labour co-chair, Paul Forder, was effectively able to control it with his forceful personality and considerable knowledge of OHS issues. He was supported by a highly cohesive group of labour representatives. The business co-chair was judged to be less effective, at least by some sectors of business, and the business representatives were not as united in their views. Small business was more hostile to the WHSA than big business, and the construction industry was often willing to compromise with labour. By 1992, a number of business representatives had resigned from the agency's board of directors.[51] Business observers believed that Forder had direct and privileged access to, and undue influence over, the NDP's labour minister, and was able to sway the government in favour of his position; interviewed government officials agreed that this was sometimes true. Labour did not use its hegemonic position to pursue a collaborative approach with business. As one interviewed former official put it, the WHSA was "bipartite in structure, but not in outcomes ... [L]abour ran the place."

In this atmosphere, the WHSA proceeded with initiatives that were opposed by most business interests. The number of employees who had to take safety training courses was expanded; an expensive generic course was prescribed for most trainees, in addition to job-specific training; and workers acquired additional rights to refuse to work in dangerous situations. Moreover, labour became much more involved in the delivery of safety training. Most safety associations that provided such courses had previously been controlled by business, but now much training was provided by a labour-controlled Workers' Health and Safety Centre. The cost of workplace safety training rose significantly during the early 1990s – from $42 million in 1990 to $62 million in 1994.[52] From labour's perspective, this was justified in pursuit of the (equity) objective of reducing workplace deaths and injuries. Business complained, however; in conjunction with a rapidly rising unfunded liability at the Workers' Compensation Board, they argued, it was becoming an important burden. In the face of these developments, labour and public service observers of the WHSA noticed that businesses were postponing compliance with the rules, awaiting the NDP government's demise to seek their elimination.[53] As Carolyn Tuohy noted in a report for the government, by 1995 the WHSA was widely seen as pro-labour.[54]

The Conservative party shared business's view that the WHSA was wasteful. While the Common Sense Revolution said nothing about the WHSA, it did devote considerable space to the general issue of waste and overspending by the government, and to the unfunded liability issue at the WCB. Shortly after the election, the new government's labour minister announced that the WHSA would be disbanded and its responsibilities probably reintegrated with the Workers' Compensation Board.[55] Again, there was no evident post-election consultation with any interests, and certainly none with labour, about this move.

The partisan landscape of OHS policy in Ontario was now reversed. Organized labour protested the WHSA's abandonment, and unsuccessfully challenged it in court shortly after the new labour minister dismissed Forder and the agency's board.[56] The minister struck a 10–member review panel to conduct hearings and to develop proposals for the health and safety field. As an example of consultation, this again differed radically from what had been practised under the NDP; public discussion would occur very much on the government's terms. The minister made it clear that the cost-saving and deregulatory objectives that the Conservatives had promoted in the election campaign would be central to any future changes. As one interviewed government official put it, the Tories made little effort "to ... get a middle-of-the-road consensus." The focus would now be on "economic viability" and "international global competitiveness." The OFL boycotted the panel; only one of the panel's 10 members was a labour representative. The panel's report, released in December, largely endorsed the business perspective. It reiterated the business view that the OHS be reintegrated with Workers' Compensation, proposed that safety training courses be shortened, and suggested administrative reforms to reduce costs. The unions, the NDP, and the Liberals all criticized the document's failure to respond to labour views.[57]

A task force was then asked to flesh out these recommendations. Completed in mid-1996, its report endorsed the business view that the number of safety associations delivering safety training be reduced, that they be organized more on sectoral lines, and that they be subject to more rigorous performance targets. While the union-controlled Workers' Health and Safety Centre would survive, its role as a safety-training deliverer was curtailed considerably. These changes, along with shortened mandatory safety courses, were expected to decrease OHS administrative costs by 30 per cent.[58] Both sets of recommendations were then incorporated into legislation to create a Workplace Safety and Insurance Board (WSIB), which would again include OHS training and workers' compensation under one roof.[59] The new board would also oversee OHS training with a much 'lighter touch' than had the WHSA; rather than developing safety-training courses in detail, it would set general standards for their development by training providers, a move opposed by unions and rejected as 'murky' by Tuohy. The government also suspended a past practice of conducting mandatory inquests when a worker died in an industrial accident.[60]

But some changes were not entirely beneficial to business. Conservative policy stressed the prevention of injuries more than earlier OHS legislation had; the new legislation increased business's responsibilities to prevent injuries in some respects. In November 1999, moreover, the government launched a review of Occupational Exposure Limits (OELs) in Ontario, which were updated and extended the following September.[61] On the other hand, as an interviewed official noted, it retreated from immediate implementation of some chemical bans when presented with evidence that doing so "would make us economically uncompetitive." In the same year, moreover, the government announced that it was dropping a requirement for mandatory on-site inspections for firms that had a good safety record; this was much resisted by unions.[62] During their second term, the Conservatives also implemented the second phase of a health and safety training requirement initiated under the NDP in 1993, and launched a campaign to reduce workplace injuries for young workers by disseminating safety information and penalizing negligent employers.[63] In December 2001, they passed legislation to reinstate the work-site inspection powers for WSIB officials that had been eroded by a recent court decision.[64]

The Conservatives reduced considerably the discretion available to outside actors to oversee OHS training in the province's firms, and tilted legislation decisively back in the direction of business interests, and of efficiency objectives. Yet, here again, Tory policy did not differ significantly from what had prevailed in the province before the mid-1980s. The new government's willingness to tighten modestly some OHS rules after its 1999 re-election suggests that, like earlier Conservative administrations, it retained an ability to address, in however subordinate a manner, the needs of labour as well as those of business. As with most other fields addressed in this chapter, moreover, the province's post-2003 Liberal administration could find little political or policy advantage in significantly changing the Tories' restored policy equilibrium. The Liberals' election program had said nothing about OHS issues. The new government hired 25 new OHS inspectors, launched a series of proactive inspections in December 2003, and undertook some sector-specific OHS consultations with employers and unions;[65] however, there was no fundamental departure from Conservative policy.

Workers' Compensation

The origins of NDP workers' compensation policy can be traced to the pre-1990 Liberal administration. As in the active measures and occupational health fields, however, the NDP nevertheless put a distinctive centre-left stamp on this field, again pursuing the twin goals of promoting concerted *forms* of policy-making and of making policy *content* more favourable for workers. In 1985, the Ontario Workers' Compensation Board acquired a private sector-dominated board of directors with considerable policy-making power;[66] previously, decision making was dominated by bureaucratic staff. The new board included representatives from business and labour; but it also had a neutral chair with considerable authority, who was judged by most observers to be independent of any constituency.[67] The Liberals' Bill 162, passed in 1989, addressed policy content. The much-criticized 'meat chart' formula for calculating compensation pensions (whereby benefits reflected the severity of an injury alone) was replaced. A new 'dual award' formula used loss of future earnings as the main basis for calculating pensions; additional benefits were available for 'non-economic' loss, such as impaired quality of life.[68] Bill 162 also laid greater stress on returning injured workers to the workforce, and increased benefits for some existing beneficiaries. These provisions increased costs significantly, though the Liberals had expected the changes to be revenue-neutral. In combination with the deep recession of the early 1990s, this resulted in a significant increase in the WCB's unfunded liability once the NDP was in power.[69]

After forming a government, the NDP restructured the board of directors to transform it into a bipartite body in which decision making depended on cooperation between its business and labour constituencies. This was accomplished in 1991 by creating full-time business and labour co-chairs for the board;[70] proceedings continued to be overseen by a neutral chair, but his position was much weakened in a situation where the co-chairs, especially labour's, increasingly asserted themselves as leaders, and where the business and labour membership of the board began to caucus separately to develop policy positions. These positions, moreover, were widely divergent. Labour argued that the unfunded liability problem had been exaggerated, and that some benefits should be expanded; it argued for an end to 'deeming,' an instrument used by the WCB to encourage workers to return to work when they were judged capable of doing so. Business members contended that the calculation of future economic loss under the new dual award system was frequently too generous, and that other decisions by WCB staff were also overly indulgent.[71] In the resulting climate of stalemate, the NDP abandoned efforts to have the board of directors address the unfunded liability issue. In June 1993, it appointed a Premier's Labour Management Advisory Committee (PLMAC), consisting of a select group of business and labour leaders, to address this concern and to propose a more workable governance model for the WCB.[72] The PLMAC reached consensus on a "framework agreement" the following March, but when the government released its legislative response (Bill 165) the next month, many business spokespersons argued that it did not reflect the earlier agreement.[73] Moreover, the government conceded that Bill 165 did not address all of the WCB's problems. In November 1994, it appointed a Royal Commission to consider these.[74] The commission was terminated by the Conservatives shortly after they came to power, but not before receiving a plethora of submissions from business and labour representatives, all proposing substantial – and divergent -- reforms.[75] As in each of the above three policy fields, then, the NDP's vigorous efforts to foster concertation between business and labour had come to naught when the party left power in 1995.

Despite the acrimony, Bill 165 did represent an attempt by the NDP to address the competing objectives of labour and business views, consistent with the party's preferred collaborative decision-making model. In response to labour concerns about the plight of permanently disabled workers now on the WCB roles, the legislation supplemented the pensions of some of these by up to $200 per month. To address concerns about cost, by contrast, the bill abandoned full inflation protection of pensions, replacing it with partial indexation. Other provisions created stronger inducements for recovering injured workers to return to work, and for employers to facilitate this.[76] The bill's cost-savings provisions were sufficient to reduce – but not eliminate, as business complained – the WCB's projected unfunded liability for the year 2014, from $31 billion (if there had been no changes) to $15 billion.[77] It also included provisions to reform the board of directors' structure and to increase the government's powers to direct policy; this was followed by a change in board membership in February 1995, designed to foster a more cooperative relationship. Business complained that the new composition favoured labour.[78]

The Conservatives had been consistently critical of NDP workers' compensation policy while in opposition, broadly echoing business views. In May 1995, one month before the provincial election, Mike Harris released a six-part proposal to reform policy in this area; among other things, it promised to abandon the bipartite governance structure, reduce benefit levels, and freeze new entitlements and define eligibility more restrictively.[79] Combined with a Common Sense Revolution commitment to reduce WCB premiums by 5 per cent,[80] these provided the Tories with specific policy direction after the election. As in other areas, Conservative policy would move in a significantly more business- and market-friendly direction, and largely abandon the NDP's attempt to cultivate concerted policy-making.

Bill 15, introduced quickly after the election and with little consultation, fulfilled part of this agenda. It terminated the bipartite board of directors, replacing it with one that would eventually be dominated by business representatives; it also extended the Minister of Labour's powers to issue policy directives to the board, tightened financial accountability controls, and increased penalties for violating the Compensation Act.[81] Meanwhile, Cameron Jackson, a Conservative cabinet minister, was asked to make recommendations for a second round of reforms. Although he conducted some consultations, he was assigned a clearly pro-business mandate at the outset. He was asked to "provide a comprehensive savings package that will stabilize the system over the long term and will eliminate the unfunded liability by 2014 and fulfil the government's commitments on benefit levels, a waiting period, entitlements and assessment rates."[82] Jackson's report, released in February 1996, made proposals consistent with these goals,[83] and formed the basis for the introduction of Bill 99 in November. The new legislation introduced substantial changes. As we saw in the previous section, it reintegrated occupational health administration with workers' compensation in a new Workplace Safety and Insurance Board. Benefit levels were reduced from 90 per cent of average earnings to 85 per cent (where they had been before 1985); inflation adjustment was further curtailed for most categories of benefits; time limits were introduced for making a claim after an injury, and for challenging board decisions; the appeals process was streamlined; benefits would no longer be available for chronic (as opposed to acute) mental stress, and would be limited for chronic pain (these claims had occasioned considerable, time-consuming, and expensive litigation); benefit eligibility would be reassessed more frequently, and stronger incentives were created for beneficiaries to return to work; employers also faced more requirements to return workers to work, as well as stronger board procedures for debt

recovery.[84] The changes, unequivocally supported by business and opposed by labour, were designed to entirely eliminate the unfunded
liability by 2014.[85]

Conservative policy over the subsequent six years did not reverse
these significant changes, but also did not push further in a market-
oriented direction. Just as proposals for truly radical policy retrenchment, such as abandoning the Rand formula, were rejected in the
industrial relations field, so the Harris and Eves governments also
spurned the potentially momentous option of privatizing workers' compensation in Ontario; this was proposed periodically by some business
commentators.[86] By the late 1990s, moreover, incremental policy adjustments were more consistent with pre-1995 initiatives than opposed to
them. In 1998, the WSIB's anti-cheating Special Investigation Unit was
expanded. According to the board's chair, it charged employers with
offences more often than it did workers. The number of charges grew
from about two dozen in 1997 to 429 in 1998.[87] A regulatory change in
2002 relaxed somewhat the exclusion of chronic stress from coverage
that was legislated by Bill 99; stress would now be recognized as acute
(and compensable) if it resulted from a cumulative series of traumatic
events.[88]

One prominent interviewed public servant commented that Bill 99
"essentially returned the situation to the 1980s," a view broadly shared
by other interviewed officials; neither it nor the Tories' subsequent
policies, then, represented a radical departure from the post-war pattern regarding workers' compensation in Ontario. By 2002, moreover, it
was evident that the radical cost-savings and reduction in the unfunded
liability sought by the Conservatives had encountered severe limits.
The average premium rate per $100 of payroll, $3.00 in 1995, was
reduced to $2.13 by 2001. But in that year, faced with a recession and a
much poorer return on its investments, the WSIB's unfunded liability
increased; it had fallen from $10.9 billion in 1995 to $5.7 billion in 2001,
but rose to $6.6 billion in 2002. Premiums were increased in 2003, to
$2.19 per $100 of payroll.[89] In fact, the WSIB's benefit costs fell only
modestly from 1995 to 1999 (from $2.4 billion to $2.2 billion), before
rising (to $2.9 billion) in 2002. The much-publicized improvement in
the WSIB's balance sheet during the late 1990s, consequently, largely
did not result from policy retrenchment, but from spectacular – and
ephemeral – gains in the value of its investments between 1997 and
2001.[90] Here, again, the Conservatives had established something of a
policy equilibrium by 2003, broadly reflecting the pre-1985 status quo·

ante. The Liberals, true to form, were largely mute about workers' compensation during the 2003 election campaign, and introduced no significant changes after coming to power.

Employment Standards

The trajectory of employment standards (including pay and employment equity) policy in Ontario after 1990 differed from the pattern observed in policy fields discussed above. Except regarding employment equity, neither the NDP in 1990 nor the Conservatives in 1995 started their terms of office with detailed proposals for employment standards; and, with that one exception, there was no significant 'swing to the left' under the NDP, and no notable effort by that party to use concerted policy-making in this field; finally, while the post-1995 Harris government undertook a now-familiar 'swing to the right,' the political and policy dynamics underlying this change were distinctive: some Tory policy was contested and delayed much more than in the fields discussed above, and went some distance towards genuine retrenchment, rather than re-establishing a pre-1985 status quo ante. But the fundamental dynamics observed in other areas of Ontario labour market policy also, in the end, were relevant to employment standards. There was a clear and decisive difference between the policy preferences of New Democrats and Conservatives in power, illustrating once more the vital importance of partisan ideology in shaping policy-making. Secondly, Tory policy regarding the Employment Standards Act (ESA) was unique, among those treated here, in not establishing a policy equilibrium by 2003; motivated in part by the changes' unpopularity, the McGuinty Liberals promised significant change, and quickly delivered on this commitment after the election. These changes, in turn, restored significant elements of the pre-1985 policy framework; the status quo ante again proved resilient.

The NDP's *An Agenda for People* was silent about the province's Employment Standards Act, but promised that "[o]ver four years we would increase the minimum wage to 60 per cent of the average industrial wage, and eliminate the lower rate for younger workers." It also committed to extending coverage under the province's pay equity legislation, passed by the Peterson Liberal government in 1987, to female workers now exempted from it.[91] In power, the NDP raised the minimum wage several times; the basic rate rose from $5.00 in 1990 to $6.85 per hour on 1 January 1995; by the latter date, however, the NDP had abandoned its commitments to increase the rate to 60 per cent of the average industrial wage (about $8.00 per hour) and to eliminate the lower rate for youth; in 1995, Ontario's rate was the second highest among the provinces.[92] The pay equity commitment was fulfilled with legislation introduced in December 1991. The original Liberal act had only provided for coverage in work sites where traditionally male and female occupations could be directly compared; the NDP legislation permitted indirect comparisons where these could be made using criteria of 'proportional value' and 'proxy comparison.'[93]

But other NDP policies evoked sufficient opposition to be reversed after 1995. A Wage Protection Act, introduced in August 1991, was designed to extend the protection of workers employed by firms that went bankrupt. The payment of back wages for such workers was already protected under existing legislation; the new bill extended this protection to termination and severance pay, created a government fund to cover the resulting costs pending their recovery from employers, and made company directors, as well as firms, liable for these costs. The legislation was vehemently opposed by small business,[94] and revoked by the Conservatives soon after they came to power. Another NDP initiative that lay partly in the employment standards field was its proposal to ensure that gay couples have the same access as heterosexual couples to, among other things, spousal employment benefits. After a lengthy and acrimonious public debate, this legislation was defeated in a free vote of the provincial legislature during June 1994, with a dozen NDP MPPs joining all Conservative and all but three Liberal legislators in opposing it.[95]

By far the most prominent NDP initiative, broadly belonging to this domain, was its introduction of employment equity to Ontario's private sector. Announced shortly after the 1990 election, the legislation took effect in mid-1994, covering approximately three-quarters of the workforce.[96] Private sector employers with more than 50 employees, and public sector ones with more than 10, were required to develop employment equity plans for categories of workers deemed to be particularly vulnerable to discrimination: aboriginal and disabled people, visible minorities, and women. The legislation required large employers to set numerical targets for the proportion of jobs in various categories that would be filled by these groups. Arm's-length bodies would oversee compliance, and, where necessary, impose fines. In other Canadian provinces, by contrast, employment equity had been introduced only in the public sector. Federal legislation did apply to federally regulated industries, but did not require that employers meet hiring targets. Passage of the legislation followed a lengthy and acrimonious consultation process that allowed considerable opposition to mobilize against it, and ensured that the legislation would remain politically prominent during the 1995 election. During that campaign, the Conservatives vowed to repeal the legislation, successfully portraying it as unaffordable in a province still experiencing weak economic growth. After the vote, it was quickly suspended, and then repealed. Reflecting its market-oriented agenda, the new government argued that "the Employment Equity Act is ... a quota-driven system that does not take into account the merit principle or advance the employer's capacity to hire the best qualified candidate for the job."[97]

The Conservatives also quickly froze the minimum wage; because the province's relatively high rate "ha[d] eroded the competitive position of many Ontario businesses;" it would not be raised again until those in neighbouring provinces and states had caught up.[98] It remained at $6.85 when the Conservatives left power in 2003; at that point it was still third highest among Canadian provinces, though only slightly ahead of Manitoba's ($6.75) and Saskatchewan's ($6.65), and modestly higher than the rate of $6.00 per hour in all four Atlantic Provinces.[99]

In May 1996, amendments to the ESA were introduced, surprising business and labour leaders, who were not forewarned. Advertised as a "minor housekeeping" measure, the changes were criticized immediately by labour. One provision sought to make it easier for employers to negotiate variances with their workers from minimum conditions defined in the act. Under existing law, employers had to obtain the consent of employees to, for instance, arrange longer work hours, alter overtime pay, and change severance and vacation pay arrangements; in addition, they had to apply to the Ministry of Labour for a permit to authorize the variance. The amendment would have abandoned this requirement. In the face of sustained criticism, the government postponed passage of the legislation in June, and then, in August, withdrew this provision; it promised to return to it as part of a broader reform in 1997.[100] The remaining amendments (Bill 49) went ahead and curtailed some worker protections: the act would no longer apply to unionized workers; workers could not seek back pay owing for more than six months (rather than the existing two years); orders under the act could not exceed $10,000; and an aggrieved employee could either file a complaint under the act or pursue the matter in court, but not both.[101]

The Conservatives did not, in fact, return to employment standards issues until 2000, after committing themselves in their 1999 *Blueprint* document to "give workers and employers more flexibility in designing work arrangements to meet their needs."[102] As promised, the second round of reforms was more extensive. New legislation (Bill 147) was preceded by more public hearings than typified most Tory legislation. A consultation based on a discussion paper transpired during the summer; legislation was passed in December. However, the government's most controversial goals, strongly opposed by unions, were largely unaffected by these discussions.[103] The bill's main feature was its renewal of the government's effort to abolish permits; it was argued that permits represented a considerable administrative burden and that many employers were simply failing to apply for them. The most controversial change allowed a variance from the rule that employees work a maximum of 8 hours a day and 48 hours a week, unless a permit authorized longer hours; now, with the employees' written consent, the latter could be asked to work up to 60 hours per week. While the existing law stipulated that overtime be paid after 44 hours, moreover, the new bill allowed work hours to be averaged over a four-week period. If this weekly mean did not exceed 44 hours, an employer – with the employee's written consent – would not have to pay overtime. Other norms that could now be waved by mutual consent included the stipulations: (a) that vacation time be allocated in blocks of at least one week; (b) that the work day not exceed 12 hours (though workers still had to benefit from 11 work-free hours per day); (c) that eating periods be at least 30 minutes long; and (d) that vacation and severance pay be granted at specified times. Some workers lost the right to time off with pay on a public holiday.[104] The government insisted that workers retained the right to refuse variances, but critics suggested that non-unionized workers would be afraid to do this; they felt that the permit requirement, however ineffective, had provided real protection.[105]

Yet not all of the new Act's provisions served to restrict the minimum standards. Fulfilling another *Blueprint* promise, Bill 147 granted workers whose employer "regularly employs 50 or more employees," the right to 10 days of emergency leave each year, which could be claimed due to personal illness or to specified family emergencies; the leave would, however, be unpaid.[106] Secondly, the legislation committed the government to increasing its enforcement of employment standards. According to interviewed sources, this was the one significant adjustment to the legislation to result from the summertime consultation. The

Labour Ministry's employment standards officers acquired enhanced investigative powers (though investigations still could be instigated only after a complaint) and could impose much higher penalties, including jail time, for non-compliance.[107] For the government, these enhanced policing powers would restrain employers from using the greater flexibility of the new act to deny workers their minimum rights as employees. Yet this claim also evoked scepticism from critics, who questioned whether the Ministry of Labour had the resources to police enforcement successfully. The Ministry's Employment Rights and Responsibilities Branch, which oversees employment standards, lost about a quarter of its budget and one eighth of its staff between the 1997–8 and 2000–1 fiscal years.[108]

Did Conservative employment standards policy represent policy retrenchment? The answer depends on the importance attributed to the permit system abolished by Bill 147; this was the most radical Tory reform, and it removed an arrangement in place for several decades. Some interviewed bureaucrats downplayed its significance: the government had been issuing an estimated 18,000 permits each year before Bill 147 (suggesting that they were easy to get), and the labour ministry's staff was far too small to ensure that employers without permits were complying with minimum standards. It is nevertheless hard to imagine that the permit requirement did not encourage employers to work within the norms: not doing so meant either going through the 'red tape' (as the Conservatives termed it) of acquiring a permit or violating the law (and risking prosecution). Unions and worker-advocacy groups probably had some grounds for their contention that the change was not unimportant. Moreover – uniquely among labour market policy fields addressed in this chapter – opposition to Bill 147 appeared to strike a chord with the public, ensuring that it never became as politically entrenched as changes in the four other fields discussed here. A union-commissioned public opinion poll in March 2001 detected widespread public opposition to the changes.[109] An official close to the legislation's preparation complained, in a July 2001 interview, that the bill's opponents had succeeded in disseminating in the media a (for him) distorted and negative interpretation of its meaning.

Unsurprising, then, the Liberals quickly reversed some features of Bill 147 once in power. A legislative amendment announced in April 2004 restored the requirement of a permit to authorize employees' working more than 48 hours a week; permits would also again be required to average employees' hours over four weeks for purposes of calculating overtime pay. The Liberals nevertheless promised a costless and electronic procedure for requesting permits to minimize its inconvenience for employers.[110] The many other changes introduced in 1996 and 2002 were not, however, reversed. The Liberals announced another amendment that would permit employees to take up to eight weeks of unpaid leave each year "to take care of a gravely ill family member."[111] When combined with a December 2003 announcement that the provincial minimum wage would be raised to $7.15 in 2004, and to $8.00 by 2007,[112] these represented the most significant adjustments to the Conservatives' labour market policy that were introduced by their Liberal successors.

Partisanship, Globalization, and Labour Market Policy in Ontario

The polarization that characterized Ontario's public life during the period examined in this chapter was atypical. The province's politics previously was characterized by most observers, at least during the post-war years, as moderate and dominated by a single party that conducted largely non-programmatic brokerage politics with consummate skill. It remains possible, moreover, that the underlying preference of Ontarians is for politics of this type, and that developments since Mike Harris's departure from office in 2002 indicate a return to a politics of moderation. In chapter 2, the contrapositive political conjuncture of the 1990s and early 2000s nevertheless led us to anticipate significant short-term political swings in Ontario labour market policy, with NDP and Conservative governments pursuing quite distinct ideological agenda; in this chapter we have uncovered conclusive evidence that this did indeed happen. Regarding the prospects for long-term policy retrenchment, the second research theme addressed in that chapter, we were unable to formulate a hypothesis. Economically polarized two-party systems, Kitschelt observed, are highly susceptible to retrenchment politics; one-party dominant and non-programmatic ones are not. Ontario's institutionally unstable party system could not, in this light, justify a clear prediction about the potential success of retrenchment there: its short-term features suggested that retrenchment was very possible; its longer-term qualities argued for the reverse. But the evidence presented in this chapter is much less ambiguous; it suggests that the longer-term characteristics prevailed; the 'Harris Revolution' of the late 1990s left Ontario with a labour market policy landscape not dissimilar to that which existed before the province entered its period of

Table 4.1. Partisan 'Swings' and Retrenchment in Ontario Labour Market Policy, 1990–2003

	Short-term partisan swings	Long-term neo-liberal retrenchment
Industrial relations	High	Low
Active measures	High	Low
Occupational health	High	Low
Workers' compensation	High	Low
Employment standards	High	Low-to-medium

political turbulence in 1985. These findings are summarized in table 3.1; the criteria used to formulate these assessments of the degree of policy change in Ontario during the period of study are set forth in the appendix.

The NDP's electoral triumph in 1990 was unprecedented and unanticipated; the party had done little to prepare for office. Nor did it elaborate a comprehensive ideological program once in power. Its labour market policies nevertheless were remarkably consistent, and embodied two main principles. NDP policy first was designed to further the party's social democratic vision of equity; this involved curtailing the unobstructed workings of the marketplace where this was deemed necessary to improve the life chances of workers, their unions, and less advantaged people. This principle was reflected in an industrial relations reform that favoured unions, the expenditure of considerable sums of money on equity-focused active measures, extension of occupational health and safety training requirements, the maintenance of a relatively expansive workers' compensation system, and more modest adjustments to employment standards and pay equity rules that favoured workers. Secondly, the NDP fostered concerted policy-making among business, labour, government, and, occasionally, other societal interests. In four of the five fields discussed here it pursued ambitious policy governance reforms that sought to reproduce in Ontario's traditionally liberal institutional environment the collaborative practices typically associated with a coordinated market economy (CME). In chapter 1 we detected a possible rationale for reforms of this type by centre-left parties in liberal settings: CMEs typically are characterized by greater income equality and less poverty, goals dear to the centre-left, than is the case in LMEs. We also noted there, however, that the comparative political economy literature traces the differences between production regimes to deeply embedded features of nations' institutional order, features that are highly resistant to change. The consistent failure of NDP governance reform therefore comes as no surprise. To the extent that the equality-favouring substance of its policies also ran against the grain of Ontario's liberal market traditions, these too encountered a formidably unfavourable environment from the outset.

Conservative labour market policy after 1995 reversed NDP initiatives in almost all important respects. The Tories' Common Sense Revolution was based on a self-consciously market-oriented philosophy, which gave priority to the free play of unfettered markets and to the fostering of an environment favourable for business investment. Conservative policy also represented a return to liberal norms regarding governance, the NDP's second focus. Consistent with the preference for executive-parliamentary norms of accountability in (British-derived) liberal settings, the Conservatives were leery of cooperative decision making. After all, they pointed out, under the NDP it had failed consistently to foster a collaborative spirit among Ontario's labour market 'partners.' On those rare occasions when the Conservatives did not eliminate collaborative forums (as in the case of local boards), the surviving arrangements were consistent with the government's preference, manifested in various fields outside of the labour market domain, for local and municipal forms of decision making. But the Conservatives' primary interest was always in policy substance ('results'), not process. Here, their direction was consistent: an industrial relations reform that eliminated the anti-scab provision of the earlier NDP legislation, the termination of the NDP's most expensive active measures, and a refocusing of training and apprenticeship on efficiency objectives; the abolition of a dedicated agency for occupational health and the curtailment of safety training; significant cuts in the generosity of workers' compensation, and the elimination of key regulatory features of the post-war model of employment standards enforcement. That their policies were far more successful than NDP reforms in gaining acceptance, or at least acquiescence, in Ontario, is not surprising. Conservative reforms championed liberal norms in an institutional setting profoundly favourable for market-oriented liberalism.

Despite Mike Harris' reputation as a policy revolutionary, however, his labour market policies looked much more like a restoration. Almost all of the major changes introduced by his administration were consistent with the status quo ante in the province before 1985. Moreover, this outcome did not arise because retrenchment-oriented, neo-liberal proposals had not been made. They were consistently available and discussed by actors seeking to influence provincial policy. There were proposals to terminate the Rand system of union dues payments, a change that would have markedly challenged union authority; entirely abandon active measures not directed at social assistance recipients, and reform all of the apprenticeship system; eliminate occupational health and safety committees in firms, and avoid updating hazardous chemicals restrictions; privatize the workers' compensation system; and reduce radically the regulatory oversight by government of its employment standards. Only in the latter instance did the Conservatives partly respond to demands for radical policy departures; and even here, changes of this type were partly compensated by regulatory extensions in other areas. It was in the employment standards field, moreover, that the institutional power of the status quo was most evident in Ontario: only in this field did Conservative policy encounter sustained public scepticism, and only here was it reversed to a significant degree by the Liberals after 2003.

5 Quebec: Legacies of Political-Economic Distinctiveness

Quebec's policy setting diverges from the Canadian norm. Its welfare state broadly reflects the Canadian pattern of liberalism tinged by social democracy.[1] But its production regime and party system possess non-liberal features that deepened during the Quiet Revolution of the 1960s. Most corporate finance in Quebec derives from equity markets or retained earnings; inter-firm relationships generally have an arm's-length character, and industrial relations are competitive and enterprise-based (see chapter two). But these liberal features are now alloyed to others more characteristic of coordinated market economies (CMEs). The Quebec state assumed an interventionist economic role during the 1960s and 1970s; it now remains more active than governments in more fully liberal settings, though *dirigisme* has attenuated since the 1980s. Secondly, significant coordination among economic actors, above all business, labour, and the state, emerged after 1980. By the 1990s, concertation was pervasive in the labour market field; the origins and significance of these arrangements are addressed in the next section. These non-liberal features of the production regime parallel attributes of the party system. Consistent with Kitschelt's expectation for coordinative settings, partisan conflict stresses social more than economic-redistributive themes. The 'national question,' the relationship of predominantly French-speaking Quebec to a Canadian state dominated by its English-speaking majority, has long been central to inter-party debate; the emergence of the pro-independence Parti Québécois (PQ) as one of the two main parties during the 1970s reinforced this. Economic-redistributive differences divide the centre-left PQ from its centre-right rival, the federalist Parti libéral du Québec (PLQ), but these are smaller than in more fully liberal two-party settings.

These features suggest specific hypotheses regarding the impact of partisanship and globalization on Quebec labour market policy after 1990, the two foci of this chapter. Moderate partisan polarization on economic issues implies that short-term partisan 'swings' after a change of government should be small. In a setting where a broad consensus was thought to exist regarding the *'fameux modèle québécois'* – a modern welfare state, combined with an activist state and considerable valuing of social cohesion – the prospects for globalization-induced policy retrenchment should also be limited. During the late 1990s, however, partisan debate in Quebec became more economically polarized than it had been for many years. This might have been expected to call these two hypotheses into question. But this chapter contends that the broad pattern of market-oriented adjustment under the Liberals after their return to power in April 2003 was modest; no changes since 1990, moreover, suggest that neo-liberal retrenchment is likely for Quebec labour market policy.

Quebec's Liberally Tinged Concertation

Some observers trace Quebec's proclivity for concertation to the central role played by the Catholic Church and its social teachings in pre-Quiet Revolution Quebec, and to the impact of the national question on its politics.[2] But cooperation has hardly been a constant of Quebec public life. Relations among government, business, and, above all, organized labour, were extremely fractious during much of the Quiet Revolution, especially between 1966 and 1976. Militantly anti-capitalist views were widespread within the union movement during these years.[3] Attempts to cultivate concerted action only became prominent during the late 1970s.[4] The Parti Québécois government organized concertation-style meetings among the 'social partners' between 1976, when it came to power, and 1983. These were highlighted by three socio-economic summits among business, labour, government, and a plethora of other nongovernmental interests; and a large number of more selective sectoral meetings. But these gave rise to few permanent deliberative structures of the kind that typify CMEs, and produced few concrete results.[5] Where permanent concertation bodies did emerge, notably in the labour market field, they had limited authority or restricted responsibilities. The meetings nevertheless revealed that big business and much of the labour movement (the FTQ more than the CSN), as well as government, were willing to engage in concertation. In part, this was because of the severe disruption caused to the province's economy during the confrontational early- to mid-1970s. In 1975–76, 41 per cent of all work stoppages in Canada had occurred in Quebec; in 1976 alone, more than four times as many workdays were lost to strikes in Quebec than in Ontario.[6] PQ legislation that rolled back provisions of public sector labour contracts after the defeat of the 1980 sovereignty referendum, combined with the market-oriented discourse of the first Bourassa Liberal government, nevertheless convinced organized labour to return to an oppositional stance for the rest of the 1980s.

A second and more consequential era of concerted action began after the Liberals were re-elected in 1989. The Bourassa administration had taken only modest steps in a neo-liberal direction earlier;[7] key ministers now decided that increasing economic competitiveness could be achieved more effectively by working cooperatively with key economic actors rather than by incurring the wrath of its large public sector and strong labour unions, the probable consequences of a firmly market-oriented stance.[8] Relatively close to the governing Liberals, and amenable to the government's characterization of concertation as likely to foster flexibility and modernization, Quebec business was generally willing to participate.[9] The unions, once Canada's most militant, now were also more amenable to cooperation. According to Bourque, the severity of the recessions of the early 1980s and 1990s, a perception that Quebec's economy was vulnerable in an era of free trade and globalization, and positive experience in limited bipartite concertation arrangements with employers during the 1980s, nurtured this change.[10]

This new period of concerted action had its greatest impact on industrial, regional development and active labour market policies. Permanent deliberative bodies emerged in each, often acquiring significant authority. Reflecting the ongoing impact of liberal and pluralist features of Quebec institutions, however, these bodies were more specialized and disaggregated, and their membership more variable, than is true in most European CMEs. The industrial strategy, launched in 1991 by Industry Minister Gérald Tremblay, involved the selection of more than a dozen industrial sectors that the province thought likely to benefit from cooperation among employers and (in most cases) unions. Within each 'cluster' (*grappe industrielle*), one or more roundtables (*tables de concertation sectorielle*), consisting of these actors, identified development strategies that could be implemented with government support.[11] The Liberals' regional development policy, designed to distribute growth more evenly, was announced at the same time and transformed by the

PQ when it returned to power in 1994. In this second incarnation, it involved the use of Conseils régionaux de développement (CRDs) and 96 municipal-level Centres locaux de développement (CLEs), dominated by community, labour, and business representatives selected by the government, to identify development projects for funding.[12] In 2004, the Charest Liberal government replaced the CRDs with Conférences régionaux des élus (CREs), consisting of elected municipal officials.[13] Other concertation bodies emerged after the government released its active labour market policy.[14] Consistent with the disaggregated pattern, these were separate from the industrial and regional development bodies. They also remained distinct from existing bodies in other fields of labour market policy. By 2003, indeed, Quebec possessed five separate provincial-level concertation forums to serve different dimensions of labour market policy. As table 5.1 indicates, their authority, composition, and responsibilities diverged considerably, with the result that concertation's role in Quebec labour market policy-making differs among these fields. The post-1976 PQ government contemplated creating a summit-level Conseil économique et social,[15] an idea that resurfaced briefly in 2003, according to interviewed sources; the PQ also convened a wide-ranging and prominent Socio-Economic Summit in 1996, at which union and some social group representatives accepted a plan to eliminate the provincial deficit in exchange for a number of policy commitments. But no European-style corporatist forum, capable of integrating policy from disparate domains, ever materialized.

Coordinative arrangements also emerged, again discretely, in the health and agriculture fields.[16] Concertation now appears to be common, though not universal, in Quebec policy-making. The considerable fragmentation among these collaborative tools, however, is consistent with the disaggregated policy-making that typifies pluralist and liberal settings. They reflect the 'institutional ambiguity' – a blending of features typical of CMEs with others more characteristic of LMEs – attributed to Quebec in chapter two.

Quebec Politics since 1990

Above, we examined the evolution of coordinative features of Quebec's production regime, one element of its political economy that diverges from the liberal norm. This section addresses the second – a party system divided more by nationalism, a social concern, than the eco-

Table 5.1. Labour Market Concertation Forums in Quebec, April 2003

Policy field	Administrative entity	Concertation forum	Composition	Authority of concertation forum
Industrial relations	Ministère de travail	Conseil consultatif du travail et de la main d'oeuvre	Bipartite (B & L)	1 (advisory)
Active measures	Emploi-Québec	Commissions des partenaires du marché du travail	Multipartite (B, L, government & educators)	2/3 (limited co-management; decision-making re 1 per cent tax)
Workers' compensation	Commission de la santé et de la sécurité du travail (CSST)	Conseil d'administration de la CSST	Tripartite (B, L & government)	3 (decision-making authority; oversees administration)
Occupational health	Commission de la santé et de la sécurité du travail (CSST)	Conseil d'administration de la CSST	Tripartite (B, L & government)	3 (decision-making authority; oversees administration)
Employment standards	Commission des normes du travail	Conseil d'administration de la Commission	Multipartite (B, L, community & government)	2 (Oversees administration; limited co-management)
Anti-poverty fund (assistance for employable persons)	Ministère de l'emploi et de la solidarité sociale	Comité aviseur; Comités régionaux d'approbation	Multipartite (community, B, L & government)	2/3 (limited co-management; decision making refund distribution)

Key to 5th Column: 3 = Substantial authority involving decision-making powers; 2 = moderate authority, including some program co-management and/or significant administrative oversight; 1 = limited authority, i.e., an advisory role.

nomic-redistributive preoccupations typically prevalent in liberal settings. No post-war Canadian provincial state experienced as sudden
and radical a transformation of its economic and social policies as did
Quebec during the Quiet Revolution. This period is associated with the
PLQ, led by Jean Lesage, which governed between 1960 and 1966. But
most observers agree that the Revolution was actually launched by
Paul Sauvé, who in 1959 replaced Maurice Duplessis as premier and as
leader of the Union Nationale, the party that had previously defended a
more traditional and minimal role for government.[17] While the pace of
change slowed when the Union Nationale returned to power for the last
time between 1966 and 1970, it did not stop.[18] Quebec's rapid transformation in economic-redistributive terms during the 1960s consequently
was not sharply contested between the province's main parties at the
time.

With the emergence of the PQ as the main alternative to the PLQ
during the 1970s, Quebec party politics became sharply polarized between federalist and independentist alternatives; these parties were
also distinguishable in economic-redistributive terms, with the Péquistes
challenging the increasingly business-oriented PLQ from the centre-
left. When the PQ's record in power (1976–85, 1994–2003) is compared
with the Liberals' (1970–76, 1985–1994), however, many observers detect far more 'convergence' than 'polarization' in their approach to the
economy and welfare state. Writing in the early 1980s, Réjean Pelletier
observed that 'the period 1968–1981 was characterized by a polarization of greater and greater force among political parties along the feder-
alist-independentist axis. ... At the same time, there began a sliding of
all the parties along the interventionist axis as the *Parti Québécois* abandoned certain forms of collectivist intervention.'[19] Raymond Hudon
reached a similar conclusion, as did Brian Tanguay, writing a decade
later.[20] François Pétry's summary of recent research on the PQ's distinctiveness, cited in chapter two, again finds only modest differences from
the Liberals, if one compares implemented programs, rather than announced policies.[21]

The first two provincial elections that are directly relevant to our
period of study reflected this pattern closely; debate between the PQ
and PLQ was dominated by the national question, not the economic or
social security role of government. In the wake of the Bourassa Liberals'
retreat from most of the market-oriented retrenchment that had preoccupied some of their ministers since 1985, their 1989 re-election campaign concentrated on their apparent success in resolving Quebec's

constitutional crisis with the Meech Lake Accord, and on their decision to pass Bill 178 to reinstate most of Bill 101's provisions for protecting Quebec's *visage français*.[22] The Parti Québécois unsuccessfully campaigned on social concerns, sovereignty, and the environment.[23] In 1994, sovereignty was the main issue; Daniel Johnson, the new Liberal leader, promoted a federalist position even more enthusiastically than had his predecessor.[24] But this time the national question worked to the PQ's advantage. The failure of the Meech agreement, which caused nationalist sentiment to rekindle in Quebec, and that of the Charlottetown Accord, allowed the PQ to return to power, promising a second referendum on independence.

During the 1999 and 2003 election campaigns, however, a broader debate occurred about the Quebec state's economic and social security responsibilities, and the relatively high taxes required to support them. The national question, no longer as prominent in wake of the narrow victory of the 'no' option in the 1995 independence referendum, was somewhat less important. In 1999, *Les orientations du programme électoral du Parti libéral* committed the Liberals to substantial and rapid cuts in the size of the Quebec state: a 25 per cent reduction in the size of the public service, and, in order to facilitate the layoffs needed to accomplish this, an end to the substantial job security enjoyed by government employees.[25] The Liberals were again defeated, but received more votes than the PQ, suggesting that this agenda may have struck a chord with voters.

The economic-redistributive debate transpired again during the 2003 campaign. The Action démocratique de Québec (ADQ), which had emerged on the right wing of Quebec politics during the 1990s, began to receive substantial support in public opinion polls. Its leader openly questioned the *modèle québécois*, and sometimes espoused radically market-oriented policies. Under severe attack from the other parties, the ADQ's support fell precipitously during the election campaign, in which it won only four seats. Yet *Un gouvernement au service des Québécois*, the Liberals' election platform, though less radical than either the ADQ's or the PLQ's own four years earlier, also advocated a smaller state. It promised to reduce provincial income taxes by an average 27 per cent over five years, cut business subsidies and taxes, and, outside of the priority spending areas of health and education, to freeze all government spending in nominal dollars (effectively a 10 per cent spending reduction) over five years.[26] But when the new Charest government announced its plans for reducing the size of the state in May 2004, these were referred to by one observer as 'about twenty essentially administrative projects'; the number of state employees would be reduced by 20 per cent, but over five years, returning the public sector to its size in 1997; all job reductions would be achieved by attrition.[27] The government's second budget, brought down a month earlier, would reduce taxes by only $219 million in 2005 (mostly for low- and middle-income earners) and cut departmental spending by a modest $276 million.[28] The 2003 election platform also made specific recommendations relevant to the labour market field. As we will see below, some of these were greeted with considerable controversy when implemented; in no case, however, did they represent more than a moderate departure from the legislation of the Liberals' Péquistes predecessors. The main parties in Quebec continue to differ less regarding economic concerns than is commonly the case in other Canadian provinces.

This chapter now examines policy developments since 1990 in relation to industrial relations, active measures, workers' compensation and occupational health, and employment standards. Consistent with other chapters in this volume, it does not consider developments that pertain exclusively to the public sector. In the final section, the evidence is analysed in relation to the two hypotheses set forth at the beginning of the chapter.

Industrial Relations

Among the Quebec policy fields examined here, concertation is least well developed regarding industrial relations. Some interviewed government officials attributed influence to the advisory Conseil consultatif du travail et de la main d'œuvre, but others – and most private sector observers – viewed it as marginal to policy-making. Industrial relations is also the field where business and labour views diverge most in Quebec; indeed, the Conseil's limited influence is often attributed to its habitual inability to achieve consensus. Interviewed observers nevertheless agreed that labour law reforms in Quebec typically are preceded by extensive private sector consultations, but often in the informal and ad hoc manner that is more characteristic of liberal settings. If business or labour remains adamantly opposed to government initiatives, these are usually abandoned. By 1990, moreover, the industrial relations climate was much calmer than it had been in 1975.[29] The first Parti Québécois government reformed the Labour Code in 1977, adding an anti-scab provision to prevent employers from hiring replacement workers for most purposes during a strike.[30] Although initially opposed by business, this and other provisions in the law that benefited unions were not repealed by the PLQ when it returned to power in 1985. After years of relative industrial relations tranquility, this comparatively labour-friendly framework was now accepted by both major parties, and, to a degree, by business: the Supreme Court of Canada authorized the Conseil du patronat du Québec, the main big business association, to challenge the constitutionality of the anti-scab provision in 1991, but it decided not to do so.[31] For the same year, the Quebec government reported a lower strike rate than at any time since 1973.[32]

Industrial relations law nevertheless was less well developed in Quebec than in other provinces in 1990 in one important respect: the province lacked a quasi-judicial labour relations board (or commission); parties to disputes made frequent, time-consuming, and expensive appeals to the courts, and many avenues of delay were available to employers or unions who were inclined to exploit them. In 1986, a Péquiste-commissioned report recommended the creation of an independent commission; the Liberals introduced legislation to this effect in 1987, and, in a modified form, again in 1990. But it encountered resistance from business (the source of most of the delays), which objected to the bill's stipulation that the commission's decisions would not be subject to external review; moreover, business and labour could not agree on a non-partisan chair for the new body.[33] The extreme animosity that characterized business-labour relations in the 1970s had attenuated; but residual distrust precluded a reform consensus from emerging, and the Liberals would not proceed without one.

The PLQ did launch two changes in labour relations law, and planned one other, over the objections of at least part of the union movement. But labour resistance was never vociferous and uniform regarding the longer-term implications of these reforms; and none of the latter was reversed – two were extended – by the Péquistes when they returned to power. First, collective bargaining in the construction sector, which had been subjected to repeated strikes in recent years, was altered. Striking workers were required to return to work and non-union workers were permitted onto residential sites involving less than eight units.[34] The change with the greatest long-term implications, however, abolished a highly fragmented bargaining process in construction by consolidating all negotiations into four sectors, to be conducted by committees representing employers and unions. The second change eliminated a three-year ceiling in the maximum length of private sector labour contracts.

After union protests, the legislation was amended to exempt first contracts; this addressed the main objection of the FTQ, the main private sector labour federation.[35] Third, the Liberals launched a reform of Quebec's CME-style decree system, introduced during the 1930s and unique in North America. A collective agreement negotiated in one firm could, under certain conditions, be extended by government decree to all other firms in the same sector; decrees are overseen by *commités paritaires* of employer and employee representatives.[36] In 1959, 120 such decrees existed, covering 250,000 workers. The number of workers affected fell to 140,000 in 1970 and to 130,000 in 1993.[37] Despite their gradual decline, employer associations demanded their abolition, especially in export-oriented manufacturing sectors where they might affect competitiveness. In response to an interdepartmental report, the Liberals planned to make it harder to create new decrees and to subject existing ones to review.[38] But legislation was not passed before they left office.

The Parti Québécois's return to power in 1994, in sharp contrast to government changes in Ontario and British Columbia since 1990, resulted in no fundamental shift in labour relations law. The new government did quickly reverse the Liberals' deregulation of smaller residential construction sites, a matter that had caused considerable friction during the election campaign.[39] But it also streamlined the sectoral bargaining arrangement introduced by the Liberals in the construction industry by granting the FTQ a predominant role in representing unionized workers in negotiations; after the inception of sectoral bargaining, industrial strife declined significantly in the industry. Shortly after the Péquistes came to power, Employment Minister Louise Harel indicated that she wanted to reinforce the decree system, the opposite of what the Liberals had planned to do. After somewhat inconclusive consultations with business and labour representatives from the Conseil consultatif du travail et de la main d'œuvre, however, this position was reversed. When legislation was introduced in November 1996, it restricted the use of decrees, despite protests from the labour movement.[40] Thereafter, decrees became much less important in Quebec: from 29 covering 126,000 workers in 1994, their number fell to 18 covering 71,000 workers in 2001.[41]

The PQ also began to work on a broader reform of the Labour Code, which had not been reviewed comprehensively since its own 1977 legislation. This involved a protracted dialogue among the government, business, and labour. Creation of a labour relations board, the focus of the Liberals' earlier abortive reforms, would be central to the new legislation. In the more relaxed industrial relations climate of the late 1990s, this objective was now shared by business and labour. Beyond this, each labour market partner used the reform to champion its own preferred modifications.

Most unhappy with the status quo, business was more insistent than labour about the need for change. Its foremost concern pertained to Article 45 of the Labour Code, introduced during the early 1960s to prevent employers from de-unionizing their enterprises by creating, among other things, parallel units. By the late 1990s, judicial interpretation had expanded the article's scope. Most controversially, a contract would remain in force if a firm subcontracted operations; employees at a subcontractor might automatically be covered by a contract negotiated at the contracting firm.[42] Such a comprehensive arrangement was unique in North America; in many jurisdictions, including Ontario (see chapter 4), moreover, legislative changes during the 1990s curtailed barriers to subcontracting in the public sector, permitting governments to achieve cost-savings by privatizing services. Business associations demanded that the clause be eliminated or that subcontracting be excluded from its remit.[43] They sought other changes: employers should be allowed to submit contract offers directly to union members (the existing code required the union's consent); union certification should require a secret ballot; and if a labour relations board was created, aggrieved parties should retain the right to appeal its decisions.[44] By contrast, organized labour largely supported Article 45, even wanting it strengthened in certain respects. Unions were also concerned that too many workers were becoming 'dependent entrepreneurs,' in effect employees of a firm who were treated as contractors to prevent their unionization; and they wanted the certification process – now often drawn out by judicial procedures – to be accelerated, an objective most likely to be attained by creating a strong board whose decisions could not be appealed.[45] Finally, labour hoped to acquire the right to unionize multiple enterprises in the same sector simultaneously, a right now confined to the construction and public sectors.

The first version of the PQ government's reform legislation, tabled in December 2000 after lengthy consultation with business and labour and a substantial delay, was greeted with hostility by the former. Bill 182 proposed the creation of a labour relations board, entitled the Commission de relation de travail (or CRT) to replace the existing and much-weaker Tribunal de travail. The CRT's decisions would be final, and it would provide all conciliation and arbitration services, as well as fulfilling its core quasi-judicial responsibility. Again paralleling labour's views, the bill proposed covering 'dependent entrepreneurs' under the code. Two other provisions represented modest concessions to business; employers could submit one contract offer to employees during negotiations, over union objections. Second, although Article 45 was left largely intact, its coverage of workers at subcontracting firms was weakened modestly: the ability of unions to appeal to the CRT against sub-contracting arrangements would be restricted if the union had been duly notified of, and agreed to, them in advance.[46] In the face of business's vociferous objections, Bill 182 was withdrawn, and replaced with Bill 31 in May 2001. This new, and final, version made two concessions to business: although the CRT's decisions still would not be subject to appeal, conciliation and arbitration services would remain independent of it. Second, the 'dependent entrepreneurs' category was dropped.[47] The concept was to be taken up by a study committee; when it reported shortly before the 2003 election, its findings were denounced by business,[48] and the idea was not subsequently taken up by the new Liberal government.

Though still not entirely mollified, business found Bill 31 much more palatable. The Conseil du patronat called it 'a step in the right direction' compared to the earlier version; even the small-business CFIB, especially vociferous in demanding change, was 'partially satisfied.'[49] Business remained much less happy with the reform than labour because it had greater reservations about the status quo ante in labour law, not because Bill 31 made changes that favoured unions more than employers. Both parties endorsed its main innovation, the creation of a labour relations board; labour's gain in relation to the CRT's robust mandate was counterbalanced by concessions to business regarding a contract vote, and, albeit modestly, the application of Article 45. But business wanted broader change, especially regarding the latter provision.

In opposition, the Liberals were critical of Bill 31. Their 2003 election program promised two specific changes: Article 45 would be amended 'to facilitate sub-contracting,' and CRT rulings would be subject to appeal.[50] The latter idea had not been addressed by late-2004; but in November 2003, the new government moved quickly, and after little private sector consultation, to modify Article 45. Under Bill 30, subcontracting was exempted from the clause (a labour contract would not be transferred to a subcontractor) if it was 'not accompanied by the transfer of most of the other characteristic elements of the subcontracting firm's work' to the subcontractor. Where such a transfer did accompany a subcontract, an existing collective agreement would automatically be transferred to the subcontractor, although it would be subject to immediate renegotiation.[51] Introduced with little advance notice, and addressing a key point of contention between business and labour, Bill 30 was greeted by loud complaints from organized labour.[52] There was considerable speculation in the Quebec media regarding whether the province's relatively high unionization rate might not fall in the new legislation's wake.[53]

Until this most recent legislation change, post-1990 industrial relations policy in Quebec conformed fairly closely to the pattern anticipated at the beginning of this chapter. There was only a limited ideological 'swing' when a new government came to power, and, in a context where labour law was relatively favourable to organized labour, there was no evidence of globalization-induced retrenchment. PLQ and PQ governments clearly had different proclivities: the pre-1994 Liberal administration took steps to restrict some elements of industrial relations regulation, while the 1994–2003 Péquistes administration was more responsive to labour's agenda. But all major initiatives undertaken by either government were accompanied by substantial, though usually informal, concertation with business and labour. Where these deliberations did not resolve disputes, substantial change was either abandoned (by the Liberals in 1990), or severely curtailed, with the final reform not clearly changing the 'playing field' to either social partner's advantage (the PQ in 2001). The change in government in 1994, moreover, was accompanied by none of the substantial policy reversals that occurred in other provinces studied here; the PQ's initial post-1994 initiatives, indeed, more often reinforced than nullified their predecessor's. The Charest Liberals' Bill 30 diverged from this pattern: it involved little concertation and clearly favoured one partner on a matter of some importance. It is unlikely, however, to signify a fundamental departure from the pre-existing pattern. Some commentators dispute how much curtailing Article 45 will alter the business-labour relationship.[54] The many other union-friendly provisions of pre-1990 Quebec labour law – above all the anti-scab clause – also remain in place, and are not seriously contested. Finally, the Liberals have not modified the Commission de relation de travail, created by the PQ only two years earlier; mandated to expedite the resolution of industrial conflicts, including those over certification, the new commission reflected union preoccupations more than those of employers.

Active Labour Market Policy

In Ontario and British Columbia, left and right policy objectives regarding active measures diverged considerably in relation to both policy *content* (a preference for equity and social or efficiency and economic objectives) and policy-making *style* (the merits of concertation). Neither of these fissures existed to nearly the same extent in Quebec, though the main parties did adopt somewhat different approaches to enhancing private sector participation in policy-making. Compared to the Péquistes, the Quebec Liberals preferred voluntary tools for stimulating private sector training and laid less stress on equity-oriented active measures for non-social assistance recipients (addressed in chapter 8). But these have been differences of degree much more than of kind. One feature unique to the active labour market policy field reinforced its largely consensual nature in Quebec: by the early 1990s, the main political and social actors – both main parties, as well as business, labour, and social groups – had reached a 'Quebec Consensus' on training measures: responsibility for these should primarily be in the hands of the province, not Ottawa.[55]

The Bourassa Liberal administration placed considerable emphasis on active labour market measures after its 1989 re-election, as part of the concertation-focused strategy for economic renewal that it adopted then. Regarding policy content, the Liberals sought to foster more skills formation in the private sector. Dependent for too long on training provided almost exclusively in public institutions, the government complained, the province's employers would have to increase their own direct contribution if the Quebec economy was to remain competitive.[56] To accomplish this, it introduced a refundable training tax credit for firms. The credit had been a 1989 campaign commitment designed to foster more training in a laissez-faire manner; that is, without government playing an important role in steering or regulating skills formation.[57] When the Liberals formally launched a labour force development policy in 1991, they promised to enhance private sector training in other ways. The already-emerging network of business-labour sectoral committees, which at the outset concentrated mostly on investment and technology issues, would also receive resources to enhance skills. Second, the province moved to expand considerably the apprenticeship system; according to the government's estimate, there were only 46 apprenticeable trades in Quebec in 1991, compared with more than 600 in Ontario.[58] A campaign was also launched to increase the appeal of vocational education among young people. These components were extended by the PQ government after 1994. The key initiative to foster concertation was creation of a Société québécoise de développement de la main-d'oeuvre (SQDM), consisting of six representatives each from the province's business, labour, and educational communities, to oversee and promote active measures. Training boards also emerged at the federal level and in six other provinces during the 1990s. But Quebec's experience with concertation regarding ALMP differed sharply from these.[59] First, concertation was already well developed in Quebec. Since 1969, a network of regional Commissions de formation professionelle (CFPs) had provided private sector advice on the delivery of training measures; the CFPs were transformed into regional complements to the SQDM after 1993. During the 1980s, Comités d'adaptation de la main-d'oeuvre (CAMOs) emerged to assist labour market adjustment in industries affected by job redundancies; some sectoral training bodies also were created then.[60] This prehistory contributed to the SQDM's relative success. Unlike other boards, with the brief exception of Ontario, the SQDM acquired decision-making authority, although the range of measures that it oversaw – largely pertaining to industry-based training – was modest. Its creation was greeted warmly by Quebec business and labour; similar arrangements in other Canadian jurisdictions often encountered a tepid reception, especially from business. The government was able to induce prominent representatives of both communities to sit on the SQDM's board of directors. Throughout its four-year existence, moreover, business-labour relations on the board were relatively tranquil, despite sometimes significant policy differences between them.[61]

Parti Québécois policy after 1994 featured both continuity and change in relation to this Liberal record; but circumstances in the province's environment – above all, evolving attitudes in Ottawa – were at least as important as partisan differences in accounting for the latter. This is especially true of the adjustment that the Péquistes made to concertation: in 1997, they abolished the SQDM, replacing it with a Commission des partenaires du marché du travail (CPMT). Unlike the SQDM, the commission's mandate was quasi-advisory, with one important exception (see below). Yet this change probably did not reflect more tepid interest in concertation by the new government than its predecessor. In 1996, in the wake of the narrow victory of the 'no' vote in the 1995 sovereignty referendum, Ottawa offered to transfer to the provinces responsibility for administering active measures financed from the

Employment Insurance (EI) fund. Quebec quickly accepted the offer, and implemented full 'devolution' in 1998.[62] In exchange, it had to agree to targets regarding the proportion of EI clients served by the measures and the savings realized for the EI account.[63] According to interviewed provincial officials, the PQ government believed that it would be impractical to assign responsibility for meeting these conditions to private sector actors. At the same time, it hoped to consolidate administration of the EI-funded programs, the SQDM's industry-based ones, and employment-related measures for social assistance recipients. This had first been advocated by the Liberals in 1991.[64] The three administrations were brought together in Emploi-Québec, an autonomous unit within a new Employment and Social Security Ministry. Through its senior official, Emploi-Québec was accountable to the province's employment minister, but also subject to an annual 'Plan of Action' negotiated between the minister and the CPMT. Quebec's private sector partners in effect lost the right to exercise direct control over a limited array of programs; in exchange, they acquired influence over a much wider range of measures that falls significantly short of this, but nevertheless is greater than the mere right to give advice.[65] Business and labour representatives interviewed in 2003 believed that the CPMT afforded them genuine, though circumscribed, influence over provincial active measures. Private and public sector observers agreed that its influence waned for a few years after its initial creation, but believed that it had largely been restored when it acquired a full-time director in 2002, and that it was then able to influence government initiatives regarding adult education and older workers.[66]

Substantive PQ initiatives also evidenced considerable continuity with, and some departures from, those of the Liberals. The post-1994 administration continued with the sectoral and apprenticeship initiatives launched earlier. The SQDM agreed to oversee the extension of the number of bipartite sectoral committees engaging in training; these committees, in turn, were assigned responsibility for identifying new apprenticeship opportunities.[67] The main Péquiste program innovation was Bill 90, in 1995, which subjected Quebec firms to a 1 per cent training tax. Dissatisfied with the laissez-faire approach reflected in the Liberals' tax credit, the PQ adopted a more compulsory approach to stimulating private sector training: firms that did not train would have to pay the tax; those that expended a sum at least equivalent to 1 per cent of their payroll on training, and met specific criteria in doing so, would not.[68] Revenue from the tax would be transferred to a Fonds national de la formation professionalle to be administered by the SQDM; when the CPMT was created in 1997, it carried on this responsibility – the one area in which it exercises full decision-making authority. Initially quite hostile, representatives of larger Quebec firms became reconciled to the legislation after intense negotiations at the SQDM regarding its regulations; these were defined sufficiently flexibly to allow many existing activities in firms to be classified as training for purposes of calculating their tax liability. At first only applied to firms with payrolls exceeding $1 million, the tax's coverage was extended by January 1998 to those with payrolls over $250,000.[69] By 2003, the substantial majority of firms that paid the tax, unable to document that 1 per cent of their payroll had been spent on training, were smaller ones. The small-business CFIB, unrepresented on the SQDM and the CPMT, remained firmly opposed to the tax.[70] On the eve of the 2003 election, it remained unclear how much the tax had increased private sector training, though it appeared to have had some effect.[71] At that time, the CPMT also launched a number of *mutuelles de formation*, or joint training funds; small businesses could use these to do more training, thereby meeting their 1 per cent tax obligation, at little administrative cost to themselves.[72]

The PQ's foremost preoccupation regarding ALMP after 1998 was the complexity involved in integrating three separate administrations in Emploi-Québec. Interviewed Quebec officials stressed that the merger resulted in a clash of organizational cultures; cost controls were also inadequate at Emploi-Québec, which had to integrate three incompatible information systems. Unable to manage expenses, the new entity quickly overspent its budget in the late 1990s. This problem eventually was resolved. In the interim, however, the PQ largely abstained from undertaking new ALMP initiatives; this crisis also diminished the CPMT's influence on policy-making between 1998 and the hiring of its new director in 2002.

The Charest Liberals introduced one significant change in active measures: in October 2003, after no consultation with the CPMT, they announced that the 1 per cent training tax would no longer apply to firms with payrolls between $250,000 and $1 million.[73] The change encountered considerable criticism from unions and other observers, who argued the government had 'killed,' 'cut the feet from under,' or 'substantially modified' Bill 90; about 25,000 of the 36,000 firms that had been subject to the training tax in 2001 now would be exempt.[74] since smaller firms were the source of most revenues generated by the tax (about $19 million of $35 million in 2001), the change automatically reduced the size of the Fonds national de la formation professionelle by the same proportion.[75] But it is important not to exaggerate the importance of this change: First, the larger firms to whom the tax still applies accounted for 62.9 per cent of total payroll in Quebec in 2001, compared to 13.6 per cent for firms affected by the change; the larger firms reported spending over $1 billion on eligible training in that year, compared to about $130 million for firms in the affected category. Finally, the $19 million in revenues generated from smaller firms is a very modest sum. If the tax stimulates firms to train more, its capacity to do this has not been changed in relation to most Quebec workers. In other respects, as well, the Charest administration made modest changes; Emploi-Québec was required to reduce its budget modestly, mostly by terminating temporary employees and merging local offices with those of another ministry, and it was asked to concentrate more of its resources on addressing the needs of immigrants.[76]

It is hard to discern fundamental differences between the approaches taken to active measures by the Quebec Liberals and the Parti Québécois. There has also been no discernible retrenchment in this policy field since 1990. After the 1989 election, the PLQ became committed to an active role for government in stimulating private sector training, and to using concertation arrangements to achieve this end. Though these arrangements were substantially altered by the PQ after 1994, this fundamental goal was preserved. Replacement of the SQDM by the CPMT, moreover, owed more to the logic of integrating the province's three ALMP administrations in the wake of federal devolution – a goal also favoured by the Liberals – than to differences between the parties regarding concertation. Some observers argued, before the 2003 election, that even if it shared the PLQ's interest in efficiency-oriented private sector training, the PQ was more concerned with also pursing equity objectives, especially regarding assistance recipients. As we will see in chapter 8, however, preliminary indications from the Charest government that it might curtail the more socially oriented of the PQ's measures were largely abandoned within a year of the election.

Workers' Compensation and Occupational Health

The broad trajectory traced in this chapter – from a polarized and fractious setting in the 1970s to the most coordinative and least partisan labour market policy milieu in Canada by the 1990s – is particularly evident for Quebec in the field of workers' compensation and occupational health. A bitter strike in Thetford Mines in 1975, impelled largely by the high mortality rate discovered among asbestos miners there, helped motivate a major reform.[77] There was also disagreement regarding medical decisions made by the Commission des accidents du travail (CAT), the province's workers' compensation board. In 1979, CAT was replaced by a Commission de la santé et de la sécurité du travail (CSST), which also assumed responsibility for occupational health and safety, previously administered in a government ministry. To ensure its effectiveness, the CSST would be overseen by a bipartite Conseil d'administration consisting of business and labour representatives in equal numbers;[78] its approval is required for any new CSST policies, the strongest mandate for any concertation forum discussed here. Legislation passed in 1985 was designed to reduce the system's cost while increasing injured workers' access to rehabilitation services and re-employment. But this measure failed to attain its objective; by 1991, the CSST's compensation fund had accumulated a substantial deficit. Resolving this issue was the main challenge faced by policy-makers after 1990; this was accomplished with only modest and ephemeral contention between the two major parties or between the most influential business and labour organizations.

Rather than returning injured workers to work faster, the CSST experienced an increase in average compensation periods, from 47 days per worker in 1989 to 74 days in 1991; in the latter year, its compensation fund experienced an $800 million deficit on an annual budget of just over $1.6 billion.[79] The Bourassa Liberal administration implemented experience-rating for some employers in 1990 to encourage them to improve workplace safety: workers' compensation payroll deductions for larger employers now reflected benefit costs for workers injured at their establishments.[80] Although this was followed by a reduction in reported accidents, these were more severe on average, resulting in no cost-savings.[81] Consequently, the CSST administration, and business, sought further changes to fulfil the 1985 legislation's objectives. The rising deficit meanwhile occasioned acrimony between business representatives on the Conseil d'administration, who wanted benefits reduced, and labour spokespersons, who attributed the rising costs to negligent employers.[82] The result of this further policy review was Bill 31, passed in 1992 and accompanied by administrative reforms. With concertation now firmly entrenched, the government was unwilling to make changes that ran contrary to the main preoccupations of either business or labour: the former wanted costs reduced, while the latter rejected any cuts in workers' benefits.[83]

The 1992 reforms accommodated these competing goals. On the one hand, average employer contributions to the compensation fund were increased, a measure sufficient to eliminate about half of the CSST's deficit. On the other hand, changes were made to ensure that injured employees returned to work as quickly as possible: if a client had received compensation benefits for 90 days, his or her case was subject to a personalized review by a CSST counselor. The counselor could arrange a partial return to work, even if the injury was not completely healed; request an alternative medical opinion to the one provided by the worker's physician; and, in the case of disagreement between these medical assessments, submit the matter to a bipartite medical panel for adjudication. A conciliation service was also established to reduce the number of CSST decisions that were appealed to the Bureau de révision paritaire (BRP), a bipartite appellate body; and some limits were imposed on the right of appeal. No changes were made in benefit levels.[84] The changes were opposed vociferously by the Péquistes and by smaller union federations, the CSN and CSD. The main business associations, while supportive, nevertheless considered them inadequate to redress the CSST's financial crisis. Some observers, including a former chair of the CSST, speculated that the use of bipartite concertation on the CSST rendered impossible the major changes putatively needed to solve the financial problem.[85] The reforms nevertheless went ahead because they were agreed to by the FTQ, which selects four of the seven labour representatives on the Conseil d'administration, as well as business.

In the event, they achieved their objective. Shortly before the Liberals left office, the CSST reported a surplus of $81 million, and reduced employer premiums modestly.[86] When the PQ returned to power in 1994 with the crisis largely resolved, moreover, its own reforms served to continue, not reverse, the trend established in 1992. The CSST ran operating budget surpluses throughout the rest of the 1990s, and employer contribution rates were cut seven times by the new government between 1995 and 2001. In the latter year, the budget returned to a deficit situation; but compensation benefit costs rose only modestly under the PQ until 1999, then declined over the next four years; they were approximately the same in 2003, when the PQ left power, as in 1994.[87]

The Parti Québécois' main reforms to workers' compensation and occupational health law, legislated in 1997, extended measures initiated by the Liberals. Bill 79 broadened the use of experience-rating, first introduced in 1990. The earlier change had applied only to large firms, as it was thought impractical to base premiums for an individual small- or middle-sized firm on its accident record. The new legislation allowed such firms to form 'safety groups' (*mutuelles de prévention*), a risk pool. Only firms whose safety record exceeded a certain standard would be allowed into each group to ensure that the group's premiums remained relatively low. By 2002, 157 safety groups existed for 21,000 employers.[88] The second change, Bill 74, took additional steps beyond those included in the 1992 statute to curtail expensive and time-consuming appeals of CSST decisions. The changes mostly reflected recommendations made by CSST staff to the Conseil d'administration in May 1994, while the Liberals were still in power.[89] The reform abolished the bipartite Bureau de révision paritaire, as well as the Commission d'appel en matière de lesions professionnelles (CALP), a tribunal without stakeholder representation that previously received appeals from the BRP. These were replaced by a one-stage appeal body, a Commission de lésions professionelles (CLP), to be overseen by the CSST and appointed along tripartite lines.[90] The CLP was expected to resolve cases much faster, and to save the CSST $35 million per year in administrative costs; employers and unions would economize an additional $13 million annually in legal expenses.[91] Bill 79 encountered no significant opposition; Bill 74, by contrast, was opposed by the Quebec Bar Association and by injured-worker advocacy groups; by eliminating the non-partisan CALP, and replacing it with the stakeholder-dominated CLP, they believed that workers were being denied an independent and impartial hearing. The legislation was also opposed, again, by the CSN and the CSD, as well as by the small-business CFIB. But the big-business Conseil du patronat and the FTQ, which controlled the majority of seats on the Conseil d'administration and would select most of the CLP's nongovernmental members, supported it.[92] Interviewed in 2003, a close observer of the CSST nevertheless opined that Bill 79 had changed very little; the number of appeals of CSST decisions had not declined during the intervening years.

Considering the deep fissures that emerged *within* Quebec's business and labour communities around workers' compensation issues, it is not surprising that organizations other than the Conseil du patronat and the FTQ complained about the Conseil d'administration's makeup. This concern was particularly strong in the business community, for which the Patronat was responsible for nominating all seven Conseil members. In the wake of Bill 74, several other business associations, including the Quebec Chamber of Commerce and the CFIB, proposed that they be allowed to select a representative. The CSST's chair disagreed, arguing, 'If I had to ask for the agreement of every association, I would never finish.'[93] The PQ government, like its Liberal predecessor, ignored the request.

During the late 1990s, there was also pressure to extend occupational health and safety regulations. When this law was updated in 1980, particular attention was paid to three sectors where work-related risks were greatest. Employers there were expected to draw up occupational safety plans with their workers, and to meet other commitments. In three other areas, including most public and private sector services, these requirements did not apply. Although this exclusion initially was an interim measure, it remained in place twenty years later. Pointing out that women were particularly present in the less-regulated sectors, Quebec unions wanted the requirements extended to all sectors; the Conseil du patronat disagreed.[94] In 2001, the government went partway to meeting this demand; it extended some regulations to several service sector industries.[95]

The CSST was again running deficits – $120 million for 2001 and $65 million in 2002 – when the Liberals returned to power in 2003; the employer contribution cuts of the previous decade were partly reversed.[96] Yet the Liberals did not respond to this (minor) financial reversal by curtailing CSST benefits, presumably accepting its chair's assurance that the deficit reflected poor investment returns, and that CSST surveys found Quebec employers and workers generally happy with the compensation system.[97] Interviews conducted in 2003 confirmed that leading business and labour spokespersons entertained no major reservations about compensation or occupational health arrangements.[98] In late 2003, the Liberal justice minister nevertheless proposed that the Commission de lésions professionelles be abolished, and its functions transferred to the Tribunal administratif du Québec, which would economize by assuming responsibility for several quasi-judicial functions previously administered separately. This would have ended the use of business and labour representatives in hearing CSST appeals. Supported by some legal proponents of a more independent appellate arrangement, the proposal nevertheless was strongly opposed by the CPQ and FTQ. It appeared to disappear from the government's agenda when the justice minister resigned in March 2004.[99]

Partisanship has played a very minor role in shaping workers' compensation and occupational health policy in Quebec since 1990. With no significant curtailment in benefit rates or occupational health regulations, there is also no evidence of globalization-induced retrenchment. In opposition, Quebec parties have often resisted government initiatives – as the PQ did regarding Bill 35 in 1992, and the Liberals did in relation to Bill 74 in 1997 – but these have not been reversed after a change in government. Policy-making has granted an effective veto to leading business and labour organizations over significant initiatives through their representation on the CSST's Conseil d'administration; the main complaint of smaller business and labour organizations has been that they have not been consulted as closely. Yet the crucial reforms undertaken after 1992 addressed the core preoccupations of business and labour as a whole: they contained costs, permitting an overall reduction in employer contributions; and they preserved existing benefits for workers, while increasing their access to rehabilitation services. Maligned by some in the early 1990s, Quebec's concerted policy-making addressed the compensation system's financial crisis as effectively, and more pacifically, as more politically polarized provinces.

Employment Standards

The setting for employment standards policy-making differs to a degree from those for other fields of Quebec labour market policy. Whereas the union movement is the strongest champion of expansive policy elsewhere, this role is assumed by interest groups that speak for the socially marginal, especially non-unionized workers, in this area. Such groups, above all Au bas de l'échelle, have more influence than in other provinces. Regarding our key preoccupations – the role of partisanship and of globalization in shaping policy since 1990 – this field nevertheless reflects the general pattern observed in this chapter. Partisanship plays a limited role in shaping policy; the PQ is more willing to extend protection than are the Liberals, but the direction of change is the same, towards higher standards, and there has been no significant reversal of policy reforms after a change of government. Concertation is again important in this field: the Conseil d'administration of the Commission des normes de Travail, with representatives from business, labour, and social constituencies, oversees standards implementation; but interviewed public and private sector observers found it much less important in policy development.

In 1990, the Bourassa Liberal administration undertook the first revision of the Employment Standards Act since the legislation's initial passage in 1979. Though modest compared to subsequent Péquiste reforms, all of the changes were in the direction of raising standards:[100] employees would have a right to at least three weeks of vacation after five years of service with an employer (instead of the previous 10 years requirement); a mother or father could take up to 34 weeks of unpaid parental leave in the first year after a child's birth; all women could claim up to 18 weeks of maternity leave (a right previously restricted to expectant mothers with at least 20 weeks of seniority); unfair dismissals could be appealed to a Commissaire de travail after three years of employment (rather than the existing five years); a parent could leave work without advance notice to tend to a sick child; employment security was guaranteed for all workers who took a leave authorized by the law; part-time workers would have to receive the same wage and vacation benefits as full-time employees; finally, fines were increased for employer violations of employment standards. Business organizations complained about the economic costs associated with the changes, arguing that the Liberal government was, in effect, extending a kind of union protection to non-unionized workers; but they acknowledged that some business reservations about an earlier version of the legislation had been addressed. By contrast, spokespersons for the non-unionized, as well as for unions and the PQ opposition, complained that the reforms were inadequate. The Liberals refused, for instance, to raise the provincial minimum wage at the same time, or to index it to the rate of inflation. They nevertheless increased the minimum rate eight times between 1985 and 1994, and abolished the lower rate for students during their first term in office. According to one calculation, the Quebec minimum wage's value remained stable as a ratio of average wages during this period; in 1994, this ratio was higher than in Ontario, Alberta, or British Columbia.[101]

During the 1994 campaign, the Parti Québécois promised pay equity for Quebec's private sector; only Ontario had previously taken this step. A consultative committee helped prepare legislation, the first version of which was tabled in December 1995. Business associations were united in opposing the proposal, which they claimed would be very costly.[102] A revised bill was introduced in May 1996 after lengthy consultations. It provided lengthy implementation periods, subjected smaller firms to looser requirements, and exempted those with fewer than 10 employees: Firms with more than 100 employees would be required to create employee-dominated and gender-balanced committees to oversee pay equity; they would have two years to evaluate gender-related pay discrepancies, and four additional years to rectify the imbalances; mid-sized firms would have two extra years for the evaluation and could rely on sector-level committees to conduct it; no committee review would be conducted in firms with 10 to 50 employees, where workers would have to appeal to a new Commission de l'équité salariale to obtain redress.[103] Creation of the Commission, which includes representatives from business, labour, and women's groups, was postponed in November 1996, effectively delaying full implementation for another year.[104] Two interviewed provincial officials argued that this time frame – the fact that equity settlements could not be retroactive, as they can under federal legislation – and the flexibility afforded firms in assessing and redressing wage discrepancies, meant that many business reservations had been addressed. Yet business associations remained opposed to the legislation, although the opposition Liberals supported it and took no steps to reverse it after 2003.

Additional piecemeal changes were made during the mid- to late-1990s; none was opposed by the opposition Liberals. Participants at the 1996 Socio-Economic Summit (including business) agreed to a reduction of the normal workweek from 44 to 40 hours; the change was implemented over four years.[105] Three other adjustments were made in 1999. Unions accepted a termination of the industrial relations decree in the clothing industry (a long-standing business demand) in exchange for a temporary enhancement of employment standards rules there.[106] After consultations with business and labour, the government adjusted the regulation of child labour to prevent it from interfering with school attendance.[107] The only initiative to occasion much controversy was the government's decision to prevent labour contracts from including inferior pay or benefits provisions for newly hired employees compared to those already working for a firm (*clauses discriminatoires*, or *clauses orphelins*); Quebec became the first jurisdiction in North America to bar these provisions. The province's leading business groups all opposed the legislation, claiming that it would destroy jobs; the final version of the legislation, supported by the Liberal opposition, made some concessions to these concerns.[108]

In May 2002, the Parti Québécois released a discussion paper that proposed the broadest reform of the Employment Standards Act ever undertaken since its initial passage. Proposed changes included the extension of coverage to agricultural workers, and assuring earnings of at least the minimum wage for restaurant servers; more holidays for part-time workers (up to 10 days of unpaid family leave each year, instead of the existing 5 days); up to 12 weeks of leave to tend to a gravely ill family member; personal illness leave of up to 26 weeks (instead of 17 weeks); up to 52 weeks of unpaid parental leave; eligibility to appeal an unfair dismissal after two years of service (rather than three years); abolition of practices that denied holiday pay in some cases; and limits on the number of hours per day (12) and per week (60) that an employee could normally be asked to work without her consent.[109] Clarifying an ambiguity in the initial document, it also indicated that the legislation would be extended to cover many domestic workers. There had been no prior discussion of these ideas with non-governmental actors on the Conseil d'administration of the Commission des normes de travail, or elsewhere. Quebec business associations responded very negatively to the proposals, arguing that some would be very costly for firms.[110] The PQ decided to proceed with the amendments, largely unchanged, in the face of this opposition. The government argued that the implementation costs would actually be quite small, amounting to less than $200 million per year.[111] When the legislation was tabled in November as Bill 143, in fact, it was extended in one important direction. Largely at the instigation of social organizations, which had made presentations at legislative hearings during the summer, the PQ added a provision to the law protecting workers against 'psychological harassment'; this immediately became a focal point for business opposition. Representatives of employer groups, which had also participated actively in the summertime consultations, complained bitterly that matters had only gotten worse for them in the wake of the discussions.[112] The government now took some steps to address these concerns; while most changes would be in force in May 2003, implementation of the psychological harassment provision was delayed for another year and would be subject to detailed regulations, elaborated in early 2003, to make it manageable for employers.[113] Although business opposition to the changes was never truly mollified, the opposition Liberals voted in favour of the bill.

The Péquiste government frequently was criticized by social groups and unions for not raising the minimum wage higher. Yet it went up eight times during its nine years in power, increasing from $5.85 in 1994 to $7.30 in 2003.[114] The PQ rejected union requests that upward adjustments be made automatically to match growth in the average industrial wage. In May 2002, they nevertheless announced plans to base future increases on a formula that included the average industrial wage and calculations of the effect of an increase on small firm competitiveness.[115] The PQ in fact allegedly sought to maintain the wage at about 45 per cent of the average industrial wage during its term in office – roughly the same ratio as the Liberals had upheld after 1985.[116]

Having supported passage of Bill 143, as well as the most recent minimum wage increase, the Liberals gave no indication during the 2003 election campaign that they would introduce major changes to employment standards if elected, and they did not. The most controversial feature of Bill 143 – its provisions regarding psychological harassment – went into effect in 2004, as planned. In the same year, the minimum wage was increased modestly, consistently with recent Péquiste practice. The Charest Liberals nevertheless made several regulatory adjustments to the new legislation, two of which modestly curtailed the legislation's generosity. Agricultural workers would still be covered by the legislation, but seasonal fruit and vegetable pickers would not be guaranteed the minimum wage; similarly, restaurant servers who normally received tips would continue to have a lower minimum wage.[117] A subsequent modification to the standards set for the clothing industry in 1999 eliminated some, though not all, of the protection that workers in that sector had then received temporarily. The Liberals also postponed until at least 2005 any new rule to allow parents to opt for a four-day week; they had promised to consider this option during the election campaign in response to a PQ proposal along these lines.[118]

In two provinces examined in this volume – Ontario and British Columbia – the centre-right's return to power after a period of centre-left government occasioned a significant market-oriented adjustment in employment standards. This did not happen in Quebec, where the broad lines of reform have been accepted by both major parties. The Péquistes, with close links to Quebec's social activist community, were more enthusiastic about reforming employment standards than was the PLQ, but the latter's return to power in 2003 occasioned only minor retreats from its predecessor's reforms. Concertation in policy-making is weaker here than in most areas of labour market policy in Quebec. The Conseil d'administration of the Commission des normes de travail plays an important role in overseeing implementation, but is less significant in policy-making; and we saw that, uncharacteristically, the PQ proceeded with pay equity and with the 2002 reform without addressing most of business's reservations. But this opposition was dampened once pay equity was subjected to a gradual phase-in, and when the regulations regarding psychological harassment were spelled out in 2003; and business associations made no effort, at least publicly, to press the Liberals to reverse these developments after the 2003 election.

Partisanship, Globalization, and Labour Market Policy in Quebec

The institutional setting for labour market policy-making in Quebec is more complex and contradictory than in other provinces, and is the most distinctive in Canada. Its welfare state and production regime are predominantly liberal; consistent with this, its party system remains of the two-party variety, despite the ADQ's recent challenge, and the main parties differ on economic-redistributive issues. Yet these features are adulterated by others more typical of European-style CMEs: its production regime has acquired important statist and coordinative features since the 1960s; and the national question, a social-cultural theme, is stronger than economic concerns in dividing the main parties. Consistent with Kitschelt's expectations (in chapter one) for such a setting, chapter two hypothesized that short-term policy 'swings' after a change in government would be comparatively modest in Quebec, and that the prospects for longer-term, globalization-induced retrenchment were also very low.

The evidence presented in this chapter, and summarized in table 5.2, substantially corroborates each of these propositions. The detailed methodology for calculating the degrees of change reported in the table is explained in the appendix. The prospects for polarization in Quebec public life appeared to be quite high when Robert Bourassa and his Liberal Party returned to power in 1985; but most commentators on that government's first term in office suggest that little retrenchment occurred. In its second term, moreover, the Bourassa administration turned to a policy style that favoured concertation with business and labour and moderate government intervention. In subsequent years, concerted action flourished in most areas of Quebec labour market policy. Uniquely among the provinces examined here, concertation has been since 1990 a preferred policy-making style for both the centre-left and the centre-right in Quebec. In an institutional setting already partly amenable to these arrangements, they have been more successful in Quebec than elsewhere in Canada; concerted policy-making, moreover, largely precluded significant short-term policy swings after changes in government, and entailed that there is very little evidence in Quebec of longer-term, neo-liberal retrenchment in the labour market policy field.

Table 5.2. Partisan 'Swings' and Retrenchment in Quebec Labour Market Policy, 1990–2003

	Short-term partisan swings	Long-term neo-liberal retrenchment
Industrial relations	Medium	Low-to-medium
Active measures	Low	Low
Occupational health & workers' compensation	Low	Low
Employment standards	Low	Low

Thus, Liberal industrial relations policy before 1994 curtailed union powers in some respects, but these changes were mostly of secondary importance, and they were not reversed – even reinforced – by subsequent Péquiste initiatives. In its final version, the PQ's own legislation in 2001 granted major concessions to neither business nor labour. Concertation was less formalized in this field than in others, but it was nevertheless extensive before major legislative changes; it played a particularly important role in alleviating conflict regarding the 2001 reforms. Both parties, similarly, pursued a mix of efficiency- and equity-oriented initiatives in active labour market policy, and promoted an active role for private sector partners in overseeing training initiatives, and, to a degree, in planning them. There were differences between the PLQ and PQ in this area – in the style of province-level concertation implemented by each, and in the degree to which they broadened economically or socially oriented skills formation – but these owed more to the evolving intergovernmental relations setting than to partisan disagreements about skills formation. Partisan disagreement was particularly absent with respect to workers' compensation and occupational health. In the early 1990s, both major political parties and the main business and labour organizations agreed that the main challenge was to resolve the CSST's budgetary crisis. In a context of entrenched formal concerted action, this required compromise by all sides: initially higher premiums for employers and a greater focus on a return to employment for workers. There sometimes was dissent – from small business and the smaller union centrals – from these goals and their execution; but in 2003, the main political and social interests were broadly satisfied with the status quo. Partisanship was again very modest regarding employment standards. The Liberals' 1990 reforms reinforced, rather than eroding, the level of protection afforded workers under this legislation. Subsequent PQ changes moved in the same direction, though more vigorously, and, in 2002, in the face of significant business opposition. In a setting where the nongovernment interests of importance differed somewhat from other labour market fields, concertation was less well developed in the employment standards area. Yet here, too, there appear to be no entrenched grievances for any of the leading political and social interests that await remedy.

The contention associated with some Liberal initiatives in the immediate aftermath of that party's 2003 election victory appeared to herald more partisan polarization, and retrenchment, in Quebec labour market policy. The greater prominence of the apparently neo-liberal ADQ in the province's politics recently points in the same direction. Yet it does not seem, in the event, that the Charest administration undertook a significant swing towards more market-oriented options. The most important change, a major amendment to Section 45 of the Labour Code, will make it easier for employers, especially government, to subcontract services; this change represents the one important example of a more than modest short-term policy swing in Quebec during the period of study, and it also had the effect of causing a real degree of retrenchment in the industrial relations field. Yet Quebec's industrial relations law continues to contain features of long standing (the anti-scab law) or recent vintage (a robust labour relations board) that offer generous legal protections to unions. The Charest industrial relations reforms also were not nearly as wide-ranging as those undertaken in Ontario after 1995, or in BC after 2001. Post-2003 policy changes in the other three domains were very modest.

6 British Columbia: Right Hegemony in a Polarized Liberal Polity

British Columbia is the most institutionally consistent of the jurisdictions examined in this study: a competitive liberal market economy (LME), a mostly market-oriented welfare state and a highly polarized party system – all hallmarks of a liberal institutional setting. Canadians have long entertained an image of British Columbia politics as 'colourful' and 'extreme.' Its labour movement was historically comparatively strong and militant, and it has long had a relatively strong centre-left party. The latter nevertheless normally finds itself on the opposition benches in the provincial legislature, facing a centre-right governing party that predominates politically, based on its secure electoral and financial support from the province's urban middle and business classes, and in its small towns and rural areas. In the four decades between the emergence of the polarized two-party system in 1952 and the 1991 election, the centre-left CCF and NDP governed for only three years (1971 to 1974). Thereafter, the centre-left enjoyed its longest period in government – elected in 1991 and re-elected in 1996 – before being routed in the 2001 election.

This NDP administration, under the successive leadership of Michael Harcourt, Glen Clarke, and Ujjal Dosanjh, made some effort to break with the polarized pattern of BC politics – a posture not unlike that adopted by the Ontario NDP during the early 1990s, including an incipiently contradictory mixture of efforts to level a 'playing field' thought to have previously disadvantaged labour, and of undertakings to promote a non-adversarial and cooperative culture in the province. Subsequent developments also had Ontario parallels: NDP undertakings were forcefully reversed by the centre-right when it returned to power in 2001, promoting a detailed market-oriented agenda that said little about the merits of coordinative policy-making. Many of these reversals, moreover, again had the immediate effect of returning the labour market policy regime to something like the status quo ante, the broad post-war pattern that existed before the NDP's accession to power; and centre-right policy change was more likely to go beyond this pre-existing norm in sectors that were most removed from the core preoccupations of business and organized labour – employment standards and (a matter addressed in chapter 8) social assistance for employable persons. Yet even in relation to these core sectors – industrial relations, workers' compensation and occupational health, and skills measures – the new pattern in BC since 2001 may have greater potential than have those in post-1995 Ontario to result in longer-term departures from post-war patterns. If globalization's impact is measured by the extent of this marketization, it is somewhat more evident in BC than in other provinces.

British Columbia Politics since 1990

Between the mid-1950s and 1991, party politics in British Columbia reflected a fairly stable pattern of right-left polarization, with the centre-right Social Credit Party confronting the centre-left CCF, and, after its launch in the early 1960s, the NDP on the centre-left (see chapter 2). Social Credit collapsed in the 1991 election, after a final term of office during which it moved considerably further to the right (with consequences in the labour market field, which are treated below) and when party leader Premier Bill Vander Zalm was forced from office by a series of damaging scandals. But by 2001, Social Credit had been displaced by the provincial Liberal Party as the centre-right alternative in a restabilized two-party system.[1] The Liberals, led by Gordon Campbell, came to power in 2001 with an overwhelming majority. It is appropriate in this analysis, then, to concentrate on the options proffered by the NDP and by their Liberal successors in power.

Unlike Bob Rae's Ontario New Democrats, the BC NDP was well prepared to take power in 1991, having been far ahead of the collapsing Social Credit Party in opinion polls long before the vote. Harcourt's determination to steer a more moderate course than the 1971–74 NDP government was remembered for, was planned in advance. The NDP's 1991 election platform, *A Better Way for British Columbia*, promised centre-left labour market policy reforms (see below); improved programs for women, such as sexual assault centres, child care, and family services; reduced poverty; a sustainable environment; the addressing of Aboriginal land claims; and improved health and education services.[2] However, it also promised to 'balance the budget over the business cycle,' to 'work with the business community' and foster 'a dynamic market economy'; and to foster small business, 'a vital part of B.C.'s free enterprise economy.'[3] Glen Clark, who replaced Harcourt as premier and NDP leader in 1995, was credited with a much more 'partisan' political style than his predecessor. Yet his 1996 election platform, *On Your Side*, similarly promised tax cuts for 'the middle class,' and promised that the NDP would 'eliminate waste and duplication,' be 'tough on crime and the causes of crime,' and 'fight fraud and abuse in the welfare system,'[4] at the same time as it vowed to protect universal health care, improve the schools, promote job creation, and, again, address the needs of women. While a 'partnership' approach to resolving disputes among conflicting stakeholders was not promoted in either document, it was pursued by Harcourt once in power. This was reflected in labour market initiatives addressed below, and in the Commission on Resources and the Environment (CORE), which attempted to use it to balance environmental and economic objectives in the forestry sector.[5] Consistent with these documents, pragmatism and moderation, though of a kind that still clearly distinguished the centre-left NDP from its Social Credit predecessors, has generally been attributed to the post-1991 NDP administration once in power.[6]

Many business-oriented observers of the province's politics nevertheless believe that the NDP was unable to undertake the radical (neo-liberal) policy changes that they judged necessary in light of the province's straightened economic circumstances by 2001.[7] The province's economic decline was, indeed, precipitous. In 1990, its per capita gross domestic product (GDP), above the national mean during most of the post-war era, had already fallen to 98.2 per cent of that average. This figure rose slightly, to 99.4 per cent, in 1996, which helped the NDP get re-elected in that year. By 2002, however, BC's per capita GDP was 89.4 per cent of the Canadian average,[8] and the province's economy was widely perceived to be in crisis. While conservative commentators were quick to blame the NDP for the decline, most observers now agree that the BC economy has encountered serious structural problems: its traditional resource industries shed employment and investment opportunities rapidly, and growth in the service sector has been insufficient to make up for the loss. That the NDP became associated with the late-1990s collapse nevertheless facilitated the introduction of a significantly more right-wing agenda by the new Liberal government after 2001: it was able to argue that radical solutions were needed for an acute problem, and (plausibly) that a much poorer province could no longer afford a level of public spending permissible in earlier decades. The resource-sector decline also facilitated this new agenda in another way, and may represent an enduring barrier to a return to power by a centre-left party in the province. As was noted in chapter 2, BC's overall unionization rate fell by more than any of the other three provinces studied in this volume between 1991 and 2002. These losses were particularly acute in the powerful forestry and construction sectors; public sector unions remain strong, but BC's private sector unions – long an important support for the NDP – have been considerably weakened.[9]

Pervasive alarm about the state of the BC economy by 2001 – similar to Ontario's mood in the depths of its early-1990s recession – encouraged the NDP's main centre-right opponent to develop a similarly comprehensive and radical alternative to the governing party's program. And, like the Ontario PC's 1995 Common Sense Revolution, the BC Liberals' *A New Era for British Columbia*, their 2001 election program, was carefully developed some time before the election in close consultation with the province's business community.[10] The Liberals promised, within their first 90 days in office, to 'introduce a dramatic cut in personal taxes,' and to balance the provincial budget; a substantial number of its more specific proposals, detailed below, pertained to labour market issues relevant to the private sector. In no other province examined in this study were labour market concerns so central to any major party program during the post-1990 era. They also pledged to restrict public sector bargaining in the education field and to 'eliminate government subsidies to businesses that give some companies an unfair advantage over their competitors.'[11] While the document pledged to 'honour [the tax-cutting] commitment without cutting funding for health and education,'[12] it was widely understood among political observers that extensive program reductions would be necessitated by the proposed changes. By the end of August 2001, the Liberals were, with some plausibility, able to claim that they had fulfilled their 90-day commitments: individual and corporate taxes had been cut significantly and further reductions were planned; public sector unions lost important bargaining rights, and had been legislated back to work in the health sector; a 'Core Services Review' had been launched to identify the dramatic spending reductions that would be required to permit the government to meet its balanced-budget objectives while proceeding with the tax cuts.[13] In January 2002, the new government announced a three-year spending freeze in the health and education fields (effectively requiring service curtailment in these areas), a reduction in other government spending that would average 35 per cent, and the elimination of 11,700 government jobs – roughly 31 per cent of the public service.[14] By the end of 2002, extensive changes had been introduced in each of the labour market policy domains examined below. There can be no doubt that 'partisanship' is alive and well in BC politics at the beginning of the twenty-first century.

The next four sections detail the effect of this broader political setting on the four labour market policy domains discussed here: industrial relations, workers' compensation and occupational health, active labour market policies, and employment standards. We again omit developments that concern the public sector exclusively. The final section assesses the broad pattern uncovered in this chapter, expanding upon the summary provided above.

Industrial Relations

In its 1991 platform, the NDP promised industrial relations reform; the twin elements of its broad approach to labour market policy-making – revising legislation to aid unions, while trying to foster collaborative decision-making with business and labour – were also hinted at in *A Better Way for British Columbians*: 'New Democrats will work with business, management and labour to develop balanced and fair labour legislation, with practical mechanisms for resolving disputes impartially ... and with proper protection of the rights of workers in both the public and private sectors.'[15] Industrial relations law manifested clearly the absence of a stable policy equilibrium in BC at the end of the postwar era. During the 1980s, the Social Credit administration was at loggerheads with the unions, culminating in a massive revision of the province's labour law. The Industrial Relations Act of 1987 (Bill 19) was widely seen, even by big business, as overwhelmingly favouring employers. It prohibited unionized workers from refusing to work alongside non-union ones outside of the construction sector, banned secondary picketing and secondary boycotts (the refusal of unionized workers to handle products from strike-bound firms), permitted an employer to decertify if he was not open for two years, restricted successor rights (of a union to continue representing workers if a firm's ownership changed hands), and compelled unions to submit employers' final offers to their members. It also created an Industrial Relations Council (IRC) to mediate labour disputes, which was seen as biased in employers' favour. The provincial deputy minister of labour resigned over the legislation, and the union movement boycotted the IRC.[16] Provincial government officials, interviewed in 2003, retained very negative memories of Bill 19, variously describing it as 'a hopeless piece of garbage' and 'infamous.'

The NDP legislation was drafted only after extensive consultations across the province by a panel that included representatives from large employers and unions. The panel agreed on most, though not all, provisions of the new Labour Relations Code (Bill 84). The legislation altered industrial relations law to the advantage of unions: it eliminated most of the changes introduced by Bill 19, including the ban on secondary boycotts, the successor rights restriction, and the two-year decertification provision; most prominently, it included an anti-scab rule, preventing employers from hiring replacement workers during a strike; and it permitted automatic certification of a worksite if 55 per cent of its employees had signed union cards. The IRC was replaced. Yet it also embodied important compromises agreed upon during the consultation process; in exchange for the anti-scab provision, Social Credit's ban on secondary picketing was retained.[17] These elements convinced media commentators that the legislation included important compromises between the agendas of labour and (at least big) business.[18]

Nevertheless, Bill 84 was attacked by small business interests during the final months of 1992. A Coalition of BC Businesses was formed, largely among small business groups, to fight the bill, and subsequently became their preferred vehicle for challenging NDP labour policies. Eventually, even spokesmen for the Business Council of British Columbia, whose corporate membership had been represented on the task force, joined the chorus of criticism.[19] By early 1993, it was clear that the NDP could not foster a genuinely cooperative atmosphere in labour market policy-making, especially if it simultaneously sought to promote union and worker interests. The province's ideological polarization, and business's disinclination to cooperate with an unusual centre-left government, arguably assured that this was the case.

Subsequent NDP industrial relations initiatives were not preceded by such extensive consultations, though the government continued, intermittently, to seek to persuade business of its even-handedness. Most business observers interviewed for this study agreed that the Labour Relations Board (LRB), which Bill 84 created to replace the IRC, initially was even-handed. Yet even more neutral observers detected a pro-labour bias in one key LRB decision, which had the effect of restricting considerably employers' ability to communicate with employees during a union certification drive. The LRB was also thought to have shown a clearer pro-labour bias later, especially after 1996 changes in the LRB's senior staff.[20]

The NDP's second significant initiative dealt with the construction sector. Union membership there declined precipitously during the 1980s, in the wake of various Social Credit initiatives; increasingly, construction workers found themselves represented by a Christian Labour Association of Canada (CLAC), widely acknowledged as adopting a relatively passive approach towards employers, and dismissed by mainstream labour organizations as not being a real union.[21] Because CLAC qualified as a union under the Social Credit labour law, however, it was largely protected against efforts by mainstream unions to recover their membership by 'raiding' CLAC work sites. Organized labour sought a form of sectoral bargaining to help reverse this pattern: if a union negotiated an agreement with an employer in one designated economic sector, its terms would automatically be extended to other employers and workers in the sector. Bill 44, introduced by the NDP in June 1997 without significant consultation, addressed this union objective; it divided the construction industry into seven sectors, in each of which 'master agreements' would be negotiated to cover all workers. But the legislation was quickly withdrawn in the face of vociferous employer opposition, including threats to remove all business representatives from provincial boards and commissions.[22] The NDP then launched consultations about further reforms. Bill 26, the subsequent 1998 legislation, gave 'organized labour only a fraction of what it would have received under Bill 44.'[23] A 'watered down' version of sectoral bargaining (in the words of one interviewed official) was created, but only for employers in the commercial and industrial construction sectors; the legislation's impact was much less dramatic than that of Bill 44, which would also have covered the residential sector, where non-unionized smaller contractors predominated. Despite the new bill's softer provisions – which angered the unions – it too was opposed strenuously by business and by the opposition Liberals.[24] When the NDP left office in 2001, each of its industrial relations initiatives remained hotly contested in the provincial media, and its attempt to foster collaborative decision making largely had failed.

Throughout the 1990s, the BC Liberals criticized NDP industrial relations policies, advocating more business-friendly alternatives. *A New*

Era for British Columbia committed the Liberals to reversing two NDP initiatives discussed above: a vote would be mandatory for union certification (overturning the Bill 84 provision for automatic certification if 55 per cent of a bargaining unit's members signed union cards); the limited sectoral bargaining introduced by Bill 26 would also be abolished. A 1999 amendment to the province's Pension Benefits Standards Act, which limited the ability of construction workers to collect a pension upon retirement while continuing to work in the field, would be eliminated as well.[25] (Construction unions had convinced the NDP that such workers often accepted lower wages, undermining wages for non-retired workers). After the election, the new administration quickly introduced Bill 18 to implement these commitments.[26] Based on an electoral platform, it was not the subject of consultations with affected interests. But the *New Era* document was surprisingly silent about Bill 84's anti-scab provision, the cause of so much controversy almost a decade earlier. In 1994, Gordon Campbell had, indeed, promised to terminate this as well.[27] However, during the 2001 campaign he reversed this commitment.[28] Campbell resisted considerable discrete business pressure after the election to abandon this stance.

Stymied in this one area, business lobbyists were more successful in persuading the Liberals to introduce other changes beyond those promised in 2001. Along with the new labour minister's own market-oriented views, these contributed to a second and potentially more important round of industrial relations law changes in May 2002. The resulting legislation, Bill 42, was preceded by a two-month consultation (though nothing on the scale used by the NDP in 1992), which allowed unions as well as employers to voice their views; but interviewed officials readily acknowledged that the bill addressed business concerns exclusively. The main change pertained to Section 2 of the Labour Relations Code, which defined the broad goals that the Labour Relations Board should apply in settling arbitration cases. The NDP's Bill 84 had referred to these goals – which included workers' rights to unionize, but also the need to maintain the viability of firms – as 'purposes.' During the 1990s, the LRB had given these purposes limited attention; employers' groups felt this had led to the LRB's paying insufficient attention to the question of firm viability. Bill 42 replaced the term *purposes* with the term *duties* in referring to these goals, thereby stipulating that the LRB was required to consider them in applying the code. The section's wording was also altered to enhance employer rights; it would now recognize the rights of employers as well as those of workers, and instruct the LRB to foster 'employment in economically viable businesses.'[29] Bill 42's second main provision authorized the preparation of regulations to clarify employers' right to communicate with their employees during a certification or decertification drive; as we have seen, business groups felt that this right, though explicitly protected in the NDP's Bill 84, had been eroded by LRB decisions during the 1990s.[30]

After Bill 42, business interest groups lobbied for further changes. Two frequently discussed proposals would restore features of Social Credit's Bill 19 that were abolished by the NDP: the restriction on successor rights, and the decertification of a bargaining unit if a firm closed for two years. In December 2002, the Liberal government struck a panel – with equal membership from business and labour – to discuss further reforms.[31] It is likely that these options, strongly resisted by unions, are among those being discussed in the panel's confidential deliberations. But it is unclear, at the time of writing, whether the Liberals, having launched a putatively bipartisan policy review of the type used by the NDP in 1992, would proceed with these changes over the objection of the panel's labour members.

Several senior provincial officials, interviewed in 2003, suggested that BC industrial relations law remains far removed from ('well to the left of,' according to one) the earlier Social Credit legislation. But it is unclear whether the new pattern will broadly correspond to that which existed before 1987, or be more market-oriented. The labour code retains one feature more favourable to unions than any before 1993: the anti-scab provision. Other pro-labour elements abandoned by the Liberals did not exist in the post-war era (automatic certification and sectoral bargaining), or were formally already a part of NDP legislation (the right to communicate). But adoption of either proposal discussed in the previous paragraph would be a major departure from post-war norms. The Liberals' Section 2 reform (the 'duties' provision), according to these officials, could also move BC's industrial relations regime in a significantly more market-oriented direction if its more business-friendly wording is applied vigorously by the LRB. The long-term implications of Liberal industrial relations policy are therefore likely to be contradictory – more market-oriented than pre-NDP arrangements in some areas, but less so in others.

Workers' Compensation and Occupational Health

NDP policy regarding workers' compensation and occupational health again reflected its twin desires to improve the lot of workers and to foster collaborative decision making. But the story of change in this sector does not fully mirror the one examined above: Social Credit had made no wild swing to the right here during the late 1980s, and had, indeed, tentatively sought to build a collaborative policy-making model in the field; the most noteworthy developments under the NDP administration, moreover, did not result from legislative initiatives but from administrative practices, and the broader setting of policy-making in BC. Liberal reforms after 2001 addressed these elements rather than reversing NDP legislation. In 1990, the broad design of workers' compensation and occupational health policy in BC had not altered since the 1970s. The 1971–74 NDP administration undertook a major reform;[32] reflecting the government's centre-left ideology, these made the legislation 'liberal, socially responsible, shifting the balance more towards individual justice,' in the words of an interviewed official. During the 1980s, there were frequent complaints that the Workers' Compensation Board's structure made it insufficiently accountable; business and labour wanted more opportunities to influence policy.[33] Social Credit responded with 1990 legislation that created a separate Appeals Division within the board; and by launching a Board of Governors, with members selected from the business and labour communities, that would concentrate on 'governance and policy.'[34]

Even before its 1991 accession to power, then, elements of the NDP's equity- and collaboration-favouring agenda were in place.[35] But these reforms were implemented under the NDP; and, in the words of one interviewee, this was done 'in a liberal way.' In October 1991, the month of the election, the new board of governors passed a controversial resolution stipulating that 'the governors' primary duty and responsibility is to represent the interests of their constituencies.'[36] This 'stakeholders' model – according to which business and labour board of governors' members mainly represented their constituency, rather than the interests of the compensation system as a whole – was favoured by the board's labour members. In its wake, it was never able to work consensually, and had trouble maintaining a full complement of business members. After a 1995 external review concluded that the 1990 governance model had failed, the NDP government eliminated the board; Workers' Compensation would now be overseen by a Panel of Administrators, consisting of professional staff.[37] Collaborative decision-making had again been unsuccessful.

The Appeals Division commenced operations in June 1991, shortly before the change in government. It quickly became the focus of employer concerns that its proceedings were expensive and resulted in 'a lack of finality'; workers appeared to have many avenues to appeal unfavourable decisions.[38] Costs also rose because of new and more generous methods adopted by the board to evaluate claims. During the early- and mid-1990s, the WCB's Accident Fund ran a series of budgetary deficits, and employer assessment rates rose to cover the shortfall; each of these trends reversed later in the decade.[39] Nevertheless, throughout the 1990s, the opposition Liberals criticized the WCB's finances and its frequently changing senior administration (deemed incompetent and labour-friendly).[40] Several interviewed provincial officials considered the WCB's escalating costs, and the NDP's failure to curtail them, as the most important development in this policy area during that party's decade in office. Indeed, total WCB payments in BC rose from $461 million in 1990 to $884 million in 1999, an increase of 92 per cent during a period when such costs rose by only 7 per cent across Canada.[41] In 2000, British Columbia was above the national average in the proportion of eligible employees who were receiving compensation benefits and in average benefit costs; benefits were also calculated more generously than elsewhere.[42]

With public opinion polls revealing considerable public disaffection with the WCB,[43] the NDP launched a Royal Commission to review its benefits and governance shortly before the 1996 election. The commission was mandated to undertake lengthy and extensive consultations. In its January 1999 report, it embraced several criticisms mentioned above: it recommended a smaller and less partisan board of governors; a simpler and less open-ended appeals system; and some benefit curtailments. The proposals, especially the last, evoked reservations from labour leaders.[44] While the NDP government promised to move quickly on reform, it had not done so when it left power two years later. Some interviewed officials believed that it was unwilling to make changes because organized labour 'liked the system the way it was,' in the words of one observer.

By contrast with these developments at the level of policy implementation and administration, the NDP's specifically legislative initiatives between 1991 and 2001 were modest, though they represented moves towards greater generosity. A bill passed in 1993 extended workers' compensation to most classes of workers (such as those working in financial institutions) previously excluded; coverage was now almost universal.[45] In 1997 and 1998 a large number of regulatory changes and one statute (Bill 14) extended occupational health and safety protection for workers (the only significant developments in this area under the NDP). These changes addressed numerous health risks (such as ergonomic ones) that had not existed when the regulations were last extensively revised 20 years earlier, protected workers' rights to refuse dangerous work, gave occupational health officials greater enforcement powers, and made health and safety committees mandatory in more work sites.[46] The reforms occasioned complaints from business representatives. But neither the occupational health changes nor those legislated in 1993 regarding WCB coverage were reversed by the Liberals after 2001.

The Liberals' 2001 election platform mentioned workers' compensation and occupational health issues only briefly.[47] Their earlier persistent criticism of NDP policy – and that of their business allies – nevertheless suggested that significant policy change was likely after the election. Shortly after coming to power, the Liberals commissioned two reviews of the WCB. The most important was conducted by Alan Winter, whose background made it clear what direction the new government was planning to take: he had been the main representative for the employer community at the Royal Commission.[48] While Winter did consult with nongovernmental interests in preparing his report, there was never any pretence that subsequent reforms would reflect a consensus between business and labour. His May 2002 recommendations largely paralleled those presented earlier to the Royal Commission. These quickly led to two major legislative initiatives,[49] which, in the words of one official, were 'based on what the business community, through its representative, Alan Winter, presented at the Royal Commission.' Another official observed that 'the employer community is very comfortable with the changes,' just as labour had been with NDP policy.

The first legislation, Bill 49, mostly addressed workers' compensation benefits, which were curtailed in several important respects: benefits would be calculated at 90 per cent of workers' previous gross earnings, rather than 75 per cent of net earnings (a change endorsed by the Royal Commission); benefits would now only be indexed to inflation less 1 per cent, not fully; they would end at age 65 (replaced by a separate retirement benefit, where needed); recipients would lose 50 per cent of the value of Canada Pension Plan benefits received while also receiving compensation; and the formula for calculating a workers' average earnings before injury was altered.[50] According to Labour Minister Graham Bruce, 'these changes will save about $100 million per year, to make the system more sustainable in the future.'[51] Bill 49 also created a seven-member board of directors, consisting of nongovernmental actors, to oversee the WCB. Business and labour were each assigned only one seat on the board. It is not, then, a business-labour collaborative body of the type that existed before 1995. The second reform, Bill 63, was introduced in October 2002. It again reflected the Royal Commission's recommendations and business views. The Appeals Division was merged with another body to eliminate a level of adjudication; and specific time limits were set for launching claims, and for decisions and subsequent appeals. While the existing system required an average of 35 months to arrive at a final decision, according to the government, a final decision would now be made in a maximum of 15 months.[52] These new constraints applied to employers as well as employees, but interviewed union and worker representatives argued that they would constrain worker appeals far more; resources at the WCB to assist non-unionized workers to prepare claims were said to be overstretched already.

A New Era for British Columbia promised to 'cut the 'red tape' and regulatory burden by 1/3 within three years.'[53] The resulting 'red tape review' quickly focused its attention on occupational health and safety, a field with many regulations.[54] The most discussed option for reducing regulations here involved replacing a 'prescriptive' model for evaluating workplace safety with a 'performance-based' one: rather than overseeing extensive safety regulations, government would allow employers to draft flexible plans for meeting desired safety objectives. It would then monitor performance to ensure that objectives were met. In 2003, ministry officials conducted public consultations about this option. While large business was supportive, the suggestion was 'diametrically opposed to what labour wants,' in the words of one official; unions complained that the change would result in more unsafe work environments. At the end of 2003, this issue remained unresolved.

The Liberal cuts curtailed a workers' compensation system judged by one study to have been the fifth most ample in North America in 1998 (second among Canadian provinces); occupational health deregulation could jeopardize BC's second-place ranking in this field.[55] The Liberals deemed the reductions necessary to stymie rapidly rising costs; critics might counter that costs had already peeked in 2001 and 2002, before the Liberal reforms could have had much effect; and that the Accident Fund was in surplus when the NDP left office.[56] In any case, the two governments clearly approached these domains differently. And while the NDP tried, abortively, to foster collaborative decision making, the

Liberals moved firmly and quickly towards a more business-friendly model. Were the Liberal reforms an unprecedented departure from a post-war norm? Many Bill 49 changes reversed more generous provisions in place since the early 1970s. The BC Federation of Labour calculated that the '90 per cent of gross salary' benefits formula would reduce payments by about 10 per cent (a figure acknowledged as accurate by an interviewed official); the 50 per cent deduction in relation to the Canada Pension Plan, the federation argued, could cut relevant benefits by about 20 per cent; other changes would also have important consequences.[57] On the other hand, the government and interviewed officials pointed out, many of these changes, including the benefit formula and CPP provisions, only 'brought BC into line' with most other provinces;[58] previously, it 'had been way out there.' Some observers argued that by the end of the 1990s, WCB settlements were much more generous than they had been two or three decades earlier, paralleling a similar rise in the value of tort settlements in the courts. But in the short term the cuts nevertheless are considerable. Moreover, the full implications of some changes – the curtailed appeals process, possible occupational health deregulation, and the fact of having a Liberal-appointed (and probably more conservative) board overseeing WCB policy-making and adjudication – will only become clear with time.

Active Labour Market Policy

The Social Credit administration had undertaken no signature policy departures regarding industrial training and labour market decision making in the years preceding the NDP's 1991 election win. BC's education and training arrangements very much reflected the LME-style norm that also characterized other Canadian provinces: far more resources were devoted to institutional instruction than to industrial training (provided mostly on the job); within the former category, moreover, the generalist university sector was much better financed than were vocationally oriented community colleges;[59] finally, the province had little experience with efforts to foster collaborative decision making among government, labour, and business in this field.[60] Social Credit's most significant initiative, indeed, had been to expand the university-based system further; a late 1980s policy review had pronounced this system underdeveloped, in comparison with those in other provinces.[61]

A Better Way for British Columbia said nothing about industrial training; the document complained that BC 'lags far behind the national

average in providing the opportunity to go to college and university,'
implying a preference for continued expansion of post-secondary institutions, rather than more on-the-job measures.[62] Expanding university
enrolment, combined with repeated tuition freezes was, in fact, a major
preoccupation under the NDP.[63] By 1993, however, the new government had embraced the social democratic skills agenda that was also
promoted by centre left-governments in Ontario and Quebec during the
1990s: in *policy* terms, an expansion of job creation and industrial training initiatives, with a particular focus on equity objectives; in relation to
labour market policy *decision making*, the creation of private sector
collaborative arrangements. These interests were piqued, in part, by
influences from outside the governing party: the federal government's
announcement, as part of its 1989 Labour Force Development Strategy
(LFDS), of a desire to create a network of federally dominated collaborative training boards across the country, and the 1991 recommendations of a Social Credit-appointed task force (popularly known as the
Strand Report) which recommended more on-the-job training, fostered
in conjunction with nongovernmental actors.[64] But the NDP quickly
embraced these goals as its own.

An interviewed BC official termed the NDP's approach to active
measures 'much more proactive, interventionist' and concerned with
'equity' than was that of the Liberals after 2001. For another, the NDP
was a 'very socially conscious government,' which had 'more of a
disposition to provide skills to the least advantaged.' This was reflected
in Skills Now!, announced in 1993, which committed $20 million over
two years to active measures designed for persons who were unlikely
to attend university. Skills Now! developed industrial apprenticeship
opportunities for high school students, expanded technical education
for these students, and provided training for social assistance recipients. 'It was,' according to a sympathetic observer, 'an attack on a
philosophy of education that made most BC school children feel inadequate because they were fated to become carpenters, waiters, or retail
clerks – positions deemed less significant than being an academic or
going to a university.'[65] Later in the 1990s, the NDP launched several
job creation initiatives aimed at young people, who were experiencing
particularly high rates of unemployment; and the government continued industry-related measures introduced before it came to power –
such as an Industrial Adjustment Service, which helped established
workers in declining industries to find new opportunities and attracted
workers to growing sectors.[66] Compared to the sums expended on

universities and colleges in the late 1990s – about $2 billion – job-focused active measures nevertheless remained minuscule. In 1995–96 all of the Education, Skills and Training ministry's industrial training measures cost $110 million.[67]

The NDP undertook two equally fruitless efforts to foster concerted active labour market policy-making. The British Columbia Labour Force Development Board (BCLFDB), launched in 1994, was the province's response to Ottawa's LFDS; in contrast with federal proposals, however, the board was entirely separate from the senior government and its Canadian Labour Force Development Board. It nevertheless shared with the CLFDB a number of features that rendered it ineffectual as a vehicle for fostering consensus among nongovernmental actors. First, alongside its business and labour representation (eight of each) the board included representatives from 'equity' communities (women, visible minorities, Aboriginal people, and the disabled), which faced particularly pressing labour market needs. This plethora of interests quickly proved incapable of generating any real agreement. The BCLFDB's staff steered its agenda away from subjects about which business and labour representatives disagreed fundamentally; 'equity' representation added to, rather than muting, the resulting latent tensions. Secondly, the BCLFDB never acquired more than an advisory mandate, resulting in its being devalued by its constituencies, above all business, which often failed to appoint senior representatives to it. The board was closed in 1996.[68] The Industry Training and Apprenticeship Board (ITAC), created in 1997, was configured very differently: it had decision-making powers; its remit was much smaller – focusing on apprenticeship and industrial training – and it lacked 'equity' representatives. Consistent with its desire to foster more vocational opportunities, the NDP wanted ITAC to modernize and expand apprenticeship. The number of apprentices had been declining for a number of years; and the apparent rigidity of the existing apprenticeship model was held responsible for this. Yet ITAC was torn by internecine conflict. Construction union representatives opposed reforms considered likely to 'de-skill' apprentices; that is, significantly reduce the breadth of aptitudes deemed essential for a recognized trade. Public sector unions resisted changes that jeopardized the employment of trainers who worked in community colleges. Representatives from non-unionized service businesses, where apprenticeship was historically absent, queried the potential extension of the apprenticeship model to these industries, fearing its perceived rigidity and the possibility that unionization

Labour Force Board consisting of marginalized groups was ineffective because of many different interests might accompany it. And there was disagreement between business and labour about where additional sources of funding for apprenticeship should come from. ITAC made little headway in addressing these concerns.[69]

As with the other dimensions of labour market policy treated in this chapter, the 2001 election resulted in major policy changes regarding active measures. But these were barely hinted at in *A New Era for British Columbia*. That document promised that the Liberals would 'work with educators and employers to expand job training and skills development,' and with ITAC 'to increase training and apprenticeships.'[70] Rather than expanding spending on active measures, as one might have expected from these statements, Liberal policy focused on maximizing efficiency, expenditure restraint, and free markets. In part, this was anticipated by the *New Era* commitment to 'eliminate government subsidies to businesses that give some companies an unfair advantage over their competitors.'[71]

The promise to end business subsidies resulted in the termination of all active measures other than industrial training and programs for social assistance recipients. The NDP's youth employment measures were terminated on these grounds, as was the province's participation in the Industrial Adjustment Service.[72] According to one senior official, elimination of the youth measures resulted in cost savings of about $35 million. These programs had had a significant equity focus, addressing the needs of persons with particular problems finding and keeping employment. By contrast, the goal of the Liberals' Human Resource Strategy, launched in 2002, was to foster labour market efficiency. Its stated objectives were 'to develop hard data on skills shortages,' and 'to ensure that economic growth is supported' by active measures.[73] To identify appropriate changes, government officials were asked to meet 'with representatives of businesses in key industry sectors.' Meetings focused on helping firms fill skills shortages.[74] Yet it was always questionable whether the Human Resource Strategy would accomplish much. The new ministry charged with overseeing it – Skills Development and Labour – administered no active measures once the youth and industrial adjustment programs were terminated. Policy changes would therefore have required complex negotiations with other provincial ministries. In the event, while ministry officials, interviewed in early 2003, anticipated presenting the Strategy to cabinet within a few months, no such document had emerged a full year after that deadline. At the end of 2003, BC was concentrating on addressing the skills needed to prepare for the 2010 Winter Olympic Games, which had been awarded to the Vancouver area.[75]

The Liberals also abandoned the NDP's preference for corporatist-style private sector consultation about active measures. The Human Resource Strategy consultation, as we have seen, was confined to the business community. In considering the future of ITAC and of the apprenticeship system, the new government consulted informally with labour as well as with business. But the subsequent reforms were broadly favoured by business and emphatically opposed by labour, suggesting that union views were given little credence. The Liberals announced ITAC's abolition in May 2002, and closed its network of 16 regional offices.[76] ITAC's replacement, it was made clear, would focus on addressing skills shortages as efficiently as possible. 'Under the new model, industry will lead the way to a strong, sustainable training system that better meets the needs of employers, apprentices and the market place.'[77] The new Industry Training Authority (ITA) was launched in April 2003; it was expected to oversee changes in apprenticeship – modularization, the 'opening up' of compulsory trades, using competency rather than time-based accreditation, and, more generally, creation of more 'flexible' and 'market-responsive' skills – long opposed by unions and supported by business, at least outside of the construction sector.[78] A Transition Advisory Committee had conducted province-wide consultations about the new body; it reported a concern that 'the new training authority board [might] consist solely of employers with no labour representatives.'[79] The concern was well-founded: 8 of the board's initial 10 members (including its CEO), appointed later in 2003, were from the business community; only one appeared to have a union background.[80] Moreover, the BC changes promise to go much further than an otherwise similar reform in Ontario during the late 1990s. As we saw in chapter four, the Ontario reforms exempted apprenticeship in the construction sector, where this form of training is most developed; a construction industry-sponsored proposal for a similar exemption in BC was rejected by the government.

Partisanship profoundly shaped active labour market policy in BC after 1990. The NDP expanded equity-focused measures and tried to foster collaborative decision making. Under their Liberal successors, active measures were curtailed and refocused to concentrate on labour market efficiency; the NDP's collaborative experiments were terminated, and replaced with a more traditional business-oriented form of consultation. It is less clear whether the Liberal reforms represent a fundamental departure from the post-war norm in British Columbia. There is little evidence of this regarding the policy-making process; the province's now-defunct active labour market corporatism did not pre-date the 1990s. Yet Liberal initiatives pertaining to policy content may represent fundamental retrenchment: eliminated active programs included some, such as the IAS, that had existed for decades. BC officials anticipate that their apprenticeship reform will be more radical than any other undertaken in Canada. But it is still at an early stage, with experimental pilot projects being implemented around the province.[81] It must also be borne in mind that, even under the NDP, ALMP measures remained very modest in BC, as is typical of liberal settings.

Employment Standards

BC's employment standards legislation had not been revised for more than a decade when the NDP came to power in 1991, a period during which significant changes were made in other provinces. In *A Better Way for British Columbia*, the NDP promised, cryptically, to 'introduce new employment standards legislation to ensure fair treatment for all B.C. workers.'[82] Here, again, they attempted to build consensus by appointing a committee, chaired by academic Mark Thompson, to prepare reform proposals after consulting with relevant stakeholders. But the NDP's congenital preference for relatively expansive employment standards, along with insistent pressure from its allies among unions and social activists for the same, once more ensured that the resulting reform evoked hostility from the business community. The terms of reference assigned to Thompson's committee made it clear that the NDP intended to expand protection for workers. The existing Social Credit legislation permitted collective agreements to include provisions that stipulated work conditions inferior to those specified in the Employment Standards Act. The British Columbia Federation of Labour long had argued that this allowed so-called 'rat unions' (broadly, pro-employer ones) to circumvent minimum standards. Consistent with this view, the Thompson committee was asked to determine how (not whether) this provision might be removed from the act.[83] Based on an interim report from Thompson, legislation (Bill 65) to ensure that all labour contracts 'meet or beat' employment standards was passed in 1993.[84]

More extensive changes followed the tabling of Thompson's final report in March 1994, and after what a provincial official termed 'very extensive' consultations during the rest of that year. The legislation, tabled in May 1995, nevertheless largely reflected the views of labour and social advocacy groups and was vehemently opposed by business. Bill 29 extended non-unionized workers' rights regarding leaves of absence, overtime pay, layoff notice periods, and severance pay. But its most important provisions pertained to enforcement. A new Employment Standards Tribunal was created to oversee compliance, and it was mandated to adopt a more aggressive policy of monitoring compliance with the act. Non-compliant firms faced stiffer fines, interest charges, and more regulatory supervision.[85] The government nevertheless sought (unsuccessfully) to mollify business opposition by withdrawing two additional changes that would have extended benefits for part-time workers and provided coverage for home-care workers employed for more than 15 hours a week.[86] Meanwhile, the government oversaw a series of increases in the provincial minimum wage, which rose from $5 per hour in 1990 to $7 in October 1995. In March 1995, the NDP also eliminated a lower minimum wage rate for workers under the age of 18; a 'differential' minimum wage for youth had existed since the early 1970s.[87] Organized business in BC consistently opposed these changes; opposition was particularly strong among small businesses, which are rarely unionized and are more likely than larger ones to pay minimum wages. The small-business-dominated Coalition of BC Businesses referred to Bill 29 as 'a rat's nest of new rules and paperwork that will drive good employers crazy and drive the rule-breakers underground.'[88]

In its second mandate, the NDP again periodically sought to mollify business. Premier Glen Clark quickly retreated from a May 1996 commitment to automatically adjust the minimum wage to inflation every six months; after the October 1995 increase, the minimum wage rose only modestly – to $7.60 – by November 2000. The government responded positively to some business requests that specific industries – such as high technology – be exempted from some employment standards.[89] The Coalition of BC Businesses, however, remained adamant that the law required a far more substantial overhaul in favour of employers.[90] A final NDP initiative would have been more significant had it been legislated earlier in the government's mandate: in January 2001, shortly before a provincial election that they knew they were almost certain to lose, the government announced that it would add a pay equity provision to BC's Human Rights Code. Under the provision, described as 'very unwieldy' by a government official, women employees who believed they were not receiving equal pay for work of equal

value could have appealed to the Human Rights Commission for resti-
tution. After the 2001 election, the Liberals quickly fulfilled a promise
(supported by business groups) to reverse the change.[91]

The Liberals' *New Era* platform said less about employment standards than about most other labour market fields. It nevertheless promised to '[g]ive workers and employers greater flexibility in Employment
Standards to negotiate mutually beneficial relationships that help them
compete and prosper,'[92] a clear indication that the Liberals would pre-
fer flexible and market-friendly changes. The first of these, introduced
in October 2001, had not been prominent among business preferences
and had not been expected by most observers. While the province's
general minimum wage would rise to $8 per hour from $7.60, a new
'training wage' of $6 was legislated for workers with less than
500 hours of work experience.[93] In effect, this was intended as a return
to the 'differential' minimum wage for youth that the NDP had abolished in 1995, but in a form that would be less likely to be deemed
by the courts to contradict provisions of the Charter of Rights and
Freedoms.

The next month, the Liberals announced a broader review of the
Employment Standards Act, after a brief consultation. Both business
and labour interests subsequently were consulted informally by ministry officials before new legislation was drafted. But, in the words of one
such official, 'all that labour asked for in 1995, they got' then, and they
now 'still wanted that, [so] any changes were bad changes.' Business
groups wanted the kind of deregulatory changes for which the Liberals
had signalled a preference. Small business organizations also were
more active than representatives of larger firms in the consultation; the
former had 'a much greater eye for detail' and were 'more knowledge-
able.' In the meantime, the government made clear that the new legislation would curtail standards enforcement substantially; a third of the
officers of the Employment Standards Branch were made redundant in
February 2002, and it was announced that the branch's budget would
be reduced from $11.5 million in 2001–02 to $8.3 million in 2004–05;
most of the branch's regional offices, responsible for most enforcement
and monitoring under the act, were closed.[94]

Bill 48, introduced to the legislature in May, made substantial changes
to the Employment Standards Act. A key change fundamentally reversed the NDP legislation's extension of the Employment Standards
Branch's capacity to monitor employers' compliance with the act. Possible violations of its regulations would now be investigated only after a

complaint was made. An aggrieved worker and his or her employer would be expected to resolve the dispute themselves, using a 'self-help' kit made available by the branch. If this failed, the branch would attempt to mediate the dispute; only if this failed could a decision be appealed to the Employment Standards Tribunal, which now had a substantially reduced role. On the other hand, employers found to have violated the rules repeatedly would be subject to significantly increased penalties.[95] In the wake of these changes, the number of complaints investigated by the branch, and the number of rulings against employers, fell dramatically – to about one-third of their previous level – by mid-2003. For the government, this suggested that its preferred 'non-confrontational' approach to rules compliance, and the severity of the penalties, was significantly reducing problems; NDP and labour critics argued, in contrast, that the rules were simply no longer being enforced.[96]

Another important change permitted employers to sign agreements with individual workers to allow 'variances' in the number of hours that a worker could be asked to work before being paid overtime. While the norm would still be payment of overtime after 40 hours in a week, a variance agreement could raise that ceiling to a maximum of 84 hours a week, and 12 hours a day, if these hours were 'averaged out,' with shorter work hours over a four-week period. Variances had been possible under the previous legislation, but only after a more regulated process, and not on an individual basis. Bill 48 also repealed the 'meet or beat' provision introduced by the NDP, again allowing unions to negotiate contracts that did not reflect provisions of the Employment Standards Act. Other changes curtailed minimum standards for holiday pay, reduced the amount of record keeping required of employers, made it easier for sectors to obtain exemptions from the legislation and (a change that even an interviewed spokesperson for large business opposed) allowed employers to call employees into work for a minimum of two hours, rather than the existing four.[97]

Employment standards legislation under the New Democrats sought to improve the lot of workers; Liberal policy after 2001 reversed most NDP changes, privileging labour market efficiency. Partisanship clearly affected employment standards legislation in BC after 1990, as it did other areas of labour market policy. But in this field, more than the others treated in this chapter, we can observe a pattern of substantial policy retrenchment under the Liberals; their policy framework differed notably from BC's post-war norm. Two features of Bill 48 are crucial in this respect. First, its provision for individually negotiated variances in the length of the work week could effectively eliminate overtime pay for many non-unionized workers, and erode the much-vaunted concept of a '40-hour week.' Second, adoption of a far more laissez-faire approach to investigating standards violations quickly led to a precipitous decline in the number of employers found to have violated the Employment Standards Act. It is likely that many employers who previously would have been found in violation of employment standards are no longer being investigated. Arguably, then, a core goal of employment standards legislation in post-war Canada – that employers will be subject to a degree of supervision to ensure their compliance with the law – has been severely contested in BC. Finally, these features of the new act are significantly more market-oriented than was the employment standards legislation passed by the Social Credit government in 1980.

Partisanship, Globalization, and Labour Market Policy in British Columbia

In chapter 2, British Columbia was characterized as conforming more closely than other provinces examined in this volume to the ideal typical liberal model presented in table 1.1 of chapter 1. Its broadly liberal welfare state is complemented by a market-oriented LME production regime; and, uniquely among our cases, an economically polarized two-party system. Our hypotheses regarding the two research questions formulated in chapter 2, therefore, paralleled those identified for liberal settings in that table: [a] endowed with a competitive production regime and a polarized party system, British Columbia should experience large short-term policy 'swings' between left and right policy options after changes in government; [b] for these same reasons, and because the province's party system includes a robustly market-oriented party, the potential for globalization to result in significant long-term retrenchment in BC's labour market policy field is high. An additional feature of BC's political economy reinforced the latter prediction: The unprecedented decline in its economic well-being since the early 1990s weakened the NDP's union base, and made voters particularly conscious of their province's economic reliance on global markets and readier to accept more radical policy departures.

The evidence presented above, and summarized in table 6.1, firmly corroborates the first hypothesis. The methodology used for arriving at

Table 6.1. Partisan 'Swings' and Retrenchment in British Columbia Labour Market Policy, 1990–2003

	Short-term partisan swings	Long-term neo-liberal retrenchment
Industrial relations	High	Low
Active measures	High	Low-to-medium
Occupational health & workers' compensation	High	Low-to-medium
Employment standards	High	Medium-to-high

the judgments of the degree of policy change reported in the table is explained in the appendix. In each policy domain, the NDP's accession to power in 1991 resulted in a significant shift to the left, both in policy content and in policy-making style. The NDP consistently favoured equity-enhancing policies designed to improve the circumstances of workers, unions, and the socially disadvantaged: industrial relations reform favoured unions; workers' compensation policy extended protection for injured workers; active measures concentrated on the disadvantaged; and employment standards were strengthened and their enforcement made more vigorous. Regarding policy-making style, the NDP consistently sought to foster collaborative decision making, above all among government, business, and labour, seen as equal partners; as one would expect in a liberal setting, these efforts broadly failed. Liberal policy after 2001 quickly and decisively reversed each of these patterns, focusing instead on the merits of efficiency- and market-oriented policies; and relying largely on informal forms of private sector collaboration that privileged business interests. Liberal reform reduced union powers, curtailed workers' compensation protection, reduced spending on active measures, and refocused policy on the problem of filling labour shortages, and significantly curtailed employment standards rules and enforcement. All of the NDP's collaborative decision-making innovations were terminated by the Liberals; if these were replaced, it was with more informal and business-dominated venues. The Liberal initiatives have been in place for less than three years at the time of writing, but they all seem secure – not fundamentally challenged by interests capable of overturning them, or deeply unpopular in popular opinion – something that was never true of NDP policy. A liberal institutional setting, as we have been led to expect by the comparative political economy literature reviewed in chapter 1, broadly 'selected for' liberal policies in British Columbia.

It is less clear whether early twenty-first century BC is experiencing globalization-induced long-term retrenchment in its labour market policy regime. Policy changes relevant to this question have been recent in BC; one can only cautiously address long-term trends with short-term evidence. Beyond this methodological concern, the data itself provides mixed signals; evidence of retrenchment is weakest (but not absent) regarding industrial relations, and strongest in relation to employment standards. In each domain, recent Liberal policy includes contradictory features: the preservation of an NDP-initiated anti-scab provision in industrial relations law, alongside changes that will likely result in less favourable treatment of union claims before the Labour Relations Board; a significant narrowing of workers' compensation benefits, but in a context where the broad pattern of settlements is more generous than a generation ago; the elimination of most equity-focused active measures alongside their extension for social assistance recipients (as we will see in chapter 8); and an increase in fines for violating employment standards, which compensates, though only very partially, for a significant curtailment of rights and enforcement. As was suggested in the summary statements at the end of the preceding four sections, however, market-oriented curtailments were much more common than benefit extensions; in many cases, the resulting policy mix is more market-oriented than was the pattern that prevailed in BC when the NDP was elected in 1991. Retrenchment has occurred in BC, though of a more moderate and uneven kind than our initial hypothesis suggested was possible.

7 Alberta: One-Party Dominance and Neo-liberalism

Alberta represents a unique case in that, unlike the other provinces studied in this book, the same party ruled the province from 1990 to 2003. Indeed the Conservatives have been in power continuously since 1971, with Social Credit previously having governed uninterruptedly from 1935. As analysed in this chapter, the lack of a change in governing party did not mean that labour market policy (occupational health and safety, labour relations, workers' compensation, employment standards, and active labour market measures) has remained static during the past 13 years, or necessarily shifted in accordance with the globalization thesis. This chapter begins with a brief overview of the province, focusing on the features that have historically influenced its labour market policy, as well as the key events during the 1990s.

The developments in Alberta cannot be separated from the unique characteristics of that province's economy and history. In 2003, the province was the third-largest natural gas producer and the ninth-largest oil producer in the world, with more than half of the oil and natural gas exported to the United States.[1] The production of oil and gas (and related petrochemicals) primarily for export, along with the associated machinery, construction, and transportation industries, dominate the Alberta economy. The energy sector accounts for one-fourth of the province's gross domestic product, half of its exports, and employs, directly and indirectly, one of every six workers in the province.[2] The industry – other than the exploration component, which is highly entrepreneurial and composed of small firms – is dominated by large companies, many of them based in the United States. The oil and gas industry 'with its culture of rugged individualism, paternalism, and laissez-faire ideology, has played an important role in shaping the province's conservative climate.'[3]

The second, albeit smaller, pillar of the provincial economic base is agriculture, primarily livestock and crops. This sector traditionally was based on the family farm but is increasingly becoming consolidated into large agri-business operations. The overriding role of a small number of large employers in the province is different from what is the case in Ontario and Quebec, with their more diversified economies. As well, the lack of a significant manufacturing base, unlike the two central Canada provinces, also distinguishes the province, and partially accounts for its low unionization rate.

The nature of the economic base of Alberta, its reliance on natural resources (oil, gas, and agriculture) with the associated dramatic swings in commodity prices, and, at least for exploration and farming, the relatively large number of small enterprises, has fostered an 'ethos of success' in the province. The frontier nature of Alberta has been further strengthened by immigration, especially from other parts of Canada, which can fluctuate spectacularly in response to labour market conditions.

Alberta Politics since the 1970s

The Conservatives under Peter Lougheed governed from 1971 to 1985, during which time, notwithstanding periodic recessions, the rising price of oil provided the provincial government with rising revenues. This was especially true of the 1970s, when the province engaged in considerable province-building and efforts to diversify its economy by financially supporting a wide variety of private sector ventures and businesses. The 1980s proved less kind to the Alberta economy, with recessions early in the decade and again in 1985–86, especially as the price of oil declined significantly during the first half of the decade. In 1985, Lougheed resigned and was replaced with Don Getty as premier. Nevertheless, the pattern of expanding state capacity continued for several more years, even as the provincial government was forced into budget deficits.

The second half of the decade saw increasing western discontent, resulting in the mid-1980s in the birth of the Reform Party of Canada. The new party reflected the rise of neo-conservatism across many parts of Canada, but especially in Alberta. In order to forestall the creation of a provincial Reform Party, and also aware of the shift in public sentiment, the Alberta Conservatives moved to the right beginning in the late 1980s, including a formal severing of ties to the federal party. A third element in creating the neo-liberal lurch was that Getty's cabinet had widely been seen as having granted civil servants considerable power, by adopting a hands-off style of governing.[4]

In 1992, Getty announced his resignation and was replaced by Ralph Klein, whose support came mainly from rural Alberta and Calgary. The transition in governments occurred at a time when the province was in the throes of a recession.[5] In the months before the June 1993 provincial election, Klein moved the government to the right by announcing massive reductions in government expenditures, including decreases to the size of the public service, as well as beginning to introduce (as discussed in more detail in the next chapter) elements of workfare.[6] Indeed, in 1993, Klein successfully campaigned as much against the Getty government as he did against the largely marginal opposition parties.[7] However, it should be noted that the Liberal Party also campaigned on a platform that included decreases to expenditures.[8] A central plank of the newly elected Klein Conservatives was that 'government should get out of the business of business.' With regard to economic and labour market policy, Klein placed increasing emphasis on the 'Alberta Advantage,' a set of statements illustrating that Alberta was the best location for business in Canada, including 'a government committed to less regulation.'[9]

The labour market policy components of the Alberta Advantage were stable labour relations, a productive workforce, and a cooperative work environment. Not prominent in the Alberta Advantage, but central to the Conservative Party's ideology and linked to reducing expenditures during the mid-1990s, was the emphasis on voluntary approaches to regulation – in other words, self-regulation, as well as less emphasis on enforcement. This implied a reliance on market-oriented approaches to regulation, and, more broadly, public policy.

It might be anticipated that implementing the Alberta Advantage, and more broadly the Klein government's ideology, would necessitate the reversal of at least some previously enacted labour market policy legislation, as was the case in Ontario when the Conservatives assumed power in 1995 and the Liberals in British Columbia in 2001. Such a proposition would also seem logical in that the minister of labour from 1992 to 1996 was Stockwell Day, who was firmly camped in the right wing of the Alberta Conservative Party.[10] However, in Alberta, for the most part, this would prove not to be the case, because the Klein 'revolution' was primarily one that questioned the *size* of the government, not so much the *role* of the government, at least with regard to labour market policy.[11] In other words, as shown in this chapter, the principal objective was, or at least became, to reduce costs rather than to achieve a strategic redesign of labour market policy.

Additionally, since the Conservatives had been in power for decades before 1993, there was no ideologically offensive legislation in place, again unlike the other provinces studied in this volume when the governing party changed. Finally, as examined in some detail below, the institutional arrangements of the province proved resilient and acted to prevent significant changes. Indeed, it was often business that proved unwilling to support government proposals to dramatically alter policy.

Occupational Health and Safety

Until 1993–94 there was a stand-alone, independent, public agency for health and safety that reported directly to the minister of labour. This was a unique arrangement in Canada (that is, a separate agency not attached either to a ministry or department or to the worker's compensation board). Quickly at the start of the Klein government's term in 1993, this agency was brought into the Department of Labour. Above all, the motivation was to reduce costs, since the agency, with 260 staff, had its own communications, finance, and human resources departments. A fringe benefit of the organizational centralization was to grant government a somewhat greater role in health and safety, while decreasing the opportunity for external criticism. However, given that this arrangement was standard in the rest of Canada, it can hardly be viewed as representing a major shift in labour market policy.

With regard to health and safety, the new government made few legislative changes, and those that were made were minor. Only a handful of regulatory amendments were made after 1993, but these confirmed existing policy. For instance, in 1996 a regulation was passed that formally exempted agriculture; however, this sector had never been covered by the regulations. In 2000, in response to public outcry over the murder of a person working alone, regulations were put in place that increased the responsibilities of employers in situations in which employees are working alone, extending the concept of safety beyond physical attack.[12]

The lack of regulatory revisions in health and safety, and more generally in labour market policy, is interesting since the opportunity for change was created by the newly elected government in 1993. Early in its first term the Klein government created the Regulatory Review

Secretariat, mandated to ensure that there was no more regulation than absolutely necessary by periodically reviewing all regulations across the government. By 2002, all health and safety regulations, comprising about 500 pages, had been reviewed with only minor changes (these are discussed at the end of this section).

Although health and safety regulations have remained largely untouched, the mid-1990s – the height of the Klein 'revolution' – were a period of considerable administrative turmoil as the Conservatives aimed to get (further) out of the way of business and save costs primarily by privatizing government operations.[13] In 1995, the labour department, largely at the behest of the minister, prepared a proposal to establish delegated regulatory agencies for health and safety, and employment standards. These bodies were to take over the role of government in enforcing the existing regulations, while also leading to cost-savings.

The proposal reluctantly prepared by the department for health and safety was ambitious: enforcement would be delegated to the provincial safety organizations. There were six of these in the province – essentially industry associations funded by the Workers' Compensation Board. However, the regulatory reform did not transpire as several pressures were brought against it. There was considerable public opposition, including from the labour movement, to such a shift, especially as it increasingly became clear that the industry associations were less than keen on taking on this unprecedented role. Furthermore, as the proposal was scrutinized more closely, including by a civil service that was opposed to it, it became less certain that any cost-savings would result in either the short or long term.

More importantly, at a variety of meetings, both public and private, business interests generally adopted the position that enforcing minimum health and safety standards was a core business of government. A public meeting of stakeholders with the minister in 1995, in which both business and labour called the proposal non-productive was a turning point, resulting in the withdrawal of proposals to alter the long-established role of government in health and safety.

Nevertheless, there has been a limited degree of experimentation with delegation of authority to nongovernment organizations and privatization in the province during the past decade. The Partners in Injury Reduction Program, introduced in 1989 and expanded in the mid-1990s, allows third-party organizations certified by the government, rather than ministry inspectors, to audit occupational health and safety management systems. Also, the medical and dental associations, both of which are non-profit, were granted responsibility to audit radiation equipment. However, in nearly all industries, health and safety inspections are conducted by government staff.

With respect to privatization, in 1994 the testing of equipment and conditions, previously done in government laboratories, was moved to private laboratories (paid for by the employers). A similar policy was adopted by the Conservatives in Ontario after assuming power in 1995. Finally, in mid-decade, the government stopped offering general health and safety courses, a task given over to the private sector. Both these changes occurred because it was believed that the government was competing with the private sector.

Alberta is unique in Canada in that it is the only province without mandatory health and safety committees.[14] That these committees, typically composed of equal numbers of employees and management representatives, are not required by statute in Alberta means that workers have a smaller role in addressing health and safety issues, than is the case in other Canadian jurisdictions. This has not changed even though the matter was assessed as part of the mandated public review of all health and safety regulations. During this review, there was – not surprisingly – a lack of consensus between business and labour, and no support from the Conservatives for such a shift in policy.

With the exception of the above, Alberta is not very different from the other provinces vis-à-vis its occupational health and safety regulations. As one senior government official expressed it: 'The similarities are greater than the differences.' Alberta and Ontario are the only two provinces that have a total exemption for agriculture, although pressure is growing on both to include agriculture under the health and safety regulations.

Notwithstanding the little regulatory change, the province has more lax enforcement of health and safety regulations than is the case in many other provinces. For example, during the early and mid-1990s there were almost no prosecutions under the Occupational Health and Safety Act because any such action would have been evidence that the government was getting in the way of business. By 2000, prosecutions had begun again, but only in particularly serious cases in which deaths occurred in the workplace, while the number of inspections also began to increase from the very low levels of the mid-1990s.[15] Minor amendments to the regulations in 2002–03 increased (to $500,000) the upper limit of fines and made other small changes emphasizing the prevention of workplace injuries.[16] At the same time, supplementary resources were allocated towards hiring additional safety inspection officers.[17] It should be noted that the increase in enforcement in the past several years, albeit gradual and from a very depressed level, was not contested by employers, some of whom (especially the larger enterprises that generally abide by the regulations) wanted increased enforcement so that all employers were on the same playing field.

Health and safety policy best illustrates the developments in the 1990s: a reduction of funding for labour market policy, resulting (in the case of health and safety) in a reorganization of departments; greater emphasis on self-regulation; and decreased enforcement, but no retreat in the legislative standards. By about 2000, as the government's fiscal situation improved dramatically, there was a gradual increase in enforcement and prosecution, often supported by the business community.[18]

Industrial Relations

As noted in chapter 2, Alberta has the lowest unionization rate in Canada, with only 22.5 per cent of workers belonging to unions in 2002.[19] Without a doubt, there is a stronger anti-union sentiment in the province than in other parts of the nation, especially in the southern and rural region of Alberta. Organized labour has 'never been significantly involved in government policy-making' and garners only modest levels of public support.[20] The culture of individualism in the province adds to the difficulty organized labour faces, particularly in the private sector. Most private sector unionized workers in Alberta are in industrial construction and the building trades associated with the large oil projects (but not drilling), while about half of the pulp and paper mills are unionized. In the construction sector there has generally existed a good relationship between the employers and unions. As such, labour relations issues are a concern for a relatively small number of private sector employers in the province, most of them large ones. The conflict between unions and employers in Alberta is first and foremost one between public sector unions and public sector employers, an aspect that is not studied in this book. Private sector strikes are relatively rare, but because of their rarity the strikes that do occur come as a shock and tend to be highly emotional.[21] Strikes, such as at the Gainers Edmonton meatpacking plant in the mid-1980s, Safeway in 1997, and at the *Calgary Herald* in 1999–2000, tend to be bitter, and, as one observer noted, are 'strikes to the death.'

Interestingly, the 1993–95 Klein revolution left the existing labour regime (as it applied to the private sector) untouched. This was primarily because the government focused on reducing expenditures, which meant battling with public sector unions.[22] In any case, the large unionized employers had reached accommodation with their unions and saw little benefit to be gained from antagonizing them by supporting changes to the industrial relations regime. Furthermore, the low unionization rate meant that the vast majority of employers operated with an unorganized workforce.

By leaving private sector industrial relations unchanged, the government was also able to partially engineer, and use to its advantage, the split in the labour movement between public and private sector unions. From 1993 to at least 1995, the government's downsizing was tenaciously fought by the public sector unions, while the private sector unions experienced a small increase in membership as the economy became stronger. The confrontational style of the Alberta Federation of Labour did not sit well with some of the private sector unions, such as in the construction sector, which were willing to work with the government or at least not oppose the downsizing of the public sector.

As part of the government's cost-cutting in 1994, the mediation service of the department of labour was privatized; however this was only an administrative adjustment, in that the mediators who were previously civil servants were rehired on contract (they were placed on a roster) as needed. More significantly, the government moved to pay only for the first two days of mediation, and thereafter the parties had to pay the cost of the mediation. This was to stimulate faster agreement among the parties, although it probably worked to the disadvantage of unions, given their more limited resources.

Another administrative change made in 1994 in response to the government-wide initiatives to decrease expenditures was granting the Labour Relations Board the power to charge fees to those bringing matters to the board. However, fees have never been charged, as the board determined that doing so would unduly affect workers, who are the most frequent users of services. As well, in 1994 the Labour Relations Board acquired the responsibilities of the Public Service Employee Relations Board, as part of a government-wide initiative to improve government efficiency and better utilize resources. However, the Public Sector Service Employee Relations Act was not altered.

In 2002, the government undertook, as part of its regular review of all statutes, a review of the Labour Relations Code, unaltered since 1988.

After a year of consultation, the three-member MLA committee concluded, and the government concurred, that 'the Labour Relations Code continues to be an effective and fair piece of legislation for workers, unions, employers and the public alike. We see few facts that support the proposition that the Code as a whole is no longer working.'[23] Again it is interesting to note that the large employers in the oil and gas industry expressed little interest in opening up the legislation, while other (usually smaller) employers were more enthusiastic in this regard. The construction sector unions and employers were especially prominent in lobbying for the status quo, having jointly argued that any change to legislation would be destabilizing.[24] The government's position has been to stress continuity and stability in labour relations, and the attendant labour peace which is seen as contributing to economic growth.[25]

Again, as with occupational health and safety, the labour relations laws as they apply to the private sector in Alberta are not significantly different from those of other provinces; there are more similarities than differences. For instance, the use of replacement workers during a strike or lockout is legal, but this is the case for other provinces, including Ontario (except during its NDP government). Alberta, Ontario (and Newfoundland) are the only Canadian jurisdictions that in all instances require a secret ballot vote before unions can be certified. Alberta, along with New Brunswick and Nova Scotia, are the only provinces in which arbitration for first collective agreements is not available. Furthermore, employers can compel employees to directly vote on a contract proposal without the union's consent, but again this is not unique to Alberta.

The evidence presented above corroborates that of Yonatan Reshef and Sandra Rastin, who concluded in their comparative review of Alberta and Ontario during the 1990s that industrial relations 'were not tampered with in any significant manner' by the Klein government.[26] Nevertheless, the province's labour relations regime has historically been less 'labour friendly' than that found in the other Canadian jurisdictions.[27] The recent work by Richard Block, Karen Roberts, and R. Oliver Clarke is the most extensive effort to compare sub-national labour market policies in Canada.[28] The authors compared all 10 Canadian provinces and 50 American states, applying an index of the strength (including enforcement, the right to appeal, etc.) of a variety of labour market policies, including workers' compensation, collective bargaining (labour relations), occupational health and safety, and so on. With respect to collective bargaining, seven provisions were utilized to create the index, including whether permanent replacements for strikers are allowed, conciliation rights, statutory protection for collective bargaining, and so forth.[29]

Block, Roberts, and Clarke found that in 1988 Alberta scored the lowest in Canada with regard to the strength (supportiveness for unions) of collective bargaining standards. The range of scores for the collective bargaining index ranged from 4.27 for Alberta to Quebec with 7.22 on a 10-point scale. British Columbia had the second highest ranking at 7.06, while Ontario was third highest.[30] Thus, with regard to the provinces we study in this book, Alberta is certainly an outlier. However, it should be noted that according to the analysis by Block, Roberts, and Clarke, Alberta's collective bargaining regime is very similar to that found in Nova Scotia (which scored 4.30), and quite distinct from the U.S. federal standards, which apply universally, scoring only 1.13.

Workers' Compensation

The most interesting developments in Alberta have been in workers' compensation, demonstrating how policy is made in what is a largely one-party province. As is the case in other provinces, the provincial workers' compensation board has a tripartite governance structure with three representatives of employers, three of workers, and three from the community, appointed by the government. However, unlike provinces such as Ontario, the Alberta Workers' Compensation Board (WCB) had historically operated with considerable independence in that the government appointed the board of directors, but not the chief executive officer.

As part of the ideological shift of the early 1990s, which sought to reduce the role, and especially the expenditures, of government, legislation was passed requiring that the Alberta WCB become self-funding. The new self-funding mandate, along with an unfunded liability of $600 million in 1992, resulted in various policy shifts. These included moving towards a wage loss system of compensating injured workers, rather than the previously used pension-based system; increasing the emphasis on returning injured workers to the workplace; decreasing some benefits; and assuming greater control of investment funds. The WCB was under immense pressure to reduce costs between 1993 and 1995, when government MLAs and the minister of labour publicly mused about privatizing the WCB, especially if the board did not operate with a surplus.[31] The notion of privatizing the compensation board was roundly rejected by both labour and the major business organizations in the province, and ultimately not seriously considered.[32] In any case, as a result of reforms, by the mid-1990s the board achieved a surplus and was able to reduce the employer contribution premium.

The overall effect of the policy changes was to make the WCB very effective and efficient in dealing with minor, simple, and short-term injuries that occurred in the workplace. But the trade-off was that the more complex injuries – soft tissues, multiple injuries, as well as chronic conditions and those with longer lag times – were not well addressed. Among the injured worker community and organized labour, but also more generally, the view came to be held that the increased autonomy had, in the words of one labour official, 'sparked a remarkable lack of accountability.' By the late 1990s, the board was under increasing pressure to address the demands of injured workers and their dependants. In 1998, the board made an overture in this regard with some modifications to the benefits for severely injured workers (at a cost of $100 million), and also made payouts (about $80,000 per individual) to disenfranchised widows who remarried, although the board initially resisted these steps.

Nevertheless, groups of injured workers, primarily those with severe or longstanding injuries, continued to demand higher benefits and a review of their claims, often asserting that the board sought to limit their compensation, and required them to return to work while injured. Additionally, the fact that staff at the WCB Appeals Commission, which reviewed and adjudicated appeals on WCB decisions, were WCB employees, led critics to question the independence of the review process. Lastly, the Appeals Commission has no enforcement powers, allowing (at least according to critics) the WCB to only partially implement, or delay the implementation of, decisions by the Appeals Commission. Not surprisingly, beginning in the mid-1990s and continuing until the end of the decade, more and more constituency offices of MLAs were dealing with complaints from workers. There were some calls for a public inquiry into an organization that seemed to operate with undue secrecy, and disregard for both political and public accountability. Labour groups expressed the same concern differently; namely, that the board was generating surpluses on the backs of injured workers.

During the summer of 1999, a group of injured workers camped out for several months on the front lawn of the WCB building, located but metres from the lawn of the Legislative Assembly.[33] The protestors were joined by the opposition Liberals, who reinforced their earlier call for a public inquiry. The WCB, and particularly its chief executive, ignored the tent city protest, taking the position that 'due diligence' had been done, and that in any case the protestors represented a very small segment of injured workers. However, the board's position was compromised when it granted its CEO a 39 per cent pay increase in 1999 to more than one-third of a million dollars. Observers quickly pointed out the irony of limiting payments to injured workers, while increasing the pay of senior executives.

The board's position was even further weakened in that 1999 marked the fifth consecutive year in which employer premiums were reduced (by 24 per cent), from $1.89 per $100 insurable earnings in 1995 to only $1.07 by 1999, which was equal to premiums in the 1950s.[34] In becoming more businesslike and arm's-length during the 1990s, the board had established a significant investment portfolio in the equity markets. The strong performance of the markets in the mid and late 1990s generated hefty returns, so that the board was able to refund premiums to employers during some years, and/or decrease premiums.

Although the WCB ignored the month-long tent city, the media did not; nor did the government. The newly appointed minister of the recently created Alberta Human Resources and Employment department, Clint Dunford, quickly appointed two committees to review the two sets of issues that were at the centre of the protest.[35] A committee of six Conservative MLAs was struck to review the service level of the WCB. Its final report concluded that 'Too often, it seems that injured workers, rather than being helped and assisted during a difficult and traumatic time, are marginalized by the WCB.'[36] Central among the recommendations were various steps to increase the transparency of the WCB and its accountability, as well as establishing a one-time independent tribunal to arbitrate and resolve long-standing contentious claims.

A second review was ordered by Dunford on the appeals system of the board. This was headed by a judge and contained one MLA (who was also a member of the MLA review committee) as well as two representatives from business and one from labour. Like its counterpart, this review also found 'what seems to be a well-entrenched culture of denial within the WCB and one which treats many long-term disability claimants with suspicion.'[37] The recommendations of the report also called for more transparency and accountability in the appeals process for injured workers, including a separation of the appeals function from the WCB, where it resided. Dunford accepted both reports and began to implement their key recommendations; namely, to intensify the degree of accountability of the compensation board, and to review long-standing, contentious WCB claims.

The legislative changes were preceded by further consultations whose objective was to ensure that stakeholders – injured workers, labour, employers, and other parties such as consultants and lawyers, not to mention MLAs – agreed on the major aspects of the legislation. The most reluctant stakeholder during 2001 was the WCB itself, which had to contend with, as one of its senior executives expressed it, 'the atypical, extraordinary degree of political involvement.' Of greatest concern for the board was the recommendation, apparently agreed to by the minister, of a special (and retroactive) review of contentious claims.

The legislation passed in 2002 significantly increased the degree of government oversight of the WCB in that it allowed the minister to set performance indicators for the board and permitted the provincial auditor to directly audit the WCB. As well, the legislation was a catalyst for a memorandum of understanding signed between the minister and the WCB, which requires the board to provide specific information to the minister, such as its business plan. Furthermore, the legislation required changes in the manner whereby the WCB processes claims and reached decisions.[38] As the legislative process unfolded, the board took a number of steps to address accountability and related issues, as well as to prevent further government incursions. At the beginning of 2002 the board of directors announced that the CEO had 'chosen to leave her position to pursue other opportunities' (amid further controversy as to her compensation level).[39] Finally, in early 2003, Dunford established a new committee consisting of two government MLAs and two members of the board of directors of the WCB to monitor the ongoing implementation of reforms to the Alberta workers' compensation system.[40]

The legislation also established a separate and independent (from the WCB) appeals commission, so as to address the conflict of interest that sparked the 1999 protest. Lastly, the legislation included a provision granting the government the authority to set up a review body on long-standing, contentious WCB claims. The review of long-standing claims, however, proved an area on which agreement proved much more difficult to obtain among the stakeholders, especially business.

With regard to the contentious claims, the minister announced, in mid 2001, the establishment of a one-time tribunal to review long-standing, contentious WCB claims. In order to prepare for this tribunal, a task force with representatives from labour, industry, injured workers, the WCB, and his department was fashioned to develop the terms of reference and a proposal for the process and criteria to be used by the tribunal.[41] This body reported in October 2001.[42] Yet Dunford did not have sufficient support within cabinet for beginning such a review, notwithstanding that both committees in 2000 had recommended one. The employer community was growing increasingly concerned and opposed to a review, whose outcome would certainly be to increase employer premiums. For example, the Alberta Construction Association urged its members to write local MLAs to oppose the proposed review.

Also opposed to any review of past decisions was the WCB, which contributed to the debate by noting that a review would doubtlessly increase premiums. Furthermore, the board began to increase premiums, in part because the collapse of the equity markets had depleted its reserves. Not surprisingly, the rate increases caused employers to oppose any of the reforms of the WCB and the proposed review of past claims, fearing a further increase in premiums. Instead of proceeding to establish the review tribunal, Dunford appointed yet another MLA committee in 2002 to review the cost implications of such a tribunal. The matter continued to be unresolved by the end of 2003, but it was increasingly unlikely that a review would ever be called.

Employment Standards

As with occupational health and safety, the period of study saw no substantial adjustments to employment standards, although there have been legislative and regulatory changes dealing with administration of the Employment Standards Code. In 1991, in the Getty era, the labour department gained a new minister (Elaine McCoy), and there was pressure to re-examine the employment standards. A number of public consultations were held with a discussion paper prepared that seemed to suggest that the government was contemplating extending employment standards to new groups (such as agricultural and domestic workers) and adding new standards (such as parental leave). The paper also noted that one of the roles of government was 'to ensure compliance with employment standards by investigating claims, mediating disputes and assisting employees to collect unpaid earnings.'[43] A lack of political leadership meant that the consultation process was slow, with some of what was originally contemplated (such as parental leave) later withdrawn. The planned white paper that was to follow the consultation process was never released as it became clear that a new premier would be assuming power.

With the Klein ascendancy in 1993, the ongoing review of employment standards took quite a different turn than what was contemplated in 1991. The focus became largely one of, in the words of the minister, 'looking for increased efficiency in terms of delivering government services.'[44] Legislation passed in 1994 (Bill 4) did not alter any standards, but rather was designed to set the stage for the eventual privatization of enforcement of the Employment Standards Code. The legislation included provisions that allowed for nongovernment staff to be hired to enforce the standards, and for user fees to be charged. In practice, none of these changes were actually implemented: nongovernment staff were never hired (see below), fees are not charged (except in two very specific situations). The legislation did not broaden, limit, or otherwise change the actual employment standards as there was no interest in doing this, because the political focus was expenditure reduction.

As well as steering employment standards towards eventual privatization, the government floated a proposal in 1995 to introduce right-to-work legislation, as existed in some two dozen jurisdictions, primarily in the southern United States.[45] Right-to-work policies allow persons to work in a union shop without having to join the union or having union dues deducted, as required by the Rand formula. A task force comprising labour (one-quarter of the members), business and others, headed by the former minister of labour, McCoy, was formed to study this issue. Labour had pressed for anonymous submissions to the consultations, a procedure that was ultimately adopted. At the end of its consultation, the task force unanimously concluded that there was no economic advantage to right-to-work legislation, and that any such legislation would disrupt the labour relations stability of the province.[46] The anonymous submissions to the commission, many from businesses, failed to provide the kind of support that would have been necessary for serious consideration of such a radical policy shift.[47] As one senior labour official explained, 'The reason we were able to beat it back [the right-to-work initiative] is that we were smart about it. We brought in the large unionized employers to say to the government: "Don't mess with this. Leave it as it is."' Notwithstanding that no action resulted, it is significant that the government would establish a commission to study it. This appears to be an exceptional development in Canadian labour market policy, and unlikely to occur in any other province.

After Bill 4 had been passed in 1994, the minister of labour moved aggressively to privatize the enforcement function of employment standards. In the spring of 1996, Bill 29 was passed to further prepare for privatization, by rewriting the Code in 'plain language' and improving the format of the regulations, but did not change the legislation or regulations. This was thought to be important for privatization, since complicated language would hinder the easy enforcement of the Code by a nongovernment organization.

Privatization of employment standards was to occur in early 1997, so that in 1996 public servants in the enforcement area were given layoff warnings and notices, and the department prepared a request for proposals from the private sector for the administration of employment standards. However, no acceptable responses or bids were received as organizations outside of government proved unwilling to undertake what was required, at least for the price that the government was willing to pay. As one participant noted, when there were no acceptable proposals, word 'started to get out that this was not going to work.' This view was fostered by labour groups, lawyers, and civil servants, but also businesses, which generally preferred the predictable and lax enforcement of regulation by government, than a leap into the unknown.[48] As the standards themselves were to be left unchanged, and administration likely to rise, most businesses saw no advantage in pursuing privatization. Indeed, when opponents began to criticize the plan, business associations pointedly remained silent.[49] Furthermore, some employers worried that third-party enforcement would open the door to 'end runs,' or special deals that their competitors might be able to arrange. The political risks of such a venture, which never had strong support from the centre, and the marginal benefits, convinced the Premier that there was no point in proceeding.[50] Consequently, in the next cabinet shuffle a new minister was brought in who, along with a new slate of senior executives, quickly announced that privatization would not occur. After 1997, as with occupational health and safety, turmoil in this area subsidized as the Klein government entered its second term and the imperative of reducing expenditures lessened.

Instead, in the beginning of 1998, the government released a discussion paper on the employment standards regulations as part of the review of all regulations under the government-wide Regulatory Review Secretariat process. This resulted in a process that involved considerable consultation, and some minor amendments that were passed in June 2000. The most significant of these was the introduction of a 12-month maternity leave provision, necessitated by the extension of maternity leave under the Employment Insurance program instituted by the federal government. As well, minimum wage protection was extended to domestic workers, who were previously exempt from employment standards legislation.[51]

Despite the lack of legislated change in employments standards, their enforcement has declined, as there are about 30 employment standards officers in the province, which is less than at the beginning of the 1990s. For the most part, workers do not use the employment standards regulations when problems arise; rather, they just get another job. In the mid-1990s, staff of the employment standards unit were instructed to answer only specific questions, and not to provide any additional information that might assist those with complaints. As one labour leader noted, 'the enforcement of employment standards is a joke, a joke.' Unlike health and safety, there is no indication that employment standards enforcement was boosted after 2000.[52] It is safe to conclude, as did Block, Roberts, and Clark, that Alberta generally ranks last among the large provinces in terms of the level of its employment standards.

Active Labour Market Policy

Unlike other provinces at the beginning of the 1990s, Alberta did not establish a corporatist labour market board. Government officials saw the tripartite model fashioned by the federal and some other provincial governments as one that would unduly privilege labour in Alberta given the province's low unionization rate and history of marginalizing unions. Concomitantly, a board was seen as interfering with government actions in labour market policy. As one senior official summarized: 'There was seen to be very little added value and many problems ... The province knew what was happening in the labour market and knew what to do ... A board would confuse the discussion.'

Although the province did not experiment with a corporatist body to provide input into active labour market policy, it had the Alberta Congress Board, a unique organization that has no counterpart in Ontario or British Columbia. The board, which titles itself as 'An Association for Cooperative Action,' was formed jointly by the Alberta Chambers of Commerce and various, primarily private sector unions in 1974 to address labour shortages during the rapid development of the oil,

natural gas, and petrochemical industries. Although its activities have
ebbed and flowed over the decades, it has provided a forum for business, labour, and government to discuss workplace and labour market
issues, even during the 'Klein revolution' of the mid 1990s.[53] On its
executive and associated committees sit the major representatives of
business, labour, and government. Although the board makes no recommendations on major policy issues, and its only major activity is an
annual conference, it does provide a mechanism for the labour market
actors to engage in a degree of dialogue.[54]

In the early 1990s, the government increasingly sought to rationalize
the various active labour programs, including the establishment of a
province-wide network of career development centres. Unlike other
areas of labour market policy, where decreases in budget and attempts
at privatization were the norm during these years, active measures
were exempt from spending reduction, with expenditures in this area
remaining constant from 1992 to 1995. The importance placed by the
government on active labour market policy is also seen in its willingness to collaborate with an unlikely partner: the federal government. In
1994, both levels of government established three co-location pilot
projects in the province, in Edmonton, Lethbridge, and Calgary. These
one-window offices incorporated all provincial services (apprenticeship, labour market programs, social welfare/income support) and all
federal services (employment insurance and training).

The federal government's offer in the mid-1990s to devolve Employment Insurance-funded active programming to the provinces fit well
with Alberta's efforts to create a more integrated and strategic set of
active measures. In December 1996, the province became the first to
sign a federal-provincial labour market development agreement.[55] Like
Quebec, which had been the catalyst for the decentralization of active
measures, the agreement was a full-devolution one involving the transfer of $97.5 million in 1997–98 federal funds and 156 staff to Alberta.[56]
On the other hand, British Columbia signed a less ambitious co-management agreement, while Ontario signed no agreement at all. Indeed,
the province during negotiations also made overtures to deliver EI
passive measures as well as youth programming, but the federal side
refused to consider this.

After the transfer, the active measures in Alberta became considerably more centralized and integrated, with a single front-line service
network for all clients, including social assistance recipients, EI clients,
apprenticeship students, and others. Previously, the local federal offices

had considerable power to fund specialized and unique programs, and tended to use non-institutional trainers. This changed after the labour market agreement as all programs needed to meet the requirements centrally set in Edmonton, with the provincial colleges assuming a more prominent role in training delivery. The centralization of active measures was further reinforced when in the late 1990s the Premier merged the social assistance and labour market policy portfolios into a mega-department: Alberta Human Resources and Employment.

After the intergovernmental developments of the mid-1990s, it was the apprenticeship program that received attention later in the decade. The province was in the midst of an economic boom that had caused skills shortages in some areas.[57] In Alberta, apprenticeship had for decades been largely an industry driven, and government-funded, training program, with unions in most occupations playing a marginal role, or no role at all.[58] The government described apprenticeship as 'totally industry driven.'[59] Indeed, the extensive use of advisory boards in the apprenticeship system, usually dominated by employers, was another reason why a corporatist labour force board was seen as redundant in the early 1990s.

For several decades Alberta has had a more extensive apprenticeship program than is found in other parts of Canada. This did not change during the 1990s, but the province sought to further enhance the apprenticeship training system. By the beginning of the twenty-first century, the province accounted for 20 per cent of the apprentices in Canada, but only 9 per cent of the nation's population.[60] One area of expansion has been the Registered Apprenticeship Program, which allows high school students to earn credits simultaneously towards an apprenticeship program as well as a high school diploma. This program grew from several dozen students annually in the early 1990s to about a thousand by 2003.[61] The government has sought to make apprenticeship more attractive via a well-funded and promoted scholarship program for apprentices.

A second feature of apprenticeship training in the province is its close links to industry, to the exclusion of labour. As with other provinces, the foundation of the apprenticeship and industry training system is a network of local committees in the designated trades and occupations. The Alberta Apprenticeship and Industry Training Board oversees the system and sets the province's training and certification standards. Half the membership of the various committees, including the provincial board, must consist of employer representatives, and the other half of representatives of 'employees' (not 'workers'). For many committees the 'employee' representatives are individuals who hold managerial positions in their workplaces.

The tilt towards employers was increased somewhat in 2001, when the apprenticeship legislation was amended to remove some program and process detail from the regulations, and thereby granted the Apprenticeship and Industry Training Board and local committees greater power to set training and certification rules. In the construction sector, where apprenticeship is organized in a more traditional tripartite manner, employers, unions, and government historically have a shared interest in avoiding boom-and-bust cycles. As such, all three focused during the 1990s on creating stability of demand and supply of apprentices (as well as good labour relations).[62]

In the past several years the government has continued to develop an integrated active labour market policy, outlined in the 2001 report, *Prepared for Growth: Building Alberta's Labour Supply*.[63] The three-pronged strategy outlined in the report was to increase the skill level of workers, the mobility of labour, and the number of skilled immigrants to Alberta. Having to draw highly trained workers from other parts of Canada and beyond has meant that the province has had no choice but to maintain relatively high employment standards and other workplace conditions. Indeed, in discussing the labour market strategy, the minister noted that attracting workers requires labour market policies that 'provide workers with good jobs,' including competitive wages and safe workplaces.[64]

With respect to active measures, Alberta represents an interesting case in that the government has placed a high priority on active measures. As such, the province has increased its role in this area, such as accepting federal funds and staff, centralizing policy decisions, and supporting the provincially funded colleges. It has also stressed, to a larger extent than other provinces, training for non-university-bound youth via apprenticeship, and has been willing to invest in such training. Unlike provinces such as Ontario, Alberta has sought to develop an integrated set of provincially controlled active measures. However, the province has also ignored organized labour in its decision making, while increasing the scope of employers to set priorities and influence decisions.

Globalization and Labour Market Policy in Alberta

In chapter 2, Alberta's political economy was characterized as more closely resembling the liberal ideal type than other provinces in Canada, and departing from a 'pure' variant of liberal institutions in the manner in which business interests are privileged. Our hypothesis was that given the hegemonic centre-right rule, in the province, reinforced by pluralities in both the 1997 and 2001 elections (51.2 per cent and 61.8 per cent of the popular vote, respectively), the prospects for radical retrenchment would be high.

The evidence of this chapter paints a somewhat more complex picture. The successful privatization of liquor stores, highway maintenance, automobile licensing and registries, and some other activities early in the first Klein term in 1993, made the government believe that other of its activities could be privatized. The success of welfare reform (discussed in the next chapter), also early in the government's first mandate, suggested that policy reform and retrenchment was relatively simple. However, the attempt to privatize the enforcement of occupational health and safety, and employment standards, demonstrated this was not the case. The fact that these policy domains remained relatively unchanged is due, in part, to the unwillingness of the business community to support a fundamental departure from the existing norms. Certainly, the opposition of labour, community groups, and the opposition parties, and, in some cases, the civil service, was important; however, it was the voice (or the lack of it) of large employers such as the Canadian Association of Petroleum Producers that was heard the loudest by the Conservatives.

As one participant noted in an interview, 'It took a couple of years after the Klein election in 1993 for the pendulum to be put back closer to the middle,' so that by the government's second term there was little further interest in altering the status quo in labour market policy. As one writer put it, 'The Ralph Klein revolution clocked in at just two frantic years. It lasted until the end of 1995, when a gusher of oil, gas and lottery revenue replenished the treasury's reservoirs and lowered the anxiety felt by Albertans.'[65] The historically relatively lax standards in the province – both in content and in enforcement – provided little incentive for business to support moving into uncharted territories, especially when tax rates and other aspects of economic policy were of greater concern. Therefore it seems that Alberta represents a ground zero environment for liberalism.

It is workers' compensation, a field that in the other provinces received little notice, in which Alberta has been the most active. The debate in Alberta was initiated by a grass-roots, street level protest, which resulted in a partial reversal of the policy directions put into place during the early and mid-1990s. The fact that it was not resistance

Table 7.1. Retrenchment in Alberta Labour Market Policy, 1990–2003

	Long-term neo-liberal retrenchment
Industrial relations	Low
Active measures	Low
Occupational health & safety	Low-to-medium
Employment standards	Low-to-medium
Workers' compensation	Low-to-medium

from institutionalized labour or opposition parties that pressured the government highlights the limited room for manoeuver faced by groups seeking policy change in a right-hegemonic setting like Alberta.

In contrast, employment standards and labour relations have been controversial in other provinces we studied, but not so in Alberta where they have remained unchanged. Although government intended to make changes, these were rejected, or at least not supported, by key actors in the employer community. Moreover, over the study period there have not been any significant regulatory changes that shifted the imbalance of power between business and labour even further to the advantage of the former. However, with employment standards there was a decrease in the – always very constrained – enforcement function. In workplace health and safety, the government lately reversed some of the deterioration in enforcement although a degree of retrenchment and deregulation occurred. Finally, in active labour market policy, the government in the past decade has invested considerable effort to design policies that would support economic growth. In this process there has been no withdrawal of the state; indeed, the province has expanded its role, albeit in a manner that supports business and ignores organized labour. Table 7.1 summarizes the degree of long-term retrenchment observed in each of the labour market policy fields; the methodology for these calculations is detailed in the appendix.

It should be noted that in a province governed for decades by the same party, the personality of the individual ministers takes on a degree of importance. When the party in power does not change, a new minister can represent the most far-reaching change that is possible. During 1992–96, most components of labour market policy were under a right-wing minister, while later in the decade, under a different fiscal environment, the responsible minister came from the left wing of the party.

In conclusion, Alberta's pervasively market-oriented setting, a long-standing feature of that jurisdiction, is reflected in policies that were more market-oriented then elsewhere. As a result, although there was some retrenchment during the 1990s and the first years of the twenty-first century, it was not high, and certainly not of the scale that appeared likely in 1993. The institutional setting of the province was such that the status quo was functional for government, the business community, and the strongest elements of the private sector labour movement, each of whom had an interest in ensuring the relative stability of labour market policies. This was particularly so in the absence of a fiscal crisis after 1995, and in the presence of an expanding economy and labour market. The stasis was further added to by the continuity of the governing party, although the relative stasis in policy, as we illustrate in the next chapter, did not extend to all policy domains. Finally, the status quo in Alberta is one that is distinctly more liberal than that of the other provinces we analysed. We return to this issue in the concluding chapter.

8 Social Assistance and Employment: An Anomaly?

Social assistance policy has an important impact on labour markets. The accessibility and generosity of assistance benefits, which employable Canadians often turn to after exhausting their entitlement to federally administered employment insurance, conditions the terms on which people enter or exit the labour market. Furthermore, social assistance is important, and indeed more so in the past decade, for those in the labour market who are ineligible for Employment Insurance benefits, such as new entrants and those with marginal work histories. In recent years, moreover, provincial governments have modified their assistance systems to redefine categories of recipients previously deemed unemployable (such as single mothers) as employable, and to encourage – or coerce – recipients to return to employment.[1] Accordingly, in this chapter we examine not only developments for single employable welfare recipients, but also those related to benefits and labour market attachment for sole-support parents and couples with children.

This volume examines developments in this area separately from the five fields treated in chapters 4 through 7. The political, ideological, and fiscal parameters of policy-making in this field were sufficiently distinctive, we believed, to warrant separate analysis, using a somewhat different conceptual framework from that elaborated in chapters 1 and 2. Examining policy developments in relation to institutional dynamics that are specific to a particular policy sector is justified by the scholarly literature on policy communities. Coleman and Skogstad define a policy community 'to include all actors or potential actors with a direct or indirect interest in a policy area or function who share a common "policy focus," and who, with varying degrees of influence shape policy outcomes over the long run.'[2] Policy communities are sectorally specific and distinctive institutional settings that shape the policy outcomes in that sector.[3] Paul Pross argued that these settings vary considerably across policy fields, because policy-making in different fields is conditioned by distinctive societal and governmental actors, and by specific policy legacies.[4] For reasons that will be explained below, moreover, social assistance for employable persons may be more likely than other fields examined in this study to generate debate among the general public; and this public, and thus partisan, debate may also be expected to shape the policy outcome.[5]

The comparative political economy literature reviewed in the first two chapters, by contrast, concentrates on macro-level institutional features of developed democracies – the key defining features of the welfare state, production regime, and party system – to generate hypotheses about the probable behaviour of key societal and governmental actors in policy-making. These actors are also understood in macroscopic terms to include those generally most salient in such societies: the state, business, and labour. However, scholarship on social assistance policy stresses the role of actors and dynamics specific to this field in shaping policy developments. For instance, Piven and Cloward's classic 1971 study of social assistance policy in the United States identified pressure from recipients themselves, rather than business or labour influence, as the key *political* determinant of benefit reforms. Moynihan's study of American assistance policy during the 1960s saw officials in welfare bureaucracies – as opposed to societal influences or macro-level features of state structure – as the crucial actors.[6] Haddow's examination of assistance and poverty reform in Canada between the 1960s and the 1980s also identified recipient groups, not labour or business, as the main societal influence on policy-making, but concluded that these interests typically had few resources and limited impact.[7] The most important proximate influences on poverty reform emanated from federal and provincial welfare bureaucracies, supplemented, in the 1980s, by the Department of Finance.

Some distinctive features of assistance policy-making can, in fact, be inferred from the comparative political economy scholarship treated earlier. For instance, Esping-Andersen identifies specific *ideological* consequences of social assistance-type programs that are likely to distinguish policy-making in this area.[8] Because assistance measures are targeted at a minority of citizens, who have been less successful in the marketplace and may therefore be considered 'unworthy,' these measures are particularly susceptible to a 'welfare backlash.' Politicians, especially those of the centre-right, have an incentive to critique these benefits, and to appeal to the broad mass of taxpaying voters with promises to reduce them. In Canada, certainly, social assistance has been much more prominent as a concern in provincial politics in recent times than have any of the fields discussed in earlier chapters; and this attention often concentrates on proposals for welfare cuts. During the era of slow economic growth and rising social security costs that began in the 1970s, this ideological factor has been compounded by a *fiscal* one: assistance costs tend to rise quickly in periods of slow growth and high unemployment. As we will see, assistance programs experienced such a cost explosion during the early to mid-1990s. Moreover, these costs are usually born directly by individual taxpayers. By contrast, other labour market policy fields examined in this study are essentially regulatory in nature and require limited expenditures (industrial relations, employment standards, occupational health); involve moderate and relatively stable costs (active measures); or (in the case of workers' compensation) are expensive, but have discrete budgets that are funded directly by business and are therefore subject to political debate between business and organized labour, the macro-level actors central to earlier chapters of this study.

Some observers have proposed the concept of a 'workfare state' to characterize the evolution of assistance programs in recent years. Pressures of the type identified above, they argue, led to the considerable strengthening of efforts to encourage assistance recipients to return to work. As we will see, provinces have indeed sought to enhance recipients' employability and their willingness to return to work since 1990. According to this argument, however, these efforts have resulted in a fundamental retreat from a post-war commitment to provide needy citizens with assistance as a matter of right.[9] Understood thus, workfare is a form of what we term neo-liberal retrenchment, reflecting pressures to curtail market-inhibiting features of welfare states. If true, this should be reflected in a significant decline of assistance benefits and caseloads below levels that existed during the post-war years, a possibility that is examined empirically in the next section; it should be reflected as well in qualitative changes in program administration, a matter explored in subsequent sections of this chapter.

Testing the Retrenchment Argument

Has the distinctive political, financial, and ideological situation of social assistance meant that partisanship and globalization shaped developments in this domain differently than in those addressed in the preced-

Figure 8.1. Provincial Expenditures on Social Assistance by Province 1989–2002

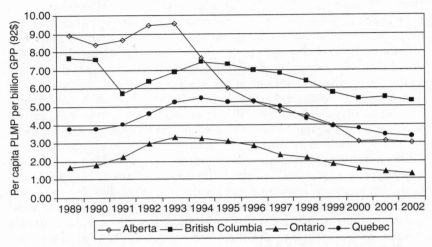

Source: Compiled by the authors from data provided by Statistics Canada, CANSIM.[11]

ing chapters? This section addresses the possibility that there has been significant globalization-induced retrenchment in assistance measures for employable persons since 1990; the detailed discussions of policy developments in each province that follow add a consideration of partisan influences as well.

Based on Statistics Canada's CANSIM database, figure 8.1 shows total social assistance expenditures per capita per GPP for the four provinces examined here since 1989. The expenditures include those for the non-employable caseload, those that are disabled or are otherwise not expected to work. They are, therefore, at best an imperfect reflection of changing benefit levels for employable recipients, our specific concern. Since 1994 for Ontario, Quebec, and British Columbia, and since 1993 for Alberta, these expenditures have decreased. The lower level of provincial expenditures in Ontario is partly a result of the municipal contribution to the social assistance program.[10]

Data from the National Council of Welfare (NCW) provides a more precise measure of policy change regarding employable recipients, as they are disaggregated by family type. Consequently, we rely mainly on these in our analysis. Tables 8.1 to 8.5 (see pp. 205–210) present assistance rate and caseload data from the NCW for our provinces. Table 8.1

Table 8.1. Provincial Social Assistance Benefits in Constant (2002) Dollars

	1990	1992	1994	1996	1998	2000	2002	2003	Change, 1990–2003
Quebec									
Single employable	6,667	7,133	7,002	6,744	6,444	6,372	6,444	6,367	– 4.5%
1 parent, 1 child	12,164	12,641	13,453	12,957	11,862	10,784	10,637	10,471	–13.9%
Couple, 2 children	14,587	15,530	15,783	15,201	13,909	12,562	12,388	12,202	–16.4%
Ontario									
Single employable	9,174	9,741	9,716	7,400	7,259	6,941	6,623	6,444	–29.8%
1 parent, 1 child	16,898	17,632	17,619	13,421	12,776	11,625	10,708	10,321	–38.9%
Couple, 2 children	22,171	23,081	22,829	17,341	16,380	14,583	13,146	12,599	–43.2%
Alberta									
Single employable	6,124	6,712	5,518	5,314	5,287	5,056	4,824	4,694	–23.4%
1 parent, 1 child	11,483	12,024	10,727	10,331	10,066	9,398	8,565	8,450	–26.4%
Couple, 2 children	16,918	18,678	16,889	16,435	15,855	14,538	13,073	12,679	–25.1%
British Columbia									
Single employable	7,400	7,507	7,720	6,891	6,720	6,478	6,251	6,062	–18.1%
1 parent, 1 child	13,214	13,534	13,918	13,448	12,726	11,691	10,543	10,083	–23.7%
Couple, 2 children	16,445	17,123	17,725	17,150	16,060	14,412	12,973	12,217	–25.7%

Sources: NCW, *Welfare Incomes 2002*, pp. 38–39; *Welfare Incomes 2003*, pp. 37, 39.

reports typical annual incomes for three family configurations in receipt of assistance; the heads of these units would now be considered employable. These figures include additional benefits, including tax credits, made available to the needy by the province. Table 8.2 combines these figures with federal income-contingent payments to recipients; these now include the federal National Child Benefit Supplement (NCBS) and the GST Credit; it shows the total income-related benefit available from both levels of government. When Ottawa created the NCBS in 1998, it increased its payments to assistance recipients. However, the provinces studied 'clawed back' these sums, leaving recipients with no net change in income; in effect, they used the federal measure to alleviate part of their own assistance costs. This is reflected in a decline in provincial assistance rates reported in table 8.1, but has no effect on data reported in table 8.2. In assessing whether there has been retrenchment in the assistance field, one must bear in mind that a cut in provincial rates, as reported in table 8.1, may not reduce total income for assistance recipients, reflected in table 8.2. Table 8.3 compares total welfare incomes (from table 8.2) to average total income for comparable family units in each province. Table 8.4 traces the evolution of provincial assistance caseloads since 1990, and table 8.5 measures these as a percentage of provincial populations.

Statistics of the type made available by the NCW have been used to suggest that there has been substantial retrenchment in Canadian social assistance since the early 1990s; that is, that benefit rates have been cut severely for most categories of recipients in almost all jurisdictions; and that caseloads have plummeted, primarily because of more severe eligibility rules. Substantial changes made by Ottawa to its cost-sharing arrangements for provincial social assistance in 1996 (discussed in chapter 3) are alleged to have contributed to this transformation. The format in which the NCW reports its data sometimes encourages this perception. In the 2002 edition of its annual report, *Welfare Incomes*, for instance, the NCW provided a consolidated table of provincial assistance benefits (such as is presented in table 8.1), stressing that these have fallen since the late 1980s. But it offered no consolidated data for total welfare incomes (table 8.2), which reflects real income available to recipients, and where reductions have been smaller. Moreover, the report displayed a table for the evolution of provincial caseloads only since 1995, when they were near their historic peak, but not for earlier years. A systematic examination of data since 1990, supplemented with more sporadic statistics available from the 1980s, suggests a more quali-

Table 8.2. Total Welfare Income in Constant (2002) Dollars

	1990	1992	1994	1996	1998	2000	2002	2003	Change, 1990–2003
Quebec									
Single employable	6,793[108]	7,145	7,160	6,924	6,599	6,560	6,654	6,576	−3.2%
1 parent, 1 child	13,806	14,466	15,283	14,565	14,005	13,572	13,800	13,691	−0.8%
Couple, 2 children	17,548	18,560	18,794	17,966	17,327	17,067	17,642	17,576	+0.2%
Ontario									
Single employable	9,261	10,082	10,092	7,722	7,524	7,128	6,833	6,653	−28.2%
1 parent, 1 child	18,738	19,667	19,645	15,372	15,007	14,418	13,871	13,541	−27.7%
Couple, 2 children	25,105	26,192	25,919	20,317	19,836	19,088	18,400	17,973	−28.4%
Alberta									
Single employable	6,541	7,243	5,964	5,703	5,615	5,317	5,034	4,903	−25.0%
1 parent, 1 child	13,205	13,920	12,616	12,132	12,153	12,080	11,634	11,576	−12.3%
Couple, 2 children	20,072	21,898	20,090	19,520	19,417	19,145	18,412	18,135	−9.7%
British Columbia									
Single employable	7,533	6,664	7,559	6,855	6,785	6,642	6,461	6,271	−16.7%
1 parent, 1 child	15,048	15,559	15,943	15,399	14,960	14,487	13,706	13,304	−11.6%
Couple, 2 children	19,488	20,234	20,838	20,126	19,516	18,917	18,227	17,598	−9.7%

Sources: NCW, *Welfare Incomes*, various years.

Table 8.3. Welfare Incomes as % of Average Total Incomes

	1990	1994	1998	2002	Change, 1990–2002
Quebec					
Single employable	26.6	29.3	26.1	23.3	−12.4
1 parent, 1 child	44.5	54.4	44.6	39.3	−11.7
Couple, 2 children	26.0	28.9	24.9	22.8	−12.3
Ontario					
Single employable	29.2	33.4	24.3	19.6	−32.9
1 parent, 1 child	59.5	60.3	40.0	34.2	−42.5
Couple, 2 children	31.5	33.1	23.5	20.2	−35.9
Alberta					
Single employable	21.6	20.4	19.7	15.6	−27.8
1 parent, 1 child	43.0	40.6	36.4	27.5	−36.0
Couple, 2 children	27.6	28.1	23.9	22.5	−18.5
British Columbia					
Single employable	24.8	26.5	23.5	21.2	−14.5
1 parent, 1 child	47.9	50.9	45.1	39.6	−17.3
Couple, 2 children	24.9	27.6	25.0	22.3	−10.4

Sources: Welfare data from *Welfare Incomes*, published in Ottawa by NCW, the year after date on cover; income data from CANSIM, table 2020403.

fied conclusion regarding retrenchment in the assistance field. Overall, the degree of retrenchment has been very uneven, varying from low in Quebec, to medium in Ontario and British Columbia, to medium-high in Alberta (see table 8.6; the methodology used for deriving this table is explained in the appendix). These variations are broadly consistent with the hypotheses presented in chapter 2, based on the distinctive institutional settings of each province: there, we anticipated that the prospects for retrenchment would be lowest in CME-tinged Quebec, higher in polarized BC, and greatest in Alberta, where the market-oriented political centre-right encounters only weak opposition.

Quebec's contribution to the incomes of two of three recipient categories reported in table 8.1 fell noticeably (by more than 10 per cent) between 1990 and 2003; but this did not cause a significant change in the real value of total incomes for recipients, reported in table 8.2. The decline in provincial benefits has been compensated by increased federal spending under the NCBS. In addition, assistance does not appear to be much harder to qualify for; the 2003 caseload was comparable to the figure for 1990 (table 8.4), and the proportion of Quebecers receiv-

Table 8.4. Estimated Number of People on Welfare, 31 March

	1990	1992	1994	1996	1998	2000	2002	2003	Change, 1990–2003	Change, 1994–2003
Quebec	555,900	674,900	787,200	813,000	725,700	618,900	560,800	544,200	–2%	–33%
Ontario	675,700	1,184,700	1,379,000	1,214,600	1,091,300	802,000	687,600	673,900	–0.2%	–51%
Alberta	148,800	188,300	138,500	105,600	77,000	64,800	53,800	57,800	–61%	–58%
BC	216,000	279,300	353,500	369,900	297,400	262,400	241,200	180,700	–16%	–49%
Canada	1,930,100	2,723,000	3,100,200	2,937,100	2,577,500	2,085,100	1,842,600	1,745,600	–5%	–44%

Sources: Data from NCW, *Welfare Incomes, 2003*, p. 83; *Welfare Incomes, 2002*, p. 78; *Welfare Incomes, 1994*, p. 46; and *Another Look at Welfare Reform*.

Table 8.5. Estimated Number of People on Welfare as a % of Population, 31 March

	1990	1992	1994	1996	1998	2000	2002	2003	Change, 1990–2003	Change, 1994–2003
Quebec	7.9	9.5	10.9	11.2	9.9	8.4	7.5	7.3	– 7.6	–34.8
Ontario	6.6	11.2	12.7	11.0	9.6	6.9	5.7	5.5	–16.7	–56.7
Alberta	5.8	7.2	5.1	3.8	2.7	2.2	1.7	1.8	–69.0	–52.6
BC	6.6	8.1	9.6	9.5	7.5	6.5	5.9	4.4	–33.3	–54.2
Canada	7.0	9.6	10.7	9.9	8.5	6.8	5.9	5.5	–21.4	–48.6

Sources: Welfare caseload data from table 8.4; population data from Statistics Canada, CANSIM, table 510001.

Table 8.6. Partisan 'Swings' and Retrenchment in Social Assistance Policy, 1990–2003

	Short-term partisan 'swings'	Long-term neo-liberal retrenchment
Ontario	High	Medium
Quebec	Low	Low
BC	High	Medium
Alberta	NA	Medium-to-high

ing assistance had declined by a modest 7.6 per cent during those years. In between, Quebec's caseload, like those of the other provinces discussed here, except Alberta, rose substantially; the generosity of assistance rates (reported in table 8.1) also increased somewhat during these years. But as with these rates, 2003 caseload levels appeared to represent a return to a status quo ante, disrupted for a time by the severe recession of the early 1990s, not a form of retrenchment unprecedented in the post-war years. Retrenchment can be said to have happened in Quebec in only one restricted sense: since 1990, the incomes of employable assistance recipients fell noticeably (a little more than 10 per cent) in relation to average incomes for comparable family units (table 8.3). Assistance recipients are not worse off than in 1990 in absolute terms, but have not shared in the province's rising incomes.

In no province has assistance been subject to such dramatic variations as in Ontario. Benefit levels fell by between 29.8 per cent and 43.2 per cent from 1990 to 2003. Even when the federal NCBS is considered (table 8.2), all three categories of Ontario recipients were about 28 per cent worse off in 2003 than in 1990. Relative to average incomes (table 8.3), welfare incomes have fallen by a third or more. The assistance caseload has declined by half since its 1994 peak (table 8.4). Yet even in Ontario, the case for retrenchment must be qualified. First, the province's caseload is again roughly comparable to its 1990 level in absolute numbers, and about five-sixths of that level in relative terms. Moreover, NCW data from the 1980s, available uniquely for Ontario, suggests that the post-1995 entitlement restrictions that contributed to these figures broadly returned the province to the situation that prevailed before the Conservatives left office in 1985. As in most policy fields discussed in chapter 4, the policies of the Harris Tory government represented a dramatic policy reversal, but one that restored the status quo ante, rather than representing an unprecedented departure from post-war norms. For instance, in inflation-adjusted dollars, total welfare incomes

for single parents with one child in Ontario in 2003 ($13,541) are compa-
rable to those available in 1985 (about $13,600) or 1975 ($13,611), and
somewhat higher than the benefit available in 1980 ($11,613) or 1970
($11,826). Assistance benefits available to a couple with two children
represented about 22.5 per cent of average incomes for families of that
type in Ontario between 1975 and 1985; the comparable figure for 2002
was 20.2 per cent (table 8.3).[12] As in Quebec, assistance recipients appear to have lost ground in relative (in relation to average incomes)
rather than absolute (the value and accessibility of benefits) terms. But
compared to 1990, at least, this relative loss was much more severe, and
these benefits were available to a significantly smaller share of the
population. The increase in benefit generosity during the late 1980s and
early 1990s was also much greater and more enduring, and the subsequent cuts no doubt were comparably more painful for employable
recipients.

British Columbia shows evidence of a pattern of medium retrenchment, although – as with the policy fields discussed in chapter 6 – one
must approach recent developments there tentatively, because the impact of Liberal policy changes since 2001 may not yet be fully manifest,
and because there is less data available for the pre-1990 era than is the
case for Ontario. In 2004, the assistance caseload had declined by more
than half (from 353,000 to 161,000) since 1994, but had fallen by a more
modest one-sixth since 1990, and was at levels comparable to those that
prevailed during the mid- to late-1980s. Assistance rates in 2003 were
lower than in 1990; but when total welfare incomes are considered, the
decline ranged between about one-tenth and one-sixth for the three
recipient categories reported in table 8.2. As a percentage of average
incomes, assistance benefits fell between 1990 and 2002, but by a magnitude – between 10.4 per cent and 17.3 per cent – that was much closer
to Quebec's modest decline than to Ontario's or Alberta's more substantial ones.

The extent of retrenchment was greatest in Alberta. The most compelling evidence of this relates to the assistance caseload. While, in absolute terms, this figure was 5 per cent below 1990 levels in 2003, and 21
per cent lower relative to the population size, for all Canadian provinces, the caseload had fallen by 61 per cent in absolute terms and by 69
per cent in relative terms in Alberta. Even in 1982, when 340,000 fewer
Canadians were on social assistance overall, almost twice as many
Albertans received assistance (92,800) as did 20 years later. Assistance
benefit rates, and benefits as a ratio of average incomes, also had fallen

markedly since 1990 (respectively, between 23.4 per cent and 26.4 per cent and between 18.5 per cent and 36 per cent); and although these reductions were lower than for Ontario, they continued a pattern of decline that originated in the 1980s, and whose cumulative impact was matched in no other province. Provincial benefits fell by between 35 per cent (for a couple with two children) and 47.8 per cent (for single employable persons) between 1986 and 2002.[13] Despite Alberta's relative prosperity, its assistance benefits for single employable persons and for single parents with one child were lower than for the other provinces discussed here in 2003 (table 8.1); they had been highest, or second highest, among all provinces for these categories in 1986.

The curtailment of assistance benefits for employable persons after 1990 did not proceed at the same rhythm or to the same degree in our four provinces. It was also accompanied by a variety of qualitative policy changes, especially in relation to employability measures and income exemptions, whose consequences are not fully reflected in the statistics discussed in this section. In three provinces, moreover, cuts followed a period of modest or substantial expansion in the generosity of benefits during the early 1990s. These specific features, which reflect the evolving and distinct partisan contexts of assistance policy making in each jurisdiction, are now examined.

Ontario

The NDP assumed power in 1990 with an election platform that called for an 'increase in social assistance rates to ensure that social assistance provides a real safety net.'[14] Indeed, the newly elected government quickly committed itself to reforming welfare in the directions proposed in a major review, entitled *Transitions*, prepared in 1988 for the previous Liberal government.[15] Shortly after assuming power the NDP increased welfare benefits in a manner that reflected the annual increases made by the previous Liberal government since 1985. But the economy was now in recession, with unemployment increasing by 54 per cent in 1991 and a further 12 per cent in 1992. Not surprisingly, caseloads swelled by 37 per cent in 1991, followed by a 22 per cent increase in 1992. The number of social assistance recipients, including children, doubled between 1990 and 1994 (see table 8.4).

In early 1991, an external advisory group on social assistance policy established by the outgoing Liberal government in 1990, released its first report, containing a number of recommendations that were immediately implemented.[16] Among these was extending eligibility (to refugees and the homeless); making the Supports to Employment program, which allowed social assistance recipients to receive employment income, more generous by increasing the amount of income a recipient could earn and still remain eligible for assistance (commonly termed *income exemptions*); and creating a permanent council of consumers, composed solely of welfare recipients, to provide advice to the government. A number of administrative changes were also made, such as eliminating mandatory home visits by social workers. These early NDP measures mirrored Liberal ones between 1985 and 1989 that also increased the benefits of, and the eligibility for, welfare. For instance, in 1987, in response to pressure from client and women's groups, the government changed a long-standing regulation that included the income of a cohabiting partner in determining eligibility. The new 'spouse in the house' regulation allowed a man and woman to live together for three years before having to demonstrate that theirs was not a spousal relationship. This represented a significant extension of eligibility.[17] As well, the Liberals included community groups and other representatives of social assistance recipients in policy consultations, a practice largely unknown under the Conservatives.

But while the NDP government initially adopted an expansionary policy towards social assistance, it inherited an economy in decline and rising social assistance caseloads. Reacting to the explosive growth in caseloads, as well as decreasing revenues, the NDP began in 1992 to embark on policies that diverged from its previous ideological position as well as the views of key stakeholders and social assistance clients.[18] In late 1992, the Supports to Employment program was revised to make it available only to those already on welfare for three months. This change prevented the working poor from being eligible for welfare payments, and was explicitly designed to reduce the growth in social assistance caseloads.[19] Increases in benefits were limited to 4.8 per cent in 1992 and 1 per cent in 1993, with benefits decreasing in 1994 for two-adult households. Administratively, after 1992 the NDP took a series of steps to contain costs, such as a comprehensive file review, where all social assistance cases were reviewed to detect overpayments.

In June 1992, the advisory group released its final report, *Time for Action*, whose recommendations again echoed those of *Transitions*, calling for rates to be increased annually based on a market basket of goods and services. As well, the report recommended that recipients who do not participate in a job search, further education, or related activities 'should not have their allowance or benefits reduced.'[20] In rejecting workfare, *Time for Action* also followed *Transitions*, which 'strongly reject[ed] the argument that the "spur of poverty" is still essential in the drive to self-sufficiency.'[21] Instead of proceeding with the *Time for Action* report, the government released its own paper, *Turning Point*, in May 1993.[22] This vague document sketched out a new income support program for all low-income families with children. However, it was silent on the question of whether some type of workfare would be introduced, as the cabinet was unable to reach consensus on this matter. The lack of consensus was partly due to the composition of the NDP cabinet, in which nearly half of the members were women who generally opposed forcing recipients, particularly single mothers, to engage in training or other activities in exchange for welfare. Also opposed to any workfare-related initiatives were labour unions, an important constituency of the NDP.[23] In any case, by 1993 the government was firmly set on a course of expenditure reduction and unsure of its ability to undertake a major overhaul of social assistance in the last stages of its mandate.[24] *Turning Point*, prepared entirely within the cabinet office, marked a major shift away from the stakeholder participation in assistance policy favoured since the late 1980s, a trend that would strengthen after 1995 under the Conservatives.

In rejecting workfare, the NDP was out of step with trends in the United States and in some other Canadian provinces. American workfare programs, implemented by both Democratic and Republican administrations, were credited with reducing program costs and caseloads, while increasingly shaping policy discussions and program design in provinces such as Alberta.[25] The dramatic increases in caseloads in Ontario during the early 1990s, and the NDP's dismissal of workfare – which putatively had reduced caseloads in other jurisdictions – allowed the opposition parties, especially the Conservatives, to criticize the NDP for inaction and mismanagement. During the 1995 election campaign the Conservatives made social assistance and the introduction of workfare a central issue.[26]

It should be noted, moreover, that the NDP government was hampered, unlike Quebec, in its policy options, not only by economic factors and the associated decline in revenues and increases in social assistance expenditures, but also by shifts in federal government policy vis-à-vis the Canada Assistance Plan discussed in chapter 3. The province estimated that by 1993, the federal government covered only 28 per cent of welfare costs compared to 50 per cent in 1989.[27]

In summary, the NDP years began with an ambitious effort to create a generous welfare program, building on similar initiatives by the previous Liberal administration, while also involving stakeholders and clients in the policy process.[28] However, the deep recession, in combination with higher benefits and broader eligibility, caused caseloads to increase dramatically and revenues to drop (aided by decreases in federal transfers). Beginning in 1992, the NDP acted to limit eligibility and benefits. In doing so, it was forced to marginalize the stakeholder groups first courted by the Liberals, and brought further into the policy-making process by the NDP. However, the NDP did resist pressure to introduce workfare.

The Progressive Conservatives assumed power in June 1995, as the economy was recovering from the deep recession. The party's election platform – The Common Sense Revolution – had social assistance as a centrepiece, and its election campaign was partially focused on this issue. The platform borrowed heavily from reforms undertaken in the United States and Alberta in the early 1990s, including the imposition of workfare requirements. It contended that assistance costs had reached a level that 'we can't afford.'[29] Among its first actions, in keeping with its election platform, the new government reduced welfare benefits (except for the disabled) by 21.6 per cent, while allowing this amount – $143 for a single individual – to be earned back under the Supports to Employment program. It also limited eligibility through a number of measures: a province-wide welfare fraud hotline was established, individuals 16 to 17 years of age were deemed ineligible for social assistance, two adults living together were made immediately responsible for household expenses (eliminating the existing three-year waiting period), and a three-month waiting period was imposed for those who left employment voluntarily without cause or were fired with cause. The new government also quickly dismantled the consultation mechanisms, including the council of consumers, established by the preceding administrations. Social action groups, such as the Ontario Coalition Against Poverty, unsuccessfully sought to influence social assistance policy through protests, marches, and the occupation of empty buildings and politicians' offices. Further restrictions were introduced in subsequent years; those convicted of assistance fraud were made permanently ineligible for welfare; health care benefits were restricted and appeals limited. In 2000, the Supports for Employment program was altered so that recipients who receive welfare for more than one year could retain only 15 per cent, rather than 25 per cent, of employment earnings. Administrative practice also shifted with the implementation of centralized call centres for the first phase of the application process. These centres have been criticized as an administrative means to discourage individuals from completing applications for welfare.[30]

In 1996, the government introduced Ontario Works, which required that all employable clients, defined as including single parents with children older than age 3, either participate in structured job search programs, or accept work placements in the public, NGO, or private sectors. Previously sole-support parents were exempt from work requirements until their children were 6 years of age. Mandatory work placements were rare under Ontario Works, with most clients in some form of job-search program, 'sometimes consisting of little more than an orientation course followed by an individual, unstructured job-search as was the case prior to the implementation of Ontario Works.'[31] It was estimated that only 2 per cent of eligible welfare recipients were actually engaged in placements.[32] The small number of placements reflected several factors, including union opposition and the fact that workfare programs are expensive to operate. Nevertheless, Ontario Works represented a major departure from the policies pursued by both the Liberals and New Democrats. Ontario Works became both rhetorical workfare – in that the government could announce that all those on welfare were required to work, even when this was not the case – and literal workfare, in that clients could be (and were) denied assistance for failing to engage in the mandated activities. In its extensive publicity campaign on social assistance, including 'reports to taxpayers on welfare reform' mailed to all households, the government stressed that its new, tougher approach to welfare was responsible for the declining caseload.[33]

A Social Assistance Reform Act was introduced in 1997, for which the government allowed a legislative committee to conduct public consultation for only four days. The legislation broadly followed the recommendations of the *Transitions and Time for Action* reports with regard to the administration of social assistance. For instance, it consolidated three previously separate acts, unified the delivery structure with municipalities given responsibility for delivering benefits for all clients other than the disabled, and reduced the number of eligibility categories, while streamlining other aspects of the program.

The Progressive Conservative era was one of policy coherence, in that its policy initiatives matched its election platforms. The buoyant economy and strong labour market, coupled with major policy changes aimed at reducing caseloads, resulted in substantial and sustained caseload reductions. Total caseloads declined continuously from their 1994 peak, so that by 2002 they had returned to their 1990 level.

The Conservatives continued the centralization trend begun by the NDP, as well as completely eliminating stakeholder involvement. The introduction of workfare, and its application to more sole-support parents, although largely rhetorical, limited caseload growth by stigmatizing those on welfare. By 2002, with the exception of workfare, the social assistance domain largely had returned to its pre-1985 state, with low benefits, limited eligibility, an intrusive role for case workers, the exclusion of stakeholders in policy-making, and considerable centralization. It was only with regard to workfare that the Conservatives shifted policy in a direction that had not existed before 1985, as the rhetoric of workfare became a feature of the social assistance regime; only a very small proportion of recipients ever became directly subject to such requirements, though many other individuals may have been affected indirectly, effectively being deterred from seeking assistance or remaining on the assistance roles.

During the late 2003 election, social assistance and workfare played little role in the election platforms of the losing Conservatives or the successful Liberals. The Liberals did campaign on a platform that included increasing welfare rates to match increases in the cost of living. Shortly after taking office the government postponed this in order to achieve a balanced budget during its first year in office.[34] However, in late 2003, the Liberals lifted the lifetime welfare ban for those convicted of welfare fraud, arguably the most severe of the policies introduced by the Conservatives.[35]

Quebec

Like Ontario and BC, Quebec experienced a significant increase in its assistance caseload and expenses during the early to mid-1990s; and by 2002 these figures had again returned to something like their 1990 levels. Unlike the two aforementioned provinces, however, partisanship played only a very modest role in shaping assistance policy for employable persons during the intervening years. The two main legislative reforms of this period, implemented by the Liberals in 1989–90 and by the Parti Québécois in 1998, both sought to enhance the availability of employability measures to assistance recipients, and to encourage them to return to study or to the workforce. But both stayed well clear of using compulsory measures to do so. Disappointed that the 1998 reforms had not had a greater impact, the Charest Liberal administration considered more restrictive reforms when it came to power in 2003, but these ambitions were quickly abandoned. This relative absence of partisan polarization is consistent with the general pattern observed in chapter 5 for other fields of Quebec labour market policy, and with the hypotheses set forth in chapter 2 about the likely impact of partisanship on labour market policy in Quebec.

The Bourassa Liberals introduced Bill 37 in May 1989; the legislation was implemented for new assistance recipients the following August, and for existing ones in August 1990.[36] Its most significant general feature was to introduce a clear distinction between claimants who were deemed employable and those who were not. Most recipients, including most single mothers, were assigned to the former category. Unemployable clients received increased benefits under the legislation. Employable ones were to be offered the option of accepting subsidized workplaces, mostly in the voluntary and public sector, or to receive employability-enhancing training. The subsidized workplace program was introduced on an experimental basis in 1989, and later expanded. These were not compulsory, but those who refused them would see their benefits cut by $100 per month (approximately from $550 to $450).[37] A recipient would also receive $89 less than before per month if he or she cohabited with another recipient, or with parents. A punitive lower assistance rate for those under 30 was eliminated by the legislation, resulting in a substantial increase of benefits for most young people; but such claimants, especially those under 21, could be subjected to a deduction if their parents were judged to be still partly responsible for their welfare.

The Péquistes opposition protested that the reforms were harsh; but the pre-1984 PQ government had, in fact, been the first in Quebec to experiment with employability measures, and it had released a white paper on this subject before leaving office in 1984.[38] Quebec's vocal social advocacy groups also denounced the reforms as punitive and unfair.[39] As the data reported in table 8.4 indicates, however, Bill 37 did not achieve its goal of reducing assistance dependency. On the contrary, in the wake of the deep early 1990s recession, the province's caseload rose sharply from about 556,000 in 1990 to 787,000 when the Liberals left office in 1994. Welfare costs also increased steeply during these years. By 1994, criticisms of the legislation as overly restrictive were overshadowed by concerns that – in a weak employment market – its employability measures were having little effect. Clients who accepted work terms or employability measures often found no permanent jobs afterwards, and ended up returning to the assistance roles.[40] Desperate to contain the swelling numbers, Employment Minister André Bourbeau expanded the use of surveillance officers – nicknamed 'boubou-macoutes' by critics – who were assigned the task of using fairly intrusive measures to ensure that recipients were not cheating the system.[41] This too did not halt the caseload's sharp upward trend.

Under these circumstances, the Parti Québécois abandoned thoughts of easing access to social assistance, or of reducing its employability features, when they came to power. In July 1995, the PQ income security minister made comments that seemed to presage a relaxing of employment-oriented provisions of Bill 37, but when a consultation paper on reform was released in December 1996, it became clear that the government would reinforce these.[42] In the interim, continuing a pattern instigated by the Liberals in 1993, it took a number of administrative steps to strengthen employment incentives; for instance, the penalty for refusing a work program increased from $100 to $150 per month. An advisory report submitted to the government by economist Pierre Fortin had recommended that a broader reform add further restrictions, including the complete denial of benefits to recipients who refused to participate in training measures. Another report, authored primarily by Camil Bouchard, proposed less coercive changes.[43]

Bill 182, the PQ's main social assistance reform, was released in December 1997. It sought to expand employability-enhancing measures, and created additional penalties for young people who refused to participate in these; it also increased benefits for recipients who found jobs and expanded some other benefits. The number of recipient classes was reduced significantly and the separate programs for employable and unemployable recipients were reconfigured, but observers considered that the assistance system's broad design had changed little. Recipients under the age of 25 would now be offered individualized *parcours vers l'emploi*, or plans for returning to work, overseen by a welfare case worker; refusal to participate in a *parcours* would result in a reduction of benefits of $150 per month. A recipient's welfare cheque could also be seized for non-payment of rent. On the other hand, the penalty for cohabiting with another recipient was eliminated, several allowable income and asset ceilings were increased (resulting in benefit increases for many), and a $500 bonus was provided for those who found and kept a job for a month; recipients deemed unemployable also received benefit increases. The changes were expected to increase annual costs by $80 million, but this would be more than offset by declining assistance roles in a stronger economy, and by the transfer of some recipients to employment programs administered by Emploi-Québec.[44]

The legislation encountered considerable criticism. The opposition Liberals referred to it as a 'coercive regime.' Social advocacy groups and some academic commentators denounced the legislation as regressive; they were particularly critical of the proposed penalty for young people who refused to participate in a *parcours*, and of the provision regarding non-payment of rent; and they demanded that all recipients, regardless of status, be guaranteed a minimum assistance benefit. In the face of this criticism, ministry officials had to engage in extensive discussions with the social groups to mollify some of their concerns. The final version of the legislation delayed implementation of the penalty for non-participation in a *parcours* by one year, and relaxed certain other provisions of the legislation; these changes added an estimated $17 million to its cost.[45] Subsequent PQ initiatives, such as Destination emploi (launched in May 1999 for employable persons under the age of 55) and Solidarité jeunesse (a voluntary re-employment measure for young recipients, started in November 2000), were designed to enhance the employment-oriented features of the assistance system.[46] This combination of increased employability measures and penalties on the one hand, and of increased benefits on the other, resulted in little evident overall change in Quebec's social assistance system, which interviewed officials judged similar to its configuration under the Liberals' Bill 37. Total welfare incomes for the categories of employable assistance recipients in Quebec reported in table 8.2 changed little between 1998 and 2002, and, as we have seen, were very similar in the latter year to their 1990 level. The many steps taken by the PQ to encourage a return to employment may have contributed to the significant decline (by about 160,000) in the province's assistance caseload between 1998 and 2002 (see table 8.4). But this decline was also facilitated by the rapid employment growth of these years, and reflected nationwide trends. Moreover, the 2002 caseload of about 561,000 was almost identical to the level that prevailed in 1990, before employment incentives had been implemented for most recipients.

Another assistance-related measure emerged from Quebec's 1996 Socio-Economic Summit, at which the province's business and labour communities agreed on a plan to eliminate the province's deficit by

2000. To mollify the opposition of social advocacy groups, who were concerned that this would be done at the expense of the least advantaged, government and the participating nongovernmental interests agreed to establish a $250 million Anti-Poverty Fund to be financed by temporary supplementary payroll deductions for workers and corporate tax charges on employers. The funds were to be expended on employment measures for poor people, especially assistance recipients; eligible measures would be decided upon by a complex network of provincial, regional, and local committees, which included business, labour, and social advocacy representatives (see table 5.1).[47] When the earmarked taxes expired in 2000, the fund was renewed for another three years with a reduced budget, now paid for from general government revenues.[48]

During the 2003 election campaign, the Liberals did not advocate major changes in assistance policy. Rather than proposing a market-oriented curtailment of benefits, they promised to index them against inflation, and to set a minimum level for assistance benefits. The latter commitment was first made the previous December, when the PQ had passed legislation designed to extend and entrench its anti-poverty initiative.[49] Following the April election, however, as the new Liberal administration encountered unexpected budgetary constraints, it appeared that significant restrictions were in the offing. The Liberals' first budget sought to reduce assistance costs by $241 million, and anticipated that the caseload would fall by over 25,000 during the next year.[50] In July, the government announced a Place à l'emploi initiative to achieve this; it proposed to have new recipients referred to Emploi-Québec within 24 hours for employment assistance, and announced monthly penalties of from $75 to $300 for those who refused to participate in employment measures.[51] When preliminary versions of the Liberals' plan for implementing the December 2002 anti-poverty law appeared in the press during the autumn, they implied a desire to go further towards enforcing work requirements and restricting access to benefits. This was greeted by loud protests from social advocacy groups, and by quieter complaints from some Liberal MNAs.[52]

By February 2004, however, it was clear that Place à l'emploi would not meet its caseload-reduction targets; moreover, internal government studies, which appeared in the press, suggested that the province's employability programs generally, including the parcours, were having little success in returning recipients to work, and that few recipients were being penalized under these measures.[53] This was followed, in early April, by release of a new anti-poverty program, which completely reversed the trajectory that the Liberals embarked upon a year earlier. It created additional incentives for recipients to return to work or enlist in employability measures, but abolished penalties for those who refused to participate in such measures. A Prime au travail was established, at a cost of $240 million, to provide a wage supplement for the working poor; a minimum assistance rate for all employable recipients, except those guilty of fraud, would commence in 2005; assistance benefits would be fully indexed against inflation for unemployable recipients, but only partly indexed for employable ones. While those participating in employment measures therefore were offered more 'carrots,' the use of 'sticks' to encourage them to do so was abandoned.[54] In light of these recent developments under the centre-right Quebec Liberals, and in view of the substantial continuity of the policies of the preceding centre-left Parti Québécois administration with those of the earlier Liberal government, it seems clear that partisanship has had a very limited impact on assistance policy in Quebec since 1990; with programs that are not noticeably less generous or more coercive than those that existed in that year, there is also little evidence of market-oriented program retrenchment in recent years.

British Columbia

Social assistance benefits in British Columbia rose modestly, or were constant, during the first half of the 1990s; but by 2002 total welfare incomes had fallen below their 1990 levels for the categories of recipients reported upon in table 8.2. The province's caseload skyrocketed between 1990 and 1996; thereafter it plummeted, but remained above 1990 levels in 2002. Throughout this period, assistance policy represented contested ground between BC's centre-left NDP and that party's centre-right opponents. But polarization was less than it was for the other areas of labour market policy discussed in chapter 6. Although different in important respects, both of BC's main parties moved assistance policy for employable persons in a similar direction after 1994 – towards greater emphasis on work incentives and some narrowing of eligibility for benefits. The post-2001, centre-right Liberal administration nevertheless went further in this direction than had its NDP predecessors. The available evidence from benefit and caseload data suggests that the Liberal changes have reduced caseloads drastically, but have had less impact on benefit levels; as with other developments in BC since 2001, it is too early to evaluate with certainty whether these

changes represent a fundamental market-oriented retrenchment of assistance programs for employable persons.

A Better Way for British Columbia, the BC NDP's 1991 election program, committed the party to 'increas[ing] minimum wage and [social
assistance] rates. We will ensure that social assistance recipients are
given the opportunity and help to find work.'[55] Consistent with this
expansive agenda – and despite fiscal pressure caused by Ottawa's
decision to freeze social assistance transfer payments to the affluent
provinces at 1990 levels – the post-1991 NDP administration increased
basic assistance rates in 1992, 1993, and 1994, and also increased the
value of some exemptions during these years. Other initiatives suggested that the new government wished to move further in this direction. Challenge of Change, a 1993 discussion paper, proposed that a
welfare reform be launched, with the objective of improving benefits
and services. The NDP also created a Minister's Advisory Council on
Income Assistance, a corporatist-style body consisting of representatives from the business and labour communities, as well as various
recipient and advocacy groups, to propose reforms. *The First Step*, the
council's first report, proposed further benefits improvements.[56] But by
1994, these progressive ambitions were overshadowed by developments that induced the NDP to undertake curtailments rather than
expansion. BC's assistance caseload rose from 216,000 in 1990 to 353,500
in 1994, a 64 per cent increase (table 8.4). In this context, the government
took a number of incremental cost-saving steps in 1994 and 1995. These
included measures to reduce overpayments; periodic requirements that
recipients claim their cheques in person; restrictions on the availability
of appeals; a reclassification of single parents of children aged 12 to 19
as employable; eliminating benefits for those who refused work or quit
jobs; a decrease in allowable asset limits; enhanced fraud detection; and
reduced access to short-term 'hardship benefits.'[57] The province briefly
attempted to deny benefits to newcomers to the province.[58]

A more comprehensive set of reforms, labeled BC Benefits, was announced in November 1995. Designed to encourage assistance recipients to return to work or to seek new skills, this initiative extended new
benefits to the working poor and curtailed them for employable people
who remained on assistance. A main component of the reform package
was the Family Bonus, an income supplement for all low-income earn-
ers with children; this resulted in a significant net benefit for the working poor, while those on social assistance – for whom the bonus was

deducted from their assistance cheque – experienced a small reduction. The working poor also benefited from a new Healthy Kids measure, which provided dental and vision care services to their children. The Youth Works and Welfare to Work components reduced assistance benefits for employable recipients under the age of 55 by 8 to 10 per cent, and required those under 60 years of age to participate in employability programs or to seek employment. Earnings exemptions were also reduced and made subject to a 12-month time limit.[59]

BC Benefits encountered strenuous criticism from both left and right; its introduction signified the definitive abandonment of the government's earlier effort to pursue policy change through corporatist-style social dialogue. The legislation was rejected as repressive by advocacy groups and unions, and the government narrowly escaped censure from the NDP's rank and file at a Provincial Council meeting. The Liberal and Reform Party opposition, by contrast, argued that the reforms did not go far enough.[60] During the 1996 provincial election campaign, assistance consequently remained a contested issue despite the NDP's turn to more restrictive policies. *On Your Side*, its 1996 election platform, defended BC Benefits as having made 'work a better deal than welfare,' but critiqued the opposition parties for proposing to 'severely weaken our safety net,' and for 'not stand[ing] up for B.C.'s poorest citizens.'[61] With the caseload still near its historic peak, the opposition parties claimed that the problems had not really been solved.

During the NDP's second term, from 1996 to 2001, only modest adjustments were made in assistance measures for employable persons, but these were consistent with the policy trend since 1994 – towards restricting benefits and enhancing employment incentives. A 1997 regulatory change reduced assistance benefits for 17,000 recipients who were classified as temporarily disabled. The following year, the government tightened information-reporting requirements for many recipients to reduce the incidence of fraud, and it launched a pilot project to assist recipients to become self-employed. In 1999, it resisted pressure from advocacy groups to have benefits increased by 25 per cent.[62] Despite the opposition criticism, in the wake of BC Benefits, and of the incremental cuts that preceded and succeeded it, the province's assistance caseload, which peaked at 374,000 in 1995, declined to 262,000 by 2000. The cost of the assistance caseload also was reigned in, though more slowly. BC's assistance system cost the province about $1.45 billion (in 1992 dollars) in 1990, a figure that rose to $1.9 billion in 1997; in

2001, it had been reduced to $1.74 billion; in per capita terms, assistance costs peaked at $716 per provincial resident in 1995, and fell to $630 per capita in 2001, slightly below their level in 1990.[63]

In this context, social assistance was not a prominent issue in the 2001 election campaign – as it had been five years earlier – and the BC Liberals made no specific commitments regarding assistance in *A New Era for British Columbia*, their election program. An interviewed Human Resources official observed that this ministry was one of very few that received no specific attention in the document. But when the new government launched its Core Services Review after the election, designed to identify areas of potential cost-savings throughout the government, it quickly decided to undertake a further tightening of the province's assistance system. A January 2002 regulatory change reclassified all single parents as employable once their children reached the age of three.[64] In February, it was revealed that the Liberal finance minister wished to use social assistance curtailments to finance approximately one-third (or $580 million) of the expenditure reductions needed to balance the province's budget in three years after the government introduced steep tax cuts.[65] The review, conducted within the ministry with little nongovernmental consultation, resulted in the tabling of two bills in the legislature in April. The Employment and Assistance Act, designed for employable recipients, included the largest changes. Most significantly, no recipient would be able to receive benefits for more than two years in any five-year period; BC thereby became the first province in Canada to set a maximum time limit for receiving assistance. New benefits claimants would also be subject to a three-week waiting period between their initial application and their eligibility for benefits. The legislation did not reduce benefit levels, but it did eliminate all earnings exemptions. A revised appeals procedure, designed to be more efficient, was created; penalties for committing fraud were increased. To assistant clients in returning to work, the government did not reduce – though it also did not increase – its overall spending on employability measures for assistance recipients. The second bill, the Employment and Assistance for Persons with Disabilities Act, narrowed the definition of disability, launched a review of the disability status of its beneficiaries, and created mechanisms to encourage those who were capable enough to take up employment opportunities.[66] Although disability advocates immediately criticized the second bill as likely to strip many unemployable persons of benefits, the government denied this; when the disability status review was completed in August 2003, moreover, only 400 of about 61,000 clients had lost their disability status.[67] The NDP opposition also warned that as continuous employable assistance clients reached the new legislation's two-year time limit, in April 2004, many would lose their benefits. But the government later introduced an exemption from the two-year limit for employable recipients who were considered to be complying with employability plans that had been drawn up for them; in February 2004, consequently, it announced that it expected only 339 clients to lose benefits due to the limit.[68]

The Liberal legislation nevertheless was followed by a precipitous decline in BC's assistance caseload, from 241,200 in March 2002 to 180,700 twelve months later. Interviewed officials cited the three-week delay in accessing benefits and fear of the time limit as important likely causes of this decline which, at 25.1 per cent, far exceeded the 5.3 per cent fall in assistance dependency in Canada as a whole during that period;[69] in 2003, the caseload – still 12 per cent above its 1990 level in 2002 – was 16 per cent below that mark. It fell more slowly thereafter, but still reached 161,000 in May 2004.[70] Because the Liberal reforms did not introduce major benefit rate reductions, these fell less dramatically, but still noticeably: in 2003, total welfare income for a single parent with one child was 7.5 per cent below its 2001 level; total benefits for a couple with two children fell by 6.5 per cent.[71]

The trajectory of assistance policy in BC since the mid-1990s parallels the pattern in Ontario and Quebec – restriction of access to benefits, and, above all, enhancement of incentives for employable recipients to seek jobs or increase their employability. But the BC experience also has distinctive features. Reflecting its institutional setting, the province's two main parties were sharply polarized on assistance policy during the early 1990s, when the NDP made the system more generous; and again in mid-decade, when the caseload and cost explosion exposed the NDP to criticism from the centre-right. Partisan debate diminished after 1996, in the wake of the NDP's restrictive BC Benefits reforms, but reignited after the 2001 election when the Liberals introduced deep cuts that had not been discussed during the campaign. Is there evidence of neo-liberal retrenchment in recent BC assistance policy for employable persons? In 2001, certainly, with caseloads still higher than at the beginning of the previous decade, and benefits not much below their 1990 level, this question would have been answered in the negative. But the Liberals' 2002 reforms resulted in a further, and substantial, reduction in the province's assistance caseload, and included unprecedented features, such (at least in principle) as fixed time limits for assistance beneficiaries. It now seems more appropriate to conclude that BC's welfare system retrenched to a degree not seen in Quebec, or, probably, in Ontario, during the post-1990 era, though less than in Alberta.

Alberta

A review of Alberta's social assistance program for non-disabled individuals was begun in 1990, partly because of a substantial increase in caseload, from 50,000 cases in 1985 to 70,000 in 1987.[72] The review concluded that assistance was becoming a long-term income support program, rather than a transitional one. That same year, the program for employables was renamed Supports to Independence, but no change was made to benefits or eligibility.[73] But, between 1990 and 1992, two important administrative changes were introduced. The model of service delivery was modified creating two types of front-line officers; financial benefits workers, and employment client support workers. Second, monthly client reporting cards were introduced (similar to those used by the Unemployment Insurance program), which clients were required to complete each month to remain eligible.

With Ralph Klein coming to power, the focus in 1993 shifted to reducing costs and caseloads. As in Ontario, central agencies became more involved in setting social assistance policy, as the line department was thought unable to meet savings targets. In the summer of 1993, to attain the announced goal of a 20 per cent decrease in the overall provincial budget over five years, the treasury ordered immediate benefits cuts, including reductions to the clothing allowance and shelter allowances for employable recipients, decreases for school supplies and transportation, and the elimination of damage deposit allowances for renters. Most significantly, monthly benefits were reduced by 17 per cent for single employables, and 7 per cent for single parents.[74] Including the decreases in the supplementary and medical benefits, the total decrease in benefits was 19 per cent for single employables and 13 per cent for parents with children.[75] Unlike Ontario in 1995, the magnitude of these reductions, and other reforms described below, were not at all signalled by the 1993 election platform of the Conservatives.

Additional regulatory changes decreased eligibility, by tightening asset rules (which excluded some individuals from being able to receive welfare), limiting appeals, and eliminating clients' entitlement to advance notice if benefits were being cut. Finally, written notice was not required for recipients to be excluded from the program. Although there are no official figures on the number of clients who were terminated, an evaluation by the Canada West Foundation in 1996–97 found that 7.3 per cent of former recipients reported being 'cut off.'[76] Significant administrative reforms were also made to assist welfare program managers to reduce caseloads. Quotas for the number of clients, and especially new clients, that should be processed, were set for field staff with instructions that their jobs were on the line if the lower caseload targets were not met. 'Perhaps the least defensible reform was a so-called minor administrative change which advised department staff that "clients were only to be issued benefits other than the standard ones if they specifically request them."'[77]

A set of 'workfare' requirements was also introduced in 1993. According to the welfare minister, the new policy emphasized employment because '(1) people want to work, (2) any job is a good job, (3) people on welfare should not be "better off" than working Albertans.'[78] Applicants now had to undergo an employability assessment and prepare formal employment plans outlining their plan to become independent. Welfare workers had the authority to deny benefits 'when expectations about becoming independent have not been met.'[79] Parents with children older than 6 months were also required to prepare these plans and to actively seek work or to enter some type of training program. Previously, parents were not required to work until the youngest child reached the age of 2.

To reduce the caseload swiftly, 11,000 welfare recipients were transferred from short-term training programs to the student income support program in 1993. This did not generate expenditure savings, as the welfare dollars went with the clients, but did reduce the number of clients and social assistance expenditures overnight. Additionally, about 2,600 welfare recipients between 60 and 64 years of age were required to apply for Canada Pension Plan benefits, either removing them from the welfare rolls altogether or reducing their benefits.[80]

The regulatory and administrative shifts were designed to make welfare extremely unattractive for potential, as well as current, recipients. The objective, in the words of one government official, was that 'people would just walk away [because the benefits were so minimal]. Go away, don't come here. That's what we wanted people to do. This became a pervasive view in the community ... [that] this is not a welcoming program.' Indeed, after 1993, local welfare offices became very good at deflecting and informally refusing to process applications, as well as denying assistance to those who were deemed not to have exhausted other options.[81] It was not uncommon for clients to be told to go bunk with a friend or come back in two weeks.[82] As such, the changes to welfare in Alberta were not rhetorical. Nevertheless, it is unclear whether the reduction of caseloads and benefits could have been achieved without decreasing monthly benefits. Senior officials within the social services department were of the view that the declining unemployment rates, in Alberta and elsewhere, largely accounted for the caseload decline, and that this decrease would have occurred regardless. In any case, caseloads decreased substantially from a peak of nearly 100,000 cases at the start of 1993 to only 40,000 by the start of 1997.[83] Even when the cases transferred to other programs are taken into account, this represents a dramatic decrease in caseload over a short span of time. As shown in table 8.4, the number of individuals on assistance decreased by 61 per cent between 1994 and 2002.

The government meanwhile enhanced somewhat the opportunities for training and employment programs. These typically subsidized the wages of recipients hired in the non-profit sector or provided a small amount of money for them to enrol in a training program. Most of the province's employment programs provided short interventions designed to move recipients quickly into an increasingly buoyant labour market. However, the expansion of training and employment funding was small. In its plan to meet the 1993 expenditure reduction targets, Alberta Family and Social Services proposed to increase spending on employment initiatives by $25 million over four years (to $35 million), while decreasing income support payments by $268 million.[84] Nevertheless, by 1996, one-third of former welfare recipients reported having participated in some type of job training and 40 per cent had attended school at some point in the previous three years.[85] The conclusion reached by most observers is that the Alberta government had 'taken its philosophy of "active support" seriously.'[86] However, there is also agreement among observers that the decline in caseloads 'came from a sharp decrease in individuals who were applying for welfare for the first time.'[87] Contributing to the effectiveness of its training efforts was the province's consolidation of its labour market services. After 1993, services for assistance recipients increasingly were integrated with the 'career centres' serving other clients, for example through the co-location of Alberta and Ottawa income security and employment preparation offices in Edmonton, Calgary, and Lethbridge. Alberta was the first province to sign a Labour Market Development Agreement with

Ottawa, which led to a realignment of federal and provincial labour market programs.[88] The integration of provincial services for non-social assistance recipients and social assistance clients was facilitated by the fact that Alberta, unlike Ontario, has had a network of field offices serving the employment and training needs of assistance recipients since the 1970s.

After the 1993 'Klein revolution,' the assistance field remained static until 2001. However, in mid-2001, the government created its own committee of MLAs to review welfare and associated programs. The all-Conservative MLA committee did not hold public consultations, but did employ a questionnaire that asked 'taxpayers if the poor and needy are receiving enough to pay for rent, medical needs and children's expenses.'[89] The committee recommended that increases in welfare rates be tied to a market basket measure, and also that a number of separate income support programs be consolidated.[90] Ignoring the call to increase benefits, the government in 2002 announced that it would integrate programs but that benefit levels would remain frozen at the 1993 level.[91] The Income and Employment Support Act was passed in 2003 to amalgamate seven previously separate pieces of social and labour market legislation. The Alberta Works program was created by integrating the Supports to Independence program with several others.[92] In a decision that was not publicly announced, in mid-2003 the government allowed a $14 per child per month increase in the National Child Benefit Supplement to flow through to families on social assistance, abandoning its previous practice of 'clawing back' that amount from social assistance payments.[93] Other than some small adjustments, Alberta Works will leave welfare rates unchanged.[94]

Poverty organizations have had very little influence in the Alberta policy process. Since 1993, civil servants have been prohibited from consulting with social assistance stakeholder groups, other than those in the disability community (where such consultation only began again in 1999). The group most active in seeking to increase welfare payments has been the Alberta College of Social Workers, rather than stakeholders representing more directly the unemployed and the poor.[95]

Although the catalyst for the 1993 changes in the welfare program was the 20 per cent across the board spending cut, the specific nature of reforms were, at least in part, a reaction to developments in the 1980s and early 1990s. During the 1980s, the welfare program became – for Alberta – uncharacteristically generous. In 1980, welfare payments in Alberta accounted for 0.4 per cent of GDP (measured in constant dollars) a figure that increased steadily until 1992 when it reached 1.4 per cent of GDP, while during these 12 years, average monthly caseloads tripled from 30,000 to 89,000.[96] According to figures prepared by M.S. Shed, the province in 1980 ranked seventh among the 10 provinces in the per capita level of expenditures for welfare, but it rose to second place in 1992.[97] Indeed, during the mid-1980s the province ranked among the most generous in its benefits. For example, in 1986, Alberta paid the highest benefits in Canada for couples with two children, second highest benefits for both single employables, and adults with one child.[98] The high point of assistance policy was reached in the mid-1980s, after nearly a decade of steady expansion of expenditures on, and eligibility for, programs.[99] Although benefit levels were decreased somewhat in the late 1980s, the recession of the early 1990s meant that total caseloads continued to climb from 1990 to 1992, when, as shown in table 8.4, the number of recipients increased by 26.5 per cent.

As noted by Boychuk, Alberta during the 1990s moved its social assistance program towards one that 'incorporates stringent enforcement of work requirements and defines employability widely so that the work requirements apply to a broad range of recipients.'[100] Notwithstanding some similarities between their welfare reforms, moreover, Alberta has embraced a much harsher approach to the 'front door diversion' of applicants than was the case in Ontario. In 2002, nearly a decade after the wave of changes, senior Alberta policy officials in the welfare program observed with dismay that the attitudes of field staff had become outdated. These officials noted that front-line staff were still in the 1993 case reduction 'mode,' failing to recognize that the nature of the caseload had changed, with those currently on assistance requiring more help because they experience greater barriers to employment. The attitude, reinforced by regulatory and administrative changes, continued to be that family and friends, not the taxpayers, should help.

Partisanship, Globalization, and Assistance for Employable Persons in Four Provinces

At the beginning of this chapter, we observed that many features of policy-making for employable social assistance recipients differ significantly from those that shape other aspects of labour market policy. We suggested that these differences reflected assistance policy's distinctive political, ideological, and fiscal nexus. The above provincial case studies do, indeed, have distinctive features: the relative absence of business and labour from policy-making, the greater – if nevertheless often less than central – position of social advocacy groups, and the intermittent saliency of assistance issues in election campaigns. The broad pattern of policy change in at least three of four provinces examined here was also parallel and quite unlike anything uncovered in earlier chapters – substantial growth in caseload and costs during the early 1990s, followed by significant cuts, the strengthening of employability requirements, and a rapid decline in program costs and caseloads after the mid-1990s. Even Alberta, which did not follow this trajectory in the same time frame, experienced not dissimilar developments a number of years earlier.

Yet social assistance policy-making since 1990 differed in important ways among these provinces; and these differences broadly mirrored interprovincial variations uncovered in earlier chapters. The macro-level institutions of each province's political economy, examined in chapter 2, consequently played a crucial role in shaping assistance policy. As Coleman and Skogstad argue, even where sector-level policy communities display distinctive features, developments there also reflect 'the impact of macro factors' such as 'the broader political, economic, and ideological environment in which they function.'[101] Parallels between the patterns of policy change observed in chapters 4 to 7 and those in the social assistance field are evident with respect to both foci of this study: the extent of short-term partisan 'swings,' and the degree of globalization-induced retrenchment. Consistent with our expectations regarding Quebec's CME-tinged liberal political economy, partisanship had a smaller impact on policy-making there than in the other three provinces; no change in government during the period of study resulted in dramatic policy change. Partisan swings were much more evident in Ontario and British Columbia; the post-1995 Conservatives in the former jurisdiction, and the post-2001 Liberals in the latter, undertook noteworthy market-oriented reforms. Both the Ontario NDP (after 1992) and its BC counterpart (after 1996) had also introduced important restrictions. But NDP reforms stopped well short of key features of their successors': Ontario's NDP rejected any form of workfare, and BC New Democrats avoided the time limits introduced after 2001. These and other differences from the policies of their centre-right successors in office suggest that in these domains, too, the degree of short-term partisan 'swing' in these provinces after the centre-right came to power was high (table 8.6, p. 211; see also appendix).

Quebec also stands out from the other cases in providing almost no evidence of longer-term neo-liberal retrenchment of assistance programs. Employment-related requirements for recipients have been strengthened, and the definition of employability considerably broadened, since 1990. Nevertheless, as we observed in an earlier section of this chapter, there is little evidence that these changes reduced benefit levels, or hindered access to them, significantly. The province's caseload is comparable to its 1990 level, and has declined only modestly as a proportion of the provincial population. Total welfare incomes were close to their 1990 level in 2003, although they had fallen modestly in relation to average incomes. Proposals for workfare and other radical curtailments of social assistance have been largely absent from mainstream political debate in the province. We characterized the degree of social assistance retrenchment in Ontario as 'medium' – greater than in most other labour market policy domains in that province. Workfare was the signature assistance policy initiative of the Harris administration. On the one hand, it has been less important than its public prominence might suggest: only a very small proportion of Ontario assistance recipients have ever received a workfare placement. On the other hand, this and other restrictions introduced by the Harris government quite likely discouraged potential recipients from applying for assistance, and facilitated the removal of persons from the welfare rolls. The province's caseload fell by about one-sixth as a proportion of the provincial population between 1990 and 2003. The continuance of workfare, even if its impact owes more to its psychological impact on recipients and on the disposition of caseworkers, could be expected to cause this proportion to fall further. On the other hand, modest reversals of the Tory cuts by the McGuinty Liberal government suggest that the retrenchment era may have ended. In British Columbia, too, one could exaggerate the degree of retrenchment; but here the pattern, far more recent, is particularly uncertain. Despite the cuts introduced by the NDP in 1996 and thereafter, there was no more reason, in 2001, to identify retrenchment as having happened there than in Quebec. The Campbell Liberals' subsequent reforms, however, resulted in a dramatic reduction in the assistance caseload, which fell to about two-thirds of its 1990 level by 2003, when calculated as a percentage of the provincial population; in the latter year, total welfare incomes were between one-tenth or one-sixth lower than in 1990. The most notable feature of the Liberals' reform, however, was its imposition of a two-years-in-five time limit on assistance eligibility. As originally conceived, this provision – unprecedented in Canada – would have caused a further substantial caseload reduction in April 2004. But the Liberals' decision to apply this restriction only to recipients who refused to participate in employability initiatives eliminated this possibility. In Alberta, evidence of retrenchment is more unambiguous; this is consistent with our expectation that in a partisan setting dominated by a market-oriented centre-right party that faces only very weak opposition from its left, the prospects for neo-liberal retrenchment will be particularly high. The province's caseload is substantially below its 1990 level, and, unlike other provinces, this decline continues a pattern that began a number of years earlier. Benefit levels, similarly, are substantially below those – relatively generous – that prevailed in the mid-1980s. The case study of Alberta policy presented above illustrates eloquently some distinctive features of reform in that province: Making the receipt of assistance so demeaning and non-remunerative that potential recipients would choose not to seek benefits was a near-explicit policy objective. Assistance caseworkers were informed that their career prospects would be affected by the extent to which they helped the province achieve its cost-savings objectives. The cuts evoked only limited political opposition. Their extent suggests that a major departure from the Canadian post-war assistance model in Canada occurred in 1990s Alberta: it became questionable if assistance as a last-resort source of income was truly available to many of the province's residents.

Employment Insurance and Social Assistance: A Stronger Case for Retrenchment?

Social assistance retrenchment was not dramatic in three of our four provinces. Some observers nevertheless contend that when the additional impact of other policy changes is considered – in the tax system, and, above all, in the federal (Un)employment Insurance (UI/EI) system – one must conclude that economically vulnerable Canadians, a population that includes most employable assistance recipients, have experienced a substantial reduction in social protection since 1990. We consider this argument here, because one cannot assess the real circumstances of assistance recipients without considering this broader setting.

McIntosh and Boychuk examine the possibility that substantial curtailment in federal income support for employable persons, in the context of additional provincial assistance cuts, could open a substantial 'gap' between these programs, leaving many people unprotected.

Table 8.7. Incidence of Low Income, before Taxes, % of All Persons

	1980	1985	1990	1995	2000	2003
Quebec	19.2	20.4	20.2	22.4	19.1	16.9
Ontario	14.1	14.0	12.5	17.2	13.9	14.3
Alberta	13.3	17.0	17.4	19.0	14.4	14.6
BC	13.1	20.4	16.7	19.5	19.4	20.1
Canada	16.0	17.5	16.2	19.3	16.4	15.9

Source: Statistics Canada, CANSIM table 2020802.

They document that the number of UI/EI recipients, between 70 and 80 per cent of the number of unemployed persons during the 1980s, represented only 42 per cent of the latter figure in 1997s; about half of this decline resulted from the massive federal program cuts of the early- to mid-1990s.[102] After reviewing recent developments in federal EI and provincial assistance policies, these authors conclude that 'both orders of government [have] been ... off-loading recipients rather than uploading or downloading them' to another level of government.[103] These developments 'restrict the level of interaction between the two programmes and contribute to a growing space between them' so that 'it is less likely that persons experiencing spells of unemployment will be eligible for [any] benefits.'[104]

There is no systematic data, of which we are aware, that documents directly the extent to which the combination of federal and provincial cuts in passive labour market programs during the 1990s created a growing cohort of unemployed Canadians who are eligible neither for EI nor social assistance. If such a trend is pronounced, however, it should entail that these vulnerable recipients are significantly more exposed to market pressures that these programs previously alleviated. One would expect such a trend to be manifested in rising levels of low income and of income inequality. Tables 8.7 to 8.9 (pp. 236–237) present data regarding these issues for recent years, and illustrate the degree to which changes in the tax system have affected the economically vulnerable.

Data regarding low income, reported in table 8.7, does not indicate that its incidence has increased in Canada in recent years. Between 1980 and 1990, the percentage of Canadians living in low-income families rose modestly, from 16.0 to 16.2 per cent, having risen to 17.5 per cent in 1985, in the wake of the early 1980s recession. This figure rose to 19.3

Table 8.8. Gini Coefficient Measure of Inequality, Market Income, All Family Units

	1980	1985	1990	1995	2000	2003
Quebec	.453	.476	.500	.525	.522	.510
Ontario	.414	.441	.457	.500	.509	.503
Alberta	.435	.440	.456	.467	.486	.448
BC	.429	.478	.477	.500	.504	.504
Canada	.437	.464	.479	.509	.515	.508

Source: Statistics Canada, CANSIM table 2020705.

Table 8.9. Gini Coefficient Measure of Inequality, After-Tax and Transfer Income, All Family Units

	1980	1985	1990	1995	2000	2003
Quebec	.344	.347	.352	.360	.376	.370
Ontario	.342	.351	.352	.364	.396	.392
Alberta	.373	.352	.356	.358	.385	.393
BC	.365	.375	.367	.373	.390	.393
Canada	.353	.357	.357	.366	.392	.389

Source: Statistics Canada, CANSIM table 2020705.

per cent in 1995, after another economic downturn, but fell to 16.4 per cent in 2000, and to 15.9 per cent in 2003. Canadian poverty levels therefore respond noticeably to changes in the business cycle and in unemployment rates, but there has been no longer-term increase in poverty. Interprovincial variations in this data – such as Alberta's relatively low incidence of low income, or the fact that British Columbia's, alone among the provinces treated here, was substantially higher in 2003 than in 1990 – probably reflect overall variations in the distribution of income among provinces, and varying provincial growth rates.

Tables 8.8 and 8.9 report Gini coefficients, a summary measure of income inequality, respectively, for market income and for final income; that is, income after taxes and transfer payments. The difference between the two effectively measures the degree to which Canada's welfare state broadly conceived – taxes and transfer payments – affects inequality. The evolution of these two coefficients between 1980 and 1995 differed strikingly, suggesting that Canada's welfare state played a substantial role in preventing final income inequality from rising in Canada; by contrast, final income inequality rose significantly in most other affluent nations.[105] While the Gini coefficient for market income rose sharply during this period for Canada as a whole (from .437 to .509), and also rose in each of its leading four provinces, it increased much less (from .353 to .366) for final income during the same period. As René Morissette et al., observed in 1995, 'in Canada, rising inequality in the labour market has so far been offset by *social transfers*, so that, unlike the US, the final distribution of total family incomes remained relatively stable.'[106]

However, most of the UI/EI cuts were too recent to have had a significant effect on inequality data in 1995; and most significant curtailments in social assistance policy began only during the mid-1990s. If the 'gap' hypothesized by McIntosh and Boychuk emerged and increased inequality, this would only become evident in subsequent years. Data for 2000 and 2003, reported in tables 8.8 and 8.9, reveal that the evolution of income inequality in Canada since 1995 has, in fact, diverged from the earlier pattern. In the face of persistent economic growth and rapid job creation, market inequality was relatively stable between 1995 and 2003 (the relevant coefficient fell from .509 to .508). By contrast, final income inequality showed its first signs of increasing, substantially, in line with the international trend, during these years; the final income Gini coefficient rose from .357 to .392 from 1995 to 2000, before declining modestly in 2003. In the latter year, final income inequality was higher in all four provinces discussed here than in 1990 or 1995. In view of the falling rate of low income before taxes (table 8.7), and of the relative economic buoyancy during these years, a rise in inequality is surprising; and since it runs counter to the stable pattern in market incomes (table 8.8), it is likely to be largely the result of changing policies. The hypothesized 'gap' between EI and assistance probably is the most important of these. The increase in final income inequality remains moderate by international standards. The final income Gini coefficient was 36 points higher in Canada in 2003 than in 1980 (.388 compared to .353). By contrast, it rose by about 75 points in the United States and 80 points in the United Kingdom between 1980 and 2000.[107] The Canadian welfare state's record of 'compensating' for substantial growth in earned income inequality is nevertheless much less impressive now than it was in the mid-1990s.

PART THREE

Reflection

9 A Perspective from Abroad: Coordinative Institutions and Labour Market Reform in Germany

STEFFEN G. SCHNEIDER

The theoretical literatures discussed in chapter 1 suggest that the impact of partisanship and globalization might be greater in a liberal welfare state and production regime than elsewhere. In order to shed light on institutional effects that cannot be captured by a study that focuses exclusively on generally liberal milieus of the type examined in the preceding chapters, this chapter examines recent developments in Germany's conservative welfare state regime and coordinated market economy. As the two nations also have very different – inter-state versus intra-state – models of federalism, the parameters of labour market policy-making in Germany differ considerably from those in Canada.[1]

The chapter focuses on post-reunification trends in Bavaria, North Rhine-Westphalia, and Saxony-Anhalt – a selection of cases that includes Germany's two largest and most populous jurisdictions and one of the five new *Länder* (federal states). It concentrates on active labour market policies, giving only cursory treatment to the other sub-fields analysed in the preceding case studies, as these are largely ultra vires for Germany's sub-national governments. Core features of the country's welfare state regime, political economy, and party system are described first. The intergovernmental distribution of responsibilities in the labour market field, as well as national programs and reform initiatives, are then examined. The chapter's third section outlines the labour market strategies and active measures of the three cases.[2]

The discussion addresses the key questions of this book: To what extent have partisanship and globalization affected policy-making? Have Germany's coordinative institutions suppressed, enhanced, or otherwise mediated the impact of partisanship? Is there a different potential for retrenchment and neo-liberal reforms in the active labour market field than in Canada? It will be argued that the effects of partisanship and globalization are indeed partly cushioned by Germany's welfare state and production regime, especially at the sub-national level. The policy swings and variations caused by the partisan complexion of governments tend to be minor. Yet while globalization has certainly not led to the full erosion of the country's regime type, active labour market policies in Germany seem to have embarked on a more strongly market-oriented trajectory in recent years.

Welfare State, Production Regime, and Party System in Germany

Using the familiar welfare state, production regime, and party system typologies, this section describes the context of national and sub-national active labour market policy-making in Germany and its Länder.

Welfare State

Germany represents Esping-Andersen's conservative welfare state regime type even if some elements were diluted during the post-war decades.[3] The four traditional branches of the country's fragmented, mandatory, and largely payroll-financed social insurance system – health, accident, pension, and unemployment insurance (UI) – cover the bulk of the population. The regime strongly relies on the family (i.e., women), labour and business, the churches, and voluntary organizations for service delivery and the governance of its para-public insurance funds. As benefits are usually earnings-related, their redistributive effect is modest. Its once-pronounced status orientation, visible in the historical distinction between blue-collar and white-collar workers, has been reduced since the 1950s, but separate funds and programs for certain occupational groups have survived. The viability of Germany's welfare state largely depends on the nation's labour market performance – that is, high and stable employment for primarily male breadwinners in standard employment, combined with female labour force participation rates well below those reached in most other advanced economies, including Canada. Most entitlements are tied to employment or family status.

Germany's peculiar brand of federalism has been no obstacle to the expansion of this comprehensive regime.[4] Although core responsibilities in the economic and social policy fields are defined as areas of concurrent legislation in the Basic (constitutional) Law, several factors have contributed to a strong centralization of legislative authority – among them, the constitutional guarantee of equal living conditions throughout the country and a political culture that is intolerant of major regional disparities. As the federal government is entitled to act pre-emptively to secure Germany's economic and legal union, the Länder have defended few legislative responsibilities or administrative duties relevant to the welfare state. Yet while the Länder have no more than a subordinate role as legislators in their own right, they participate in policy formulation and act as an important collective veto player through the second chamber of the federal parliament and other national joint decision-making institutions. Composed of Länder premiers and ministers, the Bundesrat (Parliament's Upper House) must approve most legislation. Länder can thus assume a pivotal role in federal politics. These arrangements have prevented major regional disparities in eligibility criteria or benefit levels for social programs; the contours of the German welfare state regime differ little among the Länder.

The fiscal impact of socio-economic and demographic trends since the 1970s, including rising unemployment, has increased pressure on this regime. First efforts to contain social and labour market expenditure growth date back to the post-1974 federal government coalition of Social Democrats (SPD) and Liberals (FDP) led by Helmut Schmidt. The coalition of Christian Democrats (CDU, CSU) and the FDP that came to power in 1982 initially couched its own policies in decidedly neo-liberal rhetoric. A set of cutbacks, tax abatements, privatization, and deregulation measures during the 1980s aimed at, and temporarily resulted in, economic stimulation, fiscal consolidation, reduced social expenditures, and the stabilization of contribution rates.[5]

The momentous external shock of reunification in 1990 brought these modest retrenchment efforts to an abrupt end. The swift extension of West Germany's welfare state regime to the former German Democratic Republic (GDR), whose inhabitants had to cope with economic restructuring and soaring unemployment levels, had an important legitimizing function and prevented the further pursuit of a neo-liberal agenda. Chancellor Helmut Kohl opted for a 'reluctant post-reunification Keynesianism.'[6] The federal government assumed a leadership role in the East German transition, continuing the long-standing centralization trend of German federalism and ensuring a huge volume of financial transfers from the western part of the country to the five new Länder. A large portion of these transfers had to be shouldered by the social insurance system. The resulting increase of contribution rates raised non-wage labour costs and threatened job creation and economic growth.[7] The 1992–93 downturn ushered in debates about the impact of rising social expenditures on Germany's competitiveness. The post-Maastricht criteria of fiscal convergence within the European Monetary Union also suggested a return to austerity-oriented policies, and retrenchment was therefore back on the agenda.[8] The SPD and Green Party coalition elected in 1998 initially rescinded some of Kohl's later cutbacks and expanded various benefits. In his second term, beginning in 2002, however, Chancellor Gerhard Schröder himself embarked on a highly unpopular retrenchment course.[9]

Most observers agree that Germany's conservative welfare state regime has not yet been dismantled or transformed into a liberal one. They further argue that the imposition of drastic measures dictated by economic stagnation, a dismal labour market performance, and fiscal constraints has so far been prevented by risk-averse parties, and by federal and corporatist arrangements providing reform opponents with multiple veto points. The basic elements of the social insurance system remain in place and have even been supplemented by long-term care insurance in 1994, despite the fact that a bloated welfare state and prohibitive non-wage labour costs are widely counted among the most important reasons for the failure to cope with unemployment.[10] Eligibility criteria and benefits have been tightened and reduced, forcing many people from the social insurance system into less generous means-tested programs, or back into the labour market.[11] But most of these cutbacks were consolidation or recalibration measures, driven by expenditure containment goals, rather than second- or third-order changes of the type described by Peter Hall in the typology outlined in the appendix to this volume.[12] The stronger family orientation in recent years is also in line with the logic of a conservative regime. Some reforms implemented by the current government – for example, the introduction of a voluntary, government-subsidized private supplement to the pension insurance system in 2002 – may, however, have triggered gradual processes of what Kathleen Thelen terms institutional layering and conversion, with far-reaching long-term consequences.[13]

Production Regime

Germany's conservative welfare state regime is closely linked with its Social Market Economy, a model of capitalism along the lines of Soskice's

Coordinated Market Economy (CME) ideal type.[14] The organizational capacity of labour and business is comparatively high; the system of trade unions and employers' associations is strongly integrated and centralized. Most unions belong to the German Trade Union Federation (DGB). Firms are represented by regional and sectoral employers' associations, which are in turn members of national peak associations (BDA, BDI). Coordinative arrangements and mechanisms among firms, and between labour and business, are important. The 'semi-sovereign' German state and the courts are largely restricted to defining the overall constitutional, legislative, and regulatory framework of the CME.[15] Industrial relations are characterized by the mutual recognition and ideological moderation of powerful unions and employers' associations, and a predominantly consensual style of interest accommodation. Collective bargaining takes place between regional employers' associations and the unions, without government intervention, although it results in sectoral agreements with binding legal force; inter-regional and inter-sectoral coordination ensures that national peak-level bargaining is approximated. At the firm and plant levels, coordinative arrangements and co-determination take the form of worker and union representation on boards of directors, and of works councils.

Vocational (re)training is the second key component of the German CME. The dual apprenticeship system, which epitomizes the model's emphasis on vocational skills, relies on coordination among unions and firms, the chambers of commerce and trade as regulatory agencies, and the Länder governments, which have constitutional authority over education. The large corporations of the export-oriented German manufacturing sector and its predominantly male and unionized core labour force are the principal beneficiaries of the high-productivity, high-wage, and high-skills equilibrium associated with the CME. Strike rates are low. Workers in standard employment have a strong incentive to invest in firm or industry-specific training, and in turn profit from steady, if usually moderate, wage increases. According to Wolfgang Streeck, the model's disadvantages with regard to radical innovations and short-term product market strategies are compensated by its ability to foster incremental innovations and long-term strategies that underpin diversified quality production.[16] Beyond their role in industrial relations and skills formation, labour and business participate, as shown above, in the corporatist management of Germany's welfare state. As members of tripartite advisory and decision-making bodies, the social partners are regularly involved in discussing and resolving broader social and economic issues ('concerted action').[17]

David Soskice and others underline that both major varieties of capitalism have specific comparative advantages. This view implies considerable reluctance on the part of business to drop out of coordinative arrangements.[18] Yet the expectation that this reluctance will prevent more than minor and path-dependent adjustments has been questioned lately. Many observers suggest that globalization-induced economic trends like increased capital mobility and shareholder orientation, new forms of management and production, and changing labour market structures have begun to jeopardize the German economic model. Like the generosity of its welfare state regime, the rigidity of its CME has been held responsible for the country's perceived lack of competitiveness, sluggish growth, insufficient job creation, and persistent unemployment in the last decade.[19] Yet signs abound that the model's erosion may already be underway. Union density in the private sector declined from 28.2 per cent in 1991 to a mere 17.3 per cent in 2000, although union coverage remains extensive.[20] Very much reduced to representing the core blue-collar labour force of a shrinking manufacturing sector and retired workers, the unions increasingly act as defenders of the status quo in order to secure the jobs, wage levels, and social benefits of their dwindling membership.[21]

On the business side, organizational capacity and solidarity have also shrunk. Conflicts between the more traditional BDA, responsible for collective bargaining, and the neo-liberal BDI have become more frequent, while opposition to co-determination and traditional forms of collective bargaining has grown. Aggravated divergences of interest between labour and business, and within their respective constituencies, have destabilized the industrial relations system. Employers' calls for a greater decentralization and flexibilization of collective agreements, for the creation of a low-wage sector and for the reduction of social benefits and non-wage labour costs, ushered in some 'experimentalism' and changes, especially during the 1990s.[22] The scope of collective bargaining has been reduced, the share of company-specific, rather than sector-wide, agreements rising from 27 to 39 per cent between 1990 and 2000.[23] Opening and hardship clauses with regard to wage levels, employment standards, and working times have become widespread, as have production-site agreements between managers and works councils in which job and investment guarantees are traded against cost-reduction measures and other derogations from collective agreements. Hailed as local employment pacts by employers' associations, their spread is resisted in principle, but often tolerated in practice, by the unions.[24]

According to some observers, the vocational (re)training system, with its entrenched occupational status groups, has become a comparative disadvantage, too, hindering technological and economic adjustment. Whether it continues to convey advanced technical skills and to foster innovation capacity is disputed. Moreover, social expenditures in Germany are said to crowd out funding for education and human capital formation.[25] To a considerable extent, the recent erosion of collective bargaining and apprenticeship training was caused by reunification. At first glance, the transfer of the West German model of capitalism to the east was as swift and thorough as the extension of the welfare state regime. The West German unions spread to the new Länder, and business established regional and sectoral employers' associations along West German lines, integrating them into existing national peak associations. Collective bargaining and the dual system of apprenticeship training were also introduced. Political actors and the unions even promised, against all economic rationality, to close the wage gap between East and West Germany within years. Yet the CME has never been firmly entrenched in the former GDR. Opting out of employers' associations and collective agreements, the use of opening and hardship clauses, production-site agreements, and firms managed without co-determination and works councils, are all more frequent; business participation in apprenticeship training is considerably lower than in the old Länder, forcing governments to step in with institutionalized forms of vocational training. However, although developments in the east have influenced those in the west, too, the traditional forms of collective bargaining have proven more robust there. Similarly, large corporations in manufacturing are still much more likely to stick to coordinative arrangements and mechanisms than small firms in advanced services and other sectors where standard employment relationships are less frequent.[26]

A mere stability versus erosion dichotomy, then, again cannot capture the trends unfolding since 1990, which are more aptly described as a set of gradual, uncoordinated, and unsystematic, sometimes even surreptitious and contradictory, adjustments.[27] The basic elements of the German CME remain recognizable. The unions have undeniably suffered a partial loss of their bargaining power, but remain influential. The described forms of 'experimentalism' are not comparable to American-style concession bargaining in that they modify and limit the functions and scope of collective agreements without replacing them. Again, however, observable examples of institutional layering that supplement coordinative with liberal, market-based institutions may over time translate into conversion processes, and hence ultimately result in the demise of the production regime.

Party System

As in other European countries of the conservative welfare state regime type, pronounced regional, denominational, and religious cleavages structured Germany's multi-party systems during the nineteenth and early twentieth centuries.[28] After 1945, however, political Catholicism was absorbed in the newly founded Christian Democratic Union (CDU) and its Bavarian sister party, the Christian Social Union (CSU). The Christian Democratic hegemony throughout much of the post-war era was typical for a conservative welfare state regime and CME. The SPD, for its part, came to dominate the left side of the political spectrum. It had strongly articulated economic preferences since its formation, joining several governments in the Weimar Republic, but it took a shift towards ideological moderation in the 1950s to transform it, unlike Canada's NDP, into a viable competitor to the Christian Democrats at both tiers of government. While class voting continued to play a greater role than in Canada, the two major parties moved towards the political centre, establishing broad electoral coalitions beyond their traditional class bases. And while the Christian Democrats have a more privileged relationship with business than the Social Democrats, who entertain close ties with the unions, working class interests and the Catholic labour movement have been quite well represented within the CDU and CSU. Both large parties participated in building the welfare state regime, and their electoral appeal to its beneficiaries, notably unionized workers and pensioners, reflects this fact. The logic of party competition in Germany is therefore largely centripetal; inter-party consensus on social and economic issues has usually been considerable, and hardly challenged by the FDP.[29]

Unlike Canadian party organizations, their German counterparts encompass the municipal, Länder, and national levels.[30] Moreover, while the relative strength of the CDU and CSU, SPD, and FDP fluctuates over time, and each party retains regional strongholds, the party *systems* in the eleven West German Länder have not differed much if compared with the Canadian provinces. Illustrating the dominance of national party organizations, Länder governments whose composition would have been inconsistent with the federal coalition pattern – by including, for instance, one government and one opposition party –

were usually avoided. The rise of the Greens during the 1970s and 1980s modified this picture only slightly, transforming a two and one-half-party system predominantly centred around the left-right cleavage into a system with two-dimensional cleavage structures and two blocks, each comprising one major and one smaller party. Most federal and Länder governments were coalitions between one of the large parties and the FDP until 1990. The first SPD and Green Party coalitions in the Länder were formed during the 1980s.

That inter-regional tension in German politics is low, by Canadian standards, and remained so after reunification, is not the least a result of this pronounced vertical and horizontal integration. Together with the logic of intrastate federalism, this ensures that debates within the Bundesrat, and its conflicts with the Bundestag (Parliament's Lower House), are often driven more by the strategic requirements of party competition at the national level than by regional interests. Yet despite claims to the opposite, even divergent majorities in the two chambers rarely produce legislative stalemate. Typically, conflicts in the 'grand-coalition state' are resolved through inter-party bargaining.[31]

However, reunification has ushered in more substantial transformations of the German party system, especially in the Länder. The Party of Democratic Socialism (PDS), successor to the communists in the former East Germany, failed to make inroads in the western part of the country, but remains an important force in the east, thriving on a new and pronounced regional cleavage. Representing ideological stances considerably to the left of the SPD and Greens, it has strengthened the electoral clout of the 'social-protectionist coalition,' defending the status quo of the German welfare state and production regime.[32] Moreover, it has forced the CDU and SPD into coalitions, or tolerated and joined SPD governments, in several new Länder. Yet even in the old ones, a greater range of coalition options has been explored in recent years. Despite nominal Bundesrat majorities of the SPD between 1991 and 1999, and of the CDU and CSU thereafter, squaring the requirements of national party competition with the pursuit of regional interests has therefore become more challenging than in the past.

Our cases document some of the growing specificity of political landscapes in the Länder. Bavaria is home base for the CSU, whose social conservatism places it considerably to the right of its sister party. The CSU has gained increasingly overwhelming majorities and ruled the *Land* without a coalition partner since 1962. North Rhine-Westphalia (NRW) is a stronghold of the SPD, which has continuously governed the Land since 1966, often – for example, from 1990 to 1995 – gaining majorities as well. Since the mid-1990s, NRW has been ruled by an SPD and Green coalition. Finally, Saxony-Anhalt had a CDU and FDP government from 1990 to 1994. Between 1994 and 2002, an SPD minority government, joined by the Greens until 1998, was tolerated by the PDS. This experiment went down to a crushing defeat in the 2002 election, which returned the CDU and FDP to power.

In short, the institutional arrangements of Germany's federalism, welfare state, and production regime all encourage or necessitate coordination and consensus – between the state, labour, and business in industrial relations and vocational (re)training; and among federal and Länder governments, even those of different partisan stripes, in policy-making. These features of the 'semi-sovereign' or 'grand-coalition state' were long associated with political stability, economic success, and social peace, but are now more likely to be qualified as root causes of a German disease. In this view, the wholesale transfer of the West German welfare state and production regime to the east cemented the transformation of stability, incrementalism, and policies 'of the middle way' into stagnation and lowest common denominator compromises.[33] However, while the external shock of reunification was, at first, not used for large-scale retrenchment and market-oriented institutional reforms, it would be inaccurate to describe the situation prevailing since 1990 as one of immobility. Even proponents of the reform gridlock argument concede that the heightened economic and fiscal pressures after 2002 opened a window of opportunity. Established institutional arrangements are increasingly circumvented by political actors, labour, and business precisely because their reform is difficult. The ensuing processes of layering and conversion have in turn led to fissures in the German welfare state and production regime. The arrangements of the post-war era have thus, at least to some extent, been in flux since 1990.

Regional disparities have grown considerably as a result. Table 9.1 summarizes differences and similarities in the institutional contexts faced by governments in Bavaria, NRW, and Saxony-Anhalt. As in Canada, variations are smallest – they barely exist – regarding the welfare state. They are more pronounced, at least between the old and the new Länder, with regard to the production regime, although the CME has nowhere been replaced by its liberal alternative yet. Finally, our three cases differ most strongly on the partisan dimension. While Bavaria and NRW are cases of right-wing and left-wing dominance, respectively, the extent to which the CSU controls Bavarian politics is all

Table 9.1. Institutional Contexts of Active Labour Market Policy-Making in Three German Länder

Land	Welfare state	Modified by	Political economy	Modified by	Party system	Modified by
Bavaria	Conservative	–	CME	–	3-party system	CSU dominance; single-party majority governments
NRW	Conservative	–	CME	–	4-party system	SPD dominance; majority and coalition governments
Saxony-Anhalt	Conservative	–	'Flawed' version of CME	Weaker organiza-tional capac-ity of labour and business; collective agreements, vocational training system, etc., not well entrenched	Multi-party system	High electoral volatility; minority and coalition governments
Inter-Länder variation	Low		Moderate		High	

but unique in Germany. In Saxony-Anhalt, on the other hand, the pendulum has swung back and forth between 1990 and 2002. Complementarities between the conservative welfare state regime and the CME remain strong, but the nexus with a specific type of party system is less clear than in the past.[34] Turning to the examination of national and sub-national active labour market policy-making in Germany, we might therefore hypothesize (1) relatively limited short-term policy swings whenever the partisan complexion of governments changes at both levels, (2) a comparatively modest potential for governments to implement globalization-induced retrenchment and neo-liberal reforms, and hence (3) relatively little policy convergence with liberal jurisdictions or countries like Canada.

Active Labour Market Policy-Making in Germany

The importance of adequate labour market performance for a conservative welfare state and production regime has combined with the logic of
intra-state federalism to make the labour market field predominantly a
national responsibility in Germany.[35] Labour contracts, dismissal protection, and many employment standards are tightly regulated at the
national level, too, and most of this legislation does not require Bundesrat
consent. However, like the administration of UI benefits and other
income-maintenance programs for the unemployed, the implementation of active measures has been delegated from the (rudimentary)
national bureaucracy to the Federal Employment Service (FES). As a
para-public agency, the FES enjoys considerable budgetary and operational autonomy, albeit under the oversight of the Federal Ministry of
Labour and Social Affairs and within a national legislative framework.

Although a few programs are tax-financed, UI payroll contributions
are the main funding source for both passive and active measures. FES
deficits are covered by the federal government. In keeping with the
social partnership and 'self-administration' principles of the German
regime, labour and business are represented in tripartite bodies – the
national board of governors, regional and local management committees – and share decision making with federal, Länder, and municipal
government delegates, the FES executive board, and the directors
of its subsidiaries, the regional and local employment offices. Many
FES programs are delivered by public, non-profit, or private-sector
organizations such as municipal governments, unions, and employers'
associations.[36]

Unlike Canadian provinces, the Länder have limited legislative responsibilities and administrative duties in the active labour market
field. Their authority to formulate and implement genuinely regional
labour market strategies is restricted to the few areas not covered by
national legislation. The FES dominates financially as well. Länder
programs are therefore merely supplementary, usually co-financing
FES measures. This often ensures that available national resources are
fully used: The employment offices grant their financial support to
providers on a matching basis, and many projects could not be realized
if they were not co-financed by sub-national governments, too. Moreover, the leverage effects of the co-funding approach enable the Länder
to provide additional funding for objectives that are neglected by the
FES. The approach may also be used to integrate active measures with

sub-national economic development strategies.[37] Despite limited discretion, the Länder therefore have become more proactive in the field since the late 1980s.[38]

The same is true for the municipalities. Under the Federal Social Assistance Act, they have the right, and a strong financial incentive, to support labour market (re)integration for employable social assistance recipients. The Länder may in turn encourage and co-finance municipal 'back-to-work' programs.[39] Finally, the active labour market field gained a European dimension during the 1990s with the formulation of a European Employment Strategy to complement European Union (EU) structural policies. The European Social Fund (ESF) now co-finances active measures with significant amounts of money. In Germany, both tiers of government increasingly use this opportunity. The new Länder, because of high unemployment rates, profit from this source of funding even more than the old ones. The EU encourages coordination with regional and local public actors, labour and business, and the non-profit sector, in the implementation of national action plans.[40]

However, the rising costs and doubtful effectiveness of active labour market policies have made them a retrenchment target in recent decades. Together with tightened eligibility criteria and reduced benefits in income-maintenance programs, the Schmidt and Kohl governments cut active measures to reduce growing FES deficits and to stabilize the UI contribution rate. Both governments privileged efforts to reduce the labour supply in their fight against unemployment. After 1982, repatriation incentives for foreigners and early retirement schemes were expanded.[41] These measures were complemented by the 1985 Employment Promotion Act and other neo-liberal attempts to deregulate the labour market. Most of these were, however, unsuccessful or remained modest in scope. The brighter economic and fiscal conditions after the mid-1980s even induced the government to restore some benefits and to introduce a couple of new active measures.[42]

As in other social policy fields, reunification brought retrenchment to a temporary end. The West German labour administration was immediately extended to the new Länder. The transition to a capitalist economy in the former GDR led to the virtual collapse of industrial production. The number of jobs shrank from 10 to 6 million within a couple of years. To cope with exploding unemployment levels in the new Länder, the Kohl government relied on massive infrastructure and human capital investments, industrial policies, and, again, efforts to reduce labour supply. Short-time work allowances were used generously, early retirement schemes and active measures were expanded, and new instruments were introduced in the east. Employment corporations and 'mega' job creation schemes helped stabilize the labour market. Spending on active measures, which had often become de facto income-maintenance, climaxed in 1992. The UI contribution rate had to be increased, and FES deficits reached ever new heights.[43]

Many of the special regulations and instruments for the east were therefore phased out quickly. The 1994 Employment Promotion and Working Time Acts brought more cutbacks, stricter work requirements for unemployment assistance recipients, and further deregulation, notably with regard to dismissal protection and fixed-term contracts. The placement monopoly of the FES was abolished. Cutbacks were not offset by measures like the 1994 federal-Länder initiative for vocational training in East Germany. In 1995, Chancellor Kohl initiated an Employment Alliance – that is, roundtable talks with labour and business representatives in the German tradition of 'concerted action' – that had been suggested by the Metalworkers' Union. Labour had offered wage restraint in return for the creation of more jobs and apprenticeship positions, and for an end to cutbacks. Yet the government did not refrain from unilateral action contradicting labour demands. The unions therefore pulled out of the Alliance, forcing its demise in 1996.[44] The 1996 Program for Growth and Employment, the unemployment and social assistance reforms of the same year, and the 1997 Labour Promotion Reform Act, tightened eligibility criteria, lowered UI and other income-maintenance benefits, shortened payment durations, and introduced new work requirements for employable social assistance and unemployment assistance recipients.

Since January 1998, the legislative national goal of full employment has been relaxed, replaced with increasing chances of employment retention and (re)integration, prevention of illegal employment and benefit claims, and cost reduction, as the main objectives. Target groups among the hard-to-employ were more clearly defined. While the FES board of directors had previously been responsible for fund allocation, the new legislation gave local employment offices much more budgetary discretion. To encourage competition for funds and efficiency, up to 10 per cent of their discretionary budgets were reserved for experiments linking traditional programs with broader structural objectives.[45]

By 1998, Kohl's efforts to fight unemployment were widely perceived as a failure. Unemployment in the new Länder remained stubbornly high at approximately 20 per cent, or twice the West German rate, but even in the west, the situation had not improved markedly. This greatly contributed to the electoral demise of the CDU and FDP government in the fall of that year. The incoming SPD and Green Party coalition championed welfare state inclusion. Within a year, the retrenchment and labour market deregulation efforts of the previous government were scrapped. UI benefits were improved in 2000, while work requirements for unemployment and social assistance recipients were relaxed. Active labour market policies were again expanded. A youth-employment program was launched in November 1998. The weakening of dismissal protection and the reduction of sick payments, imposed by Kohl in 1997, were rescinded. A legal right to part-time employment was entrenched in 1999, and co-determination was strengthened in 2001. Schröder also revived the 1995–96 experiment with macro-corporatist arrangements in the labour market field, initiating an Alliance for Employment in December 1998 to facilitate reforms in various policy fields and in the three tiers of government.

But the alliance quickly proved to be ineffective, 'kept alive only for public consumption' after the summer of 2001.[46] Both the unions and employers' associations increasingly shunned its tripartite logic, directly lobbying the government instead. Moreover, the post-1998 economic and labour market recovery had been short-lived and weak. The economic downturn at the beginning of the 2002 election year renewed the unemployment and fiscal challenges with a vengeance. Germany faced sanctions for infringing the EU Stability Pact. 'Modernizers' within the SPD and the governing coalition had already gained the upper hand, and the government parties lost their Bundesrat majority, in 1999. Legislative changes in 2002 curtailed the role of the social partners in the FES and gave job placement greater weight among its services; private job placement was facilitated, as were fixed-term contracts. Support for start-ups was expanded, and new instruments geared towards (re)integration into the regular labour market were introduced. In March, a regional experiment with wage subsidies in the low-wage sector became available countrywide and job placement vouchers were introduced.[47]

In 2002, a commission was also established under the chairmanship of Volkswagen executive Peter Hartz. Unlike the Employment Alliance, terminated a year later, the Hartz Commission represented a break from the tripartite philosophy and prepared unilateral government action. Labour and business were only weakly represented; the SPD caucus and the Federal Ministry of Labour were bypassed altogether.

When Hartz tabled his report in August, the debate on improved job placement and organizational changes widened to include the reform of passive and active measures, labour market deregulation, and job creation, notably in the low-wage sector.[48] Barely returned to office in 2002, the SPD and Green Party coalition enacted four related pieces of legislation (Hartz I to IV) between January 2003 and January 2005. These sought to improve placement services, but also reduced benefits and tightened obligations for job seekers. The role of the regional employment offices was adjusted, the local ones were reinvented as 'job centres,' and non-profit temporary work agencies were created. Various active measures were changed. Higher income thresholds for marginal employment with waived or reduced social insurance contributions were introduced. The new round of cutbacks limited UI payments to a year (18 months for older persons). Spending on active measures was cut further. After lengthy negotiations with the opposition-dominated Bundesrat, one of the most controversial proposals of the Hartz Commission passed the federal parliament in 2004: the replacement of social assistance for employable persons and unemployment assistance – an income maintenance program for those who had exhausted their UI benefits – with a strictly means-tested and much less generous second tier of benefits.

Active Labour Market Policy-Making in Three German Länder since 1990

As illustrated by the data in table 9.2, our three cases are characterized by quite distinct socio-economic and labour market conditions. The following analysis highlights selected indicators for the scope and nature of labour market strategies formulated and implemented by the Länder governments: How much is spent in the field? How is it organized, and which coordinative mechanisms exist? Which objectives have been pursued, which programs and instruments have been used, and to what extent have labour market strategies shifted?

Bavaria

The once marginal agrarian economy of Germany's largest and second most populous jurisdiction experienced dramatic changes during the post-war era. Unburdened by old industries, it is now prosperous, with an export-oriented manufacturing sector (automobile and electrical in-

Table 9.2. Selected Demographic, Economic, and Labour Market Indicators, Bavaria, NRW, and Saxony-Anhalt

		Bavaria	NRW	Saxony-Anhalt
Population,	1991	14.4	21.8	3.6
% total German	1996	14.7	21.9	3.3
	2001	14.9	21.9	3.1
GDP,	1991	16.8	23.6	1.3
% total German	1996	16.6	22.5	2.1
	2001	17.5	22.1	2.1
GDP per capita,	1991	116.6	108.1	37.3
% German	1996	113.2	103.0	63.4
	2001	117.0	101.0	61.8
Unemployment	1991	4.4	7.9	10.3
rate	1996	7.9	11.4	18.8
	2001	6.0	9.6	20.9
Ratio	1991	0.6	1.1	1.4
Land / Germany	1996	0.7	1.0	1.6
	2001	0.6	0.9	2.0

Sources: http://www.vgrdl.de/Arbeitskreis_VGR/tab02.asp (download 22 July 2004); http://www1.arbeitsamt.de/hst/services/statistik/200212/iiia4/multijz_heftd.pdf (download 22 July 2004).

dustry, machinery), much knowledge-intensive production, and thriving advanced services (aerospace and defense industry, biotechnology and genetics, IT). It also boasts a desirable mix of large corporations and small firms, well-developed educational and research infrastructures, and a favourable location. Bavaria's labour market performance has been one of the best in Germany since the early 1990s, with unemployment rates hovering around two-thirds of the national average. Labour market problems are mostly localized to peripheral regions.

Bavarian governments thus had few incentives to formulate explicit labour market strategies in the past. With the exception of a couple of programs for its disadvantaged regions, the Land relied on the FES and on the labour market effects of its ambitious, business-oriented industrial and technology policies. In the early and mid-1990s, however, premier Edmund Stoiber began to advocate a decentralization of the UI system and active labour market policy-making.[49] Privatization proceeds were reinvested in new structural and active labour market policies. FES and ESF programs were increasingly co-financed. Still, Bavaria remains a laggard in terms of its own budgetary labour market expenditures (see table 9.3). Its spending is dwarfed by FES expenditures in

Table 9.3. Labour Market Spending (€) – Bavaria, NRW, and Saxony-Anhalt

		Bavaria	NRW	Saxony-Anhalt
Reg. empl. office	1996	1.7 billion	3.1 billion	2.0 billion
	2001	1.4 billion	2.8 billion	1.8 billion
Reg. empl. off.,	1996	4239	3724	8433
per unemployed	2001	4282	3617	6643
Land	1996	26 million	324 million	273 million
	2001	48 million	351 million	127 million
Land,	1996	64	392	1,483
per unemployed	2001	146	458	479
Ratio	1996	1.6	12.7	13.8
Land/FES (%)	2001	3.4	12.5	7.1

Sources: Bundesanstalt für Arbeit, *Arbeitsstatistik 1996 – Jahreszahlen* (Nuremberg, 1997); Josef Schmid and Susanne Blancke, *Arbeitsmarktpolitik der Bundesländer: Chancen und Restriktionen einer aktiven Arbeitsmarkt- und Strukturpolitik im Föderalismus* (Berlin: Edition Sigma, 2001); Josef Schmid et al., *Vergleich der aktiven Arbeitsmarktpolitik der westdeutschen Bundesländer in 2001* (Tübingen: Institute for Political Science, University of Tübingen, 2003).

the Land, and by expenditures in North Rhine-Westphalia and Saxony-Anhalt. The government's goal is to fill niches left by the social partners, the municipalities, and the national labour administration.[50]

Like Ontario, the Land lacks an ample infrastructure for policy implementation and monitoring. It largely relies on the regional and local employment offices, municipal and county governments, unions and employers' associations, the chambers of commerce and trade, and other organizations. In June 1996, the Land initiated the Bavarian Employment Pact along the lines of the national Employment Alliance. Its participants – representatives of the Ministries of Labour, Economic Affairs, and Finance, the regional employment office, unions and employers' associations, and the chambers – addressed ways to stimulate growth and job creation, enhance labour market flexibility, promote work redistribution, fight unemployment, and prevent skills shortages. A working group of the Employment Pact selects projects for co-financing by the Bavarian Labour Market Fund.[51] Although modest, this fund may be the most original labour market instrument of the Land. Experimental projects in disadvantaged regions that do not meet FES or ESF guidelines are prioritized. Although the Employment Pact failed in May 2002, when labour pulled out, some working groups continued their deliberations.

Bavaria continues to focus on linkages between structural and active labour market policies. Conventional measures have outweighed innovative ones since 1990, but efficiency-related objectives and market-oriented instruments dominate; equity-related objectives and measures are usually restricted to disadvantaged regions and hard-to-place persons. Subsidized employment and direct job creation play a marginal role. Measures conducive to employment creation, job retention, and the (re)integration of unemployed persons into the regular labour market are privileged instead. The Land offers support for start-ups, including programs for female would-be entrepreneurs, or child care services for job seekers. With the Bavarian employers' associations, the government has strongly advocated reforms of the German welfare state and production regime, including a reduction of non-wage labour costs through social insurance reform, further decentralization of collective bargaining, and the development of a low-wage sector. Most labour market spending in Bavaria has been concentrated on previously neglected vocational (re)training, focusing on disadvantaged regions and target groups such as women, youth and older workers, migrants, the disabled, and the long-term unemployed. This category also includes preventive measures for workers in small firms, as well as the co-funding of local business, educational, and research networks. Apprenticeship training has been another focus, although interviewed union representatives complained about insufficient efforts. Funding for institutional providers of vocational training was terminated in 2001.

North Rhine-Westphalia

Like Bavaria, NRW – the most populous German jurisdiction – is an economic heavyweight. It comprises the urban agglomeration of the Ruhr area, the country's traditional industrial heartland. However, as its economic weight was long grounded in coal and steel production, the decline of these and related old industries during the post-war era ushered in a severe crisis. This trend has been largely responsible for the reversal of economic fortunes between the once-dominant northern and increasingly prosperous southern parts of the country. While more diverse and competitive structures have emerged in recent years, the Land economy still faces major challenges. The unemployment level greatly exceeds Bavaria's, although it has fallen below the national one. Between 1990 and 1997 alone, 100,000 jobs were shed in mining and steel production, and overall employment trends in manufacturing have been negative. Service sector growth has not yet compensated for these losses.

Unsurprisingly, then, NRW governments developed an explicit labour market strategy in the 1980s, much earlier than Bavaria. A range of programs, many co-financed with the FES and the ESF, was eventually incorporated into a coherent, regularly updated policy framework. This proactive approach is illustrated by the expenditure data in table 9.3. NRW's share of overall labour market spending in the Land is much higher than Bavaria's, compensating for low per capita spending by the national labour market administration. During the 1990s, the Land even increased its expenditures, and it now invests more in labour market programs than any other western jurisdiction, except the city states.[52]

Unlike Bavaria, the Land built a dense program infrastructure, one that has pronounced corporatist elements and greatly relies on synergies among key actors. Regional secretariats are seconded by boards of consultation in which the directors of local employment offices and representatives of municipal and county governments, unions, and employers' associations evaluate programs, formulate local strategies, and coordinate initiatives. For some complex programs, now including measures in the wake of the Hartz legislation, similar boards cover the entire Land. In December 1998, following the example of the new federal government, the NRW premier initiated his own Alliance for Employment. Pursuing a similar agenda as its federal and Bavarian counterparts, it has attempted to increase program effectiveness by involving stakeholders and coordinating policy fields. It played an important role in fighting youth unemployment, linking its own Jobs for Youth initiative with the federal program. With its range of innovative programs, NRW has assumed a leading role among the old Länder in the active labour market field. While intensive efforts are undertaken to meet equity-related objectives and to reduce the social costs of restructuring through programs that are more inclusive than in Bavaria, the Land also stresses linkages between structural and active labour market policies. More genuinely efficiency-related objectives and market-oriented instruments have recently come to the fore. In the past, by contrast, NRW relied on the co-funding of job creation schemes and other forms of subsidized employment. Funding for such measures remains at an average level. As in Bavaria, there is an employment program for social assistance recipients. However, in an effort to link structural and job creation schemes, many of the latter are tied to regional development projects. Working with other actors, the Land has also pioneered the use of non-profit temporary work placement along Dutch lines. Between 1998 and 2003, local pilot projects linked social assistance and the services of the FES.

Like Bavaria, though, the Land has recently concentrated on measures for job creation and retention, and the (re)integration of unemployed persons into the regular labour market. In 1997, support for modernization processes to enhance the productivity, flexibility, and competitiveness of firms became a central component of NRW's labour market strategy. As in Bavaria, start-up support was expanded, and the Land regularly intervenes in favour of employers in crisis situations. Women returning to the labour market and small firms have been priority areas. Again, like Bavaria, the Land has increasingly accentuated vocational (re)training. Apprenticeship has recently become a strong focus, and the Employment Alliance's working group has strengthened the commitment of firms and the NRW government to offering apprenticeship positions to young people.

Saxony-Anhalt

A small and economically peripheral jurisdiction, this Land illustrates the massive disparities between the old and new Länder.[53] Saxony-Anhalt was the industrial heartland of the GDR, home to some of its largest state conglomerates, which were closed or privatized after reunification, resulting in massive de-industrialization. Only West German and foreign investment on a very large scale ensured the survival of an extremely capital-intensive and export-oriented industrial core, primarily in the chemical industry. The economy is otherwise dominated by small firms, and agriculture is still comparatively important. While Saxony-Anhalt has broadened its economic basis, the productivity gap with the old Länder remains substantial. The post-reunification economic upheavals have translated into a dismal labour market performance and formidable policy challenges. Throughout much of the 1990s and 2000s, the Land has had the highest unemployment rate in Germany. While labour force participation has remained strong, many young and well-educated residents migrate to the west, further exacerbating this conjuncture.

Like North Rhine-Westphalia, Saxony-Anhalt therefore became proactive in the active labour market field immediately after reunification.

Like their counterparts, governments in Saxony-Anhalt concentrate on co-funding FES and ESF programs. The considerable redistribution effects between West and East Germany within the FES are illustrated by figures in table 9.3. In absolute terms, the FES spends more in Saxony-Anhalt than in Bavaria, and 'per unemployed' expenditures are even more revealing. Saxony-Anhalt's own per capita active labour market spending has ranked third among the Länder since 1992. Although its expenditures have been relatively minor in comparison with FES and overall federal spending – the latter represented as much as 12.0 per cent of its GDP in 1992, and 4.6 per cent in 2001 – Saxony-Anhalt funds active labour market policies with much more money, whether on an aggregate or on a per unemployed basis, than the average Land.[54]

Like NRW, Saxony-Anhalt has developed a relatively dense infrastructure for implementing active measures. And like the two western jurisdictions examined here, it uses coordinative arrangements extensively. Despite the lower membership and weaker organizational capacity of labour, and especially business in the new Länder, the chambers of commerce and trade, unions, and employers' associations cooperate in a range of programs. Together with the Land and the federal government, they have, for instance, co-funded and managed the important municipal employment corporations, as well as job creation schemes and vocational (re)training institutions. In 1999, the Land followed the federal example by inviting unions and employers' associations, the chambers, the FES and municipal governments, to participate in a regional Employment Alliance. Sectoral employment pacts have been initiated in the chemical and the metal industries, with a focus on preventing the out-migration of skilled labour and on supply shortages.

Given its labour market situation, it does not come as a surprise that Saxony-Anhalt has aimed both at fully using FES and ESF programs and at creating its own, innovative measures. It has tried to implement systematic monitoring and evaluation routines. In the first half of the 1990s, cushioning the social impact of exploding unemployment levels was the government's priority, but the weight of efficiency objectives has grown in recent years. Subsidized employment long played an important role in Saxony-Anhalt, though. As in the rest of East Germany, massive use of national programs greatly contributed to stabilizing its labour market after reunification. The number of participants in job creation schemes climaxed at 88,000 in 1992, but fell to less than

21,000 in 2001.[55] In co-funding them, Saxony-Anhalt accentuated economic development objectives like the rehabilitation of industrial sites, construction of transportation and tourism infrastructures, and so on. FES programs have also been topped up in order to improve benefits and services for hard-to-employ target groups. As in Bavaria and NRW, municipal social assistance recipients have been supported. In 1999, the government ensured that one form of wage subsidy, structural adjustment measures, could be extended from three to five years for workers over the age of 55.

Measures geared towards employment creation, job retention, and the (re)integration of unemployed persons into the regular labour market have therefore become more prominent. Saxony-Anhalt has supported hiring incentives for various target groups. The shift towards the regular labour market received a boost with the 2002 change of government when (re)training measures, as in Bavaria and NRW, became more important. As the dual apprenticeship system is not well entrenched in the new Länder, support for vocational training – often established with business cooperation, co-financed through the federal program for training in the east, and implemented by local employment offices – has been a priority area. Measures to encourage traditional apprenticeship have been offered as well. With the help of its Employment Alliance, Saxony-Anhalt has been relatively successful in balancing the supply of and demand for apprenticeship positions.[56]

Discussion

Does the evidence presented here corroborate the hypothesis that coordinative institutions mediate the effects of partisanship and globalization differently than liberal ones? As suggested above, the comparative political economy literature reviewed in the first and second chapters of this volume would lead us to expect relatively minor partisan variations in the active labour market field, little globalization-induced retrenchment, and hence little policy change in the direction of neo-liberal solutions. The following discussion summarizes and assesses our findings. As the strong centralization of active labour market policy-making in Germany is one of the features that distinguishes it most from Canada, both national trends and developments in the three Länder will be examined.

If one were to compare only the early phases of the Kohl and Schröder governments, or their declared goals and objectives, one might be driven towards the conclusion that policy swings – from avowedly neo-liberal to social democratic labour market strategies – were comparable in size to the ones typically experienced in Canada. Hence, at first glance, parties seem to matter just as much. Yet the policy swings *during* the Kohl and Schröder eras were hardly less considerable than the ones *between* them. The field has been characterized by a mixture of considerable stability with regard to labour market institutions and major programs, on the one hand, and cyclical spending patterns on the other. Arguably, the similarity of Christian Democratic and Social Democratic labour market strategies can be explained by the fact that both parties are closely associated with the country's welfare state and production regime. Catering to a 'social-protectionist' electoral base, they are reluctant to impose major cutbacks, relying on early retirement schemes and anti-immigration policies instead. Moreover, the two parties were confronted with post-reunification challenges that made policy experiments, let alone market-oriented cutbacks, particularly difficult. To the extent that genuine reforms were attempted by the Kohl government in the 1990s, they were resisted by the SPD opposition and its Bundesrat majority, by Länder governments of all stripes, notably in East Germany, by the unions, and even by the working class wing of the CDU itself. And although the autonomy of the FES was curtailed by Kohl, 'self-administration' and the logic of social partnership have also worked against the successful implementation of overtly partisan labour market strategies. Overall, the development of active measures was more strongly influenced by the peculiar legislative and organizational framework structuring the policy field than by the ideological stances of the two governments. Income-maintenance programs and active measures were expanded and contracted in line with economic and fiscal conditions, or with the political business cycle, but often without a clear strategic goal. In short, the veto points and coordinative mechanisms built into Germany's welfare state and production regime, its federalism, and its labour administration dampened the policy swings one might otherwise have expected to see at the national level.

A similar picture emerges at the sub-national level. Our sample does not enable us to draw firm conclusions about the relationship between changing Länder governments and the size of policy swings, but it sheds light on the extent to which the divergent partisan complexion of Länder governments causes policy variations. At first glance, active labour market policies in Bavaria, North Rhine-Westphalia, and Saxony-Anhalt are different enough in scope and nature to suggest a confirmation of the 'parties matter' hypothesis. Since 1990, the ideological distance between the Bavarian CSU and the SPD in NRW, or between CDU and FDP coalitions and the PDS-tolerated minority governments of the SPD in Saxony-Anhalt, has been great. As expected, spending on active labour market policies – in absolute terms, per unemployed, and as a percentage of accumulated FES and Länder expenditures – was considerably higher in NRW and Saxony-Anhalt than in Bavaria. Moreover, the SPD governments of NRW and Saxony-Anhalt formulated ambitious labour market strategies and established a plethora of labour market institutions and programs over the years. By contrast, Bavarian governments mostly relied on their structural policies. And while equity-related objectives have continued to figure prominently in the labour market strategies of SPD governments, their Christian Democratic counterparts have put more emphasis on efficiency-related and market-oriented instruments, even striking an avowedly neo-liberal chord in the case of the CSU. NRW and Saxony-Anhalt still invest more in job creation and subsidized employment than Bavaria. But the impact of partisanship should not be overestimated. It is exceedingly difficult, if not impossible, to disentangle partisan effects from the consequences of socio-economic context in our three cases. Many of the observed differences may have more to do with divergent unemployment rates and labour markets. NRW and Saxony-Anhalt may have been more proactive simply because they faced more severe labour market challenges and had a greater need for active measures than Bavaria. Our cases also provide quite a few examples of policy learning and convergence across the partisan cleavage.[57] The modest policy swings experienced by Saxony-Anhalt after 1994 and 2002 point in the same direction. Active labour market policies in the new Länder seem to be even more clearly problem-driven than in West Germany, where the impact of partisanship may be easier to substantiate. Compared with the Canadian provinces, then, the partisan differences among the Länder appear to be small.

Moreover, any partisan effects at the sub-national level are likely to be submerged, as it were, by the impact of the macro- and micro-institutional context in which Länder policies are made.[58] National legislation narrowly circumscribes Länder discretion in the active labour market field, and the financial dominance of the FES is overwhelming. Länder with severe labour market challenges and tight fiscal conditions (Saxony-Anhalt comes to mind) have a strong incentive to make their own labour market strategies compatible with FES and ESF guidelines, despite the strings attached. Even Bavaria, which has the fiscal capacity to do otherwise, hesitated to opt out of co-financed programs in order to concentrate on its few legislative responsibilities in the field. Major policy swings in line with the ideological stances of Länder governments are largely precluded by this national and European framework. To the extent that decentralization has occurred recently, it has been within these structures. Local employment offices now have more budgetary autonomy than in the past, and the European Employment Strategy encourages territorial employment pacts and regional networks. Yet devolution of legislative and administrative responsibilities for UI and active labour market policy-making to the Länder, as advocated by Bavaria, has not materialized, successfully resisted by jurisdictions that profit from the status quo. German federalism provides multiple veto points for the opponents of such reforms, but no opting-out provisions or tolerance for asymmetries. Ultimately, even Bavaria has been more interested in being a major player on the federal scene than in negotiating a transfer of responsibilities. German labour market institutions remain highly centralized and coordinative.

The logic of social partnership also restricts the margin of maneuver of Länder. Labour and business are involved in policy formulation, implementation, and evaluation at all tiers of the FES and in ESF-supported programs. Joint ventures are widespread in the provision of active measures. They retain clout in the field, the partisan complexion of governments notwithstanding. The ubiquity of employment alliances or pacts, networks, and roundtables initiated at all tiers of government during the 1990s is indicative of the sway that coordinative mechanisms and expectations continue to hold.[59] 'Concerted action' has been used in each of our three cases, notably in vocational (re)training. Even CDU and CSU governments have usually sought to cooperate with labour. And while the Bavarian government may lean slightly more towards business than its Social Democratic counterparts, the Bavarian Employment Pact was initiated *earlier* than its equivalents in the other two Länder. Our interviewees on the business and labour side alike confirm that the Employment Pact and its major achievement, the Labour Market Fund, were supported by a fairly broad consensus, even if the pact temporarily failed. Occasional calls for neo-liberal changes did not prevent the Bavarian government from seeking the cooperation of business and labour. Its rhetoric has been hardly more than partisan window dressing most of the time – an assessment that is further corroborated by a comparative look at the Klein and Harris governments in Alberta and Ontario. There is little evidence for an outright repudiation of social partnership by conservative governments. The Länder neither have the legislative authority nor an incentive to challenge the coordinative institutions of Germany's CME. Similarly, Bavaria may set more market-oriented accents to its active policies than the other two Länder, but it remains just as interventionist in its regional development strategies – supporting failing corporations and human capital formation. Overall it seems that active labour market policies in the Länder are largely similar in nature because they occupy the niches left by the FES and concentrate on priority areas on which all stakeholders can agree.

Does this mean, though, that coordinative institutions have blocked retrenchment and convergence towards liberal policies in the active labour market field? As suggested above, the picture is more ambivalent and inconclusive with regard to this second question. During the 1990s, retrenchment efforts were indeed comparatively modest, and there was no clear erosion. A couple of benefits and programs were even expanded by the Kohl and Schröder governments. Unlike some of its European neighbours, Germany has only recently envisaged more sweeping reforms. But the considerable stability of labour market institutions, cyclical spending patterns, and the temporary expansion of active measures in the wake of reunification should not obstruct our view of developments that might be described as a globalization-induced shift away from the policies associated with Germany's welfare state and production regime in the direction of its liberal competitor. Tightened eligibility criteria, reduced payment levels and shorter durations of UI benefits, the pending merger of the unemployment assistance and social assistance programs, and other elements of the Hartz legislation, undoubtedly constitute major retrenchment and may well be qualified as third-order changes in Peter Hall's terms. With regard to active measures, 'activation' and related terms are not just code words for neo-liberal reforms. But in Germany, they certainly refer to a pronounced shift from the inclusive thrust and entitlements of traditional programs to efficiency-related objectives and market-oriented instruments, and hence to a recommodification of the labour market field dictated by economic and fiscal imperatives. There has not yet been a globalization-induced race to the bottom among the Länder. But, as the sub-national jurisdictions depend on FES and ESF co-funding, severe cutbacks might soon be forced upon them as a consequence of the federal government's retrenchment course. In qualitative terms, the shift to efficiency-related objectives, business-oriented instruments, and 'activation' has reached the sub-national level as well. To the extent that there has been convergence in Länder policies, it too has been in a more liberal direction.

A considerable degree of inertia and path dependence has long characterized German labour market institutions and active labour market policy-making. The differences between Canada and Germany are still pronounced. And yet it is unclear if institutional hurdles against retrenchment and neo-liberal reforms will prove to be higher, in the long run, than in nations of the liberal regime type. Coordinative institutions seem to have delayed the onset of globalization-induced reforms in Germany, but their transfer to the Länder in the eastern part of the country may ultimately have provided them with no more than a breather, covering processes of institutional layering and conversion. Strikingly, the current reforms are implemented by a Social Democratic government. Hence the trajectory of German active labour market policies indicates that coordinative institutions may not as unequivocally 'select for' centre-left, egalitarian objectives and instruments as is often suggested. Together with the described fissures in the German welfare state and production regime, they shed doubt on the institutional determinism expressed in some of the recent literature on the German disease.

10 Conclusion: Stepping Back and Looking Forward

The extent to which partisan choice remains meaningful in capitalist democracies, and whether these polities are now undertaking similarly market-oriented transformations of their domestic policies, are much discussed issues both in contemporary political science and in popular commentary. Writing in the mid-1990s, the late Italian political scientist Norberto Bobbio noted that 'it is now *de rigueur* to quote Sartre who, it appears, was one of the first to argue that left and right were empty vessels,'[1] adding that 'perhaps [the] most decisive ... reason for rejecting the left/right distinction ... is the claim that the two labels have become purely fictitious, and that the left-wing and right-wing movements, faced with the complexity and novelty of current problems, say more or less the same things, formulate more or less the same programmes for consumption by their electorates, and propose the same immediate ends.'[2] Bobbio nevertheless concluded that the left-right distinction remains a pervasive reference point in public life, and that '"left" and "right" have a descriptive meaning and an evaluative meaning, [although], as with all other political terms, [they] are not very precise, because on the whole they are taken from everyday language.'[3]

Historical institutionalist scholarship of the type that inspired this study generally shares Bobbio's guarded defence of the continuing relevance of partisan choice in developed democracies; and is sceptical of claims that states, rendered powerless by globalization, will share a common neo-liberal future.[4] We addressed this theme primarily in relation to policy developments in four Canadian provinces. A secondary focus has been recent policy change in Germany, whose labour market institutions represent a paradigmatic alternative to Canada's broadly liberal ones. As was documented in chapter 3, provinces are

Table 10.1. Hypotheses and Evidence for Ontario Labour Market Policy, 1990–2003

	Short-term partisan swings		Long-term neo-liberal retrenchment	
	Hypothesis	Evidence	Hypothesis	Evidence
Industrial relations	High (4)	High (4)	Indeterminate	Low (0)
Active measures	High (4)	High (4)	Indeterminate	Low (0)
Occupational health	High (4)	High (4)	Indeterminate	Low (0)
Workers' compensation	High (4)	High (4)	Indeterminate	Low (0)
Employment standards	High (4)	High (4)	Indeterminate	Low-to-medium (1)
Assistance/employables	High (4)	High (4)	Indeterminate	Medium (2)

responsible for most labour market policy in Canada. Two questions were posed: (a) Did left and right governments after 1990 pursue different objectives in labour market policy in these jurisdictions? and (b) Was there evidence of a pervasive drift towards neo-liberal options, a pattern that could plausibly be interpreted as reflecting the impact of globalization? Examining policy in these jurisdictions required that we first model the institutional setting of policy-making in Canada as a whole (briefly), and in the four provinces studied (in more detail). Such a modelling exercise, informed by the recent historical institutionalist literature reviewed in chapter 1, has been notably underdeveloped for Canada; this was provided in chapter 2. The first section of this chapter reviews the main findings of our study; the second addresses specific problems that arise in interpreting our conclusions about the impact of globalization on labour market policy.

Summary and Discussion

The evidence reported in chapters 4 to 7 for most dimensions of labour market policy in the Canadian provinces, and in chapter 8 for social assistance, corroborates the scepticism shared by Bobbio and much historical institutionalism about the putative demise of partisanship. Our findings regarding both partisanship and globalization, along with our initial hypotheses, are summarized for each province studied in tables 10.1 to 10.4, (pp. 270 and 271) using the measures of the degree of change introduced in chapter 2 and elaborated more fully in the appendix. As is stressed in the appendix, these findings refer to the *broad pattern* of policy change in each labour market field in each province; the implications of individual program alterations are assessed in terms

Table 10.2. Hypotheses and Evidence for Quebec Labour Market Policy, 1990–2003

	Short-term partisan swings		Long-term neo-liberal retrenchment	
	Hypothesis	Evidence	Hypothesis	Evidence
Industrial relations	Low (0)	Medium (2)	Low (0)	Low-to-medium (1)
Active measures	Low (0)	Low (0)	Low (0)	Low (0)
Occupational health & workers' compensation	Low (0)	Low (0)	Low (0)	Low (0)
Employment standards	Low (0)	Low (0)	Low (0)	Low (0)
Assistance/Employables	Low (0)	Low (0)	Low (0)	Low (0)

Table 10.3. Hypotheses and Evidence for British Columbia Labour Market Policy, 1990–2003

	Short-term partisan swings		Long-term neo-liberal retrenchment	
	Hypothesis	Evidence	Hypothesis	Evidence
Industrial relations	High (4)	High (4)	High (4)	Low (0)
Active measures	High (4)	High (4)	High (4)	Medium (2)
Occupational health & workers' compensation	High (4)	High (4)	High (4)	Low-to-medium (1)
Employment standards	High (4)	High (4)	High (4)	Medium-to-high (3)
Assistance/Employables	High (4)	High (4)	High (4)	Medium (2)

Table 10.4: Hypotheses and Evidence for Alberta Labour Market Policy, 1990–2003

	Long-term neo-liberal retrenchment	
	Hypothesis	Evidence
Industrial relations	High (4)	Low (0)
Active measures	High (4)	Low (0)
Occupational health & safety	High (4)	Low-to- medium (1)
Employment standards	High (4)	Low-to-medium (1)
Workers' compensation	High (4)	Low-to-medium (1)
Assistance/Employables	High (4)	Medium-to-high (3)

of their impact on this overall pattern. To permit a ready review of whether this evidence matched our initial hypotheses, in tables 10.1 to 10.4 we attach numerical scores to each anticipated and measured degree of change – ranging from '0' for low to '4' for high. *Partisanship* had a robust impact on labour market policy-making in two of the three provinces where ideologically distinct parties governed between 1990 and 2003. We found little evidence of what Anthony Giddens has termed 'the exhaustion of received political ideologies' of both left and right in these settings.[5]

Moreover, there were important interprovincial variations in partisanship's impact that were quite consistent with our hypotheses, elaborated in chapter 2, and that reflected institutional variations among these jurisdictions. In relation to the 16 provincial policy fields for which we were able to hypothesize a likely impact for short-term policy swings on policy outcomes (6 for Ontario, and 5 each for Quebec and British Columbia), the evidence was consistent with these initial hypotheses in 15 cases: Partisan swings were consistently high, involving at least the market-relevant contesting of policy techniques and instruments after a change in government, in all 6 observed cases in Ontario, and in all 5 in British Columbia. For 4 of 5 cases studied in Quebec, partisan swings again matched our expectations by being low, involving at most the market-relevant contesting of precise policy settings after a change in government. Only in one Quebec case did the results depart from expectations; post-2003 Liberal changes to industrial relations law that weakened significantly the province's uniquely strong protection of union successor rights contested the overall pattern of policy techniques and instruments there, a medium policy swing towards the right. Thus, partisan swings resulting from a change of power were greatest, as one might expect, in party systems that reflected the economically polarized model which, for Kitschelt, typifies Anglo-Saxon liberal settings. When the right replaced the left in power (in 1995 in Ontario, in 2001 in British Columbia), the new administration quickly executed a comprehensive reversal of policies, moving from equity to efficiency goals in policy content and from corporatist experimentation to business-dominated pluralism in policy-making style. In each case, this change was planned carefully in advance, after informal consultations with the province's business community. No such pattern of rapid change is evident in Quebec and Alberta. Yet in neither of these jurisdictions would significant partisan swings have been expected: precluded by one-party dominance in Alberta, and impeded by the collaborative strain in Quebec's institutionally ambivalent political economy. Concerted forms of policy-making are accepted as normal both by the centre-left and the centre-right in Quebec politics, although the former conceives of it in more socially inclusive terms than does the latter. In this setting, ideological debate is more muted during provincial election campaigns than in the English-speaking provinces examined here that have competitive party systems.

Market-enhancing change that reflected *globalization* was evident in all provinces, but nowhere was it sufficiently potent and unambiguous to suggest an inevitable and overpowering trend. This impact, again, varied among jurisdictions in a manner that was broadly consistent with our hypotheses. Yet our findings are more tentative regarding globalization than with respect to partisanship. This uncertainty was particularly present for Quebec and BC, where changes were introduced by centre-right parties that came to power quite recently, in 2003 and 2001, respectively. The extent of industrial relations retrenchment in the former province, and of neo-liberal reform of active measures, workers' compensation, and employment standards in the latter, can be anticipated with only moderate assurance. Moreover, the degree of retrenchment generally was less than we had thought possible. We were able to venture a hypothesis about the potential extent of retrenchment in 16 cases (5 each in Quebec and BC, and 6 in Alberta). Only in 4 of these did the outcome match our hypotheses – 4 of 5 in Quebec, where there was a pervasive pattern of low retrenchment. On the other hand, the provinces that experienced the most retrenchment were, in fact, those for which we predicted that its potential was greatest. In BC and Alberta, for each of which we thought a high level of retrenchment was possible, its actual extent departed from the minimum possible (low, or '0,' in each field) by a total of 8 and 6 digits respectively. In Quebec, where we expected consistently low retrenchment, the corresponding figure was 1. In Ontario, where we ventured no hypothesis because different components of our theoretical model would have led us to make opposing predictions, the score was 3, also quite low. Retrenchment was significantly greater where we predicted considerable potential for it – BC and Alberta – than where we anticipated little or saw contradictory possibilities – Ontario and Quebec. Above and beyond short-term 'swings,' centre-right political forces in each province reaped a long-term partisan gain in relation to their centre-left rivals, but this varied, and was generally less than would be anticipated by proponents of the 'polarization' thesis discussed in chapter 1. In none of the cases examined here, conversely, was the centre-left able to 'strengthen' its long-term political hand during the period studied; that is, to move the centre of gravity for policy-making further away from market-oriented principles. The possibility of such enduring gains, even in an era of globalization, was at least hinted at in Boix's and Garrett's robust findings regarding the centre-left's contemporary prospects in relation to the supply side of the labour market.[6]

Alberta's retrenchment, low or low-to-medium for all but one field, nevertheless is particularly surprising, in light of our hypothesis that neo-liberal reform had the potential to be quite substantial there. Retrenchment in Alberta's social assistance policy was medium-high, but there was little neo-liberal retrenchment regarding industrial relations or active measures, and low-to-medium adjustment in the other three domains discussed in chapter 7. Legacies of Alberta's centre-right, one-party-dominant party system, unanticipated by the Kitschelt model of party systems examined in chapter 1, probably help explain this discrepancy between the anticipated high potential for retrenchment and the modest amount that materialized. As is pointed out in chapter 7, in many areas of labour market policy – though not social assistance, where retrenchment was, in any case, quite high – Albertan policy patterns were already significantly more market-oriented than in the other provinces studied at the *beginning* of our period of study, a phenomenon that likely reflects the long-term political hegemony of the market-oriented centre-right in that province. Its minimum wage was the lowest among the provinces examined, and industrial relations law constrained unionization more than elsewhere in Canada. Richard Block's and Karen Roberts's data, cited in chapter 2, suggests that Alberta's labour market policy regime as a whole was much more market-oriented than those of other Canadian jurisdictions in the early 1990s.[7]

In Ontario, long-term retrenchment was low in 4 of 5 fields discussed in chapter 3; it was low-to-medium in the employment standards area and medium in the assistance domain discussed in chapter 8. We had not ventured a hypothesis about the likely degree of retrenchment in Ontario, because its short-term partisan conjuncture during the 1990s was inconsistent with longer-term legacies of its party system. In the event, it was clearly the latter, not the former, that left the strongest imprint on Ontario policy. Market-oriented reforms introduced by the Harris and Eves Progressive Conservative governments only exceptionally departed substantially from patterns that existed before 1985. There was no evidence of more than very modest levels of retrenchment in any area of Quebec labour market policy discussed in chapters 5 and 8. Public reaction was quite negative to the – largely erroneous – perception that Jean Charest's post-2003 Liberal administration might substantially retrench important aspects of Quebec policy. This suggests that the degree of resistance to such change is particularly strong in Quebec, where liberal features of the political economy have been adulterated much more than elsewhere in Canada. Only in British Columbia, endowed – uniquely among the jurisdictions studied here – with a long-entrenched, economically-polarized party system, did the degree of retrenchment exceed low-to-medium in more than one policy field. Uniquely among our jurisdictions, the number of steps by which BC's policy retrenchment departed from the status quo (8) was close to the midpoint between the lowest possible score (0) and the maximum possible one (20 for BC). BC's industrial relations regime has changed little in recent years, but retrenchment was low-to-medium for occupational health and workers' compensation; medium for active measures and assistance for employable persons; and medium-high for employment standards.

The extent to which achieved retrenchment fell short of what was judged possible is nevertheless considerable for BC and Alberta. Moreover, British Columbia also experienced a significant shift towards the political right during the late 1980s. The current round of changes, consequently, could simply reflect one more swing of a pendulum that typically traces a very wide ark, rather than an inexorable move towards neo-liberalism. We return in the next section to the role that our study's relatively short and recent time frame might have played in accounting for this discrepancy between our theory and the evidence, as well as to broader issues regarding the measurement of institutional change in globalizing advanced capitalist political economies.

Because the institutional terrain of social assistance policy for employable persons – the leading societal and state interests involved in its formulation, and the fiscal and ideological stakes associated with it – was quite distinctive, this area was examined separately in chapter 8. Policy change in the assistance field did, indeed, differ in important respects from the pattern observed in earlier chapters, but it also revealed important continuities with the results reported there. On the one hand, probably reflecting the distinctiveness of this policy sector, there was more retrenchment overall in the assistance domain then in any other dimension of labour market policy. Alone among policies discussed here, the number of 'steps' by which retrenchment in all four provinces departed from the status quo (7) was close to the midpoint between the lowest (0) and highest (16) possible score. Parenthetically, the policy field that experienced the second-greatest amount of retrenchment, employment standards (where the comparable score was 5), shared some features of the assistance policy sector: in particular, much less involvement by organized labour and (at least big) business

in policy-making. In the fields of industrial relations, workers' compensation and occupational health and active labour market policy, where
the macro-institutions discussed in chapter 2 were commonly present,
the pattern of retrenchment was consistently low (an overall score of 2
for all four provinces in each of these three fields).[8] On the other hand,
partisanship's impact on assistance policy again varied considerably
among provinces, reflecting the pattern in other policy fields. It was
greatest in the polarized party systems; BC and Ontario experienced a
high swing in assistance policy for employable persons when the right
came to power, even though the left had already embarked on a pattern
of restraint before leaving office. In Quebec, partisan swings were barely
discernible, consistent with the pattern observed in other domains in
that province. 'Welfare bashing' was largely absent from public debate
in Quebec during the period of study, at least between the two main
parties.

To assess more fully the potential impact of institutional variations on
partisanship and globalization, this book includes a chapter on a jurisdiction that represents a paradigmatic contrast with predominantly
liberal Canadian jurisdictions. Chapter 9, contributed by Steffen
Schneider, examines recent labour market policy-making in Germany, a
nation where coordinative political-economic institutions have been
central to the labour market field since the Second World War, and
several of its Länder. Here, too, our findings regarding partisanship
reflect Schneider's hypotheses: consistent with expectations in a coordinative political economy, partisan swings after a change in government
were modest. It is less clear, however, that German labour market
policy has been relatively impervious to neo-liberal restraint in the
manner considered likely by much of the scholarship reviewed in chapter 1, including Hall and Soskice in their recent elaboration of the
distinction between liberal and coordinated political economies.[9] In
relation to the evidence for the Canadian provinces, this is the most
surprising finding of Schneider's chapter: This important strain of historical institutionalist theorizing suggests that in the face of globalization, distinctive political economies are likely to grow further apart,
liberal political economies will deepen their commitment to competitive and market-oriented principles; coordinative ones will reinforce
their reliance on non-market, trust-based relations. In the labour market
field, our evidence points, tentatively, in the opposite direction. Generally quite modest, albeit uneven, retrenchment has occurred in the
Canadian provinces; recent change in Germany is potentially more

decisive, although, as Schneider points out, it currently falls short of being transformative. Here, too, the question of how institutions mediate globalization, and of how we should evaluate the potential for fundamental change based on recent trends, comes to the fore.

Institutional Retrenchment in an Age of Globalization

This section addresses two themes. First, is there something in the nature of our enquiry that has made results regarding globalization inherently more difficult to measure than is the case for partisanship? Second, how might the direction and degree of globalization be assessed better than it has been by the historical institutionalist literature on welfare states and production regimes reviewed in chapter 1? What light can our findings shed on this question, and on the factors that will influence globalization's future impact on public policy-making in Canada?

Paul Pierson and Theda Skocpol identify three features as characteristic of historical institutionalist research: (1) it addresses 'big substantive questions that are inherently of interest to broad publics as well as to fellow scholars'; (2) in developing explanations, it 'takes time seriously'; (3) it analyses 'macro contexts and hypothesize[s] about the combined effects of institutions and processes.'[10] We believe that the present study fits the first and third of these criteria quite comfortably. In relation to the first, as was argued in chapter 1, labour market policy is pivotally located in the political economy of capitalist democracies – between economic and social policy and the associated imperatives to sustain growth and to alleviate the maladies associated with market societies. It stands at the crucial nexus of efficiency and equity. Regarding the third criterion, the methodology developed in chapters 1 and 2 directed our attention to multiple and intersecting macro-level aspects of the political economy of the four provinces studied here: the broad lines of their mostly-comparable welfare states, the organization of their economies, and the quite distinctive party systems which both mediate and affect the impact of these other institutional orders on policy-making.

Yet it is evident that our study falls short of Pierson and Skocpol's second, temporal criterion. To account adequately for the impact of history, they elaborate, 'usually means to analyze processes over a substantial stretch of years, maybe even many decades or centuries.'[11] Doing this 'contribute[s] to causal inference. Because theoretically grounded assertions of causal relationships imply temporal relationships among variables ... examining historical sequences is extremely useful for testing such assertions.'[12] Our study, by contrast, covers only a 14-year period in the histories of the jurisdictions studied, although the broad pattern of policy that existed during the post-war era that preceded the period of study formed an important backdrop to our enquiry. Moreover, the study's end point is very recent. These features contributed to the greater tentativeness of our findings regarding globalization, an inherently long-term process, than in relation to partisan swings which, by definition, transpire in a relatively short time frame after a change of government. Tracing retrenchment over a relatively short time period, and in relation to recent developments, many of whose indirect consequences will take years to become manifest, invites uncertainty. On the other hand, these limitations are intrinsic to any study of the impact of globalization, a process which, as defined in chapter 1, has only emerged as a potentially decisive influence on public policy after the end of the post-war 'Golden Age' of welfare capitalism in the 1970s and 1980s, and whose impact is likely to have become particularly important since 1990. Nor has historical institutionalist scholarship sought to avoid studying the impact of globalization, a dynamic that very much represents one of the 'big questions' affecting, and being affected by, multiple macro-level institutions, for which it has such an affinity.[13]

It is partly in connection with this burgeoning historical institutionalist literature on globalization that Kathleen Thelen argues for a refinement of this tradition's approach to institutional change. Referring to the 'varieties of capitalism literature' (broadly, the literatures reviewed in chapter 1), Thelen and Christa Van Wijnbergen, contend that it 'has its own characteristic blind spots. In particular, this literature tends to see all feedback as operating to sustain and reproduce the existing system.'[14] We observed this pattern in chapter 1: the welfare state and production regimes scholarship, in practice if not in principle, generally privileges structure over agency, institutions over partisanship. They suggest either that globalization has not shaken more than a few capitalist democracies from their distinctive institutional moorings, or that globalization is likely to reinforce such institutional differences. Thelen links this propensity to 'a rather strict separation of the issues of institutional innovation and institutional reproduction.'[15] This research, she argues, emphasizes the ability of established domestic institutions to persevere; institutional change is judged to occur rarely, to be truly fundamental, and to be associated with severe externally induced crises. '[I]nstitutions, once created, either persist or break down in the face of some exogenous shock.'[16] As an alternative to this 'all or nothing' conception, Thelen proposes that 'institutional survival is often strongly laced with elements of institutional *transformation* to bring institutions in line with changing social, political, and economic conditions.'[17] Institutions may experience the 'layering' of new purposes on top of old ones, 'conversion' from original purposes to entirely new ones, or simple 'atrophy' and 'drift.'[18] The pressures that lead to such evolutionary change may be endogenous. Thelen emphasizes changes in the balance of power among domestic interests in this respect: '[I]nstitutions do exert a powerful influence on the strategies and calculations of ... the actors that inhabit them ... [H]owever, institutions are the object of ongoing political contestation, and changes in the political coalitions on which institutions rest are what drive changes in the form institutions take and the functions they perform.'[19] Cultural change also may underlie endogenous institutional evolution, although 'it turns out in many cases [that] changes in power relations [i.e., among interests] hold the key to creating the opening in which new [cultural] scripts ... can become more central.'[20] Finally, Thelen observes that initial institutional endowments may differ even between broadly comparable nations (between Japan and Germany, both CMEs, and between the United States and the United Kingdom, both LMEs, regarding skills systems, for instance) in ways that lead to quite different patterns of evolution later on.[21]

To summarize, initial *institutions* may not be entirely displaced, but experience modification due to evolving power relations among *domestic interests*, not just external shocks; and this interest-based activity may affect, and be affected by, changing *ideas*, and by the latent potential of what we might term *secondary institutional* features which distinguish otherwise similar political economies. Since interests and ideas also differ from one polity to the next, institutional reform may move along paths that differ, even among nations with broadly similar institutions. Pace Hall and Soskice, globalization may not evoke a more or less uniform tendency among Coordinated Market Economies (CMEs) towards even-tighter non-market relations among economic actors, and Anglo-Saxon Liberal Market Economies (LMEs) may not all reinforce their 'comparative advantage' in competitive, comparatively unregulated market relations. These considerations permit a better understanding of the pattern of retrenchment observed in this study. Distinctive circumstances within each country can help explain why change did not proceed as anticipated in either Canada or Germany, and, by extension, within Canadian provinces.

For Germany, in contradiction to the Hall and Soskice 'polarization' thesis, Steffen Schneider uncovered significant policy reform of a liberalizing kind in chapter 9, though it as yet falls short of a fundamental break in Germany's coordinative institutional order; these conclusions are consistent with Thelen's own. To account for this, Thelen applied the above insights to the study of German labour market policy, her academic specialty. Regarding *secondary institutional* features, she argues that quite specific features of the German apprenticeship system, acquired under labour pressure during the early twentieth century, have been reconfigured in recent years, in the face of forceful pressure from German business, to meet different needs from those that they originally served.[22] By implication, other CMEs, whose training systems lacked these specific features, would be less likely to experience the same pressures for market-oriented adjustment that Schneider documented. Thelen and Schneider's evidence regarding the prominence of labour market reform in recent public policy debates in Germany, and of the role of an increasingly aggressive business community in stimulating this discussion, also suggests that an important shift in the balance of power among *domestic interests* has transpired there since the 1980s. Perceiving itself to be increasingly exposed to competitive pressures from more market-oriented political economies abroad, German business has become reluctant to continue using coordinative mechanisms in the labour market. Organized labour has been on the defensive in the face of these pressures; and, as Schneider portrays graphically, even Social Democratic governments have felt compelled to go some distance towards addressing business concerns. Germany's political centre-left has experienced a noteworthy curtailment of its agenda's long-term prospects, not just a short-term swing away from its core concerns. More broadly, the tone of recent labour market policy debate, with market-oriented ideas at the centre of policy recommendations and proposals for deeper coordination largely marginalized, suggests that an important *ideational* shift has occurred in Germany, paralleling this shift in the class balance of power. Such a shift was very much evident in interviews conducted in Germany for this research. It may, moreover, reflect a broader macro-level shift in the tone of political discourse in Germany, which is not necessarily paralleled in other coordinative political economies. Bhatia and Coleman observed such a shift in the German health care sector during the 1980s, for instance, which resulted in significant market-oriented policy changes in that domain. In Canada, by contrast, these authors documented a remarkable durability in the cultural assumptions that underlay the existing health care system, and a corresponding resistance to neo-liberal reforms.[23] Overall, these considerations lead one to suspect that the confluence of secondary institutional features and endogenous pressures for change of the type highlighted by Thelen, have entailed that pressures for neo-liberal adjustment have been greater in Germany than Hall and Soskice would have predicted, and that this explains the surprising level of change under the recent Social Democratic administration documented by Schneider.

Similarly distinctive features of the Canadian setting, by contrast, suggest an explanation for the opposite pattern here: secondary institutions and endogenous dynamics in Canada created a more hostile environment for neo-liberal retrenchment than is typical in Liberal Market Economies and than would have been expected by Hall and Soskice. *Secondary institutional* features were particularly important. As was noted in chapter 2, neo-liberal change has not been as pronounced in the Canadian welfare state as in some other liberal ones. Canada's partisan centre-left did not experience the kind of long-term historic defeat during the 1980s and 1990s that transpired in some other liberal political economies. Canada has experienced muted retrenchment, for Pierson, which he terms 'compensated restructuring,' in comparison with 'straightforward and severe cost containment and recommodification in New Zealand and the UK' and an 'intermediate' pattern in the United States.[24] He explains this in terms of secondary institutions; a particularly robust federalism dampened retrenchment in Canada. Similarly, John Myles sees the social democratic 'impurities' that Canada's welfare state acquired during the post-war era as responsible for recent policy divergence from the United States. 'Building on a legacy of universal benefits financed from general revenue, Canada has managed to pass through an era of retrenchment and cost-cutting that was comparatively successful at stabilizing though not reducing poverty rates. Failure to transcend the poor law tradition in the formative years of the US welfare state foreclosed this option.'[25] Indeed, the relative stability of Canada's rates of poverty and final income inequality in recent years is striking in comparison with their steep rise in other leading liberal welfare states, and even some Continental European ones.[26]

Varying, perhaps diverging, balances of power among *domestic interests* also distinguish liberal settings such as the United States and Canada. Hoberg et al. note that Canada's labour movement is now much stronger than its American counterpart, despite declining unionization levels; its centre-left NDP ally has no equivalent in U.S. national politics; and race, a divisive factor in American social policy debates, is largely absent from these in Canada. These provide important interest-based explanations of Canada's continuing divergence from American social policy.[27] For Jane Jenson, in addition, the regional diversity of Canadian politics, mediated by the brokerage party system, provided a partial alternative to a robust labour movement as a social underpinning of the original post-war welfare state.[28] It was argued in chapter 2, by extension, that ideology-muting brokerage politics may now also forestall the advance of neo-liberalism in federal politics. The landscape of interests has shifted less in Canada than in the United States, or, for that matter, the United Kingdom, helping to account for the relative resiliency of post-war arrangements in Canada. In sharp contrast with the German pattern, moreover, labour market policy has generally not risen to the top of federal or provincial political agendas since 1990. When it has, as we have seen, this has usually been in the context of undertakings by newly elected centre-right governments in Ontario and British Columbia to reverse relatively recent market-curtailing reforms introduced by their NDP predecessors. Among the provincial policy fields addressed here, only social assistance for employable persons acquired a relatively high profile throughout the country on a sustained basis. Canadian business, for its part, has had little of the incentive that existed in Germany to launch a sustained offensive against a labour market regime that, in view of its broadly liberal character, could not be seen as fundamentally injurious to its interests. As we have seen in various provinces in this study, proposals for more radical labour market reform, such as the ADQ's proposal to abandon the Rand formula in Quebec, similar musings in Ontario and Alberta, and even some of the more radical employment standards reforms introduced by the BC Liberals after 2001, have been regarded with ambivalence by business spokespersons.

Finally, power-distributional differences appear to parallel *ideational* ones. Summarizing 1990s data, Stephen Brooks observes that Canadians are closer to Americans than to most Europeans in their ideological views. Nevertheless, 'Canadians are more likely than Americans to value equality of results, whereas Americans are more likely to value equality of opportunity ... In Canada, egalitarianism has roots in a more collectivist tradition; in the United States, it draws on a more individualist tradition.' These differences 'help to explain Canadians' apparently greater acceptance of state measures targeted at disadvantaged groups and regions.'[29] Moreover, Canadians' ideological perspectives do not differ significantly among the provinces, including those studied here, except for Quebec, where opinions are 'clearly to the left' of those elsewhere in the country.[30] Though largely addressing other aspects of political culture, evidence of divergence over time between Canadian and American attitudes can be found in Michael Adams's recent comparative study.[31]

These general considerations regarding the specificity of Canada's experience of globalization are also relevant to the four provinces studied here. In spite of the important institutional variations that we observed among them, these provinces all reflect the constellation of secondary-institutional, interest-based, and ideational characteristics identified above as typifying the broader Canadian setting: They have quite similar welfare states, with the result that none, reflecting the national pattern identified by Myles, has witnessed an American-style increase in poverty and final income inequality in recent years. The labour movement varies in strength among these provinces, and has eroded in each of them, but in no case has this approached the near-collapse of unionism observable in the United States. Moreover, social democratic parties have not been displaced from their traditional role in the three-party systems where they were significant in the post-war era: the PQ and NDP remain the main alternative to governing centre-right parties in Quebec and BC. Ontario's NDP appears to be mired in third place in that province's party system, but it should be recalled that this is the NDP's traditional place in that province's politics; the 1990 election result represented an unprecedented – and, apparently, unique – departure from this norm. Finally, to repeat, the distinctive ideological proclivities of Canadians identified by Brooks are shared to a remarkable degree by residents of different regions of the country. It seems reasonable to conclude, then, that the same endogenous dynamics that inhibited substantial retrenchment at the national level in Canada have played a similar role in the provinces. Only in the social assistance field, where sector-specific dynamics affected policy outcomes, did the overall pattern of retrenchment approach an intermediate level. Yet organized business has consistently been least active in pursing policy change in the assistance field, and has taken little interest in workfare proposals. The popularity of these concepts owes much to the kind of welfare-bashing dynamic that Esping-Andersen long ago suggested is latent in liberal welfare states, likely to come to the fore in times of weak growth and rapidly rising cost and caseload pressures.

Uniformity and Necessity, Variety and Freedom

In this book, we sought to adapt historical institutionalism to the study of Canadian public policy in a more thorough and systematic manner than has been attempted heretofore. This required considerable attention to specific features of the Canadian political economy that have been insufficiently emphasized in available comparative research, and to institutional variability among Canadian provinces. These considerations very much militated against treating Canada as a straightforward example of a liberal political economy, where the impact of partisanship and globalization on labour market policy-making could be expected to reflect closely what available research has suggested is a typical pattern in these market-oriented settings. The findings reported in the central chapters suggest that, adapted to address these nuances, historical institutionalism nevertheless provides a valuable framework for understanding the unique and variable dynamics of labour market policy-making in Canada.

Requiring us to qualify our initial hypotheses, the evidence about partisanship and globalization reported here still reinforces this contention: institutional approaches can only be applied to Canada plausibly when they are made more sensitive than is typically the case to the subtleties of its institutional landscape. Our Canadian findings, combined with our briefer review of developments in Germany, and Kathleen Thelen's recent theoretical refinements to 'varieties of capitalism' scholarship, suggest, indeed, that this plea for nuance may also be relevant to the study of how institutions mediate partisanship and globalization in other capitalist democracies. This is certainly the case for federations or otherwise decentralized polities, but would also extend to more centralized settings, where nation-specific secondary institutions and endogenous political and cultural dynamics ensure that these variables' impact can only be predicted approximately based on the broad typological categories deployed by comparative institutional scholarship.

A final observation pertains to the question touched upon at the beginning of this study: to what extent does the contemporary conjuncture in capitalist democracies circumscribe the 'limits of the possible' available to their citizens to shape their political economies in a manner that reflects their specific values and collective wisdom? Much recent writing on globalization, especially of the popular variety, is highly pessimistic on this score. In a neo-liberal age, it is argued, public policy is determined more by international economic currents than by the autonomously developed and expressed will of voters. These arguments are often developed in highly generalized terms, and are judged to apply relatively uniformly to all countries, subject to the same anonymous and remorseless pressures. A singular merit of historical institutionalism is its attention to variability; that is, to the extent to which the boundaries that delimit what *is* from what *is not* possible depend on distinctive and historically emergent parameters of choice in different nations. And this attention to specificity is conjoined to an appreciation for the fact that agency, while always situated and constrained, also always matters. Rather than uniformity and necessity, this scholarship privileges variety and situated choice.

This study sought to radicalize and extent this proclivity in historical institutionalist scholarship by documenting how variability can occur at the sub-national level and be affected by nationally distinctive historical legacies that are not properly accounted for by 'varieties of capitalism' typologies. In doing this, it hopefully has also contributed to a deeper appreciation of the extent to which, following Thelen and Steinmo, 'political agency, conflict and choice' shape policy outcomes, but always '*within* institutional constraints' that condition the nature of 'the players, their interests and strategies, and the distribution of power among them,' resulting in 'variation[s] in political behaviour and outcomes *over time* as well as across countries.'[32] This insight can be traced at least to Hegel, who confronted the Kantian philosophical system – with its characteristic antinomies of absolute freedom and determinism, of practical and pure reason – with an alternative that stressed that humans make their own history, but in variable and distinctive circumstances. Freedom is always concrete, situated. As Charles Taylor expressed it, following Hegel, this requires seeing 'free activity as grounded in the *acceptance* of our defining situation. The struggle to be free ... is powered by an affirmation of this defining situation as ours,'[33] but as also, in context-specific ways, mutable. Based on the evidence presented here, we have no reason to believe that this is less true today than in the past.

Appendix: Criteria for Rating Labour Market Policy Change

This appendix describes the criteria used to evaluate the degree of change observed for each field of labour market policy examined in the four Canadian provinces covered by this study. It then provides a summary outline of our application of this methodology to each policy field in each province; a fuller account of these policy developments is provided in the case studies in chapters 4 to 8.

The methodology begins with a distinction used by Peter Hall to measure degrees of policy retrenchment. He described three *orders* of such change: Third-order change entails changes in the *'overarching goals* that guide policy in a particular field.' Second-order change pertains to *'techniques* or policy instruments used to attain those goals.' First-order change, finally, relates to the *'precise setting* of these instruments,' including 'level of benefits.'[1]

We then distinguished three *scores* for each of the above *orders* of change. Scores were used to indicate the extent to which new policy features replaced old ones. The highest score, *displacement*, indicates that new goals, techniques, or settings have broadly replaced old ones. The latter may survive in some areas, but are now subordinate to the new ones overall. When the degree of change is referred to as *contesting*, new goals, techniques, or settings have emerged in some areas that contest or challenge the old, which survive elsewhere. New and old patterns coexist with no evident predominance of one over the other. If new goals, techniques, or settings emerge in some areas but clearly remain subordinate to old ones, these are termed *adjustments*, and did not count in our ratings. For a score to be applied to change in a particular field, it had to characterize the *broad pattern* of goals, techniques, or settings in that field. Where some features changed in the manner described by a score, but not others, the overall score referred to the broad pattern that resulted from this mixture, not to the specific features that changed.

Different *time frames* are used to determine the degree of change in relation to globalization and to partisanship, reflecting the different objectives of these measurements: Regarding the former, the comparison was with the *pre-1990 period*. For the latter, it was the *policies of the previous government*. Consistent with the focus of our study, changes were only considered relevant for determining the degree of *partisanship* if they were (1) *market-enhancing* (i.e., served to reinforce the exposure of workers or recipients to market relations) or *market-curtailing* (inhibited the impact of market relations on workers or recipients, and protected them against market uncertainty) in relation to policy goals, techniques, or settings; and (2) if they were a subject of *partisan disagreement* between the main political parties in a province. The *overall partisanship score* for a province in any policy field reflected the *highest score* recorded for a governing party during the period of study. Consistent with this term's use in our study, changes were relevant to measuring *globalization* only if they were *market-enhancing*. Changes, however important, that were *market-neutral* (no evident impact in either direction) did not count as evidence either of partisanship or of globalization. Finally, the partisanship 'hurdle' is lower than the globalization one. This is because Hall intended his orders of change to be used to map globalization-related change, understood as fundamental and institution-shifting. Normal partisan swings of the type that we have studied here usually happen within an established institutional setting, and are likely to be less fundamental. Based on these considerations, we mapped the degree of change that would justify each of the designations described above. These are represented in figure A.1.

Applying the Map of 'Degrees of Change' to Canadian Labour Market Policy

With this framework in mind, operational definitions of specific policy changes in each labour market policy field were developed that reflected each measure of change in figure A.1. Relying on our understanding of the core elements of the post-war labour market policy regime in the Canadian provinces, outlined in chapter 3, we summarized for each policy field the key *overarching goals* of policy that emerged during the post-war era, and the distinctive *techniques and instruments*

Figure A.1. Mapping 'Degrees of Change'

Degree of change in broad pattern of policy	Globalization score	Partisanship score
Time frame	Compared to pre-1990 era	Compared to previous government
Relevant direction of change	Market-enhancing	Market-enhancing or market-curtailing
Displacement of goals	High	High
Contesting of goals or displacement of techniques	Medium-to-high	High
Contesting of techniques	Medium	High
Displacement of settings	Low-to-medium	Medium
Contesting of settings	Low	Low

used to pursue these. Within these parameters, we then determined what *precise settings* were of sufficient consequence to be considered in our evaluation of the degree of change. As is indicated in figure A.1, we judged that changes that reflected either partisanship or globalization only justified a rating of more than 'low' if they at least displaced precise settings that existed previously.

Industrial Relations

Overarching Goals

The post-Second World War model permitted union formation, organized at the enterprise level and based on majority choice; there was no incorporation of labour in broader societal decision making (with the partial exception of Quebec); the 'free collective bargaining' model minimized state interference.

Techniques or Instruments

The post-war model included the Rand formula on compulsory union dues deduction; government acting as a neutral policy arbiter and guarantor of neutral third-party oversight of certification, administration, and adjudication; the use of secret ballot voting; consistent with the 'free bargaining' and non-intervention model, no anti-scab legislation (except, again, in Quebec).

Precise Settings

These included specific provisions that a province used to implement the above: a labour relations board or a labour ministry; other secondary issues related to ease of certification and decertification, strike vote requirements, access to strike votes, and so on.

Active Measures

Overarching Goals

The market is relied upon for most industrial skills and for job creation, with the main government role assigned to institutional skills and liberal arts education; limited public-private concertation around skills formation, and a limited policy role for labour (except, to a degree, in Quebec).

Techniques or Instruments

State administration or oversight of the community college network is used for technical training, with limited private sector input; limited public spending on or monitoring of industrial training; a restricted, publicly supported, apprenticeship system concentrated in traditional trades and subject to detailed industry-mediated standards; and limited long-term direct government job creation by provinces.

Precise Settings

This included the specific level of state spending on industrial skills and apprenticeship; particulars of apprenticeship design; design of private sector advisory bodies.

Employment Standards

Overarching Goals

State oversight of minimum terms of employment, is used mostly for non-unionized workers, covering holidays, minimum wage, hours of work, overtime, severance arrangements, and so on.

Techniques or Instruments

Modestly endowed proactive investigations are used by a state agency to monitor private sector compliance; management by government of a grievance and appeals system; counselling for employers and employees about the law.

Precise Settings

These are the precise standards implemented by a jurisdiction, assuming that these are within the normal range available in the post-war era and in neighbouring jurisdictions. (If reduced to below this level, such change may be evidence of greater retrenchment; i.e., relating to techniques and instruments.)

Workers' Compensation

Overarching Goals

This model emerged during and after the First World War, whereby much of the workforce has access to a workplace injury insurance fund in exchange for losing the right to sue employers; application of actuarial principles to assure that the fund is balanced and that benefit rates are sustainable; provision of rehabilitation services.

Techniques or Instruments

The state is seen as a neutral policy-maker and guardian of independent adjudication of the right to compensation and its level and duration; appeals mechanisms; public sector management of administration and funds, with private sector advisory input only on policy and administration; a modest role for labour.

Precise Settings

These include specific benefit levels, and terms of access to them, assuming they are within the normal range available in the post-war era and in neighbouring jurisdictions. (If reduced to below this level, such change may be evidence of greater retrenchment; i.e., relating to techniques and instruments.)

Occupational Health and Safety

Overarching Goals

Rules for minimum health and safety conditions are set; these involve state-monitored, firm-level oversight of compliance.

Techniques or Instruments

Safety instruction for workers and employers is state-sponsored, with private sector advisory input only on policy and administration; modest role for labour; state mandating of safety committees in most enterprises; procedures for challenging and evaluating alleged safety risks that nevertheless minimize potential for work interruption.

Precise Settings

The specific OHS rules and the structure of enterprise committees; whether these are universal or only widely mandated; the nature of off-site health and safety education, assuming these are within the normal range available in the post-war era and in neighbouring jurisdictions. (If reduced to below this level, such change could be evidence of greater retrenchment, relating to techniques and instruments.)

Social Assistance for Employable Persons

NB: The measurement instrument for partisanship in this case was qualitative, as in the case of the policy fields discussed above. For globalization, this approach was supplemented by the statistical formula provided below.

Overarching Goals

Assistance as last-resort income support to all citizens is provided on the basis of need, to preclude absolute penury; the principle is that recipients should acquire skills for work or return to work when possible, and be deemed ineligible if unwilling to comply.

Techniques or Instruments

Needs or income tests are designed; income exemptions are used to permit modest earned income; case workers review files to determine need and availability for work; oversight mechanisms are used to suppress fraud; employability is defined for purposes of distinguishing these clients from disabled ones; there is very limited client or social group involvement in policy-making.

Precise Settings

The specific benefit rates and exemption levels, and specific provisions to deter benefit fraud and define employability, assuming that these are within the normal range available in the post-war era and in neighbouring jurisdictions. (If reduced to below this level, such changes may be evidence of greater retrenchment, relating to techniques and instruments.)

Supplementary Statistical Measure of Globalization-Induced Retrenchment for Assistance Policy

The formula used here determined the average percentage decline in welfare incomes, for the three categories of recipients identified in table 8.2, between 1990 and 2003. This figure was then averaged with the percentage decline in the provincial caseload per capita over the same period, as reported in table 8.5.

% Fall according to Formula	*Globalization*
Over 40%	High
30–40%	Low-medium
20–30%	Medium
10–20%	Low-medium
Less than 10%	Low

Summaries of Applications of the Above Scores to Labour Market Policy Change in Four Canadian Provinces

The case studies presented in chapters 4 to 8 should be consulted for detailed accounts of the policy developments summarized below. The three orders of change are referred to here, for purposes of brevity, as *goals*, *techniques*, and *settings*. Relevant policy changes are identified in point form; these are followed by our determination of the degree of change represented by each, which is provided in italics within square brackets.

ONTARIO

NB: NDP changes were only relevant to testing partisanship, since no major changes were in a market-enhancing direction. PC changes were relevant to testing partisanship where changes were market-enhancing and departed from NDP policy; they were relevant to testing globalization where they were market-enhancing and departed from pre-1990 policy.

INDUSTRIAL RELATIONS

NDP Changes, 1990–95:
– Use of LRARC and broad ongoing consultation to prepare legislation. [*Inclusion of labour suggests market-curtailing contesting of goal of restricting labour inclusion in policy-making*].
– Anti-scab provision of Bill 40 [*market-curtailing displacement of technique and market-curtailing contesting of goal of 'free bargaining'.*]
– Cards-based certification [*market-curtailing displacement of technique requiring majority vote*].
– Extension of coverage to new industries [*market-curtailing displacement of precise settings*].
Overall: High partisanship; 3 key changes contest overall pattern of techniques; it also suggests some adjustment of policy goals.

PC Changes, 1995–2003:
– Restore government control of policy-making, with conventional consultation [*market-enhancing contesting of NDP policy of involving labour, restores status quo ante technique*].
– Eliminate anti-scab provision [*market-enhancing displacement of NDP policy, restores status quo ante technique*].
– Restore majority-vote certification [*market-enhancing displacement of NDP policy, restores status quo ante technique*].
– Reverse NDP extension of coverage to new industries [*market-enhancing displacement of NDP policy; restores status quo ante precise settings*].
– End public sector successor rights [*market-enhancing displacement of an important pre-1990 setting, but for a minority of workers*].
– Suspend, temporarily, province-wide bargaining in the construction sector [*market-enhancing contesting (because change was not permanent) of an important pre-1990 technique, but for a minority of workers, and*

*displacement of settings for them; the change subjects them to the
overarching goal of enterprise bargaining that reflects the broad pattern].*
*Overall: High partisanship: NDP policy was abandoned, reversing its contest-
ing of overall framework of techniques. Low globalization: beyond reversing
NDP policy, there was only one displacement of a setting, which affected a
minority of workers; one contesting of a technique provisionally reconciled the
status of another minority with the norm regarding goals and techniques; but
there is no contesting of the overall technique framework, and the broad pattern
of settings was not displaced for the large majority of workers.*

ACTIVE LABOUR MARKET POLICY

NDP Changes, 1990–95:
– Creation of OTAB, reliance on it for policy direction [*market-neutral
  displacement of technique of limited private sector input outside of apprenticeship; market-curtailing contesting of goal of limited labour involvement*].
– jobsOntario training [*market-curtailing contesting of technique of limited
  government role in direct job creation*].
*Overall: High partisanship; displacing of technique and contesting of policy
goal in crucial policy-making area; contesting of another important technique
by expanding job creation role for government].*

PC Changes, 1995–2003:
– Elimination of OTAB, restoration of policy-making to cabinet and
  state bureaucracy [*market-enhancing displacement of NDP policy,
  restores status quo ante on a pivotal technique re private sector involvement and goal re limited role for labour*].
– Eliminate jobsOntario training [*market-enhancing contesting of NDP
  policy, restores status quo ante technique*].
– Reductions in other, modest, expenditures on active measures
  [*market-enhancing contesting of precise settings*].
– Market-oriented apprenticeship reform, with exemption for construction sector [*market-enhancing adjustment of a technique, but probably does not contest a technique; affects small proportion of all skills
  formation in province*].
*Overall: High partisanship, reversing NDP policies. Low globalization: only
one emerging new technique moves beyond NDP policy (apprenticeship reform); it could justify a score of 'medium' or 'medium-low' globalization if it*

has major long-term consequences for labour market training in Ontario overall (making it a broad displacement of settings, or a contesting of techniques); but minimal growth of apprenticeship in Ontario since the reform, esp. in affected sectors, makes this highly unlikely.

OCCUPATIONAL HEALTH AND SAFETY:

NDP Changes, 1990–95:
- Implementation of bipartite WHSA, effective labour dominance [*market-neutral displacement of crucial technique of advisory role for private sector, and market-curtailing contesting of technique of limiting labour policy role*].
- Significantly increased OHS training and expenditures [*market-curtailing displacement of precise settings*].
- Extending right to refuse work [*market-curtailing contesting of technique of minimizing work interruptions*].
- Significant expansion of labour-sponsored OHS training [*market-curtailing contesting of technique of state sponsorship and oversight*].

Overall: High partisanship, displacing technique in an important policy-making area, and contesting them in two other areas.

PC Changes, 1995–2003:
- Replacement of WHSA by WSIB, restoration of more modest private sector role [*market-enhancing displacement of NDP policy, restoring a crucial technique*].
- Curtailing of OHS training and expenditures [*market-enhancing restoration of a precise setting*].
- Restoration of labour-sponsored OHS training to smaller role [*market-enhancing restoration of a technique*].

Overall: High partisanship, as NDP policy is largely reversed. Low globalization; PC policy did little to go beyond status quo ante.

WORKERS' COMPENSATION

NDP changes, 1990–95:
- Reform of WCB board of directors along bipartite lines [*market-neutral displacement of a technique regarding private sector involvement and market-curtailing displacement of the technique of restricted labour involvement in a crucial policy-making area*].

– Modified pension levels, access to benefits and rehabilitation provisions [*market-neutral displacement of a precise settings*].
Overall: High partisanship, primarily because of displacement of technique regarding decision making; reinforced by temporary contesting of an important goal and displacement of benefit-related settings.

PC Changes, 1995–2003:
– Terminates bipartite WCB decision making [*market-enhancing reversal of NDP policy, restoring a crucial technique*].
– Tightened benefit levels and access; restored soundness of funds [*market-enhancing reversal of NDP policies, largely restoring challenged precise settings*].
Overall: High partisanship, involving reversal of NDP policies. Low globalization: decision-making structures largely restored to pre-1990 pattern, as are overall benefit costs and levels.

EMPLOYMENT STANDARDS

NDP Changes, 1990–95:
– Expanded pay equity legislation coverage [*market-curtailing contesting of precise setting*].
– Significant increase in minimum wage [*market-curtailing displacement of precise settings*].
– Wage Protection Act [*market-curtailing displacement of precise settings*].
– Employment equity legislation [*market-curtailing contesting of important goal by using standards for purposes other than setting minima; market-curtailing displacement of technique by creating much more intrusive oversight techniques*].
Overall: High partisanship due to employment equity legislation alone.

PC Changes, 1995–2003:
– Freezing of minimum wage [*market-enhancing reversal of NDP policy; adjusts precise settings*].
– Terminated WPA [*market-enhancing reversal of NDP policy; restoring precise settings*].
– Eliminated employment equity legislation [*market-enhancing reversal of NDP policy, restoring status quo ante policy and technique*].
– Bill 49 benefit curtailments [*market-enhancing contesting of precise settings*].

- Bill 147: termination of permit system [*market-enhancing displacement of an important pre-1990 technique*].
- Bill 147: relaxation of variances [*market-enhancing contesting an important pre-1990 technique*].
- Bill 147: increased enforcement [*market-curtailing contesting of precise settings*].

Overall: High partisanship by reversing NDP policy, and by displacing and contesting techniques further with Bill 147. Medium globalization: Bill 147 changes regarding permits and variances affected core technique, contesting overall pre-1990 model in market-enhancing direction.

Liberal Changes, 2003–2004:
- Partial restoration of permit system [*market-curtailing contesting of an important technique change made by PC government*].

Overall: Liberal record is too incomplete to judge its overall partisanship rating. But this one change partially reverses the Bill 147 changes that justified a score of 'medium' globalization above; the pre-1990 technique model has been restored, but with weaker enforcement (displaced settings compared to pre-1990), including electronic record keeping, and so on. The final globalization score is low-to-medium.

SOCIAL ASSISTANCE FOR EMPLOYABLE PERSONS

NDP Changes, 1990–95:
- Benefit rate increases [*market-curtailing adjustments to settings*].
- Seeking recipient and social actors' policy advice [*market-curtailing adjustment of technique*].
- *Transitions* report changes to eligibility [*market-curtailing contesting of settings*].
- Limit Support to Employment program [*market-enhancing contesting of technique*].

Overall: Low partisanship: initial benefit extensions are roughly counterbalanced by subsequent curtailments. Low globalization: no broad abandonment of generous arrangements initiated by Liberals in late 1980s.

PC Changes, 1995–2003:
- 21 per cent benefit cut in benefits for employable recipients [*market-enhancing displacement of settings, which returns them to mid-1980s levels*].

- Support to Employment program altered to encourage earning extra income [*market-enhancing contesting of technique*].
- Significant constraints on benefits access [*market-enhancing displacement of settings*].
- More complex application procedures [*market-enhancing contesting of technique*].
- Ontario Works (Workfare) [*in principle, a market-enhancing displacement of post-1960s technique, and a contesting of the goal of providing benefits based on need; in practice, given restricted application, but broader symbolic and psychological import, a contesting of post-1960s technique*].

Overall: High partisanship: PC policy moved substantially from NDP policy, displacing or contesting NDP techniques in several important areas. Medium globalization: main initiative that went beyond reversing NDP reforms, and those of the Peterson Liberals, related to Workfare and related administrative constraints; these contested post-1960s techniques.

Quantitative measure of retrenchment: –23 per cent; also medium.

QUEBEC

[*NB: PQ Changes were relevant only to measuring partisanship, because no changes above the level of contesting settings were in a market-enhancing direction; Liberal changes were relevant to partisanship where they reversed PQ or pre-1990 policy in a market-enhancing direction; they were relevant to globalization where they changed pre-1990 policy in a market-enhancing direction*].

INDUSTRIAL RELATIONS

Liberal Changes, 1990–94:
- Deregulate small residential construction sector [*market-enhancing displacement of a technique relevant to a small sub-sector; overall technique regime re union representation is unchanged*].
- Sector-level bargaining in construction sector [*market-neutral displacement of a technique*].
- Eliminate three-year ceiling on contracts, exempting first contracts [*market-enhancing contesting of a setting*].

Overall: Low partisanship: only one market-enhancing change beyond the level of contesting settings, and this applied to a very small share of the labour force. Low globalization: same reasons.

PQ Changes, 1994–2003:
- Re-regulation of small residential construction sector [*reverses Liberal policy, market-curtailing displacement of a technique relevant to a small sub-sector*].
- Streamlining sectoral bargaining [*market-neutral contesting of settings*].
- Restrict decree system [*market-enhancing contesting of a setting relevant to a small minority of workers, reinforcing broader technique of enterprise-level bargaining*].
- Create labour board [*market-neutral displacing of an important technique regarding decision making*].
- Various changes in right to submit contract offer, subcontracting rights [*market-enhancing adjustment of settings*].

Overall: Low partisanship: beyond reversing one Liberal policy, changes only contested settings or were not market-curtailing. Low globalization: market-curtailing changes never exceeded the level of contesting settings.

Liberals, 2003–
- Bill 30: comprehensively curtails previously well-entrenched successor rights [*market-enhancing displacement of an important setting, potentially relevant to many workers*].

Overall: Medium partisanship: The change potentially affects the overall pattern of settings in the direction of displacement. Low-to-medium globalization: same reasons.

ACTIVE LABOUR MARKET POLICY

Liberal Changes, 1990–94:
- Refundable training tax credit [*market-curtailing contesting of settings*].
- Expand role of sectoral committees [*market-neutral contesting of settings*].
- Creation of SQDM to supplement existing private decision-making forums [*market-neutral contesting of technique by enhancing private sector decision-making role (granting labour a policy role was not a major innovation in Quebec)*].

Overall: Low partisanship: the one change that went beyond contesting settings was market-neutral. Low globalization: same reasons.

PQ Changes, 1994–2003:
- Replacing SQDM with CPMT [*market-neutral contesting of technique by altering terms of private sector policy involvement*].
- Creation of Emploi-Québec [*market-neutral contesting of technique regarding administrative arrangements*].
- 1 per cent training grant-levy tax, with generous exemptions [*market-curtailing contesting of settings*].

Overall: Low partisanship: No market-curtailing changes went beyond contesting settings. Low globalization: same reason.

Liberal Changes, 2003–2004:
- Exempting small firms from 1 per cent tax [*market-enhancing contesting of settings*].
- Modest budgetary contraction [*market-enhancing contesting of settings*].

Overall: Low partisanship: no changes beyond level of contesting settings. Low globalization: same reason.

WORKERS' COMPENSATION AND OCCUPATIONAL HEALTH

Liberal Changes, 1990–94:
- Adoption of experience rating [*market-neutral (from a worker's perspective) contesting of settings*].
- Bill 31: contribution rate increases, expediting of return to work and conciliation reform [*market-neutral and contradictory contesting of settings*].

Overall: Low partisanship: no changes beyond level of contesting settings. Low globalization: same reason.

PQ Changes, 1994–2003:
- Broadening of experience-rating [*market-neutral adjustment to settings*].
- Curtailing availability of appeals [*market-enhancing contesting of settings*].
- Modest extension of OHS regulations [*market-curtailing adjustment to settings*].

Overall: Low partisanship: no changes beyond level of contesting settings. Low globalization: same reason.

Liberals, 2003–2004
– No significant changes.

EMPLOYMENT STANDARDS

Liberals, 1990–94:
– Extension of standards re vacations, parental leave, appeals, etc. [*market-curtailing contesting of settings*].
– Multiple minimum wage increases [*market-curtailing adjustments of settings*].
Overall: Low partisanship: no change beyond contesting settings. Low globalization: no changes in market-enhancing direction.

PQ changes, 1994–2003:
– Graduated introduction of private sector pay equity [*market-curtailing contesting of technique, but supported by opposition party*].
– Reduction in length of work week, etc. [*market-curtailing adjustment of settings*].
– Restriction of 'orphan clauses' [*market-curtailing contesting of settings*].
– 2002 Employment Standards Act revisions, including 'psychological harassment' provisions [*market-curtailing contesting of settings in most areas; market-curtailing contesting of technique regarding harassment, but supported by opposition party*].
– Multiple minimum wage increases [*market-curtailing adjustments of settings*].
Overall: Low Partisanship: Two important market-curtailing changes contested techniques, but both were supported by the main opposition party, as were some other changes. Low Globalization: No changes in market-enhancing direction.

Liberal Changes, 2003–2004:
– Two small restrictions in Employment Standards Act coverage [*market-enhancing adjustments to settings*].
Overall: Low Partisanship: No changes beyond adjustment of settings. Low Globalization: For the same reason.

SOCIAL ASSISTANCE FOR EMPLOYABLE PERSONS

Liberal Changes, 1990–94:
– Bill 37: Introduces employability test and small penalty, while extending some benefits [*overall, market-enhancing adjustment to techniques and contesting of settings*].

– Increased surveillance ('Boubou Macouttes') [*market-enhancing contesting of settings*].

Overall: Low partisanship: No change went as far as displacing settings or contesting technique at the broad level. Low globalization, for the same reasons.

PQ Changes, 1994–2003:
– Expansion of employability programs [*market-curtailing adjustment to settings*].
– Bill 182: Stronger employability incentives and penalties, combined with benefit extensions [*overall, market-enhancing adjustments to settings*].
– Subsequent increases in employability measures [*market-curtailing adjustment of settings*].
– Anti-Poverty Fund employment program increases, with some client participation [*market-curtailing contesting of settings re benefits and adjustment of technique re. client participation*].

Overall: Low partisanship: Most PQ changes were minor or included offsetting elements in terms of their market relevance. Low globalization. For the same reasons.

Liberal Changes, 2003–04:
– Abolition of penalties for refusing employment or training, enhanced employability measures [*market-curtailing adjustment of settings*].

Overall: It is too soon to evaluate Liberal policy since 2003 with assurance, but the one noteworthy change has had no significant partisanship or globalization effects.

Quantitative measure of retrenchment: –5 per cent; also low.

BRITISH COLUMBIA

[NB: NDP changes are relevant to testing partisanship; one area of change in a market-enhancing direction is relevant for measuring globalization. Liberal changes are relevant to testing partisanship where they are market-enhancing and depart from NDP policy; they are relevant to testing globalization where they are market-enhancing and depart from pre-1990 policy].

INDUSTRIAL RELATIONS

NDP Changes, 1991–2001:
– Extensive consultations preceding LRC reform [*market-curtailing contesting of important goal of limited labour policy role*].

- Bill 84: Reversal of provisions in Bill 19 [*market-curtailing displacing of settings; restoration of status quo ante before Social Credit reforms*].
- Bill 84: Anti-scab and card-based certification provisions [*market-curtailing displacement of two important techniques*].
- Presiding over a labour-friendly LRB [*market-curtailing further contesting of goal of limited labour involvement*].
- Bill 26: Limited sectoral bargaining in construction industry [*market-curtailing contesting of a technique for a minority of workers*].

Overall: High partisanship: Bill 84 process and provisions contested a key goal, and displaced important techniques. Low globalization: No changes in a market-enhancing direction.

Liberal Changes, 2001–04:
- Bill 18: Reversals of some Bill 84 provisions, restoring majority-vote certification and construction sector bargaining [*market-enhancing contesting of one important technique*].
- Bill 42: 'Duties' section of LRC; extension of 'right to communicate' [*market-enhancing contesting of two important techniques*].

Overall: High partisanship: Changes in important areas contested overall techniques. Low globalization: The 'Duties' provision, the one change that went beyond reversing NDP policy, was more market-enhancing than the post-war pattern, but other NDP reforms are kept; overall pattern 'well to the left' of 1980s' Bill 19.

WORKERS' COMPENSATION AND OCCUPATIONAL HEALTH

NDP Changes, 1991–2001:
- Presiding over cost increases at WCB, and related rule interpretations [*important market-curtailing displacement of settings*].
- 1993 extension of WC coverage [*adjusts WC settings; not opposed by opposition party*].
- Bill 18 extension of OHS rules [*adjusts OHS settings; not opposed by opposition party*].

Overall: Medium partisanship: NDP presided over WCB's broad displacement of precise settings. Low globalization: No market-enhancing changes.

Liberal Changes, 2001–2004:
- Bill 49: Curtailment of WC benefits [*broadly displacing settings re benefit levels compared to NDP pattern*].
- Bill 63: Significantly restricted appeals process for WC [*Contesting important technique*].

Overall: High partisanship: Contesting of techniques in Bill 63, along with displacement of settings, compared to NDP era, in Bill 49. Low-to-medium globalization: broad pattern of settings displaced by Bill 49; Bill 63 contests an important technique, but only adjusts the overall pattern of techniques.

ACTIVE LABOUR MARKET POLICY

NDP Changes, 1991–2001:
– *Skills Now!* initiative [*market-curtailing (equity focused) contesting of settings*].
– Post-1991 broad policy consultations [*market-curtailing contesting of technique that excludes labour from an important policy role*].
– Creation, and dissolution, of advisory BCLFDB [*market-curtailing, though abortive, contesting of technique that limited labour's policy role*].
– Creation of decision-making ITAC [*market-curtailing contesting of the technique limiting labour policy role, but in a small sector of training*].
Overall: High partisanship: Equity-focused new skills measures only contested setting; but overall technique re policy making is contested with repeated efforts to include labour. Low globalization: No market-enhancing reforms.

Liberals, 2001–2004:
– Termination of all industrial training not directed at assistance recipients [*market-enhancing displacement of important technique*].
– Termination of youth and IAS skills measures [*market-enhancing displacement of moderately important technique*].
– Cancellation of ITAC [*market-enhancing contesting of a new technique in restricted area, restoring status quo ante*].
– Anticipated comprehensive liberalization of apprenticeship [*market-enhancing displacement of technique, though one still relevant to modest skills domain*].
Overall: High partisanship: All above changes reverse NDP-era techniques by contesting or displacing them. Medium globalization: Some program eliminations, and radical apprenticeship reform, departed from pre-1990 pattern, contesting broad pattern of pre-1990 techniques.

EMPLOYMENT STANDARDS

NDP, 1991–2001:
– Bill 65: 'Meet or beat' provision [*market-curtailing contesting of technique for limited number of workers*].
– Bill 29: Extension of some standards [*market-curtailing contesting of settings*].

- Bill 29: Creation of ES Tribunal to increase enforcement [*market-curtailing displacement of important technique*].
- Frequent minimum wage increases [*market-curtailing contesting of settings*].
- Insertion of pay equity principles into Human Right Code [*belated contesting of technique*].

Overall: High partisanship: contesting and displacement of techniques in several important areas suggests contesting of broad pattern of techniques. Low globalization: no market-enhancing changes.

Liberals, 2001–2004:
- Two-tier ('training') minimum wage [*market-enhancing contesting of technique*].
- One-third ES Branch staff reduction [*market-enhancing contesting of settings*].
- Bill 48: Complaints-based ES system, curtailment of inspections [*market-enhancing contesting of goal of ES legislation to effectively set such standards; displacement of technique for achieving this goal*].
- Bill 48: Elimination of 'meet or beat' provision; extension of use of variances, and permitting of this on individual basis [*market-enhancing displacement of important technique*].
- Bill 48: Curtailment of various standards [*market-enhancing displacement of standards*].

Overall: High partisanship: substantial contesting of techniques; contesting of overall legislative goal in crucial area. Medium-high globalization: these changes suggest that the broad pattern of technique was displaced, and that the core goal of post-war legislation – effectively enforceable standards – was contested.

SOCIAL ASSISTANCE FOR EMPLOYABLE PERSONS

NDP Changes, 1991–2001:
- Early 1990s assistance benefit increases [*market-curtailing contesting of settings*].
- Minister's Advisory Council on Income Assistance [*market-curtailing adjustment of technique restricting recipient policy input*].
- 1994–95 benefits curtailments [*market-enhancing contesting of settings*].
- BC Benefits: Enhanced employment incentives and selective benefit cuts [*further market-enhancing contesting of settings; new incentives represent market-oriented contesting of techniques*].

Overall: Low partisanship: Net NDP policy moved in a somewhat market-enhancing direction, but this was not opposed by the opposition party. Low-to-medium globalization: BC Benefits broadly displaced settings at the overall level, though not techniques.

Liberal Changes, 2001–2004:
– Reclassification of many single parents as employable [*market-enhancing contesting of settings*].
– Employment and Assistance (EA) Act: '2 years in 5' limit on assistance eligibility [*in principle, a market-enhancing displacement of technique; and (as it implied challenge to principle of benefits in response to need) a contesting of a fundamental program goal. In practice, after the 2004 adjustment, it is more likely a contesting of pre-existing techniques*].
– Employment Assistance Act: extended waiting period, elimination of earnings exemptions [*market-enhancing displacement of settings*].
– EAPD Act restriction on definition of disability [*in practice, a market-enhancing contesting of settings*].

Overall: High partisanship: Changes went beyond NDP ones in contesting important technique regarding benefit access, as well as broadly displacing settings. Medium globalization: In comparison with NDP policy in 2001, and pre-1990 pattern, these changes, above all those in EA Act, further contest techniques in a market-enhancing direction, but do not yet seem to be displacing techniques or contesting overall goals.

Quantitative measure of retrenchment: –23 per cent; also medium.

ALBERTA

[NB: Only the degree of globalization is evaluated here, as only one party governed in Alberta during the period covered by our research. PC initiatives represent evidence of globalization when they are market-enhancing and depart from pre-1990 policies.]

OCCUPATIONAL HEALTH AND SAFETY

PC Changes, 1990–2003:
– Merger of OHS agency with labour ministry, accompanied by significant staff reductions [*market-enhancing contesting of techniques, which reduced state oversight, but moderately*].
– Agricultural sector formally exempted from OHS law [*market-

enhancing contesting of settings; agricultural workers had never been covered by regulations].
- New regulations for employees working alone [market curtailing contesting of settings, with limited implications].
- Partners in Injury Reduction program, permitting third-party auditing of OHS management systems [market-enhancing adjustment only of techniques, as this had little effect on the nature of the audits].
- Privatization of equipment and conditions testing [market-enhancing contesting of settings only, as employers paid for testing, which was largely unchanged].
- Termination of general health and safety courses by government [market-enhancing contesting of settings only, as most OHS training was unaffected].
- Curtailment of enforcement and prosecution during 1990s, followed by a partial reversal of this trend after 2000 [market-enhancing, but temporary, contesting of techniques].

Overall: Low-to-medium globalization: Two market-enhancing changes contested techniques, but one (curtailed enforcement) was largely reversed and the other did not affect OHS legislation or have a marked effect on its implementation. Other changes were minor. Overall, the broad pattern of techniques was adjusted and the broad pattern of settings was contested.

INDUSTRIAL RELATIONS

PC Changes, 1990–2003:
- Privatization of mediation services [market-neutral contesting of techniques, with no significant effect on nature of service].
- Curtailment of government payment for mediation services [market-enhancing contesting of techniques that reduces government administration, but with modest effect on unions].
- Labour Relations Board authorized to charge fees [potentially a market-enhancing technique, as workers would have been especially affected by this; but market-neutral in practice as no fees were charged].
- 2002 Labour Relation Code review [market-neutral, as it resulted in no policy changes].

Overall: Low globalization: Only the mediation services change was more than minor, and it did not affect the broad pattern of settings or techniques in the field.

WORKERS' COMPENSATION

PC Changes, 1990–2003:
- Early 1990s legislation requiring that WCB become self-financing; includes move from pension-based to wage-loss compensation system, increased attention to rehabilitation, and some benefit decreases [*market-enhancing contesting of techniques and displacement of settings in several important areas; effect was particularly acute for long-term cases*].
- 1998 upward adjustment of some benefits and widows' payments [*market-curtailing contesting of settings, with modest impact*].
- Successive and substantial reductions in employer premiums during 1990s, followed by rate increased after 2000 [*market-enhancing displacement of settings*].
- 2002 WCB legislation; includes increase in external oversight of the board, change in board decision making to increase attention to claims, and creation of an independent appeals commission [*market-curtailing contesting of techniques in several areas, which counteracted some of the early 1990s changes*].

Overall: Low-to-medium globalization. The early 1990s changes broadly contested techniques in this field, although they did not affect overall goals, and would have justified a score of 'medium' globalization. But the subsequent reforms served to partly counteract these changes.

EMPLOYMENT STANDARDS

PC Changes, 1990–2003:
- 1994 legislation (Bill 4), which permits nongovernmental enforcement of standards and the charging of fees [*in principle, permitted market-enhancing displacement of techniques or even a contesting of its overall goals; in practice, it had a limited effect, as its provisions were not implemented*].
- 1996 legislation (Bill 29), intended to facilitate privatization by simplifying regulations for employment standards [*in practice, this too had a limited effect, as privatization was not implemented*].
- 2000 legislation regarding maternity leave and minimum wage protection for domestic workers [*market-curtailing contesting of settings relevant to a significant share of the workforce*].
- Reduction of staff complement charged with responsibility to enforce employment standards during 1990s [*market-enhancing contest-*

ing of an important technique, which effectively reduced the law's effectiveness; but enforcement was historically low in Alberta].
Overall: Low-to-medium globalization. The one significant change, the reduction of an already-modest enforcement staff, contested techniques in an important area, but not the broad pattern, which remained comparatively lax.

ACTIVE LABOUR MARKET POLICY

PC Changes, 1990–2003:
- Co-location of federal and provincial active and passive labour market services (1994), followed by devolution of federal active measures [*market-neutral contesting of techniques*].
- Centralization and integration of active and passive measures delivery, followed by merging of social assistance and labour market portfolios with creation of Alberta Human Resources and Employment [*market-neutral contesting of techniques*].
- Expansion of apprenticeship system, including Registered Apprenticeship Program [*market-neutral contesting of settings, involving no significant change in the system's design*].
- 2001 partial deregulation of apprenticeship system [*market-enhancing contesting of settings, but without evident substantial impact*].
Overall: Low globalization. Only one policy change was market-enhancing, and it is likely to have a modest long-term impact.

SOCIAL ASSISTANCE FOR EMPLOYABLE PERSONS

PC changes, 1990–2003:
- Early 1990s separation of financial benefits and employment caseworker functions [*market-neutral adjustment of techniques*].
- Substantial benefit cuts in 1993, followed by prolonged benefits freeze [*market-enhancing displacement of settings, which moves the province from having among the most generous benefits in Canada to having some of the lowest; the extent and persistence of the cuts likely also deterred potential claimants, representing a displacement of techniques*].
- 1993 workfare requirements [*market-enhancing contesting of techniques, by requiring that some recipients meet work and training tests to receive benefits*].
- Setting of caseload reduction targets for caseworkers, and stipulation that their employment status depended on meeting them [*market-enhancing displacement of technique of a relatively neutral oversight of*

files by caseworkers; likely to have had a substantial effect on caseloads].
- Transfer of eligible clients from assistance to student income support program [*market-neutral contesting of settings for a minority of claimants, which resulted in no cost savings*].
- Requirement that claimants over the age of 60 seek CPP benefits [*market-enhancing contesting of settings for a minority of claimants*].
- Enhancement of training and employability programs [*market-curtailing (because capable of cushioning the consequences for claimants of losing benefits) contesting of settings only, because initiative was modest*].
- 2003 Income and Employment Support Act and Alberta Works [*market-neutral contesting of techniques with little effect on access to benefits or benefit levels*].

Overall: Medium-to-high globalization. The most important changes occurred during the early to mid-1990s. These included the benefit cuts, the stipulation that caseworkers seek to reduce caseloads, and the introduction of workfare requirements. Combined, these initiatives reduced caseloads much more dramatically than was the case in any other province, and effectively contested the goal of post-war social assistance regimes in Canada to provide assistance as a lost resort income where needed.

Quantitative measure of retrenchment: 42.3 per cent; high. Because this figure is close to the 'cut off' between our medium-high and high scores, and because the other evidence adduced in chapter 8 does not suggest that Alberta abandoned entirely (displaced), rather than contesting, the overall needs-based post-war social assistance model during the 1990s, we retained medium-to-high as our overall rating for this field.

Notes

1 Partisanship, Globalization and Political-Economic Institutions in Labour Market Policy-Making

1 See, for instance, Douglas Hibbs, 'Political Parties and Macroeconomic Policy,' *American Political Science Review*, vol. 71 (1977), pp. 1467–1487; Alberto Alesina and Nouriel Rosenthal, *Partisan Politics, Divided Governments, and the Economy* (Cambridge: Cambridge University Press, 1995).

2 John Myles, *Old Age and the Welfare State* (Boston: Little, Brown, 1984); Adam Przeworski and Michael Wallerstein, 'The Structure of Class Conflict in Democratic Capitalist Societies,' *American Political Science Review*, vol. 76 (1982), pp. 215–238.

3 Göran Therborn, 'The Rule of Capital and the Rise of Democracy,' *New Left Review*, no. 103 (1997), pp. 3–4; Adam Przeworski, *Capitalism and Social Democracy* (Cambridge: Cambridge University Press, 1986), pp. 35–43.

4 The industrialization thesis was defended by Harold Wilensky and Charles Lebeaux in their *Industrial Society and Social Welfare* (New York: Russell Sage, 1958); a sophisticated version of the Marxian class explanation is provided in Ian Gough, *The Political Economy of the Welfare State* (London: Macmillan, 1979).

5 Gøsta Esping-Andersen, 'Power and Distributional Regimes,' *Politics and Society*, vol. 14 (1985).

6 Leon Muszynski, 'The Politics of Labour Market Policy,' in G.B. Doern, ed., *The Politics of Economic Policy* (Toronto: University of Toronto Press, 1985), p. 251.

7 Organization for Economic Cooperation and Development, *The OECD Jobs Study: Facts, Analysis, Strategies* (Paris: OECD, 1994), n.p.

8 Kathleen Thelen and Sven Steinmo, 'Historical Institutionalism in Com-

parative Politics,' in Steinmo et al., eds., *Structuring Politics* (Cambridge: Cambridge University Press, 1992), pp. 16–18; Peter Hall and Rosemary Taylor, 'Political Science and the Three Institutionalisms,' *Political Studies*, vol. 44 (1996), pp. 937–942.

9 Esping-Andersen developed his typology using a qualitative-historical methodology; his subsequent research has combined qualitative and quantitative approaches. The most exhaustive recent historical institutionalist comparative studies do the same. See Evelyne Huber and John D. Stephens, *Development and Crisis in the Welfare State* (Chicago: University of Chicago Press, 2001); and Duane Swank, *Global Capital, Political Institutions, and Policy Change in Developed Welfare States* (Cambridge: Cambridge University Press, 2002). On this methodological evolution in comparative research, see Thomas Janoski and Alexander Hicks, 'Methodological Innovations in Comparative Political Economy: An Introduction,' in Janoski and Hicks, eds., *The Comparative Political Economy of the Welfare State* (Cambridge: Cambridge University Press, 1994), pp. 3–4.

10 Swank, *Global Capital, Political Institutions, and Policy Change in Developed Welfare States*, p. 10.

11 Alexander George, 'Case Studies and Theory Development: The Method of Structured, Focused Comparison,' in Paul Lauren, ed., *Diplomacy* (London: Macmillan, 1979), pp. 43–68.

12 The leading study in this field is Leo Panitch and David Swartz, *The Assault on Trade Union Freedoms*, 2d ed. (Toronto: Garamond Press, 1993); the book covers various aspects of industrial relations in Canada, but concentrates on federal and national trends, with particular attention to the public sector. Only chapter 6 is devoted mainly to provincial legislation affecting the private sector. See also Tom MacIntosh, 'Organized Labour in a Federal Society,' in H. Lazar and MacIntosh, eds., *Canada: State of the Federation, 1998–99*, (Kingston: McGill-Queen's University Press, 1999); and Gene Swimmer, 'Provincial Policies Concerning Collective Bargaining,' in C. Dunn, ed., *Provinces* (Peterborough: Broadview Press, 1996).

13 For a review of New Public Management theory and practice in Canada, see Leslie Pal, *Beyond Policy Analysis*, 2d ed. (Toronto: Nelson, 2001), pp. 192–223.

14 See note 12. Esping-Andersen, *The Three Worlds of Welfare Capitalism* (Princeton, NJ: Princeton University Press, 1990), pp. 13–14.

15 For a review of this literature, see Manfred Schmidt, 'When Parties Matter: A Review of the Possibilities and Limits of Partisan Influence on Public Policy,' *European Journal of Political Research*, vol. 30 (1996), pp. 155–83.

16 François Petry et al., 'Electoral and Partisan Cycles in the Canadian Provinces,' *Canadian Journal of Political Science*, vol. 32 (1999), pp. 273–292.

17 Gøsta Esping-Andersen, *Politics against Markets* (Princeton, NJ: Princeton University Press, 1985).

18 Paul Pierson, 'Coping with Permanent Austerity,' in Pierson, ed., *The New Politics of the Welfare State* (Oxford: Oxford University Press, 2001), pp. 431–456; Swank, *Global Capital, Political Institutions, and Policy Change in Developed Welfare States*. Robert Goodin et al. adopt the typology in *The Real Worlds of Welfare Capitalism* (Cambridge: Cambridge University Press, 1999). Francis Castles and Deborah Mitchell argued that there are four welfare state regimes. The putative fourth category includes Australia and New Zealand; 'Identifying Welfare State Regimes,' *Governance*, vol. 5 (1992), p. 3. Esping-Andersen contends that this fourth regime may have been ephemeral, with its member nations having evolved in a liberal direction by the 1990s; he concedes, however, that for some specific purposes, a fourth category might be said to exist that consists of various other countries: Esping-Andersen, *Social Foundations of Industrial Economies* (Oxford: Oxford University Press, 1999), pp. 89–94. Acceptance of Esping-Andersen's typology is not universal. For recent critiques see Alexander Hicks, *Social Democracy and Welfare Capitalism* (Ithaca: Cornell University Press, 1999), pp. 249–251; and Franz-Xavier Kaufmann, *Varianten des Wohlfahrtsstaats* (Frankfurt: Suhrkamp Verlag, 2003), pp. 20–24.

19 Esping-Andersen, *Social Foundations of Industrial Economies*, p. 46.

20 Ibid, chapters 6 and 7; Huber and Stephens, *Development and Crisis in the Welfare State*, chap. 4.

21 Philip Manow, 'Comparative Institutional Advantages of Welfare State Regimes and New Coalitions in Welfare State Reforms,' in Pierson, ed., *The New Politics of the Welfare State*, pp. 157, 160–161. Manow does not discuss the implications of this analysis for the social democratic model.

22 Charles Maier, 'Preconditions of Corporatism,' in John Goldthorpe, ed., *Order and Conflict in Contemporary Capitalism* (Oxford: Clarendon Press, 1984), p. 40.

23 Esping-Andersen, *The Three Worlds of Welfare Capitalism*, p. 23.

24 Paul Pierson, *Dismantling the Welfare State* (Cambridge: Cambridge University Press, 1994).

25 Gøsta Esping-Andersen and Walter Korpi, 'Social Policy as Class Politics in Post-war Capitalism: Scandinavia, Austria and Germany,' in J. Goldthorpe, ed., *Order and Conflict in Contemporary Capitalism* (Oxford: Clarendon Press, 1984), pp. 179–208.

26 Esping-Andersen, *Social Foundations of Postindustrial Economies*, p. 172.

27   Huber and Stephens, *Development and Crisis of the Welfare State*, p. 300.

28   Ibid., pp. 31–32.

29   Colin Hay and Daniel Wincott argue that in practice historical institution-alist scholarship stresses the role of institutions to the point of underemphasizing that of agency, though in principle it need not do this; 'Structure and Agency in Historical Institutionalism,' *Political Studies*, vol. 46 (1998), pp. 952–955.

30   'Structure and Agency in Historical Institutionalism,' *Political Studies*, vol. 46 (1998), pp. 952–955.

31   Kathleen Thelen, 'How Institutions Evolve,' in J. Mahoney and D. Rueschemeyer, eds., *Comparative Historical Analysis in the Social Sciences* (Cambridge: Cambridge University Press, 2003), p. 209.

32   Ibid., p. 235.

33   David Soskice, 'Divergent Production Regimes: Coordinated and Uncoor-dinated Market Economies in the 1980s and 1990s,' in H. Kitschelt et al., eds., *Continuity and Change in Contemporary Capitalism* (Cambridge: Cam-bridge University Press, 1999), p. 103.

34   Ibid., pp. 108, 111.

35   Margarita Estevez-Abe et al., 'Social Protection and the Formation of Skills: A Reinterpretation of the Welfare State,' in Peter Hall and David Soskice, eds., *Varieties of Capitalism* (Oxford: Oxford University Press, 2001), p. 154.

36   David Ashton and Francis Green, *Education, Training and the Global Economy* (Cheltenham, UK: Edward Elgar, 1996), chap. 5.

37   Hall and Soskice, 'An Introduction to Varieties of Capitalism,' in Hall and Soskice, eds., *Varieties of Capitalism*, pp. 3–40.

38   Paralleling the distinction that Castles and Mitchell made between the Australian and New Zealand welfare states and those of other Anglo-Saxon nations (see n18), Kitschelt et al. observe that strong unions and labour market regulatory bodies in the Antipodes distinguish these na-tions from other LMEs; Herbert Kitschelt et al., 'Convergence and Diver-gence in Advanced Capitalist Democracies,' in Kitschelt et al., eds., *Continuity and Change in Contemporary Capitalism*, p. 431.

39   Peter Swenson and Jonas Pontusson, 'The Swedish Employer Offensive Against Centralised Wage Bargaining,' in Torben Iversen et al., eds., *Unions, Employers and Central Banks* (Cambridge: Cambridge University Press, 2000).

40   Soskice, 'Divergent Production Regimes,' pp. 131–132; Kitschelt et al., 'Convergence and Divergence in Advanced Capitalist Democracies,' pp. 432–433.

41 'Soskice, 'Divergent Production Regimes,' p. 103.

42 Ibid, pp. 103–104, n8.

43 Vivien Schmidt, *The Futures of European Capitalism* (Oxford: Oxford University Press, 2002), p. 109; David Coates, *Models of Capitalism* (Cambridge, UK: Polity Press, 2000), p. 10. See also Robert Gilpin, *Global Political Economy* (Princeton, NJ: Princeton University Press, 2001), p. 149.

44 Schmidt, *The Futures of European Capitalism*, pp. 198–204.

45 Walter Korpi, *The Democratic Class Struggle* (London: Routledge and Kegan Paul, 1983); Esping-Andersen, 'Power and Distributional Regimes.' Esping-Andersen later abandoned this particular feature of his typology; see *The Three Worlds of Welfare Capitalism*, pp. 16–21.

46 Hall and Soskice, 'An Introduction to Varieties of Capitalism,' 4.

47 Schmidt, *The Future of European Capitalism*, p. 111.

48 Anthony Giddens, *Central Problems of Social Theory* (Berkeley: University of California Press, 1979), esp. pp. 69–73.

49 Charles Maier, 'Preconditions of Corporatism,' in J. Goldthorpe, ed., *Order and Conflict in Contemporary Capitalism* (Oxford: Clarendon Press, 1984), pp. 55–56.

50 Kitschelt et al., 'Convergence and Divergence in Advanced Capitalist Democracies,' p. 434. A similar synthesis is suggested by Peter Hall in 'The Political Economy of Europe in An Era of Interdependence,' in Kitschelt et al., eds., *Continuity and Change in Contemporary Capitalism*, pp. 147–148.

51 Based on Kitschelt et al., 'Convergence and Divergence in Advanced Capitalist Democracies,' p. 434; this table is modified to accommodate the additional model identified by Schmidt and discussed above.

52 The 'conservative' designation is disputed for these nations. One observer identifies a discrete 'Mediterranean' model; Esping-Andersen, *Social Foundations of Postindustrial Economies*, p. 74. Huber and Stephens put Japan in a category of its own: *Development and Crisis of the Welfare State*, p. 374, n1.

53 The comparative literature discussed here is inconsistent in categorizing party systems in these nations. Compare Kitschelt et al., 'Convergence and Divergence in Advanced Capitalist Democracies,' p. 434, with a revised statement of Kitschelt's analysis in 'Partisan Competition and Welfare State Retrenchment,' in Pierson et al., *The New Politics of the Welfare State*, p. 287.

54 Thelen and Steinmo, 'Historical Institutionalism in Comparative Politics,' p. 8.

55 Hall and Taylor, 'Political Science and the Three New Institutionalisms,' p. 939.

56 Recent treatments of the policy role of national parties and party systems in Canada include William Cross, *Political Parties* (Vancouver: UBC Press, 2004), chap. 3; and R. Kenneth Carty et al., *Rebuilding Canadian Political Parties* (Vancouver: UBC Press, 2000), esp. chap. 10.

57 Kitschelt, 'Partisan Competition and Welfare State Retrenchment,' p. 274.

58 Ibid., p. 278.

59 Ibid., p. 277.

60 Kitschelt et al., 'Convergence and Divergence in Advanced Capitalist Democracies,' p. 434.

61 Pierson, 'Coping with Permanent Austerity,' p. 455.

62 On the British case, see Desmond King and Stewart Wood, 'The Political Economy of Neoliberalism: Britain and the United States in the 1980s,' in Kitschelt, ed., *Continuity and Change in Contemporary Capitalism*, pp. 374–378; Conservative governments, as well as Labour ones, attempted corporatism during the 1960s and 1970s, but generally with less enthusiasm. Regarding Australian developments, see Huber and Stephens, *Development and Crisis of the Welfare State*, pp. 287–292.

63 Michael Mann, 'Globalisation and September 11,' *New Left Review*, series 2, no. 12 (2001), p. 52.

64 Gilpin, *Global Political Economy*, p. 5.

65 Ibid., p. 8.

66 Kenichi Ohmae, *The Borderless World* (New York: Harper Perennial, 1991), p. x. For a more subtle expression of a broadly similar perspective see Susan Strange, *The Retreat of the State* (Cambridge: Cambridge University Press, 1996), chap. 1.

67 Robert Boyer and J. Rogers Hollingsworth, 'From National Embeddedness to Spatial and Institutional Nestedness,' in Boyer and Hollingsworth, eds., *Contemporary Capitalism* (Cambridge: Cambridge University Press, 1997), p. 454.

68 Paul Hirst and Grahame Thompson, 'Globalisation in Question,' in Hollingsworth and Boyer, eds., *Contemporary Capitalism*, pp. 349–350. They nevertheless warn that playing this compensatory role effectively requires that nations possess institutions of the type that are associated with CMEs in Soskice's typology; ibid, p. 352.

69 This is not always true of comparative political economy research; we have seen that this is particularly true of Soskice. Nevertheless, we have hypothesized that his scholarship can be integrated with the welfare state literatures via synthetic accounts that attribute an important generative role to agency.

70 Andrew Glyn, 'Aspirations, Constraints, and Outcomes,' in Glyn, ed.,

Social Democracy in Neoliberal Times (Oxford: Oxford University Press, 2001), p. 20.

71 Gerassimos Moschonas, *In the Name of Social Democracy* (London: Verso, 2002), p. 226.

72 See, for instance, Gregory Albo, 'A World Market of Opportunities?' in Leo Panitch, ed., *Socialist Register, 1997* (London: Merlin Press, 1997), pp. 12–26; Panitch and Colin Leys, *The End of Parliamentary Socialism* (London: Verso, 1997). The latter volume focuses on the British Labour Party, but its argument is generalized to apply to other social democratic parties as well; see p. 15.

73 Adam Przeworski, 'How Many Ways Can Be Third?' in Glyn, ed., *Social Democracy in Neoliberal Times*, pp. 329, 333.

74 Fritz Scharpf, *Crisis and Choice in European Social Democracy* (Ithaca: Cornell University Press, 1991), p. 269.

75 Ibid., p. 275.

76 Ton Notermans, *Money, Markets, and the State* (Cambridge: Cambridge University Press, 2000), p. 224.

77 Ibid., p. 245.

78 Torben Iversen, 'Decentralisation, Monetarism, and the Social Democratic Welfare State,' in Iversen et al., eds., *Unions, Employers, and Central Banks*, pp. 227–228.

79 Perry Anderson, 'Introduction,' in Anderson and Patrick Camiller, eds., *Mapping the West European Left* (London: Verso, 1994), p. 16.

80 Carles Boix, *Political Parties, Growth and Equality* (Cambridge: Cambridge University Press, 1998), p. 10.

81 Ibid., p. 101.

82 Geoffrey Garrett, *Partisan Politics in the Global Economy* (Cambridge: Cambridge University Press, 1998), p. 11.

83 Ibid., p. 160.

84 Ibid., p. 85.

85 Colin Hay, 'Globalisation, Social Democracy and the Persistence of Partisan Politics: A Commentary on Garrett,' *Review of International Political Economy*, vol. 7 (2000), p. 139.

86 Ibid., p. 138. Garrett responds to Hay's critique in 'Capital Mobility, Exchange Rates and Fiscal Policy in the Global Economy,' in ibid., pp. 153–170.

87 Hall and Soskice, 'An Introduction to Varieties of Capitalism,' in Hall and Soskice, eds., *Varieties of Capitalism*, p. 58.

88 Kathleen Thelen, 'Varieties of Labour Politics in the Developed Democracies,' in Hall and Soskice, eds., *Varieties of Capitalism*, p. 102.

89 Stewart Wood, 'Business, Government, and Patterns of Labour Market Policy in Britain and the Federal Republic of Germany,' in Hall and Soskice, eds., *Varieties of Capitalism*, p. 274.
90 Duane Swank, *Global Capital, Political Institutions, and Policy Change in Developed Welfare States*, pp. 119–120.
91 However, as Richard B. Friedman points out, a nation with inferior institutions might nevertheless avoid changing them, 'because changing institutions can be expensive, so that maintaining less than ideal arrangements may be better than investing in reform.' See 'Single Peaked vs. Diversified Capitalism,' *NBER Working Paper Series*, no. 7556 (Cambridge, MA: National Bureau of Economic Research, February 2000), p. 30.
92 Garrett, *Partisan Politics in the Global Economy*, p. 157.
93 Ibid., pp. 124–125.
94 Fritz Scharpf, 'Economic Changes, Vulnerabilities, and Institutional Capabilities,' in Sharpf and Vivien Schmidt, eds., *Welfare and Work in the Open Economy*, vol. 1 (Oxford: Oxford University Press, 2000), pp. 75, 80.
95 Ibid., pp. 123–124.
96 Scharpf and Schmidt, 'Conclusions,' in Sharpf and Schmidt, eds., *Welfare and Work in the Open Economy*, vol. 1, p. 336.
97 Gøsta Esping-Andersen, 'Who Is Harmed by Labour Market Regulation?' in Esping-Andersen and Marino Regini, eds., *Why Deregulate Labour Markets?* (Oxford: Oxford University Press, 2000), pp. 91–92.
98 Gøsta Esping-Andersen and Marino Regini, 'Introduction,' in Esping-Andersen and Regini, eds., *Why Deregulate Labour Markets?*, p. 6.
99 Geoffrey Garrett and Christopher Way, 'Public Sector Unions, Corporatism, and Wage Determination,' in Iversen et al., eds., *Unions, Employers, and Central Banks*, p. 267.
100 Lane Kenworthy, 'Cooperation and Economic Performance,' *Policy Options* (October 1997), p. 33.

2 Welfare State, Production Regime, and Party System in Four Canadian Provinces

1 Gøsta Esping-Andersen, *Social Foundations of Postindustrial Economies* (Oxford: Oxford University Press, 1999), p. 73.
2 Duane Swank, *Global Capital, Political Institutions, and Policy Change in Developed Welfare States* (Cambridge: Cambridge University Press, 2002), p. 52.
3 Peter Hall and David Soskice, 'An Introduction to Varieties of Capital-

ism,' in Hall and Soskice, *Varieties of Capitalism* (Oxford: Oxford University Press, 2001), p. 8.

4 Only studies published since 1999 are included, in which case study discussions were used. The studies selected addressed at least three such cases from at least two different types of welfare state or political-economic regimes as defined in table 1.1. 'Number of cases' refers to the number that received a narrative discussion of at least one page in one place. Full references for sources can be found in Notes, chapter 1. 'Number of pages' refers to the number of pages devoted to Canada in relation to the total length of qualitative discussions in the volume. There are a number of recent studies (examined in the next subsection) that compare Canada's welfare state with other Anglo-Saxon ones including, usually, the United States and Britain.

5 Even in this one case, the Canadian discussion was not lengthy; Duane Swank, *Global Capital, Political Institutions, and Policy Change in Developed Welfare States*, pp. 238–239.

6 Paul Pierson, 'Coping with Permanent Austerity: Welfare State Restructuring in Affluent Democracies,' in Pierson, ed., *The New Politics of the Welfare State* (Oxford: Oxford University Press, 2001), p. 440.

7 On the general question of the role of region in Canadian politics, see Munroe Eagles, 'Political Geography and the Study of Regionalism,' in Lisa Young and Keith Archer, eds., *Regionalism and Party Politics in Canada* (Toronto: Oxford University Press, 2002), pp. 9–23.

8 Maureen Baker, 'Poverty, Social Assistance, and the Employability of Mothers in Four Commonwealth Countries,' in Sylvia Bashevkin, ed., *Women's Work Is Never Done* (London: Routledge, 2002), p. 88.

9 Sylvia Bashevkin, 'Road-Testing the Middle Way,' in ibid., p. 115.

10 Rodney Haddow, *Poverty Reform in Canada, 1958–1978* (Montreal: McGill-Queen's University Press, 1993), p. 14.

11 John Myles and Paul Pierson, *Friedman's Revenge: The Reform of 'Liberal' Welfare States in Canada and the United States* (Ottawa: Caledon Institute of Social Policy, 1997), p. 3.

12 Keith Banting, 'The Social Policy Divide: The Welfare State in Canada and the United States,' in Banting et al., eds., *Degrees of Freedom* (Montreal: McGill-Queen's University Press, 1997), p. 268.

13 The main exception to this pattern was insurance-based workers' compensation programs, which emerged in most provinces during and after the First World War; Dennis Guest, *The Emergence of Social Security in Canada*, 3d ed. (Vancouver: UBC Press, 1997), chap. 4.

14 Jane Jenson, 'Representation in Crisis: the Roots of Canada's Permeable Fordism,' *Canadian Journal of Political Science*, vol. 23 (1990), pp. 675–683.

15 More information on developments reviewed in this and the next two paragraphs can be found in Guest, *The Emergence of Social Security in Canada*, chaps. 8 to 13.

16 Esping-Andersen noted the proximity between the Beveridge principle and social democracy; *The Three Worlds of Welfare Capitalism* (Princeton: Princeton University Press, 1990), pp. 48–49.

17 For a similar analysis, see Paul Pierson, 'Coping with Austerity: Welfare State Retrenchment in Affluent Democracies,' in Pierson, ed., *The New Politics of the Welfare State* (Oxford: Oxford University Press, 2001), pp. 438–440.

18 Myles and Pierson, *Friedman's Revenge: The Reform of 'Liberal' Welfare States in Canada and the United States*, p. 13. They acknowledged, however, that this might change, especially in light of social assistance cuts made in many provinces after Ottawa's 1995 withdrawal from cost-sharing in this field; ibid., p. 20.

19 Gøsta Esping-Andersen, *The Three Worlds of Welfare Capitalism*, p. 74.

20 Margarita Estevez-Abe et al., 'Social Protection and the Formation of Skills: A Reinterpretation of the Welfare State,' in Peter Hall and David Soskice, eds., *Varieties of Capitalism* (Oxford: Oxford University Press, 2001), pp. 165, 168, 170.

21 Regarding PLMP developments discussed here, see Tom McIntosh and Gerard Boychuk, 'Dis-covered: EI, Social Assistance and the Growing Gap in Income Support for Unemployed Canadians,' in McIntosh, ed., *Federalism, Democracy and Labour Market Policy in Canada* (Montreal: McGill-Queen's University Press, 2000), pp. 65–158; regarding recent ALMP changes, see Thomas Klassen, 'The Federal-Provincial Labour Market Development Agreements: Brave New Model of Collaboration?' in ibid., pp. 159–204.

22 Rodney Haddow, 'How Ottawa Shrivels: Ottawa's Declining Role in Active Labour Market Policy,' in L. Pal, ed., *How Ottawa Spends, 1998–99* (Toronto: Oxford University Press, 1998), p. 104.

23 Carolyn Tuohy, *Policy and Politics in Canada* (Philadelphia: Temple University Press, 1992), p. 160.

24 Gene Swimmer, 'Provincial Policies Concerning Collective Bargaining,' in Christopher Dunn, ed., *Provinces* (Peterborough: Broadview Press, 1996), p. 352.

25 Richard Chaykowski and Terry Thomason, 'Canadian Workers' Compensation: Institutions and Economics,' in Thomason and Chaykowski, eds,

Research in Canadian Workers' Compensation (Kingston: Queen's University Industrial Relations Centre, 1995), pp. 4, 10–18.

26 Labour Canada, *Comparison of Labour Legislation of General Application in Canada, the United States and Mexico* (Ottawa: Labour Canada, 1991), pp. 6–23.

27 Carolyn Tuohy, *Accidental Logics* (New York: Oxford University Press, 1999), pp. 207, 208.

28 Ibid., p. 210.

29 Gerard Boychuk, *Patchwork of Purpose* (Montreal: McGill-Queen's University Press, 1998), pp. 15, 16, 22, 56.

30 Boychuk, 'Are Canadian and US Social Assistance Policies Converging?' *Canadian-American Public Policy*, no. 30 (1997), p. 3.

31 Esping-Andersen, *The Three Worlds of Welfare Capitalism*, pp. 22, 26.

32 Jon Pierce, *Canadian Industrial Relations* (Scarborough: Prentice Hall, 2000), pp. 279–280.

33 Richard Block and Karen Roberts, 'A Comparison of Labour Standards in the United States and Canada,' *Relations Industrielles*, vol. 55 (2000), pp. 296–297.

34 Chaykowski and Thomason, 'Canadian Workers' Compensation: Institutions and Economics,' in *Research in Canadian Workers' Compensation*, p. 13.

35 Michael Atkinson and William Coleman, *The State, Business and Industrial Change in Canada* (Toronto: University of Toronto Press, 1989), p. 33.

36 Ibid., pp. 45–48.

37 Ibid., p. 39.

38 Ibid., p. 76.

39 Daniel Drache, 'Rediscovering Canadian Political Economy,' in Wallace Clement and Drache, eds., *A Practical Guide to Canadian Political Economy* (Toronto: James Lorimer, 1978), pp. 4–14, 18–20.

40 Reginald Whittaker, 'The Quebec Cauldron,' in Michael Whittington and Glen Williams, eds., *Canadian Politics in the 1980s* (Toronto: Methuen, 1984), pp. 34–41.

41 Nelson Wiseman, 'Provincial Political Cultures,' in Christopher Dunn, ed., *Provinces: Canadian Provincial Politics* (Peterborough: Broadview Press, 1996), pp. 55–57.

42 Ian M. Drummond et al., *Progress without Planning* (Toronto: University of Toronto Press, 1987).

43 K. J. Rea, *The Prosperous Years* (Toronto: University of Toronto Press, 1985), pp. 232, 251.

44 Thomas Courchene and Colin Telmer, *From Heartland to North American*

Region State (Toronto: Centre for Public Policy, University of Toronto, 1998), pp. 11, 300.

45 Neil Bradford, 'Prospects for Associative Governance: Lessons from Ontario, Canada,' *Politics and Society*, vol. 26 (1998), pp. 541–544.

46 David Wolfe, 'Harnessing the Region: Changing Perspectives on Innovation Policy in Ontario,' in Trevor Barnes and Meric Gertler, eds., *The New Industrial Geography* (London: Routledge, 1999), pp. 147–150. Wolfe nevertheless believes that these collaborative measures had met with considerable success while they were being pursued.

47 David Wolfe and Meric Gertler, 'Globalisation and Economic Restructuring in Ontario,' *European Planning Studies*, vol. 9 (2001), p. 587.

48 A federal government study found that in 1997, about 75 per cent of all adult education and training programs in Canada were supplied by educational institutions, and only 4.7 per cent by employers, though the latter also supplied 22.3 per cent of all courses. Moreover, 86 per cent of all adult training involved a classroom component, while only 17 per cent included an on-the-job element. See Statistics Canada, *A Report on Adult Education and Training in Canada* (Ottawa: Ministry of Industry, 2001), pp. 2–3, 76–77. However, the report's authors noted that their study did not measure informal training, where employers are likely to assume a more direct role.

49 Interviewed observers from Ontario's governmental, labour, and business communities stressed this theme.

50 Sid Noel, 'The Ontario Political Culture: An Interpretation,' in Graham White, ed., *The Government and Politics of Ontario* (Toronto: University of Toronto Press, 1997), p. 53.

51 Ibid., p. 65.

52 Rand Dyck, 'The Socio-Economic Setting of Ontario Politics,' in White, ed., *The Government and Politics of Ontario*, p. 48.

53 Thomas Walkom, 'The Harris Government: Restoration or Revolution?' in White, ed., *The Government and Politics of Ontario*, pp. 413–414.

54 The classic review of neo-liberalism among Quebec's business elite was Pierre Fournier's *The Quebec Establishment* (Montreal: Black Rose, 1976). For a recent discussion, based on the views of the Conseil de patronat, see Peter Graefe, 'The Quebec *patronat*: From Neoliberalism to Neoliberalism *Fleur-de-lisé*,' paper presented at the annual meeting of the Canadian Political Science Association (Toronto, May 2002), pp. 3, 15–16, 20–21.

55 Esther Déom and Jean Boivin, 'Union-Management Relations in Quebec,' in Morley Gunderson et al., *Union-Management Relations in Canada*, 4th ed. (Toronto: Addison, Wesley, Longman, 2001), p. 489.

56 The lack of sufficienct industrial training, and an excessive reliance on institutional instruction, was one of the Quebec government's foremost critiques of the province's training system in the early 1990s; see Quebec, *Partners for a Skilled and Competitive Quebec* (Quebec City: Ministère de la Main-d'oeuvre, de la Sécurité du revenu et de la Formation professionnelle, 1991), pp. 20–21.

57 We borrow this term from Carolyn Tuohy, who used it, in another context, to describe the Canadian polity; see her *Policy and Politics in Canada: Institutionalised Ambivalence* (Philadelphia: Temple University Press, 1992), p. xvii.

58 As Peter Graefe points out, the *patronat* is unique in being structured as a 'federation of federations,' along European lines; Graefe, 'The Quebec *patronat*,' p. 4.

59 Gilles Bourque, *Le modèle québécois de développement* (Quebec City: Presses de l'Université du Québec, 2000), p. 168. Such inter-associational rivalries were also noted by business association representatives interviewed for this research.

60 Déom and Boivin, 'Union-Management Relations in Quebec,' in Gunderson, et al., *Union-Management Relations in Canada*, p. 503.

61 Clinton Archibald, 'Corporatist Tendencies in Quebec,' in Alain Gagnon, ed., *Quebec: State and Society* (Toronto: Methuen, 1984), p. 353.

62 Bourque, *Le modèle québécois de développement*, p. 184. Our translation.

63 Ibid., p. 147. Our translation.

64 Ibid., pp. 43–44, 200.

65 Yves Bélanger, *Québec inc: L'entreprise québécoise à la croisée des chemins* (Montreal: Éditions Hurtubise HMH, 1998), pp. 132–135, 156–157.

66 André Gélinas concludes his recent *L'intervention et la retrait de l'État* with the argument that since the 1980s Quebec has experienced 'neither a dismantling of its State nor even an important reduction in its inverventions' (Quebec City: Les Presses de l'Université Laval, 2002), p. 414. Our translation.

67 This is Bourque's chronology. For Alain Noël, there were important antecedents to post-1989 policies earlier in the 1980s; 'Québec inc., veni! vidi! vici?' in Jean-Pierre Dupuis, ed., *Le modèle québécois de développement économique* (Quebec City: Les Presses Inter-Universitaires, 1995), p. 73.

68 Robert Dalpé and Réjean Landry, 'Présentation,' in Dalpé and Landry, eds., *La politique technologique au Québec* (Montreal: Les Presses de l'Université de Montréal, 1993), p. 11. Our translation. Also see Daniel Latouche, 'Do Regions Make a Difference? The Case of Science and Technology Policies in Quebec,' in Hans-Joachim Braczyk et al., eds., *Regional*

Innovation Systems (London: UCL Press, 1997), pp. 319–344; and Marc Ferland et al., 'Quebec's Strategy to Foster Value-Adding Interfirm Cooperation,' in Udo Staber et al., eds., *Business Networks: Prospects for Regional Development* (Berlin: Walter Gruyter, 1996), pp. 82–96.

69 Michael Howlett and Keith Brownsey, 'The Old Reality and the New Reality: Party Politics and Public Policy in British Columbia, 1941–1987,' *Studies in Political Economy*, no. 25 (1988), p. 144.

70 On the last two points, see Rodney Haddow, 'How Malleable are Political-Economic Institutions? The Case of Labour Market Decision-Making in British Columbia,' *Canadian Public Administration*, vol. 43 (2000), pp. 391–393.

71 Howlett and Brownsey, 'Public Sector Politics in a Rentier Resource Economy,' in Brownsey and Howlett, eds., *The Provincial State* (Mississauga: Copp Clark Pitman, 1992), p. 274.

72 Edwin R. Black, 'British Columbia: The Politics of Exploitation,' in Hugh Thorburn, ed., *Party Politics in Canada*, 4th ed. (Scarborough: Prentice Hall Canada, 1979), p. 299.

73 Martin Robin, 'British Columbia: The Company Province,' in Robin, ed., *Canadian Provincial Politics*, 2d ed. (Scarborough: Prentice Hall Canada, 1978), p. 57.

74 Black, 'British Columbia: The Politics of Exploitation,' in Hugh Thorburn, ed., *Party Politics in Canada*, 4th ed., p. 299.

75 In this respect, BC's post-war infrastructure initiatives can be compared to Ontario's during the late nineteenth and early twentieth centuries, a time when Ontario governments also believed that Ottawa's efforts on their behalf were inadequate; see H.V. Nelles, *The Politics of Development: Forests, Mines and Hydro-Electric Power in Ontario, 1849–1941* (Toronto: Macmillan, 1984), esp. chap. 12.

76 Howlett and Brownsey, 'Public Sector Politics in a Rentier Resource Economy,' in Brownsey and Howlett, eds., *The Provincial State*, p. 280.

77 Norman Ruff, 'Redefining Party Politics in British Columbia,' in Hugh Thorburn, ed., *Party Politics in Canada*, 7th ed. (Scarborough: Prentice Hall Canada, 1996), pp. 490–491.

78 Jeff Taylor, 'Labour in the Klein Revolution,' in Trevor Harrison and Gordon Laxer, eds., *The Trojan Horse: Alberta and the Future of Canada* (Montreal: Black Rose Books, 1995), pp. 302–304, 312–313.

79 Peter Smith, 'Alberta: Experiments in Governance – From Social Credit to the Klein Revolution,' in Brownsey and Howlett, eds., *The Provincial State in Canada*, p. 300.

80 Kevin Taft, *Shredding the Public Interest* (Edmonton: University of Alberta Press, 1997), p. 112.

81 Réjean Landry and Chantal Blouin, 'Comparaison des Stratégies Provinciales D'Aide aux Entreprises Manufacturières,' in Crête et al., *Politiques
Provinciales Comparées*, pp. 295, 305.

82 John Richards and Larry Pratt, *Prairie Capitalism* (Toronto: McClelland and
Stewart, 1979), chap. 7.

83 Allan Tupper et al., 'The Role of Government,' in Tupper and Roger Gibbins, eds., *Government and Politics in Alberta* (Edmonton: University of
Alberta Press, 1992), p. 33.

84 Trevor Harrison, 'Making the Trains Run on Time: Corporatism in
Alberta,' in Harrison and Laxer, eds., *The Trojan Horse*, p. 120.

85 Robert Alford, *Party and Society* (Chicago: Rand McNally 1963), p. 251.

86 Janine Brodie and Jane Jenson, *Crisis, Challenge and Change: Party and Class
in Canada Revisited* (Ottawa: Carleton University Press, 1988), pp. 3–7.

87 Frank Underhill, *Canadian Political Parties* (Ottawa: Canadian Historical
Association, 1957).

88 James Bickerton et al., *Ties That Bind: Parties and Voters in Canada* (Toronto:
Oxford University Press, 1999), pp. 193–197; William Cross, 'The Increas-
ing Importance of Region in Canadian Election Campaigns,' in L. Young
and K. Archer, eds., *Regionalism and Party Politics in Canada* (Toronto:
Oxford University Press, 2002), pp. 116–128; Harold Clarke et al., 'Absent
Mandate: Canadian Electoral Politics in an Era of Restructuring,' in H.
Thorburn and A. Whitehorn, eds., *Party Politics in Canada*, 8th ed. (Toronto:
Prentice Hall, 2001), pp. 398–412.

89 William Cross, *Political Parties* (Vancouver: UBC Press, 2004), p. 33.

90 But see R.K. Carty and David Stewart, 'Parties and Party Systems,' in C.
Dunn, ed., *Provinces* (Peterborough: Broadview Press, 1996), esp. pp. 77–
86. The study of provincial political cultures might afford a fruitful starting point for developing a full comparative model of provincial party
systems in Canada; see, for instance, Nelson Wiseman, 'Provincial Political
Cultures,' in Dunn, ed., *Provinces*, pp. 21–62. Such a 10-province comparative framework, encompassing the relationship of party systems to production regimes and welfare states in each case, is beyond the scope of this
enquiry.

91 Wiseman, 'Provincial Political Cultures,' in Dunn, ed., *Provinces: Canadian
Provincial Politics*, p. 47.

92 It has been argued that the substance of Conservative policy during these
years was much more market-oriented and liberal than the party's moderate brokerage image would suggest; Rodney Haddow, 'Ontario Politics:
'Plus Ça Change'?' in James Bickerton and Alain Gagnon, eds., *Canadian
Politics*, 2d ed. (Peterborough: Broadview Press, 1994), pp. 474–476.

93 Gad Horowitz, 'Conservatism, Liberalism and Socialism in Canada: An Interpretation,' in R.S. Blair and J.T. MacLeod, eds., *The Canadian Political Tradition: Basic Readings* (Toronto: Nelson, 1988), pp. 174–180, 186–189.

94 Robert MacDermid and Greg Albo, 'Divided Province, Growing Protests: Ontario Moves Right,' in Brownsey and Howlett, eds., *The Provincial State in Canada*, pp. 163–202.

95 Haddow, 'Ontario Politics: Plus Ça Change'?' in Bickerton and Gagnon, eds., *Canadian Politics*, 2d ed., p. 481.

96 The term used to characterize Ontario's political culture by John Wilson in 'The Red Tory Province: Reflections on the Character of the Ontario Political Culture,' in Donald MacDonald, ed., *The Government and Politics of Ontario*, 2d ed. (Toronto: Van Nostrand Reinhold, 1980), pp. 210–233.

97 Vincent Lemieux, 'Heaven Is Blue and Hell Is Red,' in Martin Robin, ed., *Canadian Provincial Politics* (Toronto: Prentice Hall, 1978), pp. 248–250, 275–278.

98 At the time of writing, the Action Démocratique de Québec (ADQ), which won four seats in the province's 2003 general election, and attracted 18 per cent of the vote, has failed to break the two-party mould, as had been widely anticipated several months before the vote.

99 François Pétry, 'La Réalisation des engagements du Parti québécois: analyse d'ensemble,' in Pétry, ed., *Le Parti québécois: Bilan des Engagements Électoraux, 1994–2000* (Quebec City: Les Presses de l'Université Laval, 2002), pp. 162–177.

100 François Pétry et al., 'Electoral and Partisan Cycles in the Canadian Provinces,' *Canadian Journal of Political Science*, vol. 32 (1999), p. 287.

101 Neil Nevitte and Roger Gibbins, *New Elites in Old States* (Toronto: Oxford University Press, 1990), p. 129.

102 Nelson Wiseman, 'Provincial Political Cultures,' in Dunn, ed., *Provinces: Canadian Provincial Politics*, p. 45. This view that the left-right ideological division between Quebec's main parties is more modest than elsewhere in Canada was also expressed by many Quebec observers, in the bureaucracy and business and labour circles interviewed for this study.

103 Martin Robin, 'British Columbia: The Company Province,' in Robin, ed., *Canadian Provincial Politics*, 2d ed., pp. 49–57.

104 Rand Dyck, *Provincial Politics in Canada*, 3d ed. (Toronto: Prentice Hall Canada, 1996), p. 635.

105 Michael Howlett and Keith Brownsey, 'British Columbia: Public Sector Politics in a Rentier Resource Economy' in Brownsey and Howlett, eds., *The Provincial State*, pp. 276–279.

106 Rand Dyck, *Provincial Politics in Canada*, 3d ed. (Toronto: Prentice Hall Canada, 1996), pp. 611–614, 619–622.

107 Michael Howlett and Keith Brownsey, 'British Columbia: Public Sector Politics in a Rentier Resource Economy,' in Brownsey and Howlett, eds., *The Provincial State*, p. 272.

108 Forty-two per cent of unionized respondents to a March 2003 poll supported the NDP, compared with 24 per cent of the non-unionized. The Liberals were favoured by 50 per cent of the non-unionized, and 33 per cent of union members; they were supported by 55 per cent of those with incomes over $60,000 per year, compared to 31 per cent of respondents with incomes below $30,000. Ipsos-Reid, 'BC Provincial Political Scene,' Press release, 19 March 2003.

109 Rand Dyck, *Provincial Politics in Canada*, 3d ed. (Toronto: Prentice Hall Canada, 1996), pp. 558–559; Elections Alberta, 'Summary of Results of Past General Elections,' www.electionsalberta.ab.ca/pastelections.html/#200.

110 There is a dispute about the extent to which the Social Credit movement, which governed Alberta from 1935 to 1971, was a party of the right from the outset, or only became one during the 1940s; Peter Smith, 'Alberta: Experiments in Governance – From Social Credit to the Klein Revolution,' in Brownsey and Howlett, eds., *The Provincial State in Canada* (Peterborough: Broadview Press, 2000), p. 281.

111 Edward Bell, 'Reconsidering *Democracy in Alberta*,' in Tupper and Gibbins, eds., *Government and Politics in Alberta*, pp. 85–108.

112 Nelson Wiseman, 'The Pattern of Prairie Politics,' in Hugh Thorburn, ed., *Party Politics in Canada*, 7th ed. (Toronto: Prentice Hall Canada, 1996), pp. 440–443; Smith, 'Alberta: Experiments in Governance,' in Brownsey and Howlett, eds., *The Provincial State in Canada*, p. 283.

113 Allan Tupper, 'Debt, Populism and Cutbacks,' in Thorburn, ed., *Party Politics in Canada*, 7th ed., pp. 470–473.

114 Ibid., p. 467.

115 Peter Hall, 'Policy Paradigms, Social Learning, and the State,' *Comparative Politics*, vol. 25 (1993), p. 278.

3 Historical and Federal Context of Provincial Labour Market Policy

1 On why the state intervenes in the labour market, see Gordon Betcherman, Amy Luinstra, and Makoto Ogawa, *Labour Market Regulation: International Experience in Promoting Employment and Social Protection* (Social Protection Discussion Paper Series No. 0128. Washington: World Bank, 2001).

2 See, for example, Richard N. Block, Karen Roberts, and R. Oliver Clarke, *Labor Standards in the United States and Canada* (Kalamazoo, Michigan:

W.E.Upjohn Institute for Employment Research, 2003), chap. 3, 'Definitions and Criteria.'

3 Broadly speaking, the industrial sectors under federal jurisdiction include: interprovincial and international services such as railways, highway transport, telephone, cable and telecommunications systems, pipelines, canals, ferries, tunnels, bridges, shipping and shipping services; radio and television broadcasting; air transport and aircraft operations; banks; fisheries as a natural resource; and undertakings declared by Parliament to be for the general advantage of Canada.

4 Ronald L. Watts, *Comparing Federal Systems*, 2d edition (Kingston: Institute of Intergovernmental Relations, Queen's University, 1999); and Alain Noël, ed., *Federalism and Labour Market Policy: Comparing Different Governance and Employment Strategies* (Montreal: McGill-Queen's University Press, 2004).

5 A review of some of these dynamics and relationships for the period prior to this study can be found in Keith G. Banting, 1987, *The Welfare State and Canadian Federalism*, 2d ed. (Montreal: McGill-Queen's University Press, 1987); and Jacqueline S. Ismael, ed., *Canadian Social Welfare Policy: Federal and Provincial Dimensions* (Montreal: McGill-Queen's University Press, 1985).

6 Morley Gunderson and Douglas Hyatt, eds., *Workers' Compensation: Foundations for Reform* (Toronto: University of Toronto Press, 2000).

7 Price V. Fishback and Shawn Everett Kantor, *A Prelude to the Welfare State: The Origins of Workers' Compensation* (Chicago: University of Chicago Press, 2000), p. 1.

8 William Meredith, *Final Report on Laws Relating to the Liability of Employers to Make Compensation for Their Injuries Received in the Course of Their Employment Which Are in Force in Other Countries* (Workers' Compensation Commission) (Toronto: King's Printer, 1913), p. xix.

9 Morley Gunderson and Douglas Hyatt, 'Foundations for Workers' Compensation Reform: Overview and Summary,' in Morley Gunderson and Douglas Hyatt, eds., *Workers' Compensation: Foundations for Reform* (Toronto: University of Toronto Press, 2000), pp. 3–26.

10 The Association of Workers' Compensation Boards of Canada, composed of provincial workers' compensation representatives, was founded in 1919 but has no policy coordination authority.

11 Ontario Workers' Compensation Board, *The Workers' Compensation Board of Ontario 75th Anniversary Symposium* (Toronto: Ontario Workers' Compensation Board, 1989).

12 Terrance J. Bogyo, 'Workers' Compensation: Updating the Historic Com-

promise,' in Terry Thomason et al., eds., *Chronic Stress: Workers' Compensation in the 1990s* (Toronto: CD Howe Institute, 1995), pp. 92–135.

13 Bill Wilkerson, *Unfolding Change: Workers' Compensation in Canada: A Report for Canadians in Five Volumes*. Vol 4: *A Survey of Foreign WC Systems and Reforms* (Toronto: CorpWorld Group, 1995).

14 Gunderson and Hyatt, 'Foundations for Workers' Compensation Reform: Overview and Summary.'

15 G.B. Reschenthaler, *Occupational Health and Safety in Canada: The Economics and Three Case Studies* (Montreal: Institute for Research on Public Policy, 1979), p. 3.

16 See Eric Tucker, *Administering Danger in the Workplace: The Law and Politics of Occupational Health and Safety Regulation in Ontario, 1850–1914* (Toronto: University of Toronto Press, 1990).

17 See Tucker, *Administering Danger in the Workplace*, pp. 111–114.

18 In terms of occupational health and safety, the United States in more centralized than Canada with the federal Occupational Safety and Health Administration having jurisdiction in half of the 50 states.

19 Health and Welfare Canada, *Occupational Health in Canada: Current Status* (Ottawa: Department of National Health and Welfare, 1977).

20 Mining has always been a particularly dangerous industry in Canada.

21 Canadian Centre for Occupational Health and Safety, *A Mosaic of Mosaics: A Report of Occupational Health and Safety in Canada* (Ottawa: Canadian Centre for Occupational Health and Safety, 1983).

22 John O'Grady, 'Joint Health and Safety Committees: Finding a Balance,' in Terrence Sullivan, ed., *Injury in the New World of Work* (Vancouver: University of British Columbia Press, 2000), pp. 162–198.

23 In 1913, as the number of office workers began to increase, the Ontario Factory Act and the Shops Regulation Act of 1888 were consolidated in the Factory, Shop and Office Building Act.

24 Allan M. Dymond, *The Laws of Ontario Relating to Women and Children* (Toronto: Clarkson W. James, 1923), chap. 13.

25 Geoffrey Brennan, 'Minimum Hours and Working Time during the Last Century,' *Workplace Gazette*, vol. 3, no. 4 (2000), pp. 61–73.

26 Charles E. Reasons, Lois E. Ross, and Craig Paterson, *Assault on the Worker: Occupational Health and Safety in Canada* (Toronto: Butterworths, 1981), chap. 11.

27 See Brennan, 'Minimum Hours and Working Time during the Last Century,' for a historical review of employment standards.

28 From 1986 to 1989 Quebec and Ontario coordinated the levels of, and increases in, minimum wages. However, this pattern did not continue

after 1990, nor have there been other attempts at such interprovincial coordination.

29 Human Resources Development Canada, *Employment Standards Legislation in Canada, 1995–96* (Ottawa: Minister of Supply and Services, 1995), pp. 19–20.

30 For the HRDC data, see http://www110.hrdc-hrhc.gc.ca/psait_spila/ lmnec _eslc/ eslc/salaire_minwage/ index.cfm/doc/english. The CANSIM data vectors used in table 3.1 were the following:

Variable	Table no.	PQ Vector	ON Vector	AB Vector	BC Vector	From	To
Provincial consumer Price index (CPI)	3260001	V736152	V736288	V736696	V736831	1989	2003
Average hourly wage	2810029	V1591098	V1591285	V1591736	V1591994	1991	2003

31 Richard P. Chaykowski, 'The Arrival of Pay Equity Legislation,' in Richard P. Chaykowski, ed., *Pay Equity Legislation: Linking Economic Issues and Policy Concerns* (Kingston: Queen's University Industrial Relations Centre, 1990), p. 3.

32 In 1975 Quebec was the first jurisdiction in Canada to include a pay equity provision in its Charter of Human Rights and Freedoms.

33 In most provinces, but not all, there is pay equity legislation or policy frameworks that apply to the broader public sector.

34 Judy Fudge and Patricia McDermott, eds., *Just Wages: A Feminist Assessment of Pay Equity* (Toronto: University of Toronto Press. 1991).

35 For example, see Jan Kainer, *Cashing In on Pay Equity?: Supermarket Restructuring and Gender Equality* (Toronto: Sumach Press, 2002).

36 Stephen McBride, *Not Working: State, Unemployment and Neo-Conservatism in Canada* (Toronto: University of Toronto Press, 1992), pp. 191–192.

37 Judy Fudge and Eric Tucker, 'Pluralism or Fragmentation?: The Twentieth-Century Employment Law Regime in Canada,' *Labour*, vol. 40 (2000), pp. 251–306.

38 Eric Tucker, 'Labour Law and Fragmentation before Statutory Collective Bargaining,' in Mercedes Steedman et al. *Hard Lessons: The Mine Mill Union in the Canadian Labour Movement* (Toronto: Dundurn Press, 2000), pp. 99–116.

39 An excellent analysis of the emergence of the post-war compromise is found in Peter S. McInnis, *Harnessing Labour Confrontation: Shaping the Postwar Settlement in Canada, 1943–1950* (Toronto: University of Toronto Press, 2002).

40 Canada Department of Labour (Legislation Branch), *Labour Relations Legislation in Canada* (Ottawa: Queen's Printer, 1970), p. 3.

41 Canada Department of Labour (Economics and Research Branch), *Union Growth in Canada, 1921–1967* (Ottawa: Information Canada, 1970), table IV-A.

42 Human Resources Development Canada (Workplace Information Directorate), 'Union Membership in Canada – 2002,' *Workplace Gazette*, vol. 5, no. 3 (2003), pp. 38–45.

43 See S. Dupré et al., *Federalism and Policy Development* (Toronto: University of Toronto Press, 1973) for a review of developments in this field to about 1970.

44 For Ontario, see Ontario, *Commission on Unemployment* (interim report) (Toronto: Legislative Assembly of Ontario, King's Printer, 1915), which concluded on page six that 'nothing but a properly constituted State Employment Bureau' can meet the needs of workers, employers, and, more generally, the province.

45 John Hunter, *The Employment Challenge: Federal Employment Policies and Programs 1900–1990* (Ottawa: Government of Canada, 1993).

46 Ibid.

47 For instance, in the province of Ontario the number of individuals classified as 'employable' who were in receipt of social assistance increased five-fold to nearly 3.0 per cent of the working age population between 1991 and 1994. See Thomas R. Klassen and Daniel Buchanan, 'Getting It Backward: Economy and Welfare from 1985–95,' *Canadian Public Policy*, vol. 23, no. 3 (1997), pp. 333–338.

48 At the same time, the decentralization of active labour market policy was strongly being advocated on efficiency and effectiveness grounds by the Organisation for Economic Development and Co-Operation. See for example, OECD, The OECD *Jobs Study: Evidence and Explanations* (Paris: OECD, 1994); and OECD, *Decentralizing Employment Policy: New Trends and Challenges* (Paris: OECD, 2000).

49 Canadian Labour Market Productivity Centre, *Report of the Task Forces on the Labour Force Development Strategy* (Ottawa: Canadian Labour Market Productivity Centre, 1990).

50 The board was composed of 22 representatives: 8 from each of business and labour, 4 from social action groups (women, the disabled, visible minorities, and Natives), and 2 representatives from training providers. The members of the board were nominated by the constituencies: almost 90 national organizations. Decision-making was by consensus and the board was co-chaired by business and labour.

51 Many provinces did establish provincial boards. The boards generally mirrored the CLFDB composition, although some provinces added one or two seats for specific groups. In Quebec a somewhat different body – the

Société quebecoise de developpment de la main d'oeuvre – was established in 1993 to direct provincial training programs.

52 Andrew Sharpe and Rodney Haddow, *Social Partnerships for Training: Canada's Experiment with Labour Force Development Boards* (Ottawa: Centre for the Study of Living Standards, 1997).

53 A history of each board is found in Sharpe and Haddow, *Social Partnerships for Training: Canada's Experiment with Labour Force Development Boards.*

54 Rodney Haddow, 'Reforming Labour Market Governance: the Case of Quebec,' *Canadian Public Administration*, vol. 41 (1998), pp. 343–368.

55 The more easily understood term *transfer*, rather than the more technically accurate term *contribution*, is used to describe the flow of funds from the federal government to provincial governments for active labour market programs.

56 Furthermore, the federal government also retained three components of labour market policy: national labour market information exchange; pan-Canadian activities to be funded from the employment insurance fund at about $250 million annually; and active labour market measures for non-employment insurance clients such as youth, the disabled, Aboriginals, older workers, and recent immigrants.

57 Thomas R. Klassen, 'The Federal-Provincial Labour Market Development Agreements: Brave New Model of Collaboration?,' in Tom Mcintosh, ed., *Federalism, Democracy and Labour Market Policy in Canada* (Montreal: McGill-Queen's University Press, 2000), pp. 159–203; and Herman Bakvis, 'Checkerboard Federalism? Labour Market Development Policy in Canada,' in Herman Bakvis and Grace Skogstad, eds., *Canadian Federalism: Performance, Effectiveness, and Legitimacy* (Toronto: Oxford University Press, 2002).

58 Harvey Lazar, *Shifting Roles: Active Labour Market Policy in Canada under the Labour Market Development Agreement* (Ottawa: Canadian Public Research Networks, 2002).

59 Dymond, *The Laws of Ontario Relating to Women and Children*, points out that initially there were numerous limitations placed on such assistance, including that the mother must be a British subject and 'must have been resident in Canada for a period of three years prior to the happening of the event upon which she might be granted an allowance.'

60 Rodney S. Haddow, *Poverty Reform in Canada, 1958–1978: State and Class Influences on Policy Making* (Montreal: McGill-Queen's Press, 1993).

61 Dennis Guest, *The Emergence of Social Security in Canada*, 3d ed. (Vancouver: UBC Press, 2003), p. 146.

62 Gerard W. Boychuk, *Patchworks of Purpose: The Development of Provincial Social Assistance Regimes in Canada* (Montreal: McGill-Queen's University Press, 1998).

63 In 2004, the Canada Health and Social Transfer was replaced by the Canada Health Transfer in support of health care and the Canada Social Transfer (CST) in support of other social programs previously supported by the Health and Social Transfer.

64 Tom McIntosh and Gerard W. Boychuk, 'Dis-covered: EI, Social Assistance and the Growing Gap in Income Support for Unemployed Canadians,' in Tom McIntosh, ed., *Federalism, Democracy and Labour Market Policy in Canada* (Montreal: McGill-Queen's University Press and Queen's University School of Policy Studies, 2000), pp. 65–158.

65 Margaret Little, *'No Car, No Radio, No Liquor Permit:' The Moral Regulation of Single Mothers in Ontario, 1920–1997* (Toronto: Oxford University Press, 1998).

66 Jamie Peck, *Welfare States* (New York: Guilford Press, 2001); Patricia M. Evans, 'Linking Welfare to Jobs: Workfare, Canadian Style,' in A. Sayeed, ed., *Workfare: Does It Work? Is It Fair?* (Montreal: Institute for Research on Public Policy, 1995), pp. 75–104.

67 E. Sabatini, *Welfare – No Fair: A Critical Analysis of Ontario's Welfare System (1985–1994)* (Vancouver: Fraser Institute, 1996).

68 See James Struthers, *No Fault of Their Own: Unemployment and the Canadian Welfare State 1914–1941* (Toronto: University of Toronto Press, 1983) for a history of how the national system of unemployment insurance came into existence.

69 A recent review of developments in unemployment insurance policy, focused on gender, is found in Ann Porter, *Gendered States: Women, Unemployment Insurance and the Political Economy of the Welfare State in Canada: 1945–1997* (Toronto: University of Toronto Press, 2003).

70 Some of these were reversed in 2000, immediately prior to the federal election.

71 Tom McIntosh and Gerard W. Boychuk, 'Dis-covered: EI, Social Assistance and the Growing Gap in Income Support for Unemployed Canadians.'

72 Gavin W. Anderson, 'Filling the 'Charter' Gap?: Human Rights Codes in the Private Sector,' *Osgood Hall Law Journal*, vol. 33, no. 4 (1995), pp. 749–783.

73 For an overview of the history and limitations of human rights commissions, see R. Brian Howe and David Johnson, *Restraining Equality: Human Rights Commissions in Canada* (Toronto: University of Toronto Press, 2000).

74 For a history of immigration policy, see Ninette Kelley and Michael Trebilcock, *The Making of the Mosaic: A History of Canadian Immigration Policy* (Toronto: University of Toronto Press, 1998). Freda Hawkins, *Canada and Immigration: Public Policy and Public Concern* (Toronto: Institute of Public Administration of Canada, 1988) discusses the provinces and immigration policy in chapters 7 and 8.

75 John W. P. Veugelers and Thomas R. Klassen, 'Continuity and Change in Canada's Unemployment-Immigration Linkage (1946–1993),' *Canadian Journal of Sociology*, vol. 19, no. 3 (1994), pp. 351–369.

76 The more obvious current examples are the live-in caregiver program, which grants renewable one-year work permits to workers in other countries to enter Canada for live-in care work; and the 19,000 migrant workers, mostly from Latin America, allowed entry during planting and harvesting time under the seasonal agricultural workers program each year.

4 Ontario: Policy Continuity amid Institutional Uncertainty

1 Nelson Wiseman, 'The Pattern of Prairie Politics,' *Queen's Quarterly*, vol. 81 (1981), pp. 298–315.

2 John Wilson, 'The Red Tory Province,' in D. MacDonald, ed., *The Government and Politics of Ontario*, 2d ed. (Toronto: Van Norstrand Reinhold, 1980).

3 Rodney Haddow, 'Ontario Politics: "Plus ça change ..."?,' in J. Bickerton and A-G. Gagnon, eds., *Canadian Politics*, 2d ed. (Peterborough: Broadview Press, 1994), p. 475.

4 Ibid., p. 481.

5 Ontario Premiers' Council on Technology, *Competing in the Global Economy*, vol. 1 (Toronto: Queen's Printer, 1988); and *People and Skills in the New Economy* (Toronto: Queen's Printer, 1990).

6 Haddow, 'Ontario Politics,' p. 481.

7 See New Democratic Party of Ontario, *An Agenda for People* (Toronto: Queen's Printer, 1990).

8 Neil Bradford, 'Prospects for Associative Governance: Lessons from Ontario, Canada,' *Politics and Society*, vol. 26 (1998), pp. 544–547.

9 Progressive Conservative Party of Ontario, *The Common Sense Revolution* (Toronto: PC Party of Ontario, 1994).

10 Progressive Conservative Party of Ontario, *Blueprint: Mike Harris' Plan to Keep Ontario on the Right Track* (Toronto: PC Party of Ontario 1999).

11 Cunliffe, 'Do Political Parties Make a Difference? The Ontario NDP and Labour Law Reform' (MA thesis, University of Guelph, 1995), p. 64.

12 Ontario. *Speech from the Throne on the Opening of the First Session of the Thirty-Fifth Parliament of the Province of Ontario*, 20 November 1990, p. 5.

13 'Industry Wary of Change to Ontario Labour Law,' *Daily Commercial News and Construction Record*, 6 June 1991, p. 1.

14 Gene Allen, 'Ontario Ministry calling for ban on strike-breakers,' *The Globe and Mail*, 4 September 1991, p. A1.

15 Richard Mackie, 'Business unhappy over NDP proposal,' *The Globe and Mail*, 18 October 1991, p. A5; Virginia Galt and Richard Mackie, 'Business shudders at NDP's proposals,' *The Globe and Mail*, 8 November 1991, p. A3.

16 Harish Jain and S. Muthuchidambaram, *Ontario Labour Law Reform* (Kingston: Industrial Relations Centre, 1995), p. 26; Cunliffe, 'Do Political Parties Make a Difference?,' pp. 130–131.

17 Richard Mackie, 'NDP modifies two areas of proposed labour law,' *The Globe and Mail*, 1 October 1992, p. A8.

18 Virginia Galt, 'Business finds solidarity in war of ideologies,' *The Globe and Mail*, 4 February 1992, p. A5.

19 'Changes in Ontario Labour Law,' *The Globe and Mail*, 10 November 1995, p. A5.

20 Mel Watkins, 'Second Wind,' *This Magazine*, January/February 1998, pp. 13–14.

21 Tom Blackwell, 'Bill a green light for anti-union tactics: labour leaders,' *Canadian Press Newswire*, 22 June 1998.

22 'Proposed Changes in Ontario Construction Labour Law under fire from two sides,' *Canadian Press Newswire*, 25 April 2000.

23 Ontario Ministry of Labour, 'Improvements to Collective Bargaining in Toronto Area Residential Construction,' *Backgrounder*, 26 September 2002.

24 'Ontario Introduces Sweeping Changes in Labour Laws; unions promise to fight,' *Canadian Press Newswire*, 2 November 2000.

25 'Critics warn of "war" after Ontario government scraps construction labour bill,' *Canadian Press Newswire*, 16 October 2000.

26 Stephen Thorne, 'Supreme Court rules Ontario law on farm labour unconstitutional,' *Canadian Press Newswire*, 20 December 2001; Colin Perkel, 'Farm workers in Ontario barred from forming unions under new law,' *Canadian Press Newswire*, 18 November 2002.

27 Thomas Klassen, *Precarious Values: Organization, Politics and Labour Market Policy in Ontario* (Kingston: Queen's University School of Policy Studies, 2000), p. 18.

28 Ibid., chaps. 2, 3.

29 New Democratic Party of Ontario, *An Agenda for People*, p. 4.

30 Klassen, *Precarious Values*, chap. 4.

31 Ibid., chap. 5; Neil Bradford, 'Prospects for Associative Governance,' pp. 552–557; David Wolfe, 'Institutional Limits to Labour Market Reform in Ontario,' in A. Sharpe and R. Haddow, eds., *Social Partnerships for Training* (Kingston: Queen's University School of Policy Studies), pp. 155–188.

32 Human Resources Development Canada and Ontario Ministry of Training, Colleges and Universities, *Local Boards Evaluation*, April 2000, p. 39, www.ont-hrdc-drhc.gc.ca/english/partner/localb/.

33 Klassen, *Precarious Values*, p. 121.
34 Progressive Conservative Party of Ontario, *The Common Sense Revolution*, p. 13.
35 Klassen, *Precarious Values*, p. 140.
36 Progressive Conservative Party of Ontario, *The Common Sense Revolution*, p. 13.
37 Klassen, *Precarious Values*, p. 140.
38 Ibid., p. 178.
39 Ontario Jobs and Investment Board, 'Update from the Ontario Jobs and Investment Board,' News release, 4 August 1998.
40 The three-member panel consisted of a chartered accountant, a senior bank official, and the provincial deputy minister of education and training. Ontario Jobs and Investment Board, *Preparing People for Tomorrow's Jobs* (Toronto: Ontario Jobs and Investment Board, 1998).
41 Special Advisory Panel, *Preparing People for Tomorrow's Jobs* (Toronto: Ontario Jobs and Investment Board, 1999). The efficiency focus had been mandated by the panel's terms of reference. It had been asked 'to provide advice on practical actions and strategies designed to maximize the contributions that working people can make to our long-term economic prosperity;' p. 2 of 17.
42 'Report on the CLSC Roundtable,' in the *Report and Proceedings from the CLSC Roundtable on Creating a More Efficient Labour Market* (Ottawa: Centre for the Study of Living Standards, 2001), p. 18.
43 Canadian Auto Workers, *Appendix 'A': Trends in Employment-Related Legislative Changes between 1996 and 1999* (Toronto: CAW, 2000), p. 9.
44 Blair Setford, 'Industry wants its own rules,' *Daily Commercial News and Construction Record*, 17 March 1997, pp. A1, A7; Grant Cameron, 'Battle looming over changes to Ontario apprenticeship law Bill 55,' *Daily Commercial News and Construction Record*, 4 November 1998, p. A1.
45 Ontario Ministry of Education, 'Proclamation of the *Apprenticeship and Certification Act*, 1998,' *Backgrounder*, January 2000.
46 'Province Gives $12m to training programs for immigrants,' *Canadian Press Newswire*, 29 May 2001; Grant Cameron, 'Money earmarked for skilled trades shortage,' *Daily Commercial News and Construction Record*, 14 September 2001; 'New Ontario government web site opens the door to futures in skilled trades,' *Canadian Press Newswire*, 14 March 2002.
47 Ontario Liberal Party, *Plan for Change, 3: Achieving Our Potential* (Toronto: 2003), p. 12.
48 Ontario Liberal Party, 'McGuinty government helps build highly skilled workforce,' news release, 13 April 2004.

49 Bradford, 'Prospects for Associative Governance,' p. 547.

50 Jane Coutts, 'Unions vow to fight "watered-down" safety law,' *The Globe and Mail*, 24 February 1990, p. A12.

51 Bradford, 'Prospects for Associative Governance,' p. 551.

52 Laura Fowlie, 'Employers slam safety courses,' *The Financial Post*, 18 November 1994, p. 6.

53 Jim Middlemass, 'Safety training could cost companies $1 B.' *The Financial Post*, 8 March 1994, p. 14.

54 'WHSA review points to changes on the horizon,' *Canadian Occupational Health and Safety*, May/June 1995, pp. 11, 15.

55 'Labour minister guts workplace safety agency,' *Canadian Press Newswire*, 23 August 1995.

56 'Labour unions make bid to save safety agency,' *Canadian Press Newswire*, 30 September 1995.

57 'Business backs Witmer (labour doesn't),' *Daily Commercial News*, 25 March 1996, p. A1.

58 'Ontario Labour Worried About Government's Plans for Health and Safety,' *Canadian Occupational Health and Safety*, 1996, pp. 6, 8.

59 'New Workplace Rules in Effect,' *Human Resources Advisor; Ontario Edition*, July-August 1998, pp. 1–2.

60 'Demise of the WHSA leaves labour in Ontario in an uncertain position,' *Canadian Occupational Health and Safety*, March-April 1996, pp. 14–15; 'Ontario may scrap mandatory inquests into workplace deaths,' *Canadian Press Newswire*, 6 May 1996.

61 'Province announces funding to enforce new workplace safety limits,' *Canadian Press Newswire*, 27 June 2000; Ontario Ministry of Labour, 'Labour Minister announces consultations to keep Ontario's workplaces among the safest in the world,' news release, 18 October 2001.

62 'Ontario's unionized workers planning wildcat strike,' *Canadian HR Reporter*, 28 May 2001.

63 Lisa Wichmann, 'New safety hazard training,' *Plant*, 9 April 2001, p. 20; Grant Cameron, 'Clark issues open letter on worker safety; younger workers targeted,' *Daily Commercial News and Construction Record*, 4 September 2002, p. 1; Ontario Ministry of Labour, 'Ernie Eves government protects young workers with *Worksmartontario* website,' news release, 14 April 2003.

64 'Legislation to raise labour inspectors' authority proposed,' *Daily Commercial News and Construction Record*, 4 December 2001, p. A7.

65 Ontario Ministry of Labour, 'Minister's action group quickly to strengthen workplace health and safety,' News release, 4 February 2004; and 'Quick

start for minister's health and safety action group,' news release, 11 March 2004.

66 Ontario Workers' Compensation Board, *Policy Report*, October 1990, p. 1.

67 Andrew Stritch, 'Homage to Catatonia: Bipartite Governance and Workers' Compensation in Ontario,' in T. Thomason et al., *Chronic Stress* (Toronto: C.D. Howe Institute, 1995), pp. 139–140.

68 Ontario Ministry of Labour, *Background: Workers' Compensation Reform*, 20 June 1988, pp. 2–5.

69 'Changes to Ontario's Workers' Compensation Act,' *CLV Reports*, 27 June 1988, p. 1; Stritch, 'Homage to Catatonia,' p. 149.

70 Stritch, 'Homage to Catatonia,' p. 140.

71 Ibid., pp. 146–147.

72 'Compensation reform in Ontario: winds of change?' *Canadian Occupational Safety*, September-October 1993, p. 8.

73 'Ontario's Bill 165: Workers' Compensation Reform or Repression?' *Canadian Occupational Safety*, September-October 1994, p. 22.

74 'Government launches WCB Royal Commission,' *Canadian Press Newswire*, 4 November 1994.

75 'WCB assailed from all sides (Ontario Royal Commission on WCB hears submissions),' *Canadian Press Newswire*, 27 May 1995.

76 Workers' Compensation Board, *Policy Report*, February 1995, pp. 1–3.

77 'Ontario's Bill 165: Workers' Compensation Reform or Repression?' p. 22.

78 'WCB gets new board as labour, employers squabble,' *Canadian Press Newswire*, 2 February 1995.

79 Progressive Conservative Party of Ontario, 'Mike Harris and the WCB: Six steps to solvency,' news release, 15 May 1995.

80 Progressive Conservative Party of Ontario, *The Common Sense Revolution*, p. 15.

81 Ontario Workers' Compensation Board, *Across the Board*, November 1995, pp. 1–2; Ontario Workers' Compensation Board, 'Bill 15 Highlights,' *Policy Report*, February 1996, p. 1.

82 Ontario Workers' Compensation Board, *Across the Board*, November 1995, p. 2.

83 'Compensation board running out of control' (government report), *Daily Commercial News and Construction Record*, 2 February 1996, p. A5.

84 'Ontario cleans up its workers' compensation act,' *Canadian Occupational Safety*, January-February 1997, pp. 8–9.

85 'Employers say changes hit the mark: WCB reform upsets labour,' *Daily Commercial News and Construction Record*, 28 November 1996, pp. A1, A7.

86 'Private insurance touted as WCB alternative,' *Daily Commercial News and Construction Report*, 15 August 1997, p. B1.

87 Grant Cameron, 'More employers than employees charged by WSIB,' *Daily Commercial News and Construction Record*, 22 October 1998, p. A1; April Lindgren, 'The number of charges against companies and ...,' *CanWest News*, 30 August 1999.

88 Workplace Safety and Insurance Board, 'Traumatic Mental Stress,' *Policy Report*, December 2002, p. 1.

89 Workplace Safety and Insurance Board, *2002 Annual Report* (Toronto: 2002), pp. 12, 37; Workplace Safety and Insurance Board; 'WSIB releases 2003 premium rates,' News release, 15 November 2002.

90 Workplace Safety and Insurance Board, *2002 Annual Report*, p. 37. The board's investment income rose from $500 million in 1994 to $1,128 million in 2001, before plunging to $246 million in 2002.

91 New Democratic Party of Ontario, *An Agenda for People*, p. 4.

92 'Minimum wage to rise,' *Globe and Mail*, 23 September 1994, p. B2; 'Ontario to freeze minimum wage at $6.85 an hour,' *The Financial Post*, 30 September 1995, p. 5.

93 Richard Mackie, 'Ontario introduces bill to extend pay equity,' *The Globe and Mail*, 19 December 1991, p. A8. The NDP change was reversed by the Conservatives after 1995; but the latter legislation was struck down by an Ontario court as contrary to the Charter of Rights and Freedoms; see Marie-Thérèse Chica, ' Équité salariale,' *Le Devoir*, 28 November 1997, p. A11.

94 Nicola Pulling, 'Small businesses lament wage-protection proposal,' *The Globe and Mail*, 2 August 1991, p. A6.

95 Craig McInnes et al., 'Ontario bill on gay rights defeated,' *The Globe and Mail*, 10 June 1994, p. A1.

96 Ontario Ministry of Citizenship, *Questions and Answers on Employment Equity in Ontario* (Toronto: 1993), p. 2; and *Chronology of Consultation on Employment Equity* (Toronto: 1993), p. 3.

97 Ontario Ministry of Citizenship, Culture and Recreation, 'Harris announces government will introduce legislation to repeal Employment Equity Act,' News release, 19 July 1995.

98 'Ontario to freeze minimum wage at $6.85 an hour,' *The Financial Post*, 30 September 1995, p. 5.

99 Human Resources Development Canada, 'Hourly Minimum Wages in Canada for Adult Workers, 1995–2004,' *Databases on Minimum Wages*, www110.hrdc-drhc.gc.ca/psait-spila/lmnec-eslc/salaire-minwage/.

100 'Ontario bowing out of union-employer disputes,' *Canadian Press Newswire*, 13 May 1996; 'Labour legislation stalls in hearings (changes in employment conditions),' *Canadian Press Newswire*, 19 August 1996.

101 Legislative Assembly of Ontario, 'Employment Standards Improvement Act, 1996: Explanatory Note,' www.ontla.on.ca/documents/bills/36–parliamente/session1/G96049e.

102 Progressive Conservative Party of Ontario, *Blueprint*, p. 14.

103 'Jail time for bad bosses? Tories to draft new workplace rules,' *Canadian Press Newswire*, 25 August, 2000; 'Ontario pushes through controversial labour laws,' *Canadian Press Newswire*, 20 December 2000.

104 Ontario Ministry of Labour, 'Frequently Asked Questions (FAQ),' *Fact Sheets*, 1992, www.gov.on.ca/LAB/english/es/factsheets/fs-fax.html; 'The New Ontario Employment Standards Act,' *Labour Notes*, 5 March 2001.

105 'Critics warn proposed Ontario law overhaul will create sweatshops,' *Canadian Press Newswire*, 24 November 2002.

106 Ontario Ministry of Labour, 'Eligibility for Emergency Leave,' *Fact Sheets*, May 1992, www.gov.on.ca/LAB/english/es/factsheets/fs-fax.html;

107 'The New Ontario Employment Standards Act,' *Labour Notes*, 5 March 2001. p. 4 of 5.

108 The branch's budget fell from $32 million to $23 million over this period, and its staff complement from 296 to 266; Ministry of Labour, *Business Plan, 1997–98* (Toronto: 1997), p. 10; *Business Plan, 2000–2001* (Toronto: 2000), p. 11. An interviewed former branch official estimated that its complement of enforcement officers had fallen from about 180 in the early 1990s to 120 in 2001.

109 'Ontario government to hold meetings to determine exemptions from labour laws,' *Canadian Press Newswire*, 20 March 2001.

110 Ontario Ministry of Labour, 'McGuinty government acts to protect workers,' News release, 26 April 2004.

111 Ontario Ministry of Labour, 'McGuinty government delivering real positive change as it introduces family medical leave legislation,' News release, 13 April 2004.

112 Ontario Ministry of Labour, 'McGuinty government raises minimum wage, helps lowest-paid workers,' News release, 1 December 2003.

5 Quebec: Legacies of Political-Economic Distinctiveness

1 Its well-known effort to extend day-care services by providing them at $5 (then $7) per day arguably represents only a modest step towards social democracy beyond what is typical in Canada, considering the dearth of

spaces available in Quebec's day-care system; see, for instance, Michel David, 'La farce continue,' *Le Devoir*, 22/23 November 2003.

2 Clinton Archibald, 'Corporatist Tendencies in Quebec,' in A-G Gagnon, ed., *Quebec: State and Society* (Toronto: Methuen, 1984), pp. 353–356.

3 Carla Lipsig-Mummé, 'The Web of Dependence: Quebec's Unions in Politics before 1976,' in A-G Gagnon, ed., *Quebec: State and Society*, pp. 303–309.

4 A Brian Tanguay, 'Concerted Action in Quebec, 1976–1983,' in A-G Gagnon, ed., *Quebec: State and Society*, pp. 370–382.

5 Ibid., pp. 382–383.

6 Alain G.-Gagnon and Mary Beth Moncalm, *Quebec: Beyond the Quiet Revolution* (Toronto: Nelson, 1990), pp. 88–89.

7 Kenneth McRoberts, *Quebec: Social Change and Political Crisis*, 3d ed. (Toronto: Oxford University Press, 1999), pp. 404–421.

8 Gilles Bourque, *Le modèle québécois de développement* (Quebec City: Presses de l'Université du Québec, 2000), pp. 120–121.

9 Ibid., pp. 169–171.

10 Ibid., pp. 123–126.

11 Ibid., pp. 140–155.

12 Rodney Haddow, 'From Corporatism to Associationalism,' *Journal of Canadian Studies*, vol. 37 (2002), p. 80.

13 Kathleen Lévesque, 'Débat sur la place de la société civile au sein de la conférence régionale des élus,' *Le Devoir*, 30 April 2004.

14 Ministère de la Main-d'œuvre, de la Sécurité du revenu et de la Formation professionnelle, *Partners for a Skilled and Competitive Quebec* (Quebec City: Gouvernement du Québec, 1991).

15 A. Brian Tanguay, 'Concerted Action in Quebec, 1976–1983,' p. 374.

16 Carolyn Tuohy, *Accidental Logics* (Toronto: Oxford University Press, 1999), pp. 207–208; Eric Montpetit and William Coleman, 'Policy Communities and Policy Divergence in Canada: Agro-Environmental Policy Development in Quebec and Ontario,' *Canadian Journal of Political Science*, vol. 32 (1999), pp. 701–702.

17 Hubert Guindon, *Quebec Society: Tradition, Modernity, and Nationhood* (Toronto: University of Toronto Press, 1988), pp. 23, 62.

18 'We can discern a progressive agreement between these two parties on the form of state organization needed for Quebec society (with certain differences in the economic sector); thus, the victory of the Union Nationale in 1966 does not indicate a break with the preceding situation;' Réjean Pelletier, 'Political Parties and the Quebec State since 1960,' in A-G Gagnon, ed., *Quebec: State and Society*, p. 337. For a more qualified view, see McRoberts, *Quebec: Social Change and Political Crisis*, 3d ed., pp. 211–215.

19 Pelletier, 'Political Parties and the Quebec State since 1960,' in A-G Gagnon, ed., *Quebec: State and Society*, p. 346.

20 'One suspects that the PQ's position on the future of Quebec society has become closer to the Liberals' position;' Raymond Hudon, 'Polarization and Depolarization of Quebec Political Parties,' in A-G Gagnon, ed., *Quebec: State and Society*, p. 324. A. Brian Tanquay argued that, 'in contrast to the Parti Québécois's increasingly fuzzy thinking on economic and social matters since the mid-1980s, its position on the constitutional question has become progressively clearer during the same period;' see his, 'Quebec's Political System in the 1990s: From Polarization to Convergence,' in A-G Gagnon, ed., *Quebec: State and Society*, 2d ed., (Toronto: Nelson, 1993), p. 182.

21 See chap. 2, n97.

22 Tanguay, 'Quebec's Political System in the 1990s: From Polarization to Convergence,' in A-G Gagnon, ed., *Quebec: State and Society*, 2d ed., pp. 187–190.

23 Alain-G. Gagnon, 'Quebec,' in D. Leyton-Brown, ed., *Canadian Annual Review of Politics and Public Affairs, 1989* (Toronto: University of Toronto Press, 1995), p. 151.

24 François Rocher, 'Quebec,' in D. Leyton-Brown, ed., *Canadian Annual Review of Politics and Public Affairs, 1994* (Toronto: University of Toronto Press, 2000), p. 142.

25 Raymond Hudon, '*Fin de siècle* or *Fin de rêve* Politics in Quebec?' in H. Thorburn and A. Whitehorn, eds., *Party Politics in Canada*, 4th ed. (Toronto: Prentice Hall, 2001), p. 331.

26 Parti libéral du Québec, *Un gouvernement au service des Québécois*, pp. 22, 23, 36.

27 Tommy Chouinard, 'Québec sabre 20% des fonctionnaires,' *Le Devoir*, 6 May 2004.

28 Robert Dutrisac, 'Le dernier budget d'Yves Séguin – Comme un magicien dont on aurait vu le truc,' *Le Devoir*, 4 April 2004.

29 For a general, and critical, review of this changed atmosphere, see Mona-Josée Gagnon, 'Le nouveau modèle de relations du travail au Québec et le syndicalisme,' *Journal of Canadian Studies*, vol. 30 (1995), pp. 30–40.

30 McRoberts, *Quebec: Social Change and Political Crisis*, 3d ed, p. 269.

31 Pierre Noreau, 'Le mouvement syndical,' *L'année politique au Québec 1990–91*, www.pum.umontreal.ca/cgi-bin/texis/webinator/searchapqc/, p. 3 of 8.

32 'Labour unrest low,' *The Globe and Mail*, 3 March 1992, p. B8.

33 Peter Hadekel, 'Overhauling Quebec labour laws is all talk so far,'

Montreal Gazette, 10 January 1990, p. D1; and interviews with Quebec officials.

34 Tu Thanh Ha, 'Construction unions face tough back-to-work bill,' *Montreal Gazette*, 13 December 1993, pp. A1–A2.

35 Jean-Paul Gagné, 'Le Conseil du patronat réclame la suppressions du plafond sur la durée des conventions collectives,' *Les Affaires*, 19/25 February 1994, p. 13; 'La durée de la première convention collective n'a pas été déplafonnée,' *Les Affaires*, 28 May/3 June 1994, p. 20.

36 Jean-Paul Gagné, 'La chambre de commerce demande l'abolition de certains décrets de conventions collective,' *Les Affaires*, 26 February/4 March 1994, pp. 8–9.

37 Travail Québec, 'Évolution du nombre de décrets, d'employeurs et de salaries assujettis,' www.travail.gouv.qc.ca/presentation/services/dgpr/dpcd/decrets/evolution.html.

38 '80% des patrons veulent l'abolition de tous les décrets de convention collective,' *Les Affaires*, 5/11 June 1993, p. 3; Jean-Paul Gagné, 'Selon l'Assn des manufacturiers, les décrets de convention collective menaçent des emplois,' *Les Affaires*, 28 May/3 June 1994, p. 15.

39 'PQ scraps Liberal construction industry law,' *Canadian Press Newswire*, 8 December 1994.

40 Jean-Paul Gagné, 'Un rapport soumis à Louise Harel vise a favoriser les décrets plutôt qu'à les limiter,' *Les Affaires*, 3/9 June 1995, p. 4; Gagné, 'Décrets de convention collective: Québec modernisera la loi, mais ne parle pas d'abolition,' *Les Affaires*, 23/29 November 1996, p. 18; and interviews with Quebec officials.

41 Travail Québec, 'Évolution du nombre de décrets, d'employeurs et de salaries assujettis,' www.travail.gouv.qc.ca/presentation/services/dgpr/dpcd/decrets/evolution.html.

42 Michèle Bernard, 'Limiter la sous-traitance, *Magazine PME*, 1 April 2001, p. 10.

43 Dominique Froment, 'Les quatre grands enjeux de la reform du Code du travail,' *Les Affaires*, 24/30 April 1999, p. 5.

44 Dominique Froment, 'Le nouveau code du travail créera un fouillis juridique,' *Les Affaires*, 20 January 2001, p. 9.

45 Brian Myles, 'Le rapport Mireault sur le Code du travail,' *Le Devoir*, 31 January 1997, p. A4; Jean Charest et al, 'L'emploi 'typique'? Connais pas!' *Le Devoir*, 15 May 1999, p. A13.

46 Robert Dutrisac, 'Réforme du Code du travail,' *Le Devoir*, 21 December 2000, p. A2.

47 Robert Dutrisac, 'Code du travail,' *Le Devoir*, 16 May 2001, p. A2.

48 Josée Boileau, 'Les patrons montent aux barricades,' *Le Devoir*, 5 March 2003.
49 Dutrisac, 'Code du travail.'
50 Kevin Dougherty, 'Liberals denounce Labour Code reform,' *Montreal Gazette*, 30 May 2001, p. A11; Parti Libéral du Québec, *Un gouvernement au service des Québécois*, p. 23. Translation from the French by the authors.
51 Gouvernement du Québec, 'Le ministre du travail, M. Michel Despres, annonce des modifications au Code du Travail,' Press release, 13 November 2003. Translation from the French by the author.
52 Réginald Harvey, 'Québec 2004 – Impopulaire sous-traitance: 'Ça va être rough dans plusieurs cas,' *Le Devoir*, 14/15 February 2004.
53 See, for instance, René Roy, 'Le syndicalisme va-t-il continuer sa progression?' *Le Devoir*, 30 April 2004; Roy was Secretary General of the FTQ when he wrote this article.
54 Konrad Yakabuski, 'Charest's inaction tells real story,' *The Globe and Mail*, 12 December 2003, p. B2.
55 Andrew Johnson, 'Towards a Renewal of Concertation in Quebec,' in A. Sharpe and R. Haddow, eds., *Social Partnerships for Training* (Kingston: Queen's University School of Policy Studies, 1997), p. 132.
56 Ministère de la Main-d'oeuvre, de la Sécurité du revenu et de la Formation professionelle, *Partners for a Skilled and Competitive Québec* (Quebec City: Gouvernement du Québec 1991), pp. 19–21.
57 Bourque, *Le modèle québécois de développement*, p. 132.
58 Ministère de la Main-d'oeuvre, *Partners for a Skilled and Competitive Québec*, p. 55.
59 The fate of all of these experiments with labour market concertation is reviewed in Rodney Haddow and Andrew Sharpe, 'Labour Force Development Boards: A Viable Model?' in Sharpe and Haddow, eds., *Social Partnerships for Training*, pp. 291–318.
60 Colette Bernier et al., 'Les comités paritaires de formation profesionnelle au Québec,' *Relations Industrielles*, vol. 51 (1996), p. 666.
61 The SQDM's origins and history are discussed in more detail in Rodney Haddow, 'Reforming labour-market policy governance: the Quebec experience,' *Canadian Public Administration*, vol. 41 (1998), pp. 343–368.
62 Among the provinces examined in this study, Alberta also negotiated full devolution of the federal measures; British Columbia accepted a more restricted 'co-determination' arrangement. No agreement had been made with Ontario by mid-2004.
63 Thomas Klassen, 'The Federal-Provincial Labour Market Development Agreements,' in T. McIntosh, ed., *Federalism, Democracy and Labour Market*

Policy in Canada (Kingston: Queen's University School of Policy Studies, 2000), p. 176.

64 Ministère de la Main-d'oeuvre, *Partners for a Skilled and Competitive Québec*, pp. 50–51.

65 Haddow, 'Reforming Labour-Market Policy Governance: The Quebec Experience,' p. 349.

66 The PQ government released a policy statement on these issues in 2002; they had been discussed at the CPMT, and within the bureaucracy, for some time previously; Ministère de l'Éducation, *Government Policy on Adult Education and Continuing Education and Training* (Quebec City: 2002).

67 Haddow, 'Reforming Labour-Market Policy Governance: The Quebec Experience,' pp. 347–348; on the overall significance of bipartite training committees in Quebec, see Bernier et al., 'Les comités paritaires de formation professionelle au Québec,' pp. 665–691.

68 Alain Duhamel, 'Louise Harel propose aux entreprises un libre marché de la formation,' *Les Affaires*, 13 May 1995, p. 4.

69 Philip Authier, 'Business groups want Quebec to kill plan for payroll tax,' *Montreal Gazette*, 3 May 1995, p. A7.

70 Alec Castonguay, 'Québec allège la "loi du 1%,"' *Le Devoir*, 14 October 2003.

71 An independent assessment released in 2002 was ambivalent about the tax's impact; David Brown, 'Legislated training, questionable results: Quebec firms training more but not improving bottom line,' *Canadian HR Reporter*, 6 May 2002, pp. 1, 12. The Quebec government planned to release a study of the tax's impact in 2004; its initial tracking of it dwelt more upon the tax's incidence than on its impact on skills formation; Emploi-Québec, *Bilan quantatif sur la participation des employeurs à la loi favorisant de développement de la formation de la main-d'œuvre en vertu de l'article 3* (Quebec City: Emploi-Québec September 2003).

72 Paul Bélanger et al., 'La loi du 1% sur la formation de la main d'œuvre,' *Le Devoir*, 12 November 2003.

73 Alec Castonguay, 'Québec allège la "loi du 1%,"' *Le Devoir*, 14 October 2003.

74 Michel Venne, 'Charest tue une bonne loi,' *Le Devoir*, 20 October 2003; Alec Castonguay, 'Modification de la "loi du 1%" – Québec coupe l'herbe sous le pied des mutuelles de formation,' *Le Devoir*, 23 October 2003.

75 This and subsequent data in this paragraph are cited from Emploi-Québec, *Rapports annuel de gestion, 2002–2003* (Quebec City: Emploi-Quebec, 2003), p. 45.

76 Tommy Chouinard, 'Emploi-Québec fait des mises à pied,' *Le Devoir*,

16 March 2004; Kathleen Lévesque, 'Immigrants: Emploi-Québec résiste devant les demandes du gouvernement,' *Le Devoir*, 25 March 2004.

77 Rachel Duclos, 'Il y a vingt ans: Une grève qui a marqué l'histoire,' *Le Devoir*, 23 March 1995, p. B1.

78 Robert Bronsard, 'Vers un nouvel État-providence: l'expérience de la Commission de la santé et de la sécurité du travail du Québec,' *Canadian Public Administration*, vol. 41 (1998), pp. 78–79.

79 Ibid., pp. 79–80.

80 Dominique Froment, 'Le régime rétrospectif de la CSST pourrait être étendu à un plus grand nombre d'entreprises,' *Les Affaires*, 9 April 1994, p. B4.

81 Jean Garon, 'Seul credo en santé-sécurité du travail: que tous s'en occupent,' *Les Affaires*, 16 October 1993, p. 28.

82 Jean-Paul Gagné, 'Robert Diamant a soumis 11 recommandations – CSST: Même son président évoque des amendements à la loi,' *Les Affaires*, 9 November 1991, p. 4; Frédéric Tremblay, 'Le CPQ s'insurge contre le déficit à la CSST,' 17 October 1992; Lia Lévesque, 'La FTQ se demande si le déficit de la CSST ne fait pas l'affaire de certains employeurs,' 5 November 1992.

83 Bronsard, 'Vers un nouvel État-providence,' pp. 91–92.

84 Ibid., pp. 79–81; Jean Francoeur, 'La CSST sans menottes,' *Le Devoir*, 18 August 1992, p. 14.

85 Jean Francoeur, 'Les limites du rapiéçage,' *Le Devoir*, 24 October 1992, p. A12; Jean Francoeur, 'L'ex-pdg critique la direction bicéphale de la CSST après trois ans de silence,' *Le Devoir*, 9 December 1992, p. A5; Monique Jerôme-Forget, 'CSST : l'impossible rigeur?' *Le Devoir*, 13 January 1993, p. B8.

86 Dominique Froment, 'Pierre Shedleur fait la pari de rendre la CSST concurrentielle,' *Les Affaires*, 15 October 1994, p. B8.

87 CSST, *Rapport annuel : Appendice statistique*, www.csst.qc.ca/portail/fr/quisommes_nous/statistique.htm; 'Malgré un déficit de 114 millions, la CSST va bien, dit son président,' *Le Devoir*, 28 May 2004.

88 Sylvain Label, 'Santé et sécurité du travail: feu vert aux regroupements d'employeurs,' *Les Affaires*, 14 December 1996, p. 17; Pierre Théroux, 'Plus de 100 mutuelles de prévention ont été formées,' *Les Affaires*, 10 October 1998, p. 36; CSST, *Rapport annuel d'activité* (Quebec City: CSST, 2004), p. 19.

89 '"Déjudiciarisation" de la CSST,' *Le Devoir*, 7 May 1994, p. B8.

90 Each CLP board would consist of a government, business and labour representative. 'Déjudiciarisation et tarification de la CSST : changements importants pour les entreprises,' *Les Affaires*, 7 December 1996, p. 17.

91 'Appeal process to improve with OH&S Act changes,' *Occupational Health and Safety*, January/February 1997, p. 10.

92 Claude Masse, 'Projet de loi 79,' *Le Devoir*, 20 January 1997, p. A7; Marc Bellemare, 'La loi 79 est un recul majeur pour les accidentées du travail,' *Le Devoir*, 20 October 1997, p. A9.

93 Dominique Froment, 'Le monopole du Conseil du patronat au conseil de la CSST est remis en question,' *Les Affaires*, 8 February 1997, p. 3; Froment, 'Selon Ghislain Dufour et Pierre Shedleur, les patrons sont bien représentés à la CSST,' *Les Affaires*, 8 February 1997, p. 4.

94 Aaron Derfel, 'Job safety rules are failing women, UQAM study says,' *Montreal Gazette*, 18 March 1996, p. A1; Nathalie Vallerand, 'Les syndicats exigent que tous les travailleurs soient couverts,' *Les Affaires*, 14 October 2000, p. 49.

95 CSST, 'Changements majeurs pour tous les employeurs et travailleurs du Québec,' press release, 3 August 2001; 'New OH&S regulations in force,' *Occupational Health and Safety*, October/November 2001, p. 14.

96 'La CSST augmente de nouveau son taux de cotisation,' *Le Devoir*, 22/23 May 2004.

97 'Malgré un déficit de 114 millions, la CSST va bien, dit son président,' *Le Devoir*, 28 May 2004.

98 These interviews included three each with spokespersons for leading business and labour organizations. The main labour concern were that the 2001 occupational health regulation changes had not gone far enough, and (except for the FTQ) that smaller unions should be better represented on the Conseil d'Administration. Small business representatives also wanted representation on the Conseil.

99 Kathleen Lévesque, 'Les patrons craignent de payer pour la réforme des tribunaux administratifs,' *Le Devoir*, 5 December 2003; 'Justice administrative: la parité coûte cher aux contribuables,' *Le Devoir*, 3 February 2004; Michel David, 'Sortie de secours,' *Le Devoir*, 18 March 2004.

100 This paragraph is based on two interviews with provincial officials, and on Philip Authier, 'Bill does little for the non-unionized: PQ,' *Montreal Gazette*, 20 November 1990, p. A4; Elizabeth Kalbfuss, 'New law curbs "unscrupulous employers," minister says,' *Montreal Gazette*, 20 November 1990, p. A4; Caroline Montpetit, 'Patrons et syndicates accueillent froidement la réforme de Bourbeau sur les normes de travail,' *Le Devoir*, 15 November 1990, p. A3; Jean Leduc, 'Québec veut modifier les recours prévus à la Loi sur les normes du travail,' *Les Affaires*, 8 December 1990, p. 20.

101 Dwayne Benjamin, 'Minimum Wages in Canada,' in A. Berry, ed., *Labour*

Market Policies in Canada and Latin America (Boston: Kluwer Academic, 2001), pp. 192–193.

102 Jean-Merman Guay, 'Le patronat québécois. La nouvelle alliance,' in *L'année politique au Québec, 1995–1996*; www.pum.umontreal.ca/apqc/95_96/guay.htm.

103 Konrad Yakabuski, 'Dépot du projet de loi sur l'équité salariale: Un compromis qui ne satisfait personne,' *Le Devoir*, 16 May 1996, p. A1.

104 Mario Cloutier, ' Équité salariale: Un délai supplémentaires d'un an,' *Le Devoir*, 8 November 1996, p. A5.

105 Michel Venne, 'Québec vise la création de 35,000 emplois de plus en trois ans,' *Le Devoir*, 2 November 1996, p. A1.

106 Robert Dutrisac, 'Allégement réglementaire: La CSN et la FTQ réintègrent le Groupe Lemaire,' *Le Devoir*, 4 May 1999, p. A4.

107 Michel Hébert, 'Adoption d'une loi à l'unanimité,' *Le Devoir*, 22 October 1999, p. A3.

108 Robert Dutrisac, 'Clauses discriminatoires,' *Le Devoir*, 21 September 1999, p. A4; 'Les clauses dérogatoires seront bannies,' *Le Devoir*, 18 December 1999, p. A7.

109 Ministère du Travail, *Revoir les normes du travail au Québec* (Quebec City : Gouvernment du Québec, May 2002); Denis Lessard, 'Québec entend dépoussiérer la Loi sur les normes du travail,' *La Presse*, 3 May 2002, p. A6.

110 Josée Boileau, 'Réforme de la Loi sur les normes du travail,' *Le Devoir*, 28 May 2002, p. A4.

111 Josée Boileau, 'Jean Rochon attend les patrons de pied ferme,' *Le Devoir*, 3 December 2002, p. A8. Pierre Fortin, a respected Quebec economist, argued that the government had substantially underestimated the reform's costs to the mostly smaller and low-wage firms that would be most affected by the changes. See Josée Boileau, 'Le gouvernement entre dans une zone dangereuse,' *Le Devoir*, 8 December 2002.

112 Josée Boileau, 'Fureur et contentement,' *Le Devoir*, 8 November 2002.

113 Réginald Harvey, 'Le syndicalisme conjugué en féminin,' *Le Devoir*, 8 March 2003; Claude Lafleur, 'Vers une société plus égalitaire,' *Le Devoir*, 8 March 2003.

114 Data reported in Human Resources Development Canada, *Hourly Minimum Wages in Canada for Adult Workers;* www110.hrdc-drhc.gc.ca/psait_spila/lmnec_eslc/eslc/saliare_minwage/report2/repo...

115 Robert Dutrisac, 'Landry prend les syndicates de court – Le salaire horaire minimum passera de 7 $ à 7,30 $,' *Le Devoir*, 2 May 2002.

116 The 45 per cent target was mentioned by two officials in an interview; it

is also referred to in Denis Lessard, 'Québec entend dépoussiérer la Loi sur les normes du travail,' *La Presse*, 3 May 2002, p. A6. Data reported in Dwayne Benjamin, 'Minimum wages in Canada,' pp. 192–193., and reported above, indicates that the minimum wage remained at about 40 per cent of average manufacturing wages under the Liberal administration of 1985 to 1994. According to Benjamin, the average manufacturing wage is about 16 per cent higher than the average industrial wage (p. 191); so this is roughly comparable to the ratio of 45 per cent of the industrial wage targeted by the subsequent PQ government.

117 'Normes du travail – Un recul, selon *Au bas de l'échelle*,' *Le Devoir*, 10 June 2003.

118 'La conciliation travail-famille se fera sur une base volontaire,' *Le Devoir*, 19 June 2003; Tommy Chouinard, 'Les conditions des travailleurs du vêtement changeront,' *Le Devoir*, 2 December 2003.

6 British Columbia: Right Hegemony in a Polarized Liberal Polity

1 Norman Ruff, 'Birth Pangs: The Emergence of British Columbia's Fifth Party System, 1991–2000,' in H. Thorburn and A. Whitehorn, *Party Politics in Canada*, 8th ed. (Toronto: Prentice Hall, 2001), p. 377.

2 British Columbia New Democratic Party, *A Better Way for British Columbia* (Vancouver: BC NDP, 1991), commitments 11 to 41.

3 Ibid., commitments 4 to 6.

4 British Columbia New Democratic Party, *On Your Side. New Democrat Election Platform* (Vancouver: BC NDP, 1996), pp. 3–6, 13, 16.

5 Richard Sigurdson, 'The British Columbia New Democratic Party: Does It Make a Difference?' in R.K. Carty, ed., *Politics, Policy, and Government in British Columbia*. (Vancouver: UBC Press, 1996), p. 332.

6 Ibid., p. 336; and Daniel Gawthrop, *High-Wire Act: Power, Pragmatism, and the Harcourt Legacy* (Vancouver: New Star, 1996), pp. 347–350.

7 See, for instance, Mark Milke, *Barbarians in the Garden City: The BC NDP in Power* (Victoria: Thomas & Black, 2001). Milke was British Columbia director of the neo-liberal and business-friendly Canadian Taxpayers Federation when he published this book.

8 Calculations based on data from BC Stats. *Economic Activity, British Columbia and Canada*, www.bcstats.gov.bc.ca/data/bus_stat/bcea/tabl.htm (19 January, 2004).

9 See Statistics Canada data reported in Business Council of British Columbia, 'The Decline of Unions in the British Columbia Economy,' *Policy Perspectives*, vol. 8, no. 3 (June 2001).

10 This process was described in several interviews with business and bureaucratic participants in BC labour market policy-making.

11 British Columbia Liberal Party, *A New Era for British Columbia*. (Victoria: 2001), p. 4.

12 Ibid., p. 5.

13 Government of British Columbia, 'Government Fulfills 90–Day Agenda,' press release, 29 August, 2001; www.news.gov.bc.ca.

14 Dirk Meissner, 'B.C.'s Black Thursday: Gordon Campbell takes a huge chunk out of the provincial public service,' *Maclean's*, 28 January 2002, p. 24.

15 British Columbia New Democratic Party, *A Better Way for British Columbia*, commitment 7.

16 Gawthrop, *High-Wire Act*, pp. 63–64.

17 On the private compromises made between the government and the task force's business representative, see Vaughn Palmer, 'No more deals, Harcourt tells business,' *Vancouver Sun*, 6 November 1992, p. A18.

18 'New labour code boon for unions' (editorial), *Vancouver Sun*, 29 October 1992, p. A18; Valerie Casselton, 'Don't be fooled, measured response shows business content,' *Vancouver Sun*, 30 October 1992, p. D6.

19 Judy Lindsay, 'Goodwill squandered, NDP faces daunting task,' *Vancouver Sun*, 17 December, 1992, p. D1; 'New BC labour law could broaden anti-union stance,' *Daily Commercial News*, 14 January 1993, p. 1.

20 Rod Nutt, 'Secret ballot among recommended labour code changes,' *Vancouver Sun*, 5 March 1996, p. A1; Justine Hunter, 'NDP not playing politics in reappointment of "campaign commando," Sihota insists,' *Vancouver Sun*, 20 July 1996, p. A15.

21 Valerie Casselton, 'Non-union labour making big gains,' *Vancouver Sun*, 8 January 1990, p. B3.

22 Edward Adlen and Justine Hunter, 'NDP unveils new labour-friendly code,' *Vancouver Sun*, 26 June 1997, p. A1; Rod Nutt, 'Delay in labour-code changes draws raves,' *Vancouver Sun*, 18 July 1997; Wendy Cox, 'Labour Code changes thrown out,' *Canadian Press Newswire*, 16 July, 1997.

23 Justine Hunter and Bruce Constantineau, 'Labour code changes bring fierce reaction from critics,' *Vancouver Sun*, 18 June 1998, p. A1.

24 'B.C. introduces Labour Code bill,' *Human Resources Advisor Newsletter, Western Edition*, July/August, 1998, p. 4.

25 British Columbia Liberal Party, *A New Era for British Columbia*, p. 4.

26 British Columbia. Ministry of Skills Development and Labour, 'Government honours labour commitments,' news release, 14 August 2001; pp. 1–2.

27 Valerie Casselton, 'Campbell takes aim at contentious Code issues,' *Vancouver Sun*, 3 March 1994, p. D2.

28 'The key labour-oriented planks in the B.C. Liberal Party platform for the May 16 provincial election,' *Canadian Press Newswire*, 3 May, 2001.

29 British Columbia Ministry of Skills Development and Labour, 'Labour Code Improved to Help Revitalize Economy,' news release, 13 May, 2002, p. 1.

30 Ibid., p. 4.

31 Ministry of Skills Development and Labour, 'Independent Committee to Review Labour Relations Issues,' news release, 18 December 2002.

32 Workers' Compensation Board of British Columbia, '1973–2002: The Mature Years – Knowing More, Doing More,' *History of the Workers' Compensation Board of British Columbia*, www.worksafebc.com/wbc.history/.

33 Based on 'Questions regarding Workers' Compensation in British Columbia,' notes prepared by staff at the British Columbia Workers' Compensation Board for the authors in July 2003; p. 3.

34 Ibid. Also see 'Proposals to revamp WCB cheered by business, labour,' *Vancouver Sun*, 4 November 1988, p. A9; and 'New WCB legislation encourages cooperation between government, labour and business,' *British Columbia Policy and Politics*, vol. 3, no. 5 (June 1989), p. 4.

35 *A Better Way for British Columbia*, the NDP's 1991 election platform, made only a brief reference to workers' compensation issues, promising to 'ensure injured workers get fair competition' and to 'update and extend the coverage of our industrial health and safety laws;' commitment 40. The party's 1996 platform said nothing specifically about this policy field.

36 Cited in Patrick O'Callaghan and Judi Korban, *The Workers' Compensation Board of British Columbia Board of Governors Review: Report and Recommendations* (Victoria, 18 April 1995), p. 12.

37 Ibid., p. 11; Justin Hunter, '"Censorship" Charge Shrugged Off,' *Vancouver Sun*, 12 July 1995, p. B1; Kim Bolan, 'Labour federation defends "agenda,"' *Vancouver Sun*, 12 July 1995, p. B1; 'Purge just the latest in history of B.C. WCB troubles,' *Canadian Press Newswire*, 15 July 1995.

38 See, for instance, Coalition of BC Businesses, *Labour Policies That Work* (Vancouver, n.d.), p. 46.

39 Workers' Compensation Board of British Columbia, 'Charts: Inside the Board,' *History of the Workers' Compensation Board of British Columbia*, www.worksafebc.com/wbc.history/; 'Average Assessment Rate,' and 'Accident Fund Balance.'

40 See, for instance, Keith Baldrey, 'WCB "Administrative Nightmare,"' *Vancouver Sun*, 13 April 1994; Valerie Casselton, 'WCB masking real num-

bers, employer critique reveals,' *Vancouver Sun*, 6 May 1994, p. E7; Doug Ward, 'Business leaders, Liberals "playing politics with WCB,"' *Vancouver Sun*, 9 August 1995, p. B2.

41 Human Resources Development Canada, *Social Security Statistics. Canada and the Provinces, 1975/6 to 1999/2000*; www.hrdc=drhc.gc.ca/sp-ps/ socialp-psociale/statistics/75–76; table 250, 'Workers' Compensation, Total Payments, 1975–1999.'

42 Association of Workers' Compensation Boards of Canada, *Board/Commission Financial and Statistical Data*, various tables.

43 Workers' Compensation Board of British Columbia, 'Charts: Inside the Board,' *History of the Workers' Compensation Board of British Columbia*, www.worksafebc.com/wbc.history/; 'Public Opinion of the WCB.'

44 Greg Joyce and David Hogben, 'WCB deprives workers of fair compensation, report says,' *Vancouver Sun*, 21 January 1999, p. A1.

45 Neal Hall, 'WCB spending out of control, group charges,' *Vancouver Sun*, 6 November 1993, p. B6.

46 'A Crash Course in Over-Regulation,' *British Columbia Reports*, 6 January 1997, p. 19; 'Regs Better Reflect the Times,' *Occupational Health and Safety*, October/November 1997, p. 8; Suromitra Sanatani, 'New clothes can't conceal same old code,' *Vancouver Sun*, 20 April 1998, p. F3; 'Major Changes to B.C.'s Health and Safety Legislation,' *Human Resources Advisory Newsletter, Western Edition*, November/December 1999, p. 4.

47 British Columbia Liberal Party, *A New Era for British Columbia*, p. 10.

48 Ministry of Skills Development and Training, 'Review to Improve WCB Responsiveness and Streamline Organization,' news release, 28 September 2001.

49 A third revision (Bill 37) was introduced to the legislature in 2003; designed to make modest adjustments to Survivor's Benefits available under Workers' Compensation, it had not yet been passed at the time of writing; Minister of Skills Development and Labour, 'WCB Changes Benefit Survivors,' news release, 5 May, 2003.

50 Ministry of Skills Development and Training, 'WCB Changes Ensure Sustainable Protection for Injured Workers,' news release, 13 May 2002, p. 4.

51 Quoted in ibid., p. 2.

52 Ministry of Skills Development and Labour, 'WCB Appeal Changes Improve Responsiveness,' news release, 10 October 2002; and attached *Backgrounder*, p. 3.

53 British Columbia Liberal Party, *A New Era for British Columbia*, p. 10.

54 'Workers' Comp May Be under the Knife,' *Occupational Health and Safety*,

1 December 2001, p. 8; British Columbia Ministry of Skills Development and Labour, *2002/03 Annual Service Plan Report*, p. 19.

55 Richard Block and Karen Roberts, 'A Comparison of Labour Standards in the United States and Canada,' *Relations Industrielles*, vol. 55 (2000), p. 296.

56 Workers' Compensation Board of British Columbia, 'Charts: Inside the Board,' *History of the Workers' Compensation Board of British Columbia*, www.worksafebc.com/wbc.history/; 'Payroll and Claim Costs,' 'Cost of Claims – No Permanent Disability,' 'Cost – Permanent Disability and Fatalities,' and 'Accident Fund Balance.'

57 British Columbia Federation of Labour, *Backgrounder: Summary of the Changes to the Workers' Compensation Act*, n.d., pp. 1–3.

58 These two specific claims are corroborated by the Association of Workers' Compensation Boards of Canada, 'Preface to Accompanying Key Statistical Measures,' *Board/Commission Financial and Statistical Data*; wwww.awcbc.org/English.

59 Rodney Haddow, 'How Malleable Are Political-Economic Institutions? The Case of Labour-Market Decision-Making in British Columbia,' *Canadian Public Administration*, vol. 43, no. 4 (2000), pp. 392–393.

60 Peter Smith, 'Labour Markets and Neo-Conservative Policy in British Columbia, 1986–1991,'in A. Johnson et al., eds., *Continuities and Discontinuities: The Political Economy of Social Welfare and Labour Market Policy in Canada* (Toronto: University of Toronto Press, 1994); pp. 298–300.

61 Leif Hommen, 'The British Columbia Labour Force Development Board,' in A. Sharpe and R. Haddow, eds., *Social Partnerships for Training* (Kingston: Queen's University School of Policy Studies: 1997), pp. 222–223.

62 British Columbia New Democratic Party, *A Better Way for British Columbia*, commitment 41.

63 See, for instance, Ministry of Advanced Education, 'University Enrollment Report Shows B.C.'s Access Strategy Works,' news release, 20 October, 1998.

64 Hommen, 'The British Columbia Labour Force Development Board,' p. 221.

65 Gowthrop, *High-Wire Act*, p. 145.

66 See, for instance, Office of the Premier, 'Clark Delivers More Jobs and Training for Youth, Expanding Opportunities for Young People in B.C.,' news release, 6 April 1998; Office of the Premier, 'Clark Launches Jobs and Training Guarantee for Youth,' news release, 15 March 1996; British Columbia Ministry of Education, Skills and Training, *1995–96 Annual Report*, p. 86.

67 British Columbia Ministry of Education, Skills and Training, *1995–96 Annual Report*, p. 85.

68 The BCLFDB's history is chronicled in detail in Hommen, 'The British Columbia Labour Force Development Board,' pp. 225–241; and in Haddow, 'How Malleable Are Political-Economic Institutions? The Case of Labour-Market Decision-Making in British Columbia,' pp. 393–399.

69 Haddow, 'How Malleable Are Political-Economic Institutions? The Case of Labour-Market Decision-Making in British Columbia,' pp. 400–406.

70 British Columbia Liberal Party, *A New Era for British Columbia*, pp. 16, 17.

71 Ibid., p. 4.

72 British Columbia Ministry of Skills Development and Labour, *2001–02 Annual Report*, pp. 5–6.

73 British Columbia Ministry of Skills Development and Labour, 'What Elements Should a Provincial Human Resource Strategy Include?' October 2002, p. 1 of 3; www.labour.gov.bc.ca/skills/what-in-strategy.htm.

74 British Columbia Ministry of Skills Development and Labour, *Summary Report; Skills Shortages Meetings*, January 2003, p. 1.

75 See *Planning for Gold. Final Report of the 2010 Human Resources Planning Committee*, 15 December 2003. This committee consisted mainly of federal and provincial labour market officials. Its report focused (in a very general way) on skills shortages that would have to be filled if the province was to stage the Games successfully, but it also addressed some equity issues.

76 Colleen McKenzie, 'Training Program Continues,' *Vancouver Sun*, 17 May 2002, p. A15.

77 British Columbia Ministry of Advanced Education, 'New Model for Industry Training,' www.aved.gov.bc.ca/industrytraining/new-model.htm. n.d.

78 British Columbia Ministry of Advanced Education, 'Trainees to Have Better, More Flexible Training,' news release, 30 April 2003.

79 British Columbia Ministry of Advanced Education, *Consultation Summary of the New Industry Training Model for British Columbia*, May 2003, p. 4.

80 British Columbia Ministry of Advanced Education, 'Board to Improve Industry Training Quality, Quantity,' news release, 12 August 2003.

81 See, for instance, British Columbia Ministry of Advanced Education, '$1.94 M approved to test industry training improvements,' news release, 29 September 2003, p. 1.

82 British Columbia New Democratic Party, *A Better Way for British Columbia*, commitment 7.

83 Valerie Casselton, 'Avoiding past pitfalls could lead government into new holes,' *Vancouver Sun*, 3 March 1993, p. D1.

84 Keith Baldrey, 'Minimum standards laws will combat "rat" unions,' *Vancouver Sun*, 29 June 1993, p. A3.

85 Vaughn Palmer, 'Psst! – Wily Dan slips in some treats for labour,' *Vancouver Sun*, 25 May 1995; p. A22; Rod Nutt, 'Coalition seething over new act,' *Vancouver Sun*, 31 May 1995, p. D1.

86 Justine Hunter, 'Business groups get olive branch,' *Vancouver Sun*, 26 May 1995, p. B6.

87 'Wage hike prompts a minimum of fuss' (editorial), *Vancouver Sun*, 22 November 1994, p. A1; British Columbia Ministry of Skills Development and Labour, 'British Columbia minimum wage: 1960 – 2001,' www.labour.gov.bc.ca/minimumwage/mw–increases.htm.

88 Nutt, 'Coalition seething over new act,' p. D1.

89 Bruce Constantineau, 'Clark backtracks on minimum-wage vow,' *Vancouver Sun*, 22 May 1996; p. B1; William Boei, 'B.C. to relax high-tech employment standards,' *Vancouver Sun*, 1 August, 1998; p. H4.

90 Suromitra Sanatani, 'ESA amendments needed quickly,' *Vancouver Sun*, 14 October 1997, p. D2; Suromitra Sanatani, 'Set higher standards for economic leadership,' *Vancouver Sun*, 22 November 1999, p. C9.

91 Craig McInnes, 'NDP introduces pay-equity legislation,' *Vancouver Sun*, 3 March 2001, p. A4; Jim Beatty and Petti Fong, 'Liberals sweep away pay equity, photo radar,' *Vancouver Sun*, 9 August, 2001, p. A4.

92 British Columbia Liberal Party, *A New Era for British Columbia*, p. 11.

93 British Columbia Ministry of Skills Development and Labour, '"First-job" Wage Rate to Address Youth Unemployment,' news release, 29 October 2001.

94 Jeff Lee, 'Third of employment standards staff get notice,' *Vancouver Sun*, 22 February 2002, p. A4.

95 British Columbia Ministry of Skills Development and Labour, 'New Employment Standards Increase Workplace Flexibility,' news release, 13 May 2002, pp. 4–5 and 6 of 7; www.labour.gov.bc.ca/news/2002/2002–005.htm.

96 Craig McInnis, 'Fewer employee complaints registered,' *Vancouver Sun*, 23 July 2003, p. B7.

97 British Columbia Ministry of Skills Development and Labour, 'New Employment Standards Increase Workplace Flexibility,' news release, 13 May 2002, pp. 3 to 7 of 7; www.labour.gov.bc.ca/news/2002/2002–005.htm.

7 Alberta: One-Party Dominance and Neo-Liberalism

1 Government of Alberta, *History: Oil and Gas*; http://www.gov.ab.ca/home/Index.cfm?Page=29 (accessed 24 August 2004).

2 Government of Alberta, Department of Energy at http://www.energy
   .gov.ab.ca/com/default.htm (accessed, 24 August 2004).

3 Yonatan Reshef and Sandra Rastin, *Unions in the Time of Revolution: Government Restructuring in Alberta and Ontario* (Toronto: University of Toronto
   Press, 2003), p.14.

4 Trevor Harrison, 'The Reform-Ation of Alberta Politics' in Trevor Harrison
   and Gordon Laxer, eds., *The Trojan Horse: Alberta and the Future of Canada*
   (Montreal: Black Rose Books, 1995), pp. 47–60.

5 The GPP for the province, in constant dollars, decreased by 7 per cent in
   1991 and did not begin to recover until 1993.

6 For a review of the fiscal situation in Alberta in the early 1990s, see Robert
   L. Mansell, 'Fiscal Restructuring in Alberta: An Overview,' in Christopher
   Bruce, Ronald Kneebone, and Kenneth McKenzie, eds., *A Government
   Reinvented: A Study of Alberta's Deficit Elimination Program* (Toronto: Oxford
   University Press, 1997), pp.16–73.

7 Don Martin, *King Ralph: The Political Life and Success of Ralph Klein*
   (Toronto: Key Porter Books, 2002), pp. 105–115.

8 Robert Mansell, 'Fiscal Restructuring in Alberta: An Overview,' p. 45.

9 Government of Alberta, Minister of Finance, *Budget 2002* (Edmonton,
   19 March 2002).

10 Stockwell Day, who would become finance minister in 1997 and later the
    leader of the federal Reform Party of Canada.

11 As noted in chapter 2, the province at least since the mid-1970s has spent
    significantly on private sector subsidies. Although these declined from the
    very high levels of the mid-1980s, they remained higher than the average
    for all other provinces. See Kevin Taft, *Shredding the Public Interest: Ralph
    Klein and 25 Years of One-Party Government* (Edmonton: University of
    Alberta Press, 1997), pp. 112–113, table A.

12 See: *General Safety Regulation* (AR 448/83) as amended 4 October 2000.

13 Tom Arnold, 'Tories to privatize a dozen services,' *Calgary Herald*, 28
    March, 1995, p. A 10.

14 Nevertheless, the province has had, and continues to have, regulations
    that would allow it to mandate such committees.

15 Eric Tucker, 'Diverging Trends in Worker Health and Safety Protection and
    Participation in Canada, 1985–2000,' *Relations Industrielles*, vol. 28, no. 3
    (2003), pp. 395–426.

16 Human Resources Advisor Newsletter, 'Increased Health and Safety fines
    for Albertans,' *Human Resources Advisor Newsletter*, western ed., (January/
    February 2003), n.p.

17 Derek Sankey, 'Companies rewarded for playing safe at work,' *Calgary
    Herald*, 20 December 2003, p. CR1.

18 These conclusions are similar to those reached by Tucker, ibid., for Alberta, although his analysis is only to 2000; see note 15.

19 Comparable union membership in 2002 was 36.5 per cent for Quebec, 26.6 per cent for Ontario and 33.5 per cent for British Columbia. Source: Statistics Cananda, 'Fact-Sheet on Unionization': Perspectives on Labour and Income, vol. 4, no. 8 (August 2003), table 2A.

20 Yonatan Reshef and Sandra Rastin, *Unions in the Time of Revolution: Government Restructuring in Alberta and Ontario*, p. 15.

21 Between 1990 and 2002 there were 970,000 days lost in the private sector to strikes in Alberta, but 44 per cent of those are accounted for by two strikes. During the same time 397,000 days were lost due to public sector strikes. By contrast, British Columbia, a province with 25% more people than Alberta, had three million days of work lost due to strikes in the private sector during the same time period, and 1.1 million in the public sector. Source: Human Resources Development Canada. 'Chronological Perspective on Work Stoppages in Canada,' http://labour.hrdc-drhc.gc.ca/ millieudetravail_workplace/chrono/index.cfm/doc/english (accessed 22 February 2004).

22 Jeff Taylor, 'Labour in the Klein Revolution,' in Trevor Harrison and Gordon Laxer, *The Trojan Horse: Alberta and the Future of Canada*, pp. 301–313.

23 *Final Report: Government MLA Committee Considering a Review of the Labour Relations Code*. Richard Marz, MLA, chair (Edmonton, November 2002), p. 8.

24 Allyson Jeffs, 'Construction law flawed but bosses, unions say leave it be,' *Edmonton Journal*, 10 August 2000, p. B7.

25 Michael Lau, 'No major changes expected in labour code review,' *Calgary Herald*, 20 October, 2002, p. F1.

26 Yonatan Reshef and Sandra Rastin, *Unions in the Time of Revolution: Government Restructuring in Alberta and Ontario*, p. 228. Reshef and Rastin suggest that industrial relations for public sector workers witnessed more change and possible retrenchment.

27 Yonatan Reshef, 'The Logic of Union Quiescence,' *Journal of Labor Research*, vol. 2 (2001), pp. 635–652; also Yonatan Reshef and Sandra Rastin, *Unions in the Time of Revolution: Government Restructuring in Alberta and Ontario*, pp. 9–11.

28 Richard Block, Karen Roberts, and R. Oliver Clarke, *Labor Standards in the United States and Canada* (Kalamazoo, MI: W.E. Upjohn Institute for Employment Research, 2003).

29 Ibid., pp. 64–66.

30 Ibid.

31 'One shake-up that's working: Alberta's WCB has found a three-fold strategy to restore financial health,' *Western Report*, vol. 9, no. 14 (2 May 1994), p. 13–14.

32 Ashley Geddes, 'Plan to sell WCB runs into flak,' *Calgary Herald*, 21 October, 1995, p. A4.

33 Kevin Steel, 'A Rich Target: The Rationale for the WCB Is Under Attack from All Sides,' *Alberta Report*, vol. 26, no. 35 (September 1999), pp. 11–12.

34 Alberta Workers' Compensation Board, *Annual Report 1999* (Edmonton, 2002), pp. 4, 28.

35 Dunford has noted that he saw the protest as an opportunity to 'bring forward, to some extent, a personal agenda, but I don't feel guilty about that, because my personal agenda, I think, was very similar to 82 other MLAs.' Personal interview.

36 *Members of the Legislative Assembly Workers' Compensation Board Service Review Input Committee Final Report*, Victor Doerksen, MLA, chair (Edmonton: October 2000), p. 4.

37 Review Committee of the Workers' Compensation Board Appeal System, Samuel Friedman, chair, *The WCB Appeal Systems: Are They Working Well? Final Report* (Edmonton: November 2002), p. 1.

38 *Workers' Compensation Amendment Act, 2002*, Bill 26, SA 2002 c27.

39 Alberta Workers Compensation Board, *CEO Leaving to Pursue Other Opportunities*, News release (Edmonton, 8 January 2002).

40 Alberta Human Resources and Employment, *'New Committee to Monitor Reform of Workers' Compensation System*,' news release (Edmonton, 13 February 2003).

41 Alberta Human Resources and Employment, 'Changes Chart a New Course for Workers' Compensation System,' news release (Edmonton, 5 July 2001).

42 Alberta Human Resources and Employment. *Workers' Compensation Board Tribunal Task Force Final Report* (Edmonton, 29 October 2001).

43 Department of Labour, 'Discussion Paper: The Role of Government in a Changing Workplace' (unpublished document, 1991), p. 2.

44 Stockwell Day quoted by Claire Hoy in *Stockwell Day: His Life and Politics* (Toronto: Stoddart 2000), p. 66.

45 Canadian Press, 'Right-to-work law to be studied,' *Calgary Herald*, 13 April 1995, p. A 8.

46 Ashley Geddes, 'Committee rules out major shift in labor law,' *Calgary Herald*, 1 December 1995, p. A6.

47 Allen Ponak and Daphne Taras, 'Give right-to-work a rest: Even major employers fear RTW laws would rock peaceful labor boat,' *Calgary Herald*, 18 March 1996, p. A8.

48 Allan Chambers, 'Lawyers protest privatization of labor standards,' *Calgary Herald*, 5 September 1996, p. A4.
49 Allan Chambers, 'Privatization of labor complaints blasted,' *Calgary Herald*, 10 September 1996, p. A4.
50 Editorial, 'Privatize with care: Some – not all – things government does best,' *Calgary Herald*, 22 June 1995, p. A4; also James Stevenson, 'Ottawa watching privatized labor standards,' *Edmonton Journal*, 14 September 1996. p. A 7.
51 Jodie Sinnema, 'Domestic workers now due a protected minimum wage: New employment standards go into effect today,' *Edmonton Journal*, 1 July 2000, p. B3.
52 Mike Sadava, 'Workers shafted by standards branch, says labour expert,' *Edmonton Journal*, 15 July 1999, p. B2.
53 David Howell, '"Superior labour relations" urged,' *Edmonton Journal*, 17 October, 1999. p. A11.
54 The board's history and activities can be found at: http://www.congressboard.ab.ca/index.html (accessed August 26, 2004).
55 Harvey Lazar, *Shifting Roles: Active Labour Market Policy in Canada under the Labour Market Development Agreements*, conference report (Ottawa: Canadian Policy Research Networks, 2002).
56 See table 7 in Thomas R. Klassen, 'The Federal-Provincial Labour Market Development Agreements: Brave New Model of Collaboration?' in T. McIntosh, ed., *Federalism, Democracy and Labour Market Policy in Canada* (Montreal: McGill-Queen's University Press), p. 178.
57 Peter Verburg, 'People needed. Apply anywhere: Alberta employers can't find enough workers to fuel the province's economic bonanza,' *Canadian Business*, vol. 70, iss. 15 (14 November, 1997), p. 36.
58 Alberta Federation of Labour, Education Committee, 'The Future of Advanced Education in Alberta' (Edmonton, February 1994), p. 7.
59 Wallace Immen, 'Alberta leads the way in getting apprentices trained and ready to work,' *The Globe and Mail*, 21 January 2004. p. C 2.
60 Ibid.
61 Alberta Apprenticeship and Training Board, *Meeting the Challenges of the Future, Annual Report, 2003–04* (Edmonton: Minister of Learning, 2004), table 5, p. 71.
62 Raquel Exner, 'Trades push apprenticeship: Construction industry seeks to stabilize workforce,' *Calgary Herald*, 26 August 2000, p. B7.
63 Alberta Labour Force Planning Committee, *Prepared for Growth: Building Alberta's Labour Supply* (Edmonton: Human Resources and Development, October 2001).
64 Clint Dunford, Minister of Human Resources and Employment, 'Speaking

Notes to the Workplace Conference of the Alberta Congress Board'
(Edmonton: Human Resources and Employment, 24 October 2001.)
65 Martin, *King Ralph*, p. 161.

8 Social Assistance and Employment: An Anomaly?

1 For Ontario this development is explored in some detail by Margaret Little
   in *'No Car, No Radio, No Liquor Permit': The Moral Regulation of Single
   Mothers in Ontario, 1920–1997* (Toronto: Oxford University Press, 1998).
2 William D. Coleman and Grace Skogstad. 'Policy Communities and Policy
   Networks in Canada: A Structural Approach,' in Coleman and Skogstad,
   eds., *Policy Communities and Policy Networks in Canada: A Structural Approach* (Mississauga and Toronto: Copp Clark Pittman, 1990), p. 25.
3 Ibid., p. 29.
4 Paul Pross, *Group Politics and Public Policy*, 2d ed. (Toronto: University of
   Toronto Press, 1992) p. 127.
5 See, for example, Maeve Quaid, *Workfare: Why Good Policy Ideas Go Bad*
   (Toronto: University of Toronto Press, 2002).
6 Frances Fox Piven and Richard Cloward, *Regulating the Poor* (New York:
   Vintage, 1971), pp. xiii–xvii; Daniel Patrick Moynihan, 'The Professional-
   ization of Reform,' *Public Interest*, vol. 1 (1965), pp. 6–16.
7 Rodney Haddow, *Poverty Reform in Canada* (Montreal: McGill-Queen's
   University Press, 1993), chaps. 4, 8; Haddow, 'The Poverty Policy Community in Canada's Liberal Welfare State,' in Coleman and Skogstad, eds.,
   Policy Communities and Public Policy in Canada, pp. 226–230.
8 Gøsta Esping-Andersen, *Politics against Markets* (Princeton: Princeton
   University Press, 1985), pp. 245–247.
9 See, for instance, Jamie Peck, *Workfare States* (New York: Guilford Press,
   2001), pp. 9–12. The term was earlier used by Bob Jessop to refer to a more
   pervasive change in welfare states as a whole, which is designed to accen-
   tuate the development of skills and work habits appropriate for a more
   technologically advanced economy; see his 'Post-Fordism and the State,'
   in A. Amin, ed., *Post-Fordism: A Reader* (Oxford: Blackwell, 1994), pp. 263–
   268. For our purposes, Peck's narrower definition is of greater utility.
10 In Ontario, municipalities contribute 20 per cent of the cost of social
   assistance. The only other province to require a municipal contribution is
   Manitoba, which requires the city of Winnipeg to make payments to the
   social assistance program.
11 The following CANSIM tables and vectors were used in these calculations:

Variable	Table no.	PQ Vector	ON Vector	AB Vector	BC Vector	From	To
Social assistance	3850002	V206792	V206857	V207052	V207117	1989	2003
Gross provincial Product (GPP)	3840013	V691901	V691924	V691993	V692016	1989	2002
Provincial consumer Price index (CPI)	3260001	V736152	V736288	V736696	V736831	1989	2003
Population	510001	V468546	V468861	V469806	V470121	1989	2003

12 The 1970s and 1980s data is calculated from statistics presented in the NCW's *Welfare in Canada: The Tangled Safety Net* (Ottawa: NCW, 1987), p. 76.

13 NCW, *Welfare Income 2002*, p. 41. Alberta's rates had declined by more than any other province's for two of the three recipient categories reported in this source. They were second to Quebec's reductions for single employable persons, but the Quebec rate for this category of recipients was much higher a few years before, and after, 1986.

14 Ontario New Democratic Party, *An Agenda for People* (Toronto, 1990), pp. 5–6.

15 Ontario Ministry of Community and Social Services. *Statement by the Honourable Zanana Akande, Minister of Community and Social Services* (Toronto, 29 November 1990).

16 Advisory Group on New Social Assistance Legislation, *Back on Track*, prepared for the Ontario Ministry of Community and Social Services (Toronto: Queen's Printer, 1991).

17 Enrico Sabatini, *Welfare – No Fair: A Critical Analysis of Ontario's Welfare System, 1985–1994*. (Vancouver: The Fraser Institute, 1996), pp. 105–115.

18 See Stephen McBride, 'The Continuing Crisis of Social Democracy: Ontario's Social Contract in Perspective,' *Studies in Political Economy*, vol. 50 (1996), pp. 65–93; and A. Moscovitch, 'Participatory Reform in Canada: The Case of Social Assistance in Ontario,' *Social Policy & Administration*, vol. 28, no. 2 (1994), pp. 120–127.

19 Thomas R. Klassen and Daniel Buchanan, 'Getting it Backward? Economy and Welfare in Ontario 1985–1995,' *Canadian Public Policy*, vol. 23, no. 3 (1997), pp. 333–338.

20 Advisory Group on New Social Assistance Legislation, *Time for Action*, prepared for the Ontario Ministry of Community and Social Services (Toronto: Queen's Printer, 1992), p. 86.

21 Social Assistance Review Committee, *Transitions: Report of the Social Assistance Review Committee*, prepared for the Ontario Ministry of Community and Social Services (Toronto: Queen's Printer, 1988), p. 13.

22 Ontario Ministry of Community and Social Services, *Turning Point: New Support Programs for People with Low Income* (Toronto: Queen's Printer, 1993).

23 Jamie Peck, *Welfare State* (New York: Guilford Press, 2001).

24 Malcolm Fairbrother, 'The Freedom of the State: Recent NDP Governments and a Reply to the Globalization Sceptics,' *Canadian Review of Sociology and Anthropology*, vol. 40, no. 3 (2003), pp. 311–329.

25 Patricia M. Evans, 'From Workfare to the Social Contract: Implications for Canada of Recent US Welfare Reforms,' *Canadian Public Policy*, vol. 19, no. 1 (1993), pp. 54–67; and Patricia M. Evans, 'Linking Welfare to Jobs: Workfare, Canadian Style,' in A. Sayeed, ed., *Workfare: Does It Work? Is It Fair?* (Montreal: Institute for Research on Public Policy, 1995), pp. 75–104.

26 Ernie Lightman, '"It's Not a Walk in the Park": Workfare in Ontario,' in E. Shragge, ed., *Workfare: Ideology for a New Under-Class* (Toronto: Garamond Press, 1997).

27 Ontario Ministry of Community and Social Services, *Turning Point: New Support Programs for People with Low Income* (Toronto: Queen's Printer, 1993), p. 9.

28 R.M. Sheldrick, 'Welfare Reform under Ontario's NDP: Social Democracy and Social Group Representation,' *Studies in Political Economy*, vol. 55 (1998), pp. 37–63; and A. Moscovitch 'Participatory Reform in Canada: The Case of Social Assistance in Ontario,' pp. 120–127.

29 Ontario Progressive Conservative Party, *The Common Sense Revolution*, p. 11.

30 Dean Herd, 'Cutting caseloads by design: The Impact of the New Service Delivery Model for Ontario Works,' *Canadian Review of Social Policy*, vol. 51 (2003), pp. 114–120.

31 Organisation for Economic Cooperation and Development, *The Battle against Exclusion: Social Assistance in Canada and Switzerland* (Paris: OECD, 1999), p. 108.

32 M. Quaid, *Workfare: Why Good Social Policy Ideas Go Bad* (Toronto: University of Toronto Press, 2002), p. 172; and Organization for Economic Cooperation and Development, *The Battle against Exclusion: Social Assistance in Canada and Switzerland*, p. 109.

33 Ontario Ministry of Community and Social Services, *Making Welfare Work: Report to Taxpayers on Welfare Reform* (Toronto: Queen's Printer for Ontario, 2000); see also press releases such as Ontario Ministry of Community, Family and Children's Services, 'Twelve People an Hour Moving Off Welfare in Ontario' (Toronto, 12 November 2000).

34 Hansard (Ontario), Legislative Assembly, First Session, 38th Parliament.

Hon. Sandra Pupatello, Minister of Community and Social Services (17 December 2003), p. 868.

35 Ontario Ministry of Community and Social Services, 'McGuinty Government Scraps Lifetime Welfare Ban,' press release, Toronto, 9 January 2004.

36 A detailed overview of the legislation is provided in the National Council of Welfare's *Welfare Reform* (Ottawa: 1992), pp. 15–22; Catherine Burke, 'Group aims to clog welfare system,' *Montreal Gazette*, 27 July 1990, p. A3.

37 Michael Orsini, 'Sinking farther below the line,' *Montreal Gazette*, 28 July 1990, p. B1; 'La reforme de l'aide sociale entre en vigeur aujourd'hui,' *Le Devoir*, 1 August 1989, p. 1.

38 Jean Francoeur, 'Le jour J a l'aide sociale,' *Le Devoir*, 1 August 1989, p. 12.

39 Michel Venne, 'Bourbeau défie les assistés sociaux qui voudraient embourber la machine,' *Le Devoir*, 30 July 1990, p. 3; Venne, 'Les réductions de prestations touchent 79,000 assistés sociaux,' *Le Devoir*, 2 August 1990, p. 3.

40 Louise Boivin, 'Quebec's Workfare Experiment,' *This Magazine*, May 1995, pp. 32–36; Hazel Porter, 'Welfare reforms a bust: report,' *Montreal Gazette*, 25 March 1993, p. G1.

41 Jean Francoeur, 'Des 'boubou-macoutes' dotés de pouvoirs élargis,' *Le Devoir*, 8 October 1992, p. B1.

42 Carolyn Adolph, 'Welfare's fatal flaw: no way out,' *Montreal Gazette*, 29 July 1995, pp. B1–B2; National Council of Welfare, *Another Look at Welfare Reform* (Ottawa: Ministry of Public Works and Government Services Canada, 1997), pp. 44–45.

43 National Council of Welfare, *Another Look at Welfare Reform*, pp. 39–40.

44 Campbell Clark, 'Welfare reform gives, takes away,' *Montreal Gazette*, 19 December 1997, p. A5; Mario Cloutier,, 'Harel bonifie le régime d'aide sociale,' *Le Devoir*, 19 December 1997, p. A1.

45 Clément Trudel, 'Réforme de l'aide sociale: Les ponts se rompent entre Harel et les groupes sociaux,' *Le Devoir*, 27 May 1998, p. A4; Mario Cloutier, 'Harel assouplit sa réforme,' *Le Devoir*, 18 June 1998, p. A1.

46 Robert Dutrisac, 'Mesures d'insertion au marché du travail,' *Le Devoir*, 17 September 1999, p. A1; Kathleen Lévesque, 'Résultats décevants d'un autre programme d'Emploi-Québec,' *Le Devoir*, 26 February 2004.

47 Elizabeth Thompson, 'Quebec imposes "solidarity tax,"' *Montreal Gazette*, 2 November 1996, p. A13; Sarah Scott, 'Business puts on a happy face,' *Montreal Gazette*, 2 November 1996, p. A13; National Council of Welfare, *Another Look at Welfare Reform*, p. 43.

48 Linday Guylai, 'City to get lion's share of fund,' *Montreal Gazette*, 13 June 2000, p. A3.

49 Tommy Chouinard, 'Un emploi pour sortir de la pauvreté – Des programmes à enricher,' *Le Devoir*, 20 September 2003.
50 Kathleen Lévesque, '50 millions de moins pour l'aide sociale,' *Le Devoir*, 15 June 2003.
51 Tommy Chouinard, 'Un emploi pour sortir de la pauvreté – Des programmes à enricher,' *Le Devoir*, 20 September 2003.
52 Tommy Chouinard, 'Le colère gronde chez les libéraux,' *Le Devoir*, 2 October 2003; Kathleen Lévesque, 'Plan d'action contre la pauvreté,' *Le Devoir*, 15 December 2003.
53 Kathleen Lévesque, 'Place à l'emploi ne remplit pas ses promesses d'économies,' *Le Devoir*, 15 February 2004; Kathleen Lévesque, 'Résultats décevants d'un autre programme d'Emploi-Québec,' *Le Devoir*, 28 February 2004.
54 Tommy Chouinard, '240 millions consacrés aux bas salaries,' *Le Devoir*, 31 March 2004; Tommy Chouinard, 'Québec abolit les sanctions,' *Le Devoir*, 3 April 2004, p. A1.
55 British Columbia New Democratic Party, *A Better Way for British Columbia* (Victoria: BC NDP, 1991), commitment 15.
56 National Council of Welfare, *Another Look at Welfare Reform* (Ottawa: NCW 1997), pp. 92–94.
57 Justine Hunter, 'Welfare changes draw fire from all political sides,' *Vancouver Sun*, 21 January 1994, p. A1; Hunter, '5,000 to lose emergency welfare benefits,' *Vancouver Sun*, 14 September 1995, p. C16; Jim Beatty, 'Labour minister stirs anger by saying workfare like tough love,' *Vancouver Sun*, 2 November 1995, p. B1.
58 The measure was eventually thwarted by Ottawa's determination to penalize BC for doing this, using a provision of the Canada Assistance Plan Act that required provinces not to deny benefits to newly arrived claimants; National Council of Welfare, *Another Look at Welfare Reform*, p. 96.
59 Justine Hunter, 'B.C. to provide working poor a family bonus: Up to $103 a month per child,' *Vancouver Sun*, 9 November 1995, p. A1; Robert Sarti and Jim Beatty, 'Welfare effort to train thousands for high-tech jobs,' *Vancouver Sun*, 10 November 1995, p. A16; National Council of Welfare, *Another Look at Welfare Reform*, pp. 97–98.
60 Stephen Hume, 'The way we work – or not – critical to our welfare debate,' *Vancouver Sun*, 15 November 1995, p. A15; Tom Barrett, 'NDP averts split over welfare plan, NDP,' *Vancouver Sun*, 20 November 1995, p. A1; Doug Ward, 'Labour tells NDP to rescind welfare,' *Vancouver Sun*, 23 November 1995, p. B13; Jim Beatty, 'Liberals want photo-ID cards:

Campbell vows to wage war on welfare fraud,' *Vancouver Sun*, 15 May 1996, p. B4.

61 British Columbia New Democratic Party, *On Your Side* (Victoria: BC NDP, 1996), p. 16.

62 Jon Kesselman, 'Compassion dictates B.C. lower minimum wage,' *Vancouver Sun*, 11 April 1997, p. A21; Patti Fong, 'Benefit consent form too intrusive, groups say,' *Vancouver Sun*, 29 January 1998, p. B7; 'Pilot Project: New program helps move from welfare to work,' *Vancouver Sun*, 30 July 1998, p. B1; Lori Culbert, 'Welfare sit-in participants vow to stay in Clark's office,' *Vancouver Sun*, 20 April 1999, p. A1.

63 For the CANSIM tables and vectors used in these calculations, see n11.

64 Tom Barrett, 'Reforms to reduce welfare roll,' *Vancouver Sun*, 18 January 2002, p. A4. The NDP government, whose BC Benefits legislation had lowered this threshold age for children from 19 to 13 in 1996, later had reduced it to 7 years.

65 Craig McInnes, '30,000 of 240,000 who are on welfare to lose it,' *Vancouver Sun*, 23 February 2002, p. A1.

66 British Columbia Ministry of Human Resources, 'New Acts Provide Assistance, Opportunity and Independence,' News release, 15 April 2002, and attached 'Backgrounder'; ibid., 'Income assistance changes protect disabled and promote jobs,' News release, 30 September 2002, and attached 'fact sheets'; Craig McInnes and Jim Beatty, 'Disabled on welfare to get help finding jobs,' *Vancouver Sun*, 16 April 2002, p. A4.

67 British Columbia Ministry of Human Resources, 'Review confirms disabilities status for vast majority,' News Release, 11 August 2003.

68 Dirk Meissner, 'NDP says leaked document forecasts 30,000 people cut off welfare in April,' *Canadian Press Newswire*, 20 October 2003; 'More than 125 organizations call for end of welfare time limit,' *Canadian Press Newswire*, 13 February 2004; British Columbia Ministry of Human Resources, 'Time Limit Policy to Protect People in Need,' news release, 6 February 2004.

69 National Council of Welfare, *Welfare Incomes 2003* (Ottawa: NCW, 2004), p. 82.

70 British Columbia Ministry of Human Resources, *BCEA Summary Reports – May 2004*, p. 2.

71 Ibid., p. 53.

72 Canada West Foundation, *Welfare Reform in Alberta: A Survey of Former Recipients* (Calgary, CWF, 1997), fig. 1, p. 3.

73 Some clients in Supports to Independence – those in the Assured Support stream – were not expected to work because they have multiple barriers to employment.

74 Jonathan Murphy, 'Alberta and the Welfare Myth,' in Eric Shragge, ed., *Workfare: Ideology for a New Under-Class* (Toronto: Garamond Press. 1997), pp. 109–127.
75 M.S. Shed, 'Family and Social Services: the Alberta Deficit Elimination Program,' in Christopher Bruce, Ronald Kneebone, and Kenneth McKenzie, eds., *A Government Reinvented: A Study of Alberta's Deficit Elimination Program* (Toronto: Oxford University Press, 1997), table 6, p. 258.
76 Canada West Foundation. *Welfare Reform in Alberta*, p. 2.
77 Murphy, 'Alberta and the Workfare Myth,' p. 117.
78 Robert Howe, *Workfare: Theory, Evidence and Policy Design* (Toronto: University of Toronto Faculty of Law, 1996), p. 23.
79 Carolyne Gorlick and Guy Brethour, *Welfare-to-Work Programs: A National Inventory* (Ottawa: Canadian Council on Social Development, 1998), p. 207.
80 Murphy, 'Alberta and the Workfare Myth.'
81 Kenneth J. Boessenkool, *Back to Work: Learning from the Alberta Welfare Experiment* (Toronto: C.D. Howe Institute, no. 90, April 1997), p. 5.
82 There are stories of welfare clients being given bus fare to other provinces. Although these are most likely apocryphal, it is the case that applicants and recipients were encouraged, if not told, to seek opportunities in other parts of Canada.
83 Canada West Foundation, *Welfare Reform in Alberta*, fig. 1, p. 3.
84 Government of Alberta. *A Better Way: A Plan for Securing Alberta's Future* (Family and Social Services), (Edmonton: Government of Alberta, 24 February 1994), p. 6.
85 Canada West Foundation, *Welfare Reform in Alberta*, p. 2.
86 Ibid., p. 8.
87 Kenneth J. Boessenkool, *Back to Work*, p. 11.
88 Alberta Family and Social Services, *Business Plan 1996–97 to 1998–99* (Edmonton: Alberta Family and Social Services, 7 February 1996), pp. 227–228.
89 'Public to rule if welfare rates are adequate, says Dunford,' *Edmonton Journal*, 8 June 2001, p. A8.
90 MLA Committee to Review Low-Income Programs, *Low Income Programs Review: What We Recommend* (Edmonton, November 2001).
91 Mitchell Gray, 'Alberta won't raise welfare rates,' *Calgary Herald*, 23 May 2002. p. A13.
92 The government also sought to include the Assured Income for Severely Handicapped program in this integration, but fierce opposition from the disabled community, which feared their benefits would be reduced, prevented this from occurring.

93 Edmonton Social Planning Council, 'National Child Benefit and the Alberta Government,' news release (Edmonton: ESPC, 23 July 2003).

94 'From welfare to work: Social assistance reforms will help more people become self-sufficient' *Calgary Herald*, 3 April 2004, p. A 22.

95 Baldwin P. Reichwein, *Benchmarks in Alberta's Public Welfare Services: History Rooted in Benevolence, Harshness, Punitiveness and Stinginess*, research report, Alberta College of Social Workers (Edmonton, 2003). See also 'Social workers plot campaign for welfare hikes: Government needs political will to raise rates, says Social Workers Association,' *Edmonton Journal*, 4 July 2002, p. A7.

96 These figures are from table 2 and table 3, respectively, from M.S. Shed, 'Family and Social Services, the Alberta Deficit Elimination Program,' in Bruce, Kneebone, and McKenzie, eds., *A Government Reinvented*, pp. 252–253.

97 Ibid., table 4, p. 255.

98 National Council of Welfare, *Welfare Income 1999* (Ottawa: NCW 2000), table 5.

99 See, *Caring and Responsibility: A Statement of Social Policy for Alberta* (Edmonton: Government of Alberta, 1988) for a review of this expansion.

100 Boychuk, *Patchworks of Purpose: The Development of Provincial Social Assistance Regimes in Canada* (Montreal: McGill-Queen's University Press, 1998), p. 75.

101 William Coleman and Grace Skogstad, 'Conclusion,' in Coleman and Skogstad, eds., *Policy Communities and Public Policy in Canada*, p. 14.

102 The remainder of the decline reflected the increased presence in the labour force of individuals who had too little prior labour market attachment to have qualified for UI benefits even under the earlier, more generous, eligibility rules. Tom McIntosh and Gerard Boychuk, 'Dis-Covered: EI, Social Assistance and the Growing Gap in Income Support for Unemployed Canadians,' in McIntosh, ed., *Federalism, Democracy and Labour Market Policy in Canada* (Montreal: McGill-Queen's University Press, 2000), pp. 93–95.

103 Ibid., p. 99.

104 Ibid., p. 101.

105 This was especially true for the United States and the United Kingdom, but also for Germany, Belgium, the Netherlands, and Norway. However, Canada's Gini coefficient remained higher (its overall final income inequality was greater) than for all of these other nations in 1995, except for the United States. It was also higher than in France, where final income inequality fell considerably in this period. See Timothy Smeeding, *Public*

Policy and Economic Inequality: The United States in Comparative Perspective (Syracuse: Campbell Public Affairs Institute, Syracuse University, 20 February 2004), fig. 3.

106 René Morissette et al., 'Earnings Polarization in Canada, 1969–1991,' in K. Banting and C. Beach, eds., *Labour Market Polarization and Social Policy Reform* (Kingston: School of Policy Studies, Queen's University, 1995), p. 24; emphasis in the original.

107 Timothy Smeeding, *Public Policy and Economic Inequality: The United States in Comparative Perspective*, working paper no. 367 (Syracuse, NY: Luxembourg Income Studies, 2004), fig. 3.

108 The calculation of this figure is based on the National Council of Welfare's revised estimation of basic assistance benefits for single employable individuals in Quebec in 1990, as reported in *Welfare Incomes 2002*, p. 37. This figure differs from the sum originally reported by the Council in *Welfare Incomes 1990*.

9 A Perspective from Abroad: Coordinative Institutions and Labour Market Reform in Germany

1 Thomas R. Klassen and Steffen Schneider, 'Similar Challenges, Different Solutions: Reforming Labour Market Policies in Germany and Canada during the 1990s,' *Canadian Public Policy*, vol. 28 (2002), pp. 51–69.

2 The chapter draws on expert interviews undertaken in 2002 and 2003 with Rodney Haddow and Thomas R. Klassen. I thank all experts for sharing their time and knowledge.

3 Franz-Xaver Kaufmann, *Varianten des Wohlfahrtsstaats: Der deutsche Sozialstaat im internationalen Vergleich* (Frankfurt/M.: Suhrkamp, 2003); Manfred G. Schmidt, *Sozialpolitik in Deutschland: Historische Entwicklung und internationaler Vergleich* (Opladen: Leske & Budrich, 1998).

4 Heinz Laufer and Ursula Münch, *Das föderative System der Bundesrepublik Deutschland* (Opladen: Leske & Budrich, 1998); Ursula Münch, *Sozialpolitik und Föderalismus: Zur Dynamik der Aufgabenverteilung im sozialen Bundesstaat* (Opladen: Leske & Budrich, 1997); Philip Manow, 'Germany – Cooperative Federalism and the Overgrazing of the Fiscal Commons,' in Stephan Leibfried et al., eds., *Federalism and the Welfare State: European and New World Experiences* (Cambridge: Cambridge University Press, 2005), pp. 222–262.

5 Jens Alber, 'Der Wohlfahrtsstaat in der Wirtschaftskrise – Eine Bilanz der Sozialpolitik in der Bundesrepublik seit den frühen siebziger Jahren,' *Politische Vierteljahresschrift*, vol. 27 (1986), pp. 28–60.

6 Klaus von Beyme, 'Verfehlte Vereinigung – verpaßte Reformen? Zur Problematik der Evaluation der Vereinigungspolitik in Deutschland seit 1989,' *Journal für Sozialforschung*, vol. 34 (1994), p. 265.

7 Wendy Carlin and David Soskice, 'Shocks to the System: The German Political Economy under Stress,' *National Economic Institute Review*, vol. 159 (1997), pp. 57–76; Charlie Jeffery, 'The Non-Reform of the German Federal System after Unification,' *West European Politics*, vol. 18 (1995), pp. 252–272; Rainer-Olaf Schultze, 'Statt Subsidiarität und Entscheidungsauton-omie – Politikverflechtung und kein Ende: Der deutsche Föderalismus nach der Vereinigung,' *Staatswissenschaften und Staatspraxis*, vol. 4 (1993), pp. 225–255; Heiner Ganßmann, 'After Unification: Problems Facing the German Welfare State,' *Journal of European Social Policy*, vol. 3 (1993), pp. 79–90.

8 Charlie Jeffery and Roland Sturm, eds., *Federalism, Unification and European Integration* (London: Frank Cass, 1993); Jens Alber, 'Der deutsche Sozial-staat in der Ära Kohl: Diagnosen und Daten,' in Stephan Leibfried and Uwe Wagschal, eds., *Der deutsche Sozialstaat: Bilanzen – Reformen – Perspek-tiven* (Frankfurt, M./New York: Campus, 2000); pp. 235–275; Manfred G. Schmidt, 'Sozialstaatliche Politik in der Ära Kohl,' in Göttrik Wewer, ed., *Bilanz der Ära Kohl* (Opladen: Leske & Budrich, 1998), pp. 59–87.

9 Antonia Gohr and Martin Seeleib-Kaiser, eds., *Sozial- und Wirtschaftspolitik unter Rot-Grün* (Wiesbaden: Westdeutscher Verlag, 2003); Manfred G. Schmidt, 'Rot-grüne Sozialpolitik (1998–2002),' in Christoph Egle et al., eds., *Das rot-grüne Projekt* (Wiesbaden: Westdeutscher Verlag, 2003), pp. 239–258.

10 Philip Manow and Eric Seils, 'Adjusting Badly: The German Welfare State, Structural Change, and the Open Economy,' in Fritz W. Scharpf and Vivien A. Schmidt, eds., *From Vulnerability to Competitiveness: Welfare and Work in the Open Economy* (Oxford: Oxford University Press, 2000), pp. 264–307; Karl-Heinz Paqué, 'Unemployment and the Crisis of the German Model: A Long-Term Interpretation,' in Herbert Giersch, ed., *Fighting Europe's Unemployment in the 1990s* (Berlin/Heidelberg: Springer, 1996), pp. 119–155; for more sanguine views, see Jens Alber, 'Der deutsche Sozialstaat im Licht international vergleichender Daten,' *Leviathan*, vol. 26 (1998), pp. 199–227; Elmar Rieger and Stephan Leibfried, *Limits to Global-ization. Welfare States and the World Economy* (Cambridge: Polity Press, 2003).

11 Martin Seeleib-Kaiser, 'A Dual Transformation of the German Welfare State?' *West European Politics*, vol. 25 (2002), pp. 25–48.

12 Stephan Leibfried and Herbert Obinger, 'The State of Germany's Welfare

State: Social Policy between Macro-economic Retrenchment and Micro-economic Recalibration,' *West European Politics*, vol. 26 (2003), pp. 199–218; for interpretations that give more weight to major structural changes, see Frank Bönker and Hellmut Wollmann, 'Sozialstaatlichkeit im Übergang: Entwicklungslinien der bundesdeutschen Sozialpolitik in den Neunziger-jahren,' in Roland Czada and Hellmut Wollmann, eds., *Von der Bonner zur Berliner Republik* (Wiesbaden: Westdeutscher Verlag, 1999), pp. 514–538; Stephan Lessenich, *Dynamischer Immobilismus: Kontinuität und Wandel im deutschen Sozialmodell* (Frankfurt, M./New York: Campus, 2003); Mark I. Vail, 'Rethinking Corporatism and Consensus: The Dilemmas of German Social-Protection Reform,' *West European Politics*, vol. 26 (2003), pp. 41–66.

13 Kathleen Thelen, *How Institutions Evolve: The Political Economy of Skills in Germany, Britain, the United States and Japan* (Cambridge: Cambridge University Press, 2004).

14 Berndt Keller, *Einführung in die Arbeitspolitik* (Munich/Vienna: Olden-bourg); Wolfgang Streeck, 'German Capitalism: Does It Exist? Can It Survive?' *New Political Economy*, vol. 2 (1997), pp. 237–256; Kathleen Thelen, *Union of Parts: Labor Politics in Postwar Germany* (Ithaca/London: Cornell University Press, 1991).

15 Peter J. Katzenstein, *Policy and Politics in West Germany: The Growth of a Semisovereign State* (Philadelphia: Temple University Press, 1987).

16 Wolfgang Streeck, 'On the Institutional Conditions of Diversified Quality Production,' in Egon Matzner and Wolfgang Streeck, eds., *Beyond Key-nesianism: The Socio-economics of Production and Full Employment* (London: Edward Elgar, 1991), pp. 21–61; Pepper D. Culpepper and David Finegold, eds., *The German Skills Machine: Sustaining Comparative Advantage in a Global Economy* (New York/Oxford: Berghahn Books, 1999).

17 Bernhard Weßels, 'Die deutsche Variante des Korporatismus,' in Max Kaase and Günther Schmid, eds., *Eine lernende Demokratie* (Berlin: Edition Sigma, 1999), pp. 87–113.

18 David Soskice, 'Globalisierung und institutionelle Divergenz: Die USA und Deutschland im Vergleich,' *Geschichte und Gesellschaft*, vol. 25 (1999), pp. 201–225; Kathleen Thelen, 'Why German Employers Cannot Bring Themselves to Dismantle the German Model,' in Torben Iversen et al., eds., *Unions, Employers, and Central Banks* (Cambridge: Cambridge Univer-sity Press, 2000), pp. 138–172; Stewart Wood, 'Labour Market Regimes under Threat? Sources of Continuity in Germany, Britain and Sweden,' in Paul Pierson, ed., *The New Politics of the Welfare State* (Oxford: Oxford University Press, 2001), pp. 368–409.

19 Rebecca Harding, 'Standort Deutschland in the Globalising Economy: An

End to the Economic Miracle?' *German Politics*, vol. 8 (1999), pp. 66–88; Stefan Immerfall and Peter Franz, *Standort Deutschland: Stärken und Schwächen im weltweiten Strukturwandel* (Opladen: Leske & Budrich, 1998).

20 Wolfgang Streeck and Anke Hassel, 'The Crumbling Pillars of Social Partnership,' *West European Politics*, vol. 26 (2003), p. 110.

21 Jürgen Beyer, ed., *Vom Zukunfts- zum Auslaufmodell? Die deutsche Wirtschaftsordnung im Wandel* (Wiesbaden: Westdeutscher Verlag, 2003); Reiner Hoffmann et al., eds., *German Industrial Relations under the Impact of Structural Change, Unification and European Integration* (Düsseldorf: Hans-Böckler-Stiftung, 1995).

22 Wade Jacoby and Martin Behrens, 'Experimentalism as a Tool of Economic Innovation in Germany,' *German Politics and Society*, vol. 16 (2001), pp. 1–33; Klaus Schmierl, 'Vielfalt im Umbruch. Auflösungserscheinungen, Anpassungsprozesse und neue Interessenvertretungsmodelle in den Arbeitsbeziehungen,' in Beyer, ed., *Vom Zukunfts- zum Auslaufmodell?*, pp. 36–60.

23 Streeck and Hassel, 'The Crumbling Pillars of Social Partnership,' p. 108.

24 Britta Rehder, 'Konversion durch Überlagerung. Der Beitrag betrieblicher Bündnisse zum Wandel der Arbeitsbeziehungen,' in Beyer, ed., pp. 61–77.

25 Jutta Allmendinger and Stephan Leibfried, 'Education and Social Policy: The Four Worlds of Competence Production,' *Journal of European Social Policy*, vol. 13 (2003), pp. 63–81; Wolfgang Lehmann, 'Is Germany's Dual System Still a Model for Canadian Youth Apprenticeship Initiatives?' *Canadian Public Policy*, vol. 26 (2000), pp. 224–240.

26 Steve French, 'The Impact of Unification on German Industrial Relations,' *German Politics*, vol. 9 (2000), pp. 195–216; Lowell Turner, *Fighting for Partnership: Labor and Politics in Unified Germany* (Ithaca/London: Cornell University Press, 1998).

27 Schmierl, 'Vielfalt im Umbruch,' Rehder, 'Konversion durch Überlagerung,' Beyer, 'Einleitung: Unkoordinierte Modellpflege am koordinierten deutschen Modell,' in *Vom Zukunfts- zum Auslaufmodell?*, pp. 7–35.

28 Oskar Niedermayer, 'Die Entwicklung des deutschen Parteiensystems bis nach der Bundestagswahl 2002,' in Niedermayer, ed., *Die Parteien nach der Bundestagswahl 2002* (Opladen: Leske & Budrich, 2003), pp. 9–41.

29 Gøsta Esping-Andersen and Walter Korpi, 'Social Policy as Class Politics in Post-War Capitalism: Scandinavia, Austria and Germany,' in John H. Goldthorpe, ed., *Order and Conflict in Contemporary Capitalism* (Oxford: Clarendon Press, 1984), pp. 179–208; Herbert Kitschelt, 'Political-Economic Context and Partisan Strategies in the German Federal Elections, 1990–2002,' *West European Politics*, vol. 26 (2003), pp. 125–152.

30 Charlie Jeffery, 'Party Politics and Territorial Representation in the Federal Republic of Germany,' *West European Politics*, vol. 22 (1999), pp. 130–166.

31 Gerhard Lehmbruch, *Parteienwettbewerb im Bundesstaat: Regelsysteme und Spannungslagen im politischen System der Bundesrepublik Deutschland* (Wiesbaden: Westdeutscher Verlag, 2000); Manfred G. Schmidt, 'Germany: The Grand Coalition State,' in Josep M. Colomer, ed., *Political Institutions in Europe* (London: Routledge, 1996); Stephen J. Silvia, 'Reform Gridlock and the Role of the Bundesrat in German Politics,' *West European Politics*, vol. 22 (1999), pp. 167–181.

32 Kitschelt, 'Political-Economic Context and Partisan Strategies.'

33 Manfred G. Schmidt, 'The Policy of the Middle Way,' *Journal of Public Policy*, vol. 7 (1987), pp. 135–177; Herbert Kitschelt and Wolfgang Streeck, 'From Stability to Stagnation: Germany at the Beginning of the Twenty-First Century,' *West European Politics*, vol. 26 (2003), pp. 1–34; Helmut Wiesenthal, 'German Unification and "Model Germany": An Adventure in Institutional Conservatism,' *West European Politics*, vol. 26 (2003), pp. 37–58.

34 It should be underlined that the yardstick used to describe variations as low, medium, and high differs from the one used in the Canadian chapters – in comparison with Canada, Germany remains a fairly homogeneous society and political system.

35 Berndt Keller, *Einführung*, chaps. 13, 14; Günther Schmid, 'Beschäftigungs-und Arbeitsmarktpolitik,' in Klaus von Beyme and Manfred G. Schmidt, eds., *Politik in der Bundesrepublik Deutschland* (Opladen: Westdeutscher Verlag, 1990), pp. 228–254; Christine Trampusch, 'Dauerproblem Arbeitsmarkt: Reformblockaden und Lösungskonzepte,' *Aus Politik und Zeitgeschichte*, vol. 53 (B18–19, 2003), pp. 16–23.

36 Michael Fertig and Christoph M. Schmidt, 'Discretionary Measures of Active Labor Market Policy: The German Employment Promotion Reform in Perspective,' *Schmollers Jahrbuch*, vol. 120 (2000), pp. 537–565; Karsten Schuldt et al., *Das finanzielle Volumen der aktiven Arbeitsmarktpolitik in den östlichen Ländern Deutschlands* (Rostock, Teltow: PIW, 2003), pp. 24–34; Christine Trampusch, *Die Bundesanstalt für Arbeit und das Zusammenwirken von Staat und Verbänden in der Arbeitsmarktpolitik von 1952 bis 2001* (Cologne: Max-Planck-Institut für Gesellschaftsforschung, Working Paper 5/2002).

37 Ulrich Jürgens and Wolfgang Krumbein, eds., *Industriepolitische Strategien: Bundesländer im Vergleich* (Berlin: Edition Sigma, 1991).

38 Josef Schmid and Susanne Blancke, *Arbeitsmarktpolitik der Bundesländer: Chancen und Restriktionen einer aktiven Arbeitsmarkt- und Strukturpolitik im Föderalismus* (Berlin: Edition Sigma, 2001).

39 Adalbert Evers and Matthias Schulze-Böing, 'Öffnung und Eingrenzung: Wandel und Herausforderungen lokaler Beschäftigungspolitik,' *Zeitschrift für Sozialreform*, vol. 45 (1999), pp. 940–960; Michael Puhlmann, 'Perspektiven, Chancen und Risiken kommunaler Arbeitsmarkt- und Strukturpolitik,' in Berthold Dietz et al., eds., *Handbuch der kommunalen Sozialpolitik* (Opladen: Leske & Budrich, 1999), pp. 285–304.

40 Eschel Claus Alpermann, 'Die neue Beschäftigungspolitik der Europäischen Union – Aktuelle Entwicklungen und Initiativen,' in Rolf Prigge et al., *Strategien regionaler Beschäftigungsförderung: Schweden, Österreich und Deutschland im Vergleich* (Frankfurt, M./New York: Campus, 2000), pp. 383–407; Berndt Keller, *Europäische Arbeits- und Sozialpolitik* (Munich/Vienna: Oldenbourg, 2001).

41 Klaus Jacobs et al., 'Germany: The Diversity of Pathways,' in Martin Kohli et al., eds., *Time for Retirement: Comparative Studies of Early Exit from the Labor Force* (New York: Cambridge University Press, 1991), pp. 181–221; Gaby von Rhein-Kress, *Die politische Steuerung des Arbeitsangebots* (Opladen: Westdeutscher Verlag, 1996).

42 Heidrun Abromeit and Bernhard Blanke, eds., *Arbeitsmarkt, Arbeitsbeziehungen und Politik in den 80er Jahren* (Opladen: Westdeutscher Verlag, 1987); Friedbert W. Rüb and Frank Nullmeier, 'Die Flexibilisierung der Arbeitsgesellschaft,' in Werner Süß, ed., *Die Bundesrepublik in den 80er Jahren: Innenpolitik, politische Kultur, Außenpolitik* (Opladen: Leske & Budrich, 1991), pp. 121–136; Reimut Zohlnhöfer, 'Institutions, the CDU and Policy Change: Explaining German Economic Policy in the 1980s,' *German Politics*, vol. 8 (1999), pp. 141–160.

43 Martin Eichler and Michael Lechner, 'Die aktive Arbeitsmarktpolitik in den neuen Bundesländern,' in *Zehn Jahre Deutsche Einheit – Bilanz und Perspektiven* (Halle: IWH, 2001), pp. 148–167; Hubert Heinelt et al., eds., *Arbeitsmarktpolitik nach der Vereinigung* (Berlin: Edition Sigma, 1994); Josef Schmid and Susanne Blancke, 'Arbeitsmarktpolitik in Ostdeutschland: Aufstieg und Fall einer Policy?' *Deutschland-Archiv*, vol. 31 (1997), pp. 938–947.

44 Reinhard Bispinck, 'The Chequered History of the Alliance for Jobs,' in Giuseppe Fajertag and Philippe Pochet, eds., *Social Pacts in Europe* (Brussels: European Trade Union Institute, 1997), pp. 63–78.

45 Karin Gottschall and Irene Dingeldey, 'Arbeitsmarktpolitik im konservativ-korporatistischen Wohlfahrtsstaat: Auf dem Weg zu reflexiver Deregulierung?,' in Leibfried and Wagschal, *Der deutsche Sozialstaat*, pp. 306–339; Hubert Heinelt and Michael Weck, *Arbeitsmarktpolitik: Vom Vereinigungskonsens zur Standortdebatte* (Opladen: Leske & Budrich, 1998);

Günther Schmid, 'Das Nadelöhr der Wirklichkeit verfehlt: Eine beschäf-
tigungspolitische Bilanz der Ära Kohl,' in Wewer, ed., *Bilanz der Ära Kohl*,
pp. 145–181; Steffen Schneider, 'Labour Market Policy and the Unemploy-
ment Crisis in the Federal Republic of Germany: Institutional Sclerosis or
Corporatist Renewal?' in Alain Noël, ed., *Federalism and Labour Market
Policy: Comparing Different Governance and Employment Strategies* (Mon-
treal/Kingston: McGill-Queen's University Press, 2004), pp. 83–142;
Reimut Zohlnhöfer, *Die Wirtschaftspolitik der Ära Kohl: Eine Analyse der
Schlüsselentscheidungen in den Politikfeldern Finanzen, Arbeit und
Entstaatlichung, 1982–1998* (Opladen: Leske & Budrich, 2001).

46 Streeck and Hassel, 'The Crumbling Pillars of Social Partnership,' p. 118;
Gerhard Lehmbruch, 'Institutionelle Schranken einer ausgehandelten
Reform des Wohlfahrtsstaates. Das Bündnis für Arbeit und seine
Erfolgsbedingungen,' in Czada and Wollmann, eds., *Von der Bonner zur
Berliner Republik*, pp. 89–112; Werner Reutter, 'Das Bündnis für Arbeit,
Ausbildung und Wettbewerbsfähigkeit,' in Gohr and Seeleib-Kaiser, eds.,
Sozial-und Wirtschaftspolitik unter Rot-Grün, pp. 289–306.

47 Susanne Blancke and Josef Schmid, 'Bilanz der Bundesregierung Schröder
in der Arbeitsmarktpolitik 1998–2002: Ansätze zu einer doppelten Wende,'
in Egle et al., eds., *Das rot-grüne Projekt*, pp. 215–238; Hubert Heinelt,
'Arbeitsmarktpolitik – von 'versorgenden' wohlfahrtsstaatlichen Inter-
ventionen zur 'aktivierenden' Beschäftigungsförderung,' in Gohr and
Seeleib-Kaiser, eds., *Sozial- und Wirtschaftspolitik unter Rot-Grün*, 125–146;
Edgar Rose, 'Arbeitsrechtspolitik zwischen Re-Regulierung und Deregulierung,' in Gohr and Seeleib-Kaiser, op. cit., pp. 103–124; Josef Schmid,
'Große Probleme und kleine Lösungen? Aktuelle Entwicklungen in der
deutschen Arbeitsmarktpolitik,' *Deutschland-Archiv*, vol. 35 (2002), 97–104.

48 Peter Hartz et al., *Moderne Dienstleistungen am Arbeitsmarkt: Bericht der
Kommission* (Berlin: Federal Ministry of Labour and Social Affairs, 2002);
Günther Schmid, 'Moderne Dienstleistungen am Arbeitsmarkt: Strategie
und Vorschläge der Hartz-Kommission,' *Aus Politik und Zeitgeschichte*, vol.
53 (B6–7, 2003), pp. 3–6; for a critical perspective, see Rudolf Hickel,
'Hartz-Konzept: Arbeitslose effektiver in billige Jobs – Deregulierungs-
schub auf den Arbeitsmärkten,' *Aus Politik und* Zeitgeschichte, vol. 53
(B6–7, 2003), pp. 7–16.

49 As advocated by a joint commission established by Bavaria and Saxony;
see Kommission für Zukunftsfragen der Freistaaten Bayern und Sachsen,
*Erwerbstätigkeit und Arbeitslosigkeit in Deutschland: Entwicklung – Ursachen –
Maßnahmen*, 3 vols. (Munich, 1996, 1997).

50 Wolfgang Ismayr and Gerhard Kral, 'Bayern,' in Jürgen Hartmann, ed.,

Handbuch der deutchen Bundesländer (Frankfurt, M./New York: Campus, 1997), pp. 84–126; Schmid and Blancke, *Arbeitsmarktpolitik der Bundesländer*, pp. 170–177; Josef Schmid et al., *Vergleich der aktiven Arbeitsmarktpolitik der westdeutschen Bundesländer in 2001* (Tübingen: University of Tübingen, Institut für Politikwissenschaft, 2003), pp. 62–74.

51 Bayerisches Staatsministerium für Arbeit, *Der Arbeitsmarktfonds Bayern 1997 bis 2001: Eine Zwischenbilanz* (Munich, 2001).

52 Dagmar Biegler et al., 'Nordrhein-Westfalen,' in Hartmann, ed., *Handbuch der deutschen Bundesländer*, pp. 383–432; Schmid and Blancke, *Arbeitsmarktpolitik der Bundesländer*, pp. 138–147; Schmid et al., *Vergleich der aktiven Arbeitsmarktpolitik*, pp. 131–146.

53 Although the *political* importance of the divide between East and West Germany equals the one between Quebec and the rest of Canada, Saxony-Anhalt is thus more comparable with the Atlantic provinces in terms of its fiscal, economic, and labour market situation.

54 Bernhard Boll and Everhard Holtmann, 'Sachsen-Anhalt,' in Hartmann, ed., *Handbuch der deutschen Bundesländer*, pp. 546–580; Schmid and Blancke, *Arbeitsmarktpolitik der Bundesländer*, pp. 193–197; Schuldt et al., *Das finanzielle Volumen*, pp. 104–118.

55 Rodney Haddow et al., *Contrasting Milieus and Common Constraints: The Labour Market Policy-making Capacity of Peripheral Regions in Canada and Germany* (Toronto: Canadian Centre for German and European Studies, York University, Working Paper 4/2003), p. 26.

56 Pepper D. Culpepper, 'Powering, Puzzling, and "Pacting": The Informational Logic of Negotiated Reforms,' *Journal of European Public Policy*, vol. 9 (2002), pp. 774–790.

57 Susanne Blancke, *Politikinnovationen im Schatten des Bundes: Policy-Innovationen und -Diffusionen im Föderalismus und die Arbeitsmarktpolitik der Bundesländer* (Wiesbaden: VS Verlag für Sozialwissenschaften, 2004).

58 A point made by Josef Schmid in our interview.

59 Godehard Neumann, 'Bündnisse für Arbeit in Deutschland – Ein Überblick,' *WSI-Mitteilungen* (7/2000), pp. 419–429.

10 Conclusion: Stepping Back and Looking Forward

1 Norberto Bobio, *Left and Right: The Significance of a Political Distinction* (Chicago: University of Chicago Press, 1996), p. 3.

2 Ibid., p. 16.

3 Ibid., p. 35.

4 See, for instance, Kathleen Thelen and Christa Van Wunbergen, 'The

Paradox of Globalization: Labour Relations in Germany and Beyond,' *Comparative Political Studies*, vol. 36 (2003), pp. 859–860.

5 Anthony Giddens, *Beyond Left and Right* (Stanford: Stanford University Press, 1994), p. 10.

6 Carles Boix, *Political Parties in the Global Economy* (Cambridge: Cambridge University Press, 1998), p. 101; Geoffrey Garrett, *Partisan Politics in the Global Economy* (Cambridge: Cambridge University Press, 1998), p. 85.

7 Richard Block and Karen Roberts, 'A Comparison of Labour Standards in the United States and Canada,' *Relations Industrielles*, vol. 55 (2000), pp. 296–297.

8 Retrenchment for occupational health exclusively, which is only examined for Ontario and Alberta in this volume, is excluded from this calculation; the score for this was 0 for the former province, 1 for the latter.

9 Peter Hall and David Soskice, 'An Introduction to Varieties of Capitalism,' in Hall and Soskice, eds., *Varieties of Capitalism* (Oxford: Oxford University Press, 2001), p. 57.

10 Paul Pierson and Theda Skocpol, 'Historical Institutionalism in Contemporary Political Science,' in I. Katznelson and H. Milner, eds., *Political Science: The State of the Discipline* (New York: W.W. Norton, 2002), pp. 695–696.

11 Ibid., p. 698.

12 Ibid., p. 699.

13 For a recent comparative examination of institutionalist approaches to studying neo-liberalism, see John Campbell and Ove Pederson, eds., *The Rise of Neoliberalism and Institutional Analysis* (Princeton: Princeton University Press, 2001), part 2 specifically addresses historical institutionalism.

14 Kathleen Thelen and Christa Van Wijnbergen, 'The Paradox of Globalization: Labour Relations in Germany and Beyond,' *Comparative Political Studies*, vol. 36 (2003), p. 860.

15 Kathleen Thelen, 'How Institutions Evolve: Insights from Comparative Historical Analysis,' in J. Mahoney and D. Rueschemeyer, eds., *Comparative Historical Analysis in the Social Sciences* (Cambridge: Cambridge University Press, 2003), p. 209.

16 Ibid.

17 Ibid., p. 211. Emphasis in the original.

18 Ibid., pp. 225–226.

19 Thelen, *How Institutions Evolve* (Cambridge: Cambridge University Press, 2004), p. 31.

20 Thelen, 'How Institutions Evolve: Insights from Comparative Historical Analysis,' p. 217.

21 Thelen, *How Institutions Evolve*, pp. 5, 22–23, 212–213.

22 Thelen, 'How Institutions Evolve: Insights from Comparative Historical Analysis,' pp. 222–225.
23 Vandna Bhatia and William Coleman, 'Ideas and Discourses: Reform and Resistance in the Canadian and German Health Systems,' *Canadian Journal of Political Science*, vol. 36 (2003), pp. 715–739.
24 Pierson, 'Coping with Permanent Austerity,' in Pierson, ed., *The New Politics of the Welfare State* (Oxford: Oxford University Press, 2001), p. 438.
25 John Myles, 'How to Design a Liberal Welfare State: A Comparison of Canada and the United States,' in E. Huber, ed., *Models of Capitalism* (Philadelphia: Pennsylvania University Press, 2002), p. 363. Similarly to Thelen, Myles distinguished broad welfare state *regimes* from more secondary *program designs*. The latter may diverge even among liberal welfare states with important long-term political consequences; see p. 340.
26 Canada's Gini coefficient measure of final income inequality changed very little between 1977 and 2000, while those of most OECD nations, other than France, rose appreciably. In the latter year, inequality in Canada nevertheless remained higher than in Western Europe, though it was now much lower than in the United States. See Timothy Smeeding, *Public Policy and Economic Inequality: The United States in Comparative Perspective* (Syracuse: Campbell Public Affairs Institute, Syracuse University, 20 February 2004), fig. 3.
27 George Hoberg et al., 'The Scope of Domestic Choice: Policy Autonomy in a Globalizing World,' in Hoberg, ed., *Capacity for Choice: Canada in a New North America* (Toronto: University of Toronto Press, 2002), pp. 270–271.
28 Jane Jenson, 'Representation in Crisis: The Roots of Canada's Permeable Fordism,' *Canadian Journal of Political Science*, vol. 33 (1990), pp. 653–683.
29 Stephen Brooks, 'Political Culture in Canada: Issues and Directions,' in J. Bickerton and A. Gagnon, eds., *Canadian Politics*, 4th ed. (Peterborough: Broadview Press, 2004), p. 66.
30 Ibid., p. 60.
31 Michael Adams, *Fire and Ice* (Toronto: Penguin, 2003).
32 Kathleen Thelen and Sven Steinmo, 'Historical Institutionalism in Comparative Politics,' in Steinmo et al., eds., *Structuring Politics* (Cambridge: Cambridge University Press, 1992), pp. 12–13. Emphasis in the original.
33 Charles Taylor, *Hegel and Modern Society* (Cambridge: Cambridge University Press, 1979), p. 160.

Appendix: Criteria for Rating Labour Market Policy Change

1 Peter Hall, 'Policy Paradigms, Social Learning, and the State,' *Comparative Politics*, vol. 25 (1993), p. 278.

Index

Studies in Comparative Political Economy and Public Policy